A Dictionary of Mind and Body

A DICTIONARY OF
MIND AND BODY

Therapies, techniques and ideas
in alternative medicine, the healing arts
and psychology

DONALD WATSON

ANDRE DEUTSCH

First published in Great Britain in 1995 by
André Deutsch Limited
106 Great Russell Street
London WC1B 3LJ

CIP data for this title is available
from the British Library.

ISBN 0 233 98890 4

Printed in Great Britain by
WBC, Bridgend

This book is dedicated to David Yarnell

The cure of a part should not be attempted without treatment of the whole. No attempt should be made to cure the body without the soul, and if the head and body are to be healthy you must begin by curing the mind, for this is the greatest error of our day in the treatment of the human body, that physicians first separate the soul from the body.

Plato

Introduction

There is no illness of the body apart from the mind.

It is impossible to separate 'mental' and 'physical' processes in any form of human activity.

Any illness is a signal that there is something amiss in the unity of mind, body and emotions.

The primary concern of the authors of these remarks, which clearly say much the same thing, was respectively philosophy, physical posture, and the treatment of cancer. (They are Socrates, F. M. Alexander[1] and Carl Simonton.[2]) From whatever direction one approaches this subject, the conclusion is the same: body and mind are inseparable.

Practically all alternative therapies, physical and psychological, subscribe to the view that neither the mind nor the body can be treated in isolation, as the medical establishment has long maintained. Many of the key figures in the movement away from orthodox medicine started off as part of that establishment, which for too long ignored or even denied all links between the mind and the body. Among them was F. M. Alexander: 'When I began my investigation, I, in common with most people, conceived of "body" and "mind" as separate parts of the same organism, and consequently believed that human ills, difficulties and shortcomings could be classified as either "mental" or "physical" . . . My practical experiences, however, led me to abandon this point of view . . . it is *impossible* to separate "mental" and "physical" processes in any form of human activity.'[3]

There had been no real separation between mind and body until the seventeenth century, when Descartes established the dualism that still dominates western medical theory and practice. The mind was henceforth excluded from the factors which governed physical health: 'I consider the human body as a machine. My thought compares a sick man and an ill-made clock with my ideas of a healthy man and a well-made clock.' Medical students are still taught as if being a doctor were like being a watch repairer: the body is made up of bits and pieces which are studied as separate entities; medical treatment involves tinkering with those parts somehow to make them work more efficiently; the mind, if it ever comes into the picture at all, is just another distinct entity separate from the body.

Some people in the medical establishment are starting to recognize the failings inherent in this reductionist view. One such, Patrick Pietroni, writes: 'Medical education, with its emphasis on "parts" and on the need for distinct entities in disease labelling, sees its causative base as increasingly molecular, and emphasises the importance of numeracy, measurement and the technological apparatus for arriving at precision.'[4] There are many unfortunate consequences of this almost obsessive preoccupation with finding, labelling and measuring a single cause in each pathological condition: the use of an arcane language to describe the labelling and measuring makes doctors unable to communicate with patients about their condition in ways that they understand; and newly qualified doctors leave medical school with a certain type of understanding of disease but no real knowledge of health.

Medicine is increasingly referred to as 'health care', but this belies the true situation in which the real concern of the medical establishment is disease. Health was defined by WHO in 1946 as a 'state of complete physical, mental and social well being'. This insistence on the social dimension may seem exaggerated, but once the mental aspect has been admitted, the social can hardly be excluded, since environmental factors and particularly interpersonal relationships inevitably affect the mental condition.

Most healing systems other than orthodox western medicine are based on the principle that the body heals itself and the physician simply facilitates this natural process. (This was also the view of Hippocrates.) As Albert Schweitzer said, 'Each patient carries his own doctor inside him. They come to us knowing that truth. We are at our best when we give the doctor who resides within each patient a chance to go to work.' Perhaps most people still instinctively feel this, and it is because conventional doctors seldom seem to take cognizance of it that their patients are often so dissatisfied with the treatment they receive. This was not the conclusion of the BMA survey on alternative medicine in the 1980s, but people were presumably not asked 'Do you believe in an inner doctor?' or even 'Do you think your body knows how to get better?' What the BMA survey did show was that patients consulted alternative practitioners because of the amount of time they offered and their willingness to listen. So presumably those patients were able to voice their feelings about their condition to physicians who respected what they had to say; they were given the opportunity to grant that 'inner doctor' self-expression; and they were given permission to regard body, mind and emotions as a unity.

The increased interest in alternative therapies was recognized by the Council of Europe in 1984, when it declared, 'It is not possible to consider this phenomenon as a medical side-issue. It must reflect a genuine public need which is in urgent need of definition and analysis.'[5] In 1985 one in seven of the 28,000 members of the Consumers Association had visited some form of alternative therapist in the preceding year. Although the membership of this organization is far from representative of the whole population, it is significant that in 1991 this figure had risen to one in four. Osteopathy accounts for a third to 40 per cent of all consultations. In 1990 one in three American adults used some form of alternative therapy.[6] With ever-growing demand, both therapies and therapists are increasing in number. Lord Skelmersdale, Under-Secretary of Health, told Parliament during a debate on complementary medicine in November 1987 that he had identified 160 such therapies, and the British Holistic Medical Association estimates that alternative therapists are increasing in number by 11 per cent a year.[7]

In this dictionary I have tried to include terms associated with psychological therapies that are often classified collectively as 'personal growth', with physical therapies that come under the general heading of 'alternative medicine', and with the common philosophy underlying and linking many, if not most, of these therapies. This underlying philosophy concerns our understanding of the mind-body relationship, questions such as: How do mind and body affect each other? What can the state of the body tell us about the state of the mind? How do our mental and emotional states affect physical well-being? To what extent might 'physical' therapies (such as the Alexander Technique) affect psychological health?

Inclusion of a therapy in this dictionary is no guarantee of its effectiveness. When considering how people sometimes become over-enthusiastic about particular alternative remedies Lawrence LeShan quotes an aphorism coined by the psychoanalyst, Jules Eisenbud, and known as Eisenbud's First Theorem: 'Just because an idea has been rejected by modern science does not mean that ipso facto it is valid.' It is a human characteristic to want 'magic bullets'. The same trait can manifest itself in some people's attitude towards alternative medicine:

people do like to be able to take a single cure, and the charisma and mystery surrounding some practitioners and their therapies cannot disguise the fact that many of their patients are still asking for a simple recipe. Having tried the magic bullets of medical science, perhaps they now want to sample something of the healing arts.

This is not just a reference book. The length of entries and the full use of cross-referencing means that each entry can be regarded as a way in to the whole structure of the book. Despite the linear quality of an alphabetical list of headwords, the abundance of cross-references can for the interested reader work rather like hypertext in electronic data: when a word is marked as a cross-reference the reader can choose whether or not to investigate that idea further by looking up the new headword. One could eventually read most of the book by starting from a limited number of entries and following up the cross-references.

Some people see the use of hypertext as a sign that a new non-linear way of thinking is coming into being. Such a 'multi-dimensional' way of thinking would be particularly appropriate in the field of health and medicine. It is the linear approach, characteristic of reductionist thinking, that has made it so difficult for people to appreciate the complex relationships between mind and body, between predisposition and cause or between immediate cause and contributory factors in disease, and between inner state and external conditions in the maintenance of health. The single-cause/single-remedy principle of orthodox western medicine belongs to a rigid type of linear thought. More and more people are beginning to realize that there are few if any 'magic bullets'; even when one such bullet appears to be effective, there is a tendency for other problems suddenly to arise and, like Jason fighting the soldiers growing from the dragon's teeth he had sown, we are faced with a worse situation than before. We have no Medea's charm to turn those soldiers against each other, but we do have an array of therapies, old and new, of which at least some may enable us to escape the pattern of attacking disease at the cost of undermining health, and many point to new ways of understanding the unity of mind and body.

Donald Watson
February 1994

Notes

1   Alexander, F.M.: *The Use of the Self*, London, Methuen, 1932; Gollancz, 1985.
2   Simonton, O. Carl, Matthews-Simonton, Stephanie, and Creighton, James L.: *Getting Well Again*, J. P. Tarcher, 1978.
3   Alexander, F.M.: *The Use of the Self*.
4   Pietroni, Patrick: *The Greening of Medicine*, London, Gollancz, 1991.
5   Council of Europe: *Legislative and Administrative Regulations on the Use by Licensed Health Service Personnel of Non-Conventional Methods of Diagnosis and Treatment of Illness*, Brussels, 1984.
6   Eisenberg, D. M. *et al.*: 'Unconventional Medicine in the United States: prevalence, costs and patterns of use', *New England Journal of Medicine*, 328 (1993).
7   British Holistic Medical Association: *A Response to the Government's Green Paper 'The Health of the Nation'*, London, BHMA, 1991.

NOTE

Entries cover therapies, techniques and ideas in alternative medicine, the healing arts and psychology. People are not included as headwords but the index shows under which entries they are mentioned. The index also includes many terms that do not appear as headwords. Superior figures refer to the publications listed in the bibliography. Small capitals indicate a cross-reference.

For safety's sake, readers are advised not to try any of the practices or techniques described in this book without first seeking professional advice.

ABDOMINAL SEGMENT In REICHIAN THERAPY the body is regarded as divided into seven areas, the sixth of which is the abdominal segment. Massage and deep breathing exercises are used to release the muscular ARMOURING which often manifests in this area as a result of sexual repression.

ABRAMS BOX The American neurologist and founding father of RADIONICS, Albert Abrams (1863–1924), designed a diagnostic instrument with which a patient's electromagnetic radiation or BIOCURRENTS could purportedly be measured by connecting the individual, or a sample of diseased tissue, a drop of blood or a lock of hair (a DIAGNOSTIC WITNESS) to a variable resistor. This instrument was in the form of a box – the Abrams box, also referred to as the 'black box' or, as Abrams himself called it, the Biodynamometer. Abrams was ridiculed by the medical and scientific community. After his death his work was continued in California by Ruth Drown, who developed new instrumentation which the Food & Drugs Administration of California condemned as 'not scientifically able', despite the evidence of many patients. An early British version of the Abrams box was the EMANOMETER, and its best known successor is probably the Rae POTENCY SIMULATOR.

ABREACTION One of the main purposes in many mind and body therapies (such as REICHIAN THERAPY, PRIMAL THERAPY and REBIRTHING as well as orthodox PSYCHOANALYSIS and PSYCHOTHERAPY) is the recollection of repressed memories and the release of and from the emotions that are associated with experiences buried in the unconscious. This release is known as abreaction.

ABSOLUTES Absolutes are a type of essential oil used in AROMATHERAPY. They are produced by the process known as ENFLEURAGE rather than the simpler, more common method of steam distillation and are consequently much more concentrated.

ACCIDIE Abraham Maslow, a key figure in HUMANISTIC PSYCHOL-
OGY, said that 'the ultimate disease of our times is valuelessness'.
At the root of this lack of values lies a profound sense of apathy or
spiritual sloth – accidie. 'The state of being without a system of
values is psychopathogenic. Human beings need a philosophy of life,
a religion, or a value system, just as they need sunlight, calcium,
and love.'[125] People whose basic needs are satisfactorily met may
still feel that life is meaningless unless they have what he calls
METAMOTIVATIONS and a sense of BEING-VALUES or 'B-values', the
values that self-actualizers (see SELF-ACTUALIZATION) naturally seek.

ACCOMMODATION In the BATES METHOD of sight improvement
accommodation is the eye's act of changing focus between near and
far. Accommodation exercises in the form of focusing alternately on
close and distant objects strengthen the eye muscles, which Bates
believed to be the key factor in good vision.

ACTIVE PSYCHOTHERAPY In the 1950s a Los Angeles psychotherapist, Dr Francis I. Regardie, developed a system of therapy he
called Active Psychotherapy. His process involved actual regurgita-
tion by the patient to achieve the therapeutic effects of ABREACTION,
in a manner which resembles the 'primal scream' in PRIMAL
THERAPY.

ACUPOINT An acupoint is a point on the body used in ACU-
PUNCTURE, ACUPRESSURE and related therapies. Treating such
points with needles, MOXIBUSTION or pressure is intended to affect
the flow of CH'I and restore balance in the body's energies.

ACUPRESSURE Although the first part of the word is derived from
acus (Latin) meaning 'needle', acupressure is the treatment of ACU-
PUNCTURE points (and meridians) not with needles but with finger
pressure or massage. (When these points are treated with sound or
laser, the practice is known as *sonopuncture* and *laserpuncture*.) It also
goes under the name of G-Jo (Chinese for 'first aid') and SHIATSU
(the Japanese version). Other forms of acupressure are JIN SHIN
DO (which uses only selected meridians), DO-IN (which is self-
administered), and TUI NA (which uses a wider variety of massage
techniques). REFLEXOLOGY and ZONE THERAPY are later western
versions which make use of pressure points on the hands and feet.
    Since needles were never used with babies and small children, in
such cases traditional Chinese acupuncturists practised acupressure.

As a form of first aid, acupressure can be used to relieve pain in sudden emergencies, and to treat common ailments such as toothache, insomnia and diarrhoea. It can be used as a form of self-help; the pressure points can be massaged by the patient without a practitioner. Mental problems such as depression and stress are also susceptible to treatment with acupressure.

In Santa Cruz, California, teachers started using acupressure as an effective means of relaxing children at school. The technique was also adopted with slow learners and their learning ability subsequently improved. Teachers from all over the USA are now trained in the use of these techniques.

ACUPUNCTURE The Latin derivation of 'acupuncture', 'pierced with a needle', is more objectively precise but perhaps less picturesque than the Chinese term, which consists of two ideograms: *zhen* meaning metal, and *jiu* meaning fire, expressing the idea of 'metal that burns'.

The earliest known reference to acupuncture is in the *Nei Ching* (or *Nei Jing*), the principal Chinese *Classic of Internal Medicine*, begun as legend has it by the Yellow Emperor, Huang Ti (c. 2700–2600 BC). This collection of writings took over 1,500 years to assemble and traditional Chinese medicine still adheres to most of its teachings. The version that has survived to this day was written down around 300 BC. Much later, around 1026, Wang Wei Yi wrote the *Classic of the Bronze Man*, in which he named 657 acupuncture points, and he organized the casting of bronze statues on which the meridians were engraved, the points being marked by tiny holes.

Although it is in China that acupuncture has been developed to its highest degree and practised most consistently, there is evidence that it has been used in many other parts of the world. Egyptian writings from around 1000 BC describe a system of energy channels around the body resembling that used in acupuncture, and a similar system was described in the eleventh century by the Persian physician Avicenna. Drawings at least one thousand years old have been found in Sri Lanka showing the acupuncture points of an elephant. A tribe in Brazil treats illness with small darts shot from blowpipes, the Bantus in southern Africa scratch the skin in specific places to prevent disease, and Eskimos use sharpened stones in similar ways.

Acupuncture is based on the notion that a healthy body depends on the balance of negative and positive (yin and yang) in the flow of energy around the body. This *ch'i* or life-force follows specific

3

pathways, called meridians, and when it is blocked or becomes sluggish, or when it flows too strongly, illness results. It is the physician's task therefore to identify where the flow of ch'i is either too strong or too weak and to restore a more balanced, even flow. The flow is either boosted or reduced by inserting very fine needles into the skin at precise points. These needles may be left in the skin for a while, they may be manipulated while in the skin (by gently rotating them between finger and thumb), or they may be inserted and immediately withdrawn again (a process known as 'tonification').

The earliest needles were made of stone and quartz. Then bone, bamboo and thorns were used. From about 400 BC metal needles were adopted – iron, copper and bronze, although the wealthy preferred gold (to stimulate) and silver (to sedate). Modern acupuncturists use stainless steel needles.

There are about 800 acupuncture points on the human body. Some of these can be detected today electronically as areas of high electrical conductivity (low electrical skin resistance) relative to nearby tissues, and this conductivity changes according to other changes in the body. For example, an increase or decrease in the heart rate is accompanied by a matching and proportionate change in the conductivity at heart acupuncture points.[224] But how these points came to be discovered thousands of years ago is not known. The first to be identified were probably those that are particularly sensitive to the touch in specific illnesses. By imagining that those points associated with the same organ were joined together, the early acupuncturists might then have discovered more points lying on the same line. According to traditional Chinese medicine there are twenty-six such lines, called meridians, along which the life-force, ch'i, flows around the body. Two of these pathways run down the middle of the body, front and back. The other twenty-four are paired off as mirror images of each other on the left and right side of the body, each pair linked with a particular organ.

The Chinese concept of an organ includes its function and the system which it controls. So in Chinese medicine, the Lungs includes the whole breathing apparatus – nose, trachea etc. as well as the lungs themselves; the Chinese concept of the spleen includes the digestive system. (The conceptual unity of organ and function was perhaps encouraged by the taboo on dissecting bodies.)

Many aspects of the basic Chinese theory behind what constitutes health and how to maintain it sit very uncomfortably with western medicine's preoccupation with disease, finding a single cause and knocking it out. Because of this totally different ethos, many regard acupuncture as alternative (where western medicine is concerned) rather than complementary, although it could reasonably complement other alternative therapies such as homoeopathy. As one recent popularizer has said, 'Any person who professes to practise acupuncture without having studied Chinese medical theory and who maintains that it can be used as an adjunct to Western medicine has failed to grasp its essence.'[131]

The traditional Chinese view recognizes that it is the natural disposition of the body to gravitate back towards a state of equilibrium, which we now call homoeostasis. The aim of the acupuncturist is to assist these homoeostatic functions by helping to balance the energies in the body. As well as helping to prevent illness that might otherwise be induced by the imbalances in the body, acupuncture treatment also enhances resistance to infectious disease. The imbalances which cause disease and make the body susceptible to infection result from the interaction between the body and the environment. This interaction is influenced by qualities or 'excesses' in the environment (cold, heat, etc.) and internal factors or 'moods' (joy, anger, fear, etc.).

It was the traditional Chinese doctor's task to help the patient to overcome or counteract any of these possible adverse effects *before* they resulted in illness, i.e. before the manifestation of any symptoms. Treatment was therefore what we would understand as preventive, and according to Chinese tradition the doctor was only paid when the patient was well. As soon as the patient became ill payment ceased and was resumed only when the patient was restored to health again.

The need for preventive treatment is a fundamental axiom of traditional Chinese medicine, as stated in the *Nei Jing*: 'To administer medicines to diseases which have already developed and to try to restore order only after chaos has already broken out is comparable to the behaviour of people who wait until they are already weak from thirst before they begin to dig a well, or who begin to forge a spear when they are already engaged in battle.'

Before deciding on treatment the acupuncturist must diagnose the pattern of disharmony. This involves much more than a review of the symptoms. The patient is a unique individual and must be appreciated as such. As Chuang Tse wrote in the fourth century BC,

Natures differ, and needs with them, hence the wise men of old did not lay down one measure for all.

This is clearly very different from the philosophy behind conventional western medical practice.

A most important part of making a diagnosis is the feeling of the pulses. The acupuncturist feels the pulse of the radial artery in six different positions (three on each wrist) and at two different pressures (superficial and deep) so as to feel the pulse of each of the twelve so-called Officials corresponding to the twelve major meridians (those pairs of pathways associated with particular organs). Each of these twelve pulses is evaluated in terms of twenty-eight different qualities, described for example as full, empty, floating, rapid, slow, intermittent, wiry, slippery, hollow, knotted, deep or tight. (Although this seems alien to our modern understanding of what constitutes the pulse, it is not unique to China; in the second century, the Greek physician, Galen of Pergamum, wrote eighteen works on subtle pulse diagnosis, describing over a hundred different pulse qualities.)

By feeling the pulses the acupuncturist recognizes in which meridians the energy flow is out of balance. Discussing the patient's basic constitution and emotional condition also plays an important part in any diagnosis. In deciding which points to treat the acupuncturist will naturally consider the relationship between all organs and meridians according to the ways in which they influence each other. This interrelationship is mapped out according to the Chinese system of elements.

There are five elements in the Chinese system: Wood, Fire, Earth, Metal and Water. Each element contains yin and yang and an organ is linked with these aspects of each element. The organs associated with the yin element are said to be in a nourishing cycle – each yin element is regarded as the 'mother' of the next in the above order (Wood fuels Fire, which produces ash or Earth, which provides Metal, which holds Water, which nourishes Wood). The yang elements are in an inhibiting relationship with each other; Wood covers Earth, which absorbs and dams Water, which extinguishes Fire, which melts Metal, which cuts Wood.

ELEMENT	YIN ORGAN	YANG ORGAN	SEASON	EMOTION
Wood	Liver	Gall bladder	Spring	Anger
Fire	Heart	Small intestine	Summer	Joy
Earth	Spleen	Stomach	Late summer	Sadness
Metal	Lungs	Colon	Autumn	Grief
Water	Kidneys	Bladder	Winter	Fear

So if there is a problem with the kidneys, the acupuncturist may, depending also on the pulse diagnosis, decide to direct treatment to the 'mother' organ, the lungs, which will then provide more energy for the kidneys. All yin organs are also 'solid organs', which store ch'i; the 'hollow' yang organs are concerned with transforming this vital energy and discharging waste.

Each element is also associated with other external and internal factors, in particular the seasons and the emotions. The above chart can give only a simplified picture of these complex relationships. For example, Wood is seen as the initiator of action, responsible for planning and organizing, having a personal sense of purpose and hope for the future. Point names on the liver meridian (associated with Wood) include 'Gate of Hope'. But Wood is also particularly associated with anger. 'When anger rises to the head and does not descend, the liver is injured.' (*Nei Jing.*) In other words, excessive or unresolved anger is harmful to the liver and Wood element, and it causes headache. For some people alcohol is an intensifier of anger as well as being harmful to the liver. (The description 'gung-ho' has a Chinese etymology and in one version the expression derives from *gan* [liver] and *ho* [fire], indicating a person in whom the element of fire is in excess especially in relation to the liver, which having the attributes of the element Wood can be 'consumed' by fire.) People who have difficulty with anger should avoid excessive consumption of food that is toxic to the liver – alcohol, drugs, chocolate and fatty foods. Just as anger damages the liver, joy (excessive excitement) may harm the heart (how many comedians die of heart attacks?), anxiety the spleen, grief the lungs, and fear the kidneys.

As well as having acupuncture points needled, some patients may be treated with MOXIBUSTION. This involves burning the dried or powdered leaves of the herb mugwort (*Artemesia vulgaris latiflora*), also known as moxa, and holding the smouldering substance close to the skin.

Other therapeutic techniques which may form part of treatment with acupuncture include massage (particularly ACUPRESSURE) and CUPPING. Acupuncture is also commonly used in combination with herbal and naturopathic remedies, and it may be combined with HOMOEOPATHY (homoeopuncture).

In the West, acupuncture is often tried as a last resort, when other remedies have failed, and when according to Chinese medical theory it is already too late for the sort of cure the patient is looking for. Perhaps for this reason acupuncture is regarded as less effective in life-threatening diseases, but it is very useful in dealing with a variety of conditions that do not respond well to conventional treatment, such as migraine, frozen shoulder, headache, impotence, asthma, and skin problems. It is often used today to help people when they want to stop smoking. It helps them to relax and improves general vitality, so reducing the habitual need to smoke, as well as reducing the withdrawal symptoms.

As a substitute for anaesthetic, acupuncture analgesia was not used in a surgical operation until 1958 in Shanghai and not witnessed by western (American) scientists until 1971. For analgesic purposes a form of electro-acupuncture is usually used, in which the needles are electrically stimulated. Dr David Eisenberg, an American trained doctor who also studied Chinese medicine in China, has described several operations in which acupuncture analgesia was used.[37] However, acupuncture is regarded as not as effective as conventional anaesthetics for most people, because most people cannot relax the muscles adequately while still conscious. Nevertheless it has definite advantages; acupuncture avoids many problems associated with anaesthetics such as post-operative bleeding, nausea, respiratory difficulties and temporary suppression of the immune system, and recovery rates tend to be quicker after an operation with acupuncture.

ACU-YOGA In acu-yoga specific movements and postures are used which activate the energy meridians of ACUPUNCTURE and ACUPRESSURE.

ADAPTATION ENERGY/(GENERAL) ADAPTATION RESPONSE According to Hans Selye, the Canadian pioneer of STRESS research, every individual is born with a certain amount of 'adaptation energy', which is gradually used up as stressful events are encountered. It has been likened to a bag of coins: once spent it cannot be replaced. Every individual may inherit a different quantity of it, but once it is gone, burnout occurs. In studies of shell-shocked soldiers, Lord Moran, Sir Winston Churchill's personal physician, referred to this energy as 'courage'. In terms of adaptation energy and the effects of its depletion, shell shock in young soldiers is similar to senility in the elderly.

According to the theory of the *general adaptation response* as proposed by Selye, the effects of severe stress follow a pattern of three basic stages: the alarm stage, the adaptation stage (or stage of resistance, during which the organism adapts or withstands the 'attack') and the exhaustion stage. This pattern is followed in all situations of stress, whether physical or emotional. The alarm stage may be characterized in the case of physical injury by pain or inflammation and in cases of emotional trauma by shock. In the adaptation stage the body adjusts to the crisis or resists it, perhaps by stiffening a joint or suppressing hurt feelings. (It has been suggested that during recovery from chronic conditions there is often a return to this stage of resistance, giving rise to what is known as a HEALING CRISIS.) If there is still no relief from the stressful situation there follows the exhaustion stage, in which there is physical degeneration or emotional collapse.

Morale studies of bomber crews in the Second World War showed that the alarm stage lasted for the first five or six missions; the adaptation stage lasted for only about another five missions; after about the eleventh flight the exhaustion stage was reached, the equivalent of shell shock, in which young men, in a state of war-weary resignation, aged almost overnight.

ADJUSTMENT The founder of CHIROPRACTIC adopted the use of the word 'adjustment' to refer to the thrust used by chiropractors to shift misaligned vertebrae back into their proper position.

ADULT See TRANSACTIONAL ANALYSIS.

AERION THERAPY The use of ionizers to increase the number of negative ions in the air we breathe is sometimes called aerion therapy. It is more commonly known as air IONIZATION THERAPY.

AFFIRMATIONS Affirmations are statements of intention which are made as if they were already facts. In their simplest form they are an element of POSITIVE THINKING, as in the famous dictum 'Every day, in every way, I am getting better and better' – an affirmation devised as a mantra by Emile Coué, the creator of AUTOSUGGESTION. It is in combination with various therapies allied to hypnosis, such as autosuggestion, SILVA MIND CONTROL and HYPNOTHERAPY that affirmations can best be exploited. They are used, for example, at certain points in AUTOGENIC THERAPY, where the desired aim is 'autogenic modification' – improvement in the functional use of a particular part of the body or the overcoming of a chronic condition. In treating hay fever, for example, one could use the affirmation 'Pollen doesn't matter' while in the autogenically induced state of deep relaxation.

AH SHI POINTS See ALARM POINTS.

AIKIDO Aikido means literally the road (*do*) to union or harmonization (*ai*) with the life-force (*ki*); the name can be translated more idiomatically as the 'way to spiritual harmony'. It is one of the most recently developed of the Japanese MARTIAL ARTS, having been invented in the 1920s by Morihei Ueshiba (1883–1969), a martial arts expert skilled in the use of traditional weapons (sword, spear and staff) as well as in judo and jujitsu. He maintained that the true purpose of *budo* (the Japanese term for martial arts) was to develop love for all creation. Although aikido is a form of self-defence, it depends on cultivating a sense of harmony between oneself and the aggressor. As in other martial arts, power is seen not to depend on size and strength; the force of the aggressor is not resisted but rechannelled so as to neutralize the attack. But unlike judo and jujitsu, aikido is not competitive: it is based on cooperation, on a relationship of give and take. Combat is regarded as a metaphor for life, with victory and defeat being unimportant except as a reflection of the changing fortunes of life. Although aikido is always practised with a partner, in other respects it has much in common with T'AI CHI: both stress the importance of allowing the body to act in a smooth, natural way, reducing tension and promoting a sense of balance and harmony.

AIR IONS See IONIZATION THERAPY.

ALARM POINTS In ACUPUNCTURE alarm points are points on the skin which become particularly sensitive in acute conditions. These may have been the first points to be discovered, before the system of acupuncture was developed. On the front of the body they are called *mu* points, and on the back, *shu* points. Each one is associated with a particular organ. Other points which become tender in certain conditions and are used as indicators of an incipient problem are called *Ah Shi* points (*Ah Shi* meaning 'That's it!').

ALARM STAGE See general ADAPTATION RESPONSE.

ALEXANDER PRINCIPLE/ALEXANDER TECHNIQUE The

Alexander technique is a process of psycho-physical re-education: by inhibiting automatic habitual responses it allows one to eliminate old behaviour patterns. It is not manipulation, and strictly speaking it is not a therapy or a treatment. Although it improves body posture it is wrong to define it as posture-training. It gets rid of many other faulty habits as well as bad posture, including tension, poor breathing, and speech defects, by enabling the individual to acquire conscious control over the body, its reactions and behaviour.

Alexander's fundamental discovery was that the wrong use of the body plays an important part in disease. He wrote: 'The majority of people have developed a manner of use of themselves which is constantly exerting a harmful influence not only upon their functioning but also upon their manner of reaction. We should be able to see that this wrong use can be a source of individual failings, peculiarities, wrong ideas and ills of all kinds, as well as that inward unrest and unhappiness which is evident in the social life of today.'[2]

Frederick Matthias Alexander (1869–1955) was born in Tasmania and trained as an actor. He started to specialise in giving dramatic and humorous monologues, and found that his voice disappeared. Self-observation convinced him that he was misusing his body, which prevented him from speaking properly. His head, neck and back were in a state of tension.

Alexander: 'I saw that as soon as I started to recite, I tended to pull back the head, depress the larynx, and suck in breath through the mouth in such a way as to produce a gasping sound.'[2] The trouble was caused not by his vocal organs, but by the way he was using them, and in particular the way he was using his spine. He achieved insight into this by self-observation, both while he was behaving in his habitual way and while he was trying to change this behaviour.

Part of the problem, both of our 'wrong' behaviour and of our attempts to change it, is that we are unaware of what we are actually doing with our bodies. In this respect we cannot rely on our feelings and sensory apparatus to give us accurate information: we suffer from what Alexander called 'debauched kinaesthesia'.

The technique that Alexander developed changes behaviour by changing the individual's sensory experiences. It is not a set of exercises, nor can it be learnt from a book. By using hand contact and verbal directions the teacher gives the student a new experience in bodily coordination. The aim is to re-educate the kinaesthetic senses. It is notoriously difficult to describe in words how this is achieved; as Aldous Huxley (one of Alexander's 'pupils') wrote,

'One cannot describe the experience of seeing the colour red. Similarly, one cannot describe the much more complex experience of improved physical coordination.'[89]

A significant aspect of changing one's behaviour and one's sensory experience is the process of 'attending to oneself'. For example, by thinking of 'going up' (but without looking up) when making a downward movement one can learn to prevent the 'collapse' that affects the posture of most people. Thinking of maintaining an erect posture would most decidedly not achieve this.

Typically we worry too much about the end result instead of focusing on the *how*, the 'means whereby'. As Wilfred Barlow put it, 'As human beings, we are so constructed that we work best when we concern ourselves with process. When we are concerned with *ends* rather than *means*, our bodies don't function as well. The human organism is built for process-operation, not for end-gaining.'[8] Inhibiting old patterns of behaviour means first of all inhibiting even the initial intention, because the mere intention initiates the body's 'wrong' response and reinforces the old habits before new patterns can be established. Re-educating the body's reactions through the Alexander technique means developing a 'refusal to do' and a willingness to 'let it happen' which is akin to the way of Zen.

Human reactions tend to be too quick and too strong, as well as automatic and habitual. Even getting up from a chair can put harmful pressure on the body. According to Alexander the chair is humanity's worst invention, since it encourages bad habits: people who squat or sit cross-legged on the ground suffer far less from arthritis and back problems. Furthermore, crossing the legs when sitting on a chair interferes with circulation and raises one side of the pelvis, creating a sideways curve of the spine.

Our modern lifestyles give less opportunity for natural physical stimulation, and we seem to have lost the ability to relax properly. For example, after any movement the body should return to a state of balanced rest but is often rigid or collapsed or a combination of the two. One reason why people lose height as they get older is the constant over-contraction of muscles and the inability to allow them to return to their lengthened resting state.

Alexander believed that at this stage in human evolution we have lost the instinct to use the body well; others maintain that each generation loses it in childhood. Whichever view is closest to the truth, Alexander realized that the key area to focus on when 'unlearning' the body's habitual reactions and tensions is at the top of the spine – the head and neck area. This he called the Primary

Control of Use, believing that it had a profound effect on the whole organism. Tension in this area, for example, has a deleterious effect on breathing, which can result in shortening and curvature of the spine, causing backache, more tension and problems in other parts of the body. Since such tension also interferes with circulation, resistance is lowered and one is more open to infection and disease.

Alexander moved to London in 1904. As an actor himself he first took on other actors as pupils. (He never referred to his clients as patients.) Among these were Henry Irving, Lillie Langtry and Herbert Beerbohm Tree. He started teaching regularly in New York, and gained the support of the philosopher and educationist, Professor John Dewey, who wrote an introduction for his second book, *Constructive Conscious Control of the Individual* (1924). Until 1930 there were only three other teachers of the new technique, including his brother (A. R. Alexander), but then with growing awareness of his methods among doctors and educationists he started to train others to teach the technique. He continued to take on pupils, including such figures as Aldous Huxley, Adrian Boult and Bernard Shaw, who started lessons when he was eighty.

Aldous Huxley wrote, 'It is now possible to conceive of a totally new type of education, affecting the entire range of human activity . . . which would preserve children and adults from most of the diseases and evils that now affect them.'[89] He also referred to 'a general heightening of consciousness on all levels' which the technique brought about. Alexander recognized that muscular balance and control are inseparably linked with mental states, so it was no surprise to him that his pupils often noted that they were mentally calmer, more open-minded and tolerant, with a corresponding improvement in their personal relationships and greater self-confidence. Those who had come to him with some weakness in the back discovered that, both literally and figuratively, they had backbone after all. The Alexander technique combines well with YOGA: it is said to make both breathing exercises and meditation more effective.

ALLOPATHIC MEDICINE/ALLOPATHY One of the most basic tenets of conventional medicine is that treatment aims to counteract the symptoms manifested in a disease, in an attempt to create a condition which is different from the one that caused the disease. So any imbalance is countered by intervention to rectify the balance: by the introduction of food or drugs, by raising or lowering the body temperature, or by depriving the body of something. Such treatment is *allopathic* (from the Greek roots *allo*, different, and *pathos*, suffering). Allopathy was defined by Hahnemann (who introduced the term) as 'the curing of a diseased action by the inducing of another or a different action, yet not necessarily diseased'. Difficulties arise when such treatment fails to distinguish adequately between physiological conditions which are at the root of the problem and those which are a natural part of the self-healing process. It was this inadequacy which led Hahnemann to develop HOMOEOPATHY, based on the principle of treating like with like.

ALPHA RHYTHMS See BRAIN RHYTHMS.

ALTERED STATE OF CONSCIOUSNESS See STATES OF CONSCIOUSNESS.

ALTERNATIVE MEDICINE 'Alternative' is one of several ways of referring to a variety of therapies and types of health care which are not normally available from the so-called general practitioner trained in orthodox medicine. It is probably the one description which carries the fewest overtones.

The term of 'fringe', whilst not being as derogatory as 'quack', has pejorative connotations, and to some ears 'unorthodox' or 'unconventional' may polarize the issue, sounding unduly subversive, more obstinately outside the mainstream, whose position as 'orthodox' and 'conventional' is not actually challenged. At the other end of the spectrum, to talk of 'natural' remedies may sound too partisan, and in any case it is a rather loose term to apply to some systems: is acupuncture natural? Some remedies may be described as 'traditional', but not all alternative therapies have long traditions behind them, and many are much more sophisticated than the term 'folk medicine' suggests. 'Holistic' seems to imply that alternative therapies have a monopoly on HOLISM and that they are inherently holistic, ignoring the fact that in the wrong hands they too can be practised in a most 'unholistic' way.

The designation 'complementary' has often been seen as an attempt to show how conventional and unconventional therapies may work in conjunction with each other, but this tends to conceal a basic rivalry between the two: if treatment is given according to theories which are actually rejected by medical science, how can the two approaches live harmoniously together? Too often they are diametrically opposed. Homoeopathic remedies, for example, can never be used to 'complement' the antibiotics of mainstream medicine.

So along the spectrum of descriptions – fringe, unorthodox, unconventional, alternative, complementary, traditional, folk, natural, holistic – 'alternative' is probably the most accurate and the least contentious. Terms such as 'alternative' and 'complementary' seem to be used less often in this context in North America (perhaps because in Canada and the USA, unless the law specifically permits the practice of a named alternative therapy, it is illegal). Lawrence LeShan refers to alternative therapies as 'adjunctive modalities'[116] and to practitioners of alternative medicine as 'adjunctive professionals'. A different problem arises with the American use of 'traditional': in the USA people imbued in the modern western tradition of medical science often refer to mainstream, orthodox, conventional medicine as 'traditional medicine'. Whenever we hear or read this description we have to remember to ask ourselves, 'Whose tradition are we talking about?'

Alternative medicine takes many forms. There are complete systems of healing, such as acupuncture, herbalism, and homoeopathy. Then there are specific methods of diagnosis which are not part of any grand system of medicine; these include kinesiology (for allergies), iridology (for hidden disease), hair analysis (for nutritional defects). Other therapies which do not belong to any particular system may lend themselves more readily to use as a supplement to other (perhaps conventional) treatment: massage, reflexology, aromatherapy and hydrotherapy may be considered in this category. And there are various 'self-help' therapies, some of which may have started life as part of whole systems of medicine: in this category we could put meditation, visualization, breathing and relaxation, exercise therapies such as t'ai-chi, and aspects of food and diet.

The various alternative therapies can be categorized in another way, according to the method used rather than the purpose. Food and diet may be considered as types of NATURAL REMEDIES, which use naturally occurring substances directly on the body (whether externally or internally). Some can be classified as MANIPULATIVE THERAPIES which work on the musculo-skeletal structure; despite their apparently physical orientation, claims are often made for the beneficial mental effects of such therapies. Similar claims are made by the BODY AWARENESS or 'exercise and movement' therapies, which include yoga and martial arts as well as dance therapy. Other SENSORY THERAPIES using colour, art and music more obviously exploit the ability of the mind consciously or unconsciously to influence the body in order to achieve their results, as do the many kinds of psychological or MENTAL THERAPY from hypnosis to the different therapies based on forms of humanistic psychology. Although these five categories may at first sight seem fairly clear-cut, it is not always easy to ascribe a particular therapy to one group alone. Aromatherapy is both natural and sensory; bioenergetics is mental but involves body awareness; t'ai chi is a therapy of movement but also involves mental discipline; in the Alexander Technique body awareness is achieved partly by manipulative and partly by psychological means. So these categories represent rather vague areas on a spectrum of entry points into the body-mind system.

In Britain, people are allowed to set themselves up as therapists of any kind without interference from the state, the only legal restriction being that an alternative practitioner should not claim to be a medical doctor. This goes some way to explaining the proliferation and availability of different kinds of alternative therapies in Britain, but it does not explain why the demand for them has grown so much in recent years. To answer that question we need to consider how and why people's attitude to mainstream medicine has changed.

There was a time when the medical profession was respected above all others; sadly that is probably no longer the case. There is some justification for saying that the seeds of dissent were sown in the 1940s and 1950s, when mainstream medicine seemed to be having unprecedented success. That was the time when many new drugs were introduced, often with spectacular results, when belief in the MAGIC BULLET approach received its greatest boost. The belief grew that medicine would ultimately find a cure for everything, that all disease was purely organic (in a strictly materialistic sense), and only a doctor really understood the workings of the body. The reaction against such blind faith and unrealistic expectations was probably inevitable.

One of the key triggers may have been the thalidomide tragedy in the early 1960s. This drew public attention to the fact that modern drugs can have disastrous side-effects. Having been encouraged to put all their faith in doctors, who had assumed total responsibility for the health of patients ('The doctor knows best'), people suddenly started to feel betrayed. It was also found that at any one time a significant proportion of patients in hospital were there as a result of their treatment rather than their original condition; their illness was IATROGENIC – caused by doctors. People like Ivan Illich started drawing the public's attention to this and complained of the MEDICALIZATION of life – our increasing dependency on professionals – which the medical establishment fostered. At the same time evidence was growing that personality and lifestyle were important factors in the genesis and development of disease, an idea which had always been one of the basic premises of many non-mainstream systems of medicine.

Whilst the public's perception of doctors underwent drastic change, the doctors themselves were slow to adapt and did little to remedy the loss of confidence. If anything, whether out of conviction that their methods were right or for lack of time to do anything else, doctors seemed even more inclined to address illnesses and symptoms rather than the individuals suffering from them, and seemed content to be dispensers of drugs. (Yet there is perhaps indirect evidence that doctors have long been well aware that they have not been satisfying the real needs of their patients: alcoholism among doctors is about three times the figure for other professional groups, and mental illness, including depression and suicide, is twice as common amongst doctors as amongst men of equal professional standing.)

Dissatisfaction with an orthodox doctor's manner, which is a direct consequence of the general ethos of orthodox medicine, lies at the root of many people's decision to go to an alternative practitioner. Of the four main reasons given for consulting such therapists, three are concerned with the desire to be treated as an individual – the alternative practitioners are said to offer more time, more compassion, and they actually touch the patient. Ivan Illich has suggested that most traditional healing methods were a way of consoling, caring and comforting people while the body did what was necessary for the natural process of healing to occur. The fourth reason people give for consulting alternative therapists is their charisma; this is in stark contrast to and perhaps partly a result of the public's loss of faith in orthodox doctors: patients still need healers with some kind of mystique.

This sense of mystique not only compensates for people's loss of confidence in orthodox doctors; somehow it also seems to engender faith in the new therapy, and faith contributes to the therapy's effectiveness. Those who approach a particular therapy with enthusiasm report 70–90 per cent effectiveness, whilst the effectiveness for sceptics is reduced to 30–40 per cent. Doctors themselves are not immune to this phenomenon and trials have shown that their own faith in the treatment they administer is also significant: doctors report better results from a new drug as compared with a PLACEBO, even when what they are actually comparing is one placebo with another (i.e. unknown to them, the new drug has been replaced with another placebo).

17

The ease with which this mystique can be manufactured by charlatans is a constant danger which inevitably handicaps genuine alternative practitioners, but for too long mainstream doctors used this as an excuse to ignore alternative medicine altogether. They often characterize the alternative lobby as unscientific and credulous, seizing on anything science rejects. An American psychoanalyst, Jules Eisenbud, has coined an aphorism which he calls Eisenbud's First Theorem: 'Just because an idea has been rejected by modern science does not mean that ipso facto it is valid.'

The medical profession is certainly now modifying its stance, but it is a very slow process. 1986 was an interesting year in terms of the debate between conventional and alternative medicine in Britain. In that year the *Lancet* published a report of studies on acupuncture and homoeopathy (areas which are still avoided in comparable American journals such as the *New England Journal of Medicine*), and in May 1986 the report of the British Medical Association's Board of Science and Education on Alternative Therapy was published.

In that report the BMA accepted that acupuncture, osteopathy and chiropractic might have a valid role in pain relief, but this was less a result of well-documented clinical evidence than a consequence of the discovery in laboratory research in 1975 that the body's central nervous system produced its own analgesics, endorphins. Too often the crucial test in the eyes of mainstream medicine is not whether a therapy works, but whether some sort of biochemical mechanism can be identified to explain *how* it works. The report concluded that there was 'no logical class of alternative therapies: only therapies with and without good evidence for their efficacy' (in other words, scientifically controlled CLINICAL TRIALS).

Yet none of this diminished the public's inclination to consult alternative practitioners. In that same year a survey in *Which?* magazine (October 1986) revealed that in 1985 one in seven readers had visited an alternative therapist of some kind, and the numbers have been steadily growing. The underlying mood of the public had been caught well by the Prince of Wales in his address to the BMA in 1983. (It was partly as a result of this address that the BMA had set up the working party which reported in 1986.) Prince Charles claimed that 'the whole imposing edifice of modern medicine' was 'slightly off balance'. He issued a warning to his audience: 'Don't underestimate the importance of an awareness of what lies beneath the surface of the visible world and of those ancient unconscious forces which still help to shape the psychological attitudes of modern man. Sophistication is only skin-deep and when it comes to healing people it seems to me that account has to be taken of those sometimes long-neglected complementary methods of medicine.'

If the BMA report of 1986 did little to answer this challenge, two years later the Royal Society of Medicine conceded that the medical establishment might have something to learn from alternative practitioners. In 1988 the RSM published a brief survey of the relationship between orthodox and alternative medicine in which members of the medical establishment recognized that 'Conventional medicine may be guilty of imposing its own illness model on patients and the doctor may therefore fail to understand patients' needs, and as a consequence fail to help them.' In contrast to this, it was acknowledged, 'The complementary practitioner would probably take a more thorough history than the conventional doctor and might therefore be better able to isolate the environmental and psychological elements aggravating or causing the ulcer.'[177]

The establishment is now having to admit that it does not have all the answers and that many of its oft-stated objections to alternative medicine were not wholly objective. Similar reports have been appearing in many western countries. For example, the Commission for Alternative Systems of Medicine set up by the Netherlands Ministry of Health and Environmental Protection said in 1981 that the division between orthodox and alternative systems of medicine was not primarily scientific but had its origin in political and social as much as scientific factors.

Nevertheless there is an enormous difference between orthodox western medicine and the main systems of alternative medicine. It is not just a difference in the manner of the doctor: there is often a profound difference in belief regarding the human organism. Orthodox medicine regards the human body as a mechanism; if it breaks down somewhere, the doctor intervenes to eradicate all symptoms of disease and to get everything working properly again. Most alternative systems of medicine see the human organism as multidimensional: matter and energy are interchangeable, and disease is a late manifestation of underlying imbalances. It is these imbalances which need rectifying, and the disease is generally the body's own attempt to re-establish harmony; intervention should not therefore attack symptoms indiscriminately, since they are part of the body's natural coping mechanism. Alternative systems of medicine stress the interconnectedness of all things; the western separation of mind and body is seen as artificial, and consciousness is seen as playing an integral role in the physical universe. At the same time the linear model of cause and effect is only partly applicable to disease and health, so that it is pointless to look for a single cause for a disease as western medicine does. Health and disease lie along a continuum and represent the organism's degree of harmony with the universe. It is the task of the (alternative) healer to encourage the innate capacity of the individual to restore their state of balance and harmony.

Most alternative systems of medicine are essentially preventive, in that all is done to help the individual to preserve that crucial balance. This is true health-care, whereas orthodox medicine has become 'sick-care', with doctors being consulted only when something has obviously gone wrong; the orthodox system dispenses treatment but does not invest in health. The increasing popularity of alternative medicine, regardless of whether or not orthodox medicine is seen to have failed, is perhaps also due in part to the opportunity it offers for self-responsibility. People who subscribe to orthodox medicine depend on medicine rather than on themselves; alternative medicine hands responsibility back to the individual, and health is then one of the few remaining areas of life in which the individual can maintain a sense of power, of self-control and self-determination, and perhaps a truer sense of 'self'.

AMMA Amma is a form of traditional Chinese massage. It is a technique of rubbing and pressing the body in order to stimulate circulation and the flow of CH'I. It forms the original basis of massage technique used in ACUPRESSURE, and its Japanese equivalent, *anma*, has been incorporated into SHIATSU.

ANAGOGIC INTERPRETATION Used in religious discussion, 'anagogic' (from Greek, 'lifting up') refers to the spiritual or allegorical interpretation of scriptures. Jung used the term when referring to the spiritual interpretation of DREAMS. It was part of his 'progressive' method which aimed at synthesis rather than analysis.

ANALYSIS See PSYCHOANALYSIS and PSYCHOTHERAPY.

ANALYTICAL PSYCHOLOGY In 1911 Jung named his work 'analytical psychology' to distinguish it from that of Freud. It can be defined as the science of mapping out the inner workings of the psyche. (See EGO, SELF, SHADOW, ANIMA/ANIMUS, INDIVIDUATION, EGO FUNCTIONS, ARCHETYPE, etc.)

ANIMA/ANIMUS 'Anima' (Latin for 'soul', that which gives life to or 'animates' the body) is the word chosen by Jung to refer to the image of a woman which a man carries in his own psyche, 'animus' being the masculinzed form referring to the masculine image within a woman. From puberty (if not before) children assimilate the characteristics associated with their sex in their conscious personality, whilst the contrasexual characteristics remain unconscious. These also become polarized so that we carry both idealized and SHADOW versions of our anima/animus. Jung believed that this happens at a collective as well as a personal level. For example, the (masculine) Roman Catholic church projects its anima positively onto the Virgin Mary and negatively as the Whore of Babylon (or even, perhaps, women in general).

When people fall in love, it is claimed, they have found someone who fits or corresponds fairly closely to the positive version of this unconscious image they carry within, love at first sight being an indication that it has probably been projected onto the other person. The other is then appreciated only in a rather idealized form, as it was with Dante's obsession with Beatrice. Recognition of one's 'other half' brings a passionate desire to unite with it in order to become whole. When love 'wears off' it is a sign that the two people must start to appreciate each other as individuals, a process which is made easier if they each also start to recognize the power and quality of their own anima/animus. This is one of the tasks in INDIVIDUATION. As Emma Jung wrote in her study *Animus and Anima* (Jung himself had devoted most of his attention to the anima rather than the animus), 'Redemption is achieved by recognizing and integrating these unknown elements of the soul.'[107]

ANIMAL MAGNETISM See MESMERISM.

ANMA Anma was a form of traditional Japanese massage with the purpose of stimulating circulation. It has been incorporated into SHIATSU.

ANOREXIA NERVOSA Anorexia is literally 'loss of appetite', and the 'nervous' description indicates that its origin is believed to be psychological. (We still use words like 'nerves' and 'nervous' when referring to a variety of mental and emotional conditions in which the actual nerves are not directly involved at all: a bundle of nerves, a nervous breakdown, lose your nerve, unnerving, etc.)

Although anorexia nervosa is commonly regarded as an illness of our modern age, this is not the case: the term was first used in the nineteenth century by the English physician, William Gull (1816–90), and there are accounts of the condition going back several centuries. However, the preoccupation among women today with slimness may account for a higher incidence of anorexics, who typically have a distorted sense of their own body-image. Although commonly associated with girls and young women, it can also affect men.

It is one of the growing number of illnesses in which the medical establishment is increasingly obliged to acknowledge an interplay of psychological and biological factors. It is thought that the condition is initiated somewhere in the hypothalamus, the region of the brain controlling the emotions, appetite and sexuality, all of which are involved in anorexia. The initial trigger is often an extreme family situation, the death of a parent or a decision to marry against the wishes of a parent. In 10 per cent of cases it results in death.

ANTHROPOSOPHICAL MEDICINE Anthroposophical medicine is a philosophy of health and medicine developed by Rudolf Steiner (1861–1925) in accordance with the principles of anthroposophy as a response to questions brought to him by doctors. Steiner started delivering lectures to medical audiences in 1920 but had already formulated ideas and given advice on cures, as reported by Kafka in a diary entry as early as 1911. As a belief system anthroposophy was based primarily on the ideas of Theosophy, but Steiner adopted a fundamentally Christian view (as opposed to the Hindu-cum-Buddhist worldview of the Theosophists) and his whole approach was more human. The name 'anthroposophy' is derived from the Greek *anthropos*, 'man', and *sophia*, wisdom, and Steiner said that the aim in studying anthroposophy is to become fully aware of what it means to be human. According to this interpretation anthroposophy means 'awareness of one's humanity'.

Only medically qualified doctors are allowed to train and practise in anthroposophical medicine. Although this might suggest that anthroposophical medicine can be regarded as complementary to mainstream medicine (anthroposophists claim that it is an extension of orthodox medical practice rather than an alternative), the materialism and mechanistic reductionism of mainstream medicine has meant that the two have become increasingly incompatible and represent totally different ways of looking at the human organism. Their attitudes towards illness, for example, are almost diametrically opposed. As with many ALTERNATIVE systems of medicine, anthroposophists regard illnesses not so much as conditions to be eradicated as processes to be helped along so that balance is restored and a greater wholeness achieved. In contrast to the reductionist view that a living organism is no more than an aggregation of cells and that to understand the body it is sufficient to understand the mechanism and pathology of its basic units, i.e. the cell, Steiner stressed the importance of unquantifiable qualities of life such as the processes of growth and healing, which follow different laws from those that govern the behaviour of inert matter and which are not susceptible to chemical analysis.

In any living organism there are two invisible forces at work – one for growth and expansion, the other limiting and organizing such growth. If these two forces are in harmony the body is healthy. If the organizing force is weak, cancer can result (cells growing out of control). The organizing force is linked to a sense of individuality and personal uniqueness, so something of what was to be understood much later as the 'CANCER PERSONALITY' was foreshadowed in Steiner's teachings.

A fundamental premise of anthroposophy and of anthroposophical medicine is the existence of three 'worlds', three levels or modes of existence and consciousness beyond that of inanimate matter: they are – in ascending order from the physical – the etheric, the astral and the spiritual. Etheric forces are the formative forces that underlie and shape all animate matter. Astral bodies underlie the etheric bodies in animals and human beings, and spiritual bodies underlie the astral in humans only. These 'bodies' develop at different rates in early life: at the end of each of the first three seven-year periods of life there is according to Steiner a new 'birth'. At the age of seven, coinciding roughly with the loss of the milk teeth, there is the etheric birth, when the etheric body finally detaches itself completely from the mother; at the age of fourteen the astral body is born, accompanied by the onset of much emotional confusion; and at twenty-one, the traditional age of majority, the ego is born.

Disease results when a person's four 'bodies' malfunction in some way. This allows for a wide range of causative and contributory factors, since food and the environment can directly affect both the physical and the etheric levels of the organism, whilst the astral is affected by the inner life of emotions and drives, and the spiritual by a sense of conscious identity and the will. The interrelationship of these four levels is reflected in the anthroposophical belief that PSYCHOSOMATIC processes work both ways: the mind can produce physical disorders and bodily malfunctions can result in psychological disturbances (e.g. liver disorders can cause depression). Steiner never recognized the validity of talking about the unconscious mind; no such separate entity could exist in his scheme, although his 'physical psychotherapy' might deal with the same basic issues. For these reasons Steiner always recommended that any physical treatment should be supported by treatment for the mind in the form of ART THERAPY or EURHYTHMY.

According to Steiner the human organism has a triune structure consisting of two 'poles' and a system which links and harmonizes them. The upper 'thinking' or 'nerve-sense' pole, also referred to as the *cephalic* pole, includes the brain, nerves and sense organs and is associated with thinking, consciousness, perception and the means by which the individual absorbs the outside world. The lower pole, also called the *metabolic* pole, deals with food conversion and energy transformation and is associated with locomotion and the means by which the individual influences the outside world through action. The third part of the human organism is the *rhythmic* system, centred in the chest and consisting of the heart, lungs and blood vessels; it is concerned with breathing and the circulation of the blood, harmonizing and balancing out the centripetal (cephalic) and centrifugal (metabolic) aspects of the two poles. These three aspects of the human organism parallel the three basic faculties – thinking, the will and the emotions.

upper (cephalic) pole	brain, nerves, senses	perception, thinking
linking, rhythmic system	heart, lungs, respiration, circulation	feeling, emotions
lower (metabolic) pole	limbs, locomotion, metabolism, energy	action, will

The principle of polarity is reflected in specific types of illness: over-activity of the metabolic pole tends to result in inflammatory conditions, whilst a lack of control in the nerve-sense pole leads to degenerative conditions and tumours. But whatever the immediate causes of a disease the ultimate causes arise from imbalances between the forces of the ego (spirit), the astral body and the etheric body, and the activities of the cephalic, metabolic and rhythmic systems. For example, anything that causes an excessive reduction in astral and spiritual activity at the cephalic (nerve-sense) pole can result in an attack of migraine. This can happen through stress, overwork, or by too much sense data being received too quickly.

Excessive demands on the nerve-sense system result in inadequate transference of astral energies to the digestive system to strip food of its etheric forces. This means that more energy is taken from the cephalic pole to restore balance, and migraine results.

Steiner also linked the traditional (western) temperaments – or HUMOURS – and the four elements to the four 'bodies'. So, for example, someone with a nervous temperament, susceptible to quick changes, just as the wind changes, has therefore an affinity with the element Air; the emotions are controlled by the astral body, which is said to be dominant in such people. The anthroposophical correlations for all four humours, elements and bodies are as follows.

HUMOUR	BODY	ELEMENT	ORGAN
melancholic	physical	Earth	lungs
phlegmatic	etheric	Water	liver
sanguine/nervous	astral	Air	kidneys
choleric	Ego/spirit	Fire	heart

From an anthroposophical viewpoint, illness is not an evil to be eliminated so much as an opportunity to achieve greater freedom and wholeness. This is similar to the concept of disease in many traditional alternative systems of medicine, but at the same time it goes further than most. For example, it is common to most alternative systems to regard inflammation not as a symptom to be eradicated but as an integral part of the healing process, so to reduce it artificially does not help the underlying condition. Anthroposophical medicine goes further than most other schools of thought in suggesting that the root causes of disease are mental, emotional and, most essentially of all, spiritual. The illness should therefore be worked with constructively, since it is often a means of overcoming the spiritual imbalance. Many of today's illnesses in the West, for example, result from overstimulation and a failure of will – a loss of the 'will-to-life'.

The anthroposophical physician has to work with the patient to find what lies behind an illness, a task which requires spiritual awareness to a degree which few if any other systems of medicine demand of their practitioners. Remedies are, of course, also administered, for all such substances act on more than just the physical level. Anthroposophical medicine recognizes the value of HOMOEOPATHY, and Hahnemann, the creator of homoeopathy, referred to the 'spirit-like medicinal powers' of POTENTIZED medicines – a clear reference to the 'energies' attributed to all natural substances by anthroposophical medicine. (The equivalent term in anthroposophy for potentization in homoeopathy is DYNAMIZATION.)

In anthroposophical medicine plants are thought to be a way of directing particular metals to particular organs in the body. In BIODYNAMIC AGRICULTURE plants are grown in a systematic way so that they absorb the required metals. Animals as well as minerals and plants are used as medication, often derived from the whole creature (spiders and bees) or from a mammalian organ, which is often used homologically (i.e. to treat the same organ in the human). Subcutaneous injection is often preferred to taking medicine orally, especially if the rhythmic system is to be influenced. Oral intake may be more common when the metabolic system is targeted, and external applications – oils, ointments, lotions and baths – are more effective when treating the nerve-sense system.

In continental Europe, especially Germany, Switzerland and the Netherlands, there are many more anthroposophical physicians and surgeons than in Britain or America. There are also at least ten anthroposophical hospitals in Europe, and in the Netherlands anthroposophical medicine is increasingly popular: its principles are used by teachers in primary schools and by those who care for the mentally handicapped, and many general practitioners are also qualified in anthroposophical medicine.

ANTIPSYCHIATRY Antipsychiatry was the name given to the movement that grew up in Britain around the ideas of the Scottish psychiatrist, R. D. Laing, but it had antecedents in the work of Thomas Szasz in America. The realization that patients confined in mental hospitals, far from being cured of their illness, became increasingly institutionalized, led to many questions being asked in the 1960s; to what extent was their treatment responsible for their condition? Were they actually ill at all? Who was to judge?

The American psychiatrist Thomas Szasz was one of the first to draw attention to the MEDICALIZATION of mental illness. In his view mental hospitals are simply a modern version of former lunatic asylums, using chemical straitjackets instead of physical ones, and substituting labels like psychopath and schizophrenic for witch and lunatic. According to his labelling theory or *social reaction theory*, someone who is labelled 'mad' will suffer stigmatization, which will accentuate their sense of alienation and thus formalize the 'illness' into a lifelong career of 'madness'. The humiliating experience of being confined and 'treated' in a psychiatric hospital, far from equipping the patient for a more normal life, actually strips away what sense of identity the individual has.

Some supporting evidence for these ideas was found through an experiment in which nine professional and academic people feigned mental illness and presented themselves for psychiatric help, complaining of hearing voices. Eight of these perfectly healthy individuals (with no particular acting ability) were diagnosed as schizophrenic, and all nine as manic depressive. While they were in the mental hospital, behaving normally, medical staff did not detect their previous subterfuge although other patients did.

Similar ideas were put forward by the American sociologist, Erving Goffman. From his observations while working for several months as a nurse's aide in a mental hospital, he came to the conclusion that instead of helping their patients the hospital tended to perpetuate the same kind of 'crazy' family situations and relationships which drove them 'mad' in the first place. Mental hospitals are 'maddening' places.[65]

According to Ronald Laing, our definition of mental illness is false, a product of a fault in society itself. Schizophrenics are not mad, but are searching for sanity in an insane society. Laing goes beyond Szasz's labelling theory, claiming that in developed cultures mental illness is a label attached to behaviour that is socially unacceptable. In his later work he suggests that this may be western society's way of silencing its mystics. However, he did not go as far as some of his followers in trying to explain all psychiatric illness in this way, for one cannot deny that there are people with psychiatric problems. Even tribal societies which have healers and shamans, acceptable identities for people who hear voices, do classify certain other members of their communities as mad.

The problem, as Laing sees it, lies both with society and with psychiatry. People with feelings of disintegration, consulting a psychiatrist given to making an impersonal objectification of psychic states, are put through a process of reductive analysis which can only add to their sense of alienation, depersonalization and unreality. Even if the elements revealed by the psychiatrist as underlying a patient's condition are true, the way in which they are communicated as facts can actually make them more significant and more difficult to overcome. 'Patients seeking help because they feel like dead and shattered objects find themselves further petrified by the viewpoints of psychiatry.'[74]

Laing points out that both patient and psychiatrist are 'split', schizoid, each having a TRUE SELF and a FALSE SELF. The patient, unable to feel real, has invented a false self with which to confront the outside world, and which absorbs and introjects all the judgments and criticisms of others, such that the individual has the experience of behaving like an automaton with no real freedom. ('So the person who says he is a machine is mad, while many of those who say men are machines are considered great scientists.'[74]) But the psychiatrist also has a false self, a professional self, in the form of a theory armed with its vocabulary of denigration and with which the patient, or rather the patient's false self, is objectified and analysed. Little wonder that the patient complains of not being truly understood: the true self is not really being addressed. 'It's a most terrible feeling to realize that the doctor can't see the real you, that he can't understand what you feel, and that he's just going ahead with his own ideas.'[113]

Only by recognizing first of all what is false can the psychiatrist and the patient hope to be successful in their enterprise. The false self must then be reconnected to the true self and unified with it. This does not invalidate the joint venture of psychiatrist and patient, but it does mean that the relationship between the two should be more honest, less authoritarian, allowing for more subjectivity. 'Psychotherapy must remain an obstinate attempt of two people to recover the wholeness of being human through the relationship between them.'[114]

APPLIED KINESIOLOGY Kinesiology is the science of muscle activation, literally the study of movement (from the Greek for 'to move'), but as a therapy, more often referred to as 'applied kinesiology' (or 'touch for health' in Britain), it is a technique of diagnostic muscle testing and a method of correcting imbalances in the body's energy system through touch. Although it was developed by a chiropractor, touch is not used to manipulate but more in the manner of ACUPRESSURE or SHIATSU.

In 1965 George Goodheart, an American chiropractor, discovered that some of his standard tests for muscle strength and tone gave indications of the working of the entire body. His first realization was that back problems could result not necessarily from the fact that certain muscles were in spasm or too taut, but rather that muscles on the opposite side of the body were too weak, causing the other muscles to tighten. This muscle imbalance could also be a result of energy imbalance in the eastern sense – the irregular flow of energy (or CH'I) along the pathways (or MERIDIANS). So through muscle testing the applied kinesiologist can diagnose not only structural imbalances but also organ dysfunctions, dietary deficiencies and allergies. To test for allergies, for example, the patient holds in one hand a phial containing a substance to which there may be an allergic reaction, and the flexibility or rigidity of the other arm when the kinesiologist applies pressure indicates whether that substance is safe for the patient or not. (The technique of combining muscle-testing with questions can also be used to probe the psychological roots of physical conditions. Investigating a patient's inner state in this way is sometimes called BIOKINESTHESIOLOGY.)

Applied kinesiology is said to chart electrical potentials in the body and hence the activity of the brain. In this way the kinesiologist discovers the individual polarity pattern of the patient, the relative dominance of the left or right hemisphere, the degree of communication between the two sides and the amount of 'switching' – rapidly alternating between the two sides instead of using them together. Realignment of the energy flow of the whole body can sometimes be achieved by a light touch on a specific point on the cranium. Other pressure points may be held for longer and meridians may be stroked lightly. Dietary factors are also considered in the treatment.

ARCHAEOPSYCHE/ARCHAEOPSYCHIC EGO STATE In TRANSACTIONAL ANALYSIS the archaeopsychic ego state is more commonly referred to as the CHILD.

ARCHETYPE In Jungian psychology archetypes are images in the collective unconscious which embody powerful forces in the psyche. Since they are 'in the collective unconscious' they are universal. For example, all over the world children have stories of witches, an archetype which represents simply their awareness of the negative side of the mother, every aspect of the mother which the child fears. As Jung made clear, it is not the images themselves that we inherit but the tendency to create them and use them. The term archetype 'is not meant to denote an inherited idea, but rather an inherited mode of functioning, corresponding to the inborn way in which the chick emerges from the egg, the bird builds its nest . . . In other words it is a "pattern of behaviour".'

Different archetypes will be more influential at different stages of life as the EGO grows and develops. Because of archetypes we are predisposed to approach life's experiences and deal with them in certain ways, according to patterns laid down in the psyche. There are archetypal figures (mother, father, child, God), archetypal events (birth, death, separation, marriage) and archetypal objects (sun, moon, snakes, animals, water). There are also certain archetypes which are crucial to the development of the EGO and its relationship with the SELF: the SHADOW and the ANIMA or ANIMUS. All such archetypes are manipulated in DREAMS and play the most important part in dream interpretation.

ARICA The Arica system is a training programme in self-development, compiled by the Bolivian-born mystic, Oscar Ichaza. The Arica Institute was founded in New York in 1972, following a visit by fifty Americans to Ichaza in Arica, Chile. Arica is sometimes called 'scientific mysticism' and aims at a scientific understanding of the psyche and the transformation of society. It represents a synthesis of several disciplines, combining aspects of eastern esoteric traditions such as Tibetan Buddhism, yoga and Zen with western HUMANISTIC PSYCHOLOGY and a scientific approach to MEDITATION and altered STATES OF CONSCIOUSNESS. Central to Arica is the new discipline called *psychocalisthenics* and its systematic programme of breathing and movement exercises and meditation aimed at achieving unity of body, mind and emotions at each of nine levels of consciousness.

ARMOUR/ARMOURING Armouring is a physical condition resulting from mental and emotional factors. 'Muscular armour' is a term coined by Wilhelm Reich to describe the chronic tightness of muscles caused by the repression of emotions. Typical inappropriate responses to anxiety, for example, result in restricted breathing and tightening of the stomach muscles. Muscular armouring can also manifest in the eye muscles, thus impairing vision, and astigmatism is often reduced when tension decreases. Alexander Lowen developed his BIOENERGETICS around the same basic premise, and the new sense of freedom felt by students of the ALEXANDER TECHNIQUE suggests a similar link, in this case from body to mind.

As well as muscular armour, Reich talked of 'character armour', resulting from years of being conditioned to be submissive in society. Reich himself focused on the deleterious effect of both types of armouring on orgastic potency and renewal of the body's life energy, and many other schools of therapy have shown how such character armour hinders an individual's ability to communicate, to form and maintain satisfactory relationships, and to grow psychologically.

ASSERTIVENESS TRAINING, for example, suggests simple ways to shed some of this character armour.

AROMATHERAPY A narrow interpretation of aromatherapy is that healing and preventive treatment is administered via the sense of smell alone. An alternative term for this interpretation is *ophresiology* from the Greek *ophresis* meaning 'smell'. But aromatic plant material can be used in various ways on the body too, and nowadays aromatherapy usually means the medicinal use of aromatic plant essences, applied by massage and in baths as well as through inhalation. In its widest interpretation aromatherapy may also include the ingestion of these essences, although many aromatherapists specifically exclude such practices.

The word was coined in 1937 (as the French *aromathérapie*) by René Maurice Gattefossé, a chemist and perfume manufacturer. Knowing something of the medicinal history of essential oils, he was impelled to write a study of the use of oils in dermatology following an incident in which his hand had been badly burned in a laboratory explosion. He had plunged his hand into a container of pure lavender oil and within hours it had healed completely.

The earliest aromatic oils were not distilled from the herbs themselves but were prepared by infusing the herbs in oils such as castor oil in ancient Egypt and olive oil in classical Greece. The basic method of *distillation* – by passing steam over the plant material, condensing it and syphoning off the oil – was discovered around the year AD 1000, reputedly by Avicenna. Rose, lavender and camomile were among the first essences to be distilled. In the twelfth century, with the travels of the crusaders, these essences and the method of distillation were introduced into Europe from the Arab world, and essential oils were added to existing HERBAL remedies. By the middle ages in Europe, the antiseptic power of certain essences was recognized: hospitals were fumigated by burning incense, and aromatic candles were used in sickrooms.

The olfactory nerve is connected to the limbic system, part of the brain that is concerned with memory and the emotions, which may explain why aromatherapy is considered to be particularly appropriate in conditions which are thought to have a strong psychosomatic component. The limbic system is connected to the hypothalamus and the pituitary gland, the master gland which controls all the other glands and the entire hormonal system. So smelling something not only influences mood, but can also affect the autonomic nervous system, the hormonal system and the wide range of responses which they control.

When molecules are inhaled, some will pass into the bloodstream along with the oxygen and will be transported around the body. When essential oils are mixed with natural vegetable oils and lotions and applied to the skin they pass through the pores, into the lymphatic system and again into the bloodstream. This *transcutaneous absorption* is generally regarded as the most effective method of administering essential oils. They can also be taken with food or drink, thus entering the bloodstream via the digestive system, but this is much slower and many aromatherapists disapprove of this method, considering it to be less safe. The alimentary canal is more sensitive, and less tolerant of essential oils, than the skin (incidentally the largest single organ in the body), which can absorb oil more easily, in greater quantities and with more immediate effect.

How the essences achieve their medicinal effect is not fully understood. The reductionist scientific method has so far failed to answer this basic question. For example, the active constituent in cloves, eugenol, can be isolated and used as an antiseptic, but as such it is not as effective as clove oil itself. Most essential oils consist of anything between 50 and 500 chemical constituents, so it is perhaps not surprising that they are more effective than one or two of those chemicals alone. Using isolated active constituents (which is what many conventional drugs are) can also result in unwanted side effects. In the absence of a satisfactory mechanistic explanation, many people are led to support the view that essential oils contain some 'vital energy' which acts at a more subtle level. Some talk of the 'personality' of a plant being preserved in this subtle form. As with homoeopathic remedies, which also defy mechanistic explanation, light causes the oils to deteriorate so they are kept in dark glass bottles.

Aromatherapy is often used in combination with various 'touch' therapies such as REFLEXOLOGY, APPLIED KINESIOLOGY and SHI-ATSU. Some aromatherapists may use dowsing with a pendulum (RADIESTHESIA) as a diagnostic tool and aspects of COLOUR THERA-PY may also be introduced.

AROMATIC OILS Aromatic oils, used in AROMATHERAPY, are of two kinds: they are either pure essential oils, obtained from plants in a variety of ways, or infused oils. Some essences can be obtained more easily than others: certain resins can be tapped directly from the trunk or branch, or the oil can be pressed out of plants such as cloves. But for most plants the process of oil extraction is more complex: by *distillation* (steaming the plant and collecting the concentrated oil from the condensation) or ENFLEURAGE (absorption of the plant oil by a fatty substance from which it is then separated). *Infusion*, the common practice for thousands of years before distillation was discovered, involved immersing the plant material in vegetable oil and heating the mixture. Infused oils are less concentrated than essential oils, they are very greasy and do not evaporate, whereas essential oils are actually non-oily and evaporate readily. (Modern perfumes generally speaking contain only 20 per cent natural ingredients, the rest being synthetic chemicals.)

AROUSAL DISORDER In modern life we often find ourselves in situations which evoke in us the FIGHT-OR-FLIGHT RESPONSE. But to give vent to this flood of hormonal activity in the body by actually fighting or fleeing is seldom deemed appropriate, and the accumulation of such events burdens us with almost constant physiological arousal – muscles tensed and metabolism heightened. Herbert Benson has called this counter-productive and damaging frustration of the fight-or-flight response an arousal disorder. His recommended antidote is to evoke the RELAXATION RESPONSE.

ART THERAPY In art therapy people express themselves through drawing, painting or modelling in clay. Immediate effects are usually a sense of relaxation, a release of tension, an increase in self-confidence and a reduction of anxiety. If art therapy is practised as part of Freudian or Jungian analysis the analyst will probably offer interpretations of the symbols used. Humanistic psychotherapists are more likely to invite the client to suggest interpretations. But overt interpretation is by no means always necessary: the simple act of self-expression is often sufficient to release the individual from past emotional problems, help to establish a clearer sense of identity and draw attention to new directions for the future, without the need for verbalization. For this reason it is often suitable for the less articulate or for people who are not well served by a 'talking cure'. In this sense it is comparable to some forms of MUSIC THERAPY. For those with little patience to wield a pencil or paintbrush SANDPLAY is another kind of creative therapy.

ARTIFICIAL SOMNAMBULISM The Marquis de Puységur, who

learned the technique of MESMERISM from Franz Mesmer, compared the trance-like state which was induced by so-called 'animal magnetism' with sleep-walking and referred to it as artificial somnambulism, a term that was used well into the nineteenth century by such people as William Gregory, an Edinburgh professor of chemistry who also researched HYPNOTISM. The Abbé de Faria (1755–1819) referred to the same phenomenon as 'lucid sleep'.

ASANAS The body postures used in HATHA YOGA are known by the Sanskrit name *asanas*, from the root meaning 'to sit'.

ASSERTIVENESS TRAINING Although assertiveness training was first developed as long ago as 1949 (by Andrew Salter in America), it was only in the mid-1970s that it really caught the public's imagination and became popular on both sides of the Atlantic. Demand for it grew initially as a result of the women's movement: reacting against society's imposition on them of a passive role, which made it difficult for many women even to express their needs let alone satisfy them, and realizing that adopting the stereotypically aggressive behaviour of men was counter-productive, women recognized probably before most men that 'assertive' behaviour represented the best strategy available for effective communication generally. Eventually many men, who had been conditioned to be more aggressive, also came to realize that aggressive behaviour was not the best way to preserve their self-esteem.

People are often unassertive simply because they think it is wrong to be assertive. This mistaken belief comes in part from an inability to distinguish between assertive and aggressive behaviour. The two natural responses an animal has to choose between in an emergency are to fight or to flee, the so-called FIGHT-OR-FLIGHT RESPONSE. But for humans the choice is not simply between aggression and passivity: because of our facility with language we need not feel obliged either to argue angrily (fighting with words) or to give in, letting the other person have the last say (submission and flight); we can also discuss and negotiate. Some of the verbal strategies adopted in assertive behaviour may at first sound like 'fighting talk', but they are in fact a non-aggressive way of dealing with aggression. It is perhaps the sense of victory over someone else's aggression (e.g. taking the wind out of their sails) that makes it difficult for some people to distinguish between assertive behaviour and aggression: assertive behaviour frustrates aggression by questioning or deflecting it, but with aggressive behaviour one simply locks horns with the aggressor.

The aggressive, passive and assertive attitudes are demonstrated not just in what we say but also in the way we use our voice and in our body language. An aggressive response is typified by shouting, standing with a rigid posture and with folded arms or pointing a finger. Signals of a passive attitude are a whining voice, clenched or wringing hands, shuffling feet, a stoop and an avoidance of eye contact. In assertive behaviour the voice is calm and controlled, the posture relaxed and upright, and eye contact is maintained.

People who are unassertive are often over-tolerant of the mistakes of others but surprisingly intolerant of their own shortcomings. Their readiness to accept blame is recognized and taken advantage of by the aggressive manipulators who are attracted to them. Ultimately the manipulators will also feel dissatisfied with their behaviour, which leads to distrust, antagonism and generally unsatisfactory relationships. Understanding the GAMES people play is one of the first lessons to learn in assertiveness training. It might also be helpful to recognize *why* one is too aggressive or passive, by recalling perhaps how one managed to get one's own way as a small child, but in assertiveness training one tends not to delve into the past in this way.

Much of assertiveness training is concerned with separating inappropriate aggression – anger – from simple assertive statements such as 'Please don't do that.' It aims to convert extreme anxiety and panic about one's own future performance to healthy concern, and to change guilt about having caused someone pain into sincere regret and an apology. It often involves modifying the behaviour of one's inner parent (see TRANSACTIONAL ANALYSIS) or replacing it with behaviour more typical of the inner adult.

Changing long-established behaviour patterns involves considerable 'reprogramming', or reconditioning. Certain aspects of POSITIVE THINKING come into play in this mental reprogramming. Unassertive people have often got into the habit of 'playing it safe'; they need to learn how to take risks, which requires a degree of self-confidence, developed while increasing one's self-esteem. This demands a recognition of self-worth – the ability, for example, to accept compliments as well as give them.

Learning how to deal with criticism confidently and in a way which does no damage is another major part of developing one's assertiveness. Too often we react aggressively to criticism, hitting back in a way which makes effective communication impossible. Or we take it too much to heart, thereby allowing what self-confidence we have to be destroyed (and incidentally building up anger and resentment). Or else we avoid criticism altogether by adopting ingratiating behaviour in a denial of our own rights. In assertive behaviour we acknowledge what is valid criticism and recognize that it can be useful, whilst pointing out (calmly) where we think criticism has been overgeneralized or exaggerated in some way. We also need to appreciate the difference between justified and manipulative criticism.

Three different techniques for dealing with criticism have been proposed by Manuel J. Smith.[161] *Negative assertion* means accepting valid criticism. If the criticism is manipulative, intended as a *put-down* to make one feel small, one again accepts it but in a modified way, saying that there may be some truth in it, but avoiding being cowed, or hurt, or drawn into a slanging match. This is called *fogging*. Denying the critic the satisfaction of seeing that one is upset makes it less likely that such an attempt to cause hurt will be made again. Another way of taking the sting out of a put-down is the *negative enquiry*, in which one asks for specific information about a general criticism that has been made.

At the same time one has to learn how to offer criticism constructively and sympathetically. This involves first acknowledging what is positive, and then being specific in one's criticism, avoiding labels, stereotypes and generalizations, limiting the criticism clearly and expressing it with empathy.

Clearly, whilst assertiveness is about recognizing and asserting one's rights, it is important to grant others their rights too. One cannot develop one's own assertiveness without at the same time encouraging and promoting assertiveness in others.

ASSIST In DIANETICS (and Scientology) an assist is an action which encourages an individual to overcome both the effects of an injury or harmful experience and the tendency to allow the event to recur.

ASTON PATTERNING Aston patterning is a method of identifying and correcting stress-induced movement habits, developed by Judith Aston, a dancer and choreographer who worked with Ida Rolf (see ROLFING). The technique stems from her main insight that people's bodies are asymmetrical and their movements occur in spirals, two factors which should be taken into consideration when learning more comfortable and effective ways of moving. First the therapist (or teacher) observes the client's movements, noting where movement is restricted, which movements cause bracing or protective changes in speed, where certain movements start, and which parts of the body are held unnaturally. The teacher can then teach the client to loosen certain areas and be more aware of the body. Treatment also includes massage to release unnecessary tension.

AT See AUTOGENIC TRAINING.

ATARAXIS See ATAVISTIC REGRESSION.

ATAVISTIC REGRESSION The Australian psychotherapist Ainsley Meares believes that the hypnotic trance is a throwback to a state of mind which predates the development of reason. It is a commonplace that animals instinctively know what food or herbs to seek out for their physical ailments, and under hypnosis people have also diagnosed their own condition far beyond their conscious knowledge of anatomy or medicine. Through atavistic regression, a blend of hypnosis and meditation, Meares seeks to reproduce this atavistic state of mind by removing the patient's immediate fears and worries in order to allow the body free rein to continue its natural self-healing process. This method is also called mental *ataraxis*, from the Greek for 'without disturbance'.

ATTAR The essential oil of plants, as used for example in AROMATHERAPY, is also known as attar. This term is most commonly used when referring to attar of roses (or rose *otto*), which is obtained from the petals of the damask rose, grown in the Balkans.

ATTENUATION In HOMOEOPATHY and ANTHROPOSOPHICAL MEDICINE remedies are prepared by a process of progressive dilution or attenuation, such that the doses which are administered contain a minimal amount of the original substance, if any at all. According to the LAW OF POTENTIATION the greater the degree of attenuation (i.e. the less of the original substance a remedy contains) the more potent the remedy is.

ATTITUDE There are at least three positions it is possible to adopt regarding the relationship between mental attitude and physical health, and each one includes many differences of degree. One position maintains that all illness originates at a non-physical level, whether mental, emotional or spiritual. HOLISTIC MEDICINE of all kinds regards mental attitude and physical condition as inseparable, as do many ALTERNATIVE therapies. Groddeck's notion of the IT falls into this category as does the more spiritual viewpoint of Edward

Bach (creator of the BACH FLOWER REMEDIES): 'Nothing in nature can hurt us when we are happy and in harmony, on the contrary all nature is there for our use and our enjoyment. It is only when we allow doubt and depression, indecision or fear to creep in that we are sensitive to outside influences. It is, therefore, the real cause behind the disease, which is of the utmost importance; the mental state of the patient himself, not the condition of his body.'[86] If this is the case, physical cure can only be effective if there is some change in attitude, some sort of ATTITUDINAL HEALING. This is an important part of SELF-HEALING and can involve the patient determining what might have been the root cause of the condition, or what purpose it might serve. It has been shown that mental attitude is often linked with cancer (the CANCER PERSONALITY) and EXPECTATION with the rate of recovery, although opinions vary enormously on the extent to which these attitudes are significant.

There is a growing amount of research on the question of whether positive states of mind enhance the functioning of the immune system. Whilst many accept the evidence that there is probably a connection between attitude (as demonstrated by EMOTIONS, the response to STRESS, LAUGHTER, etc.) and general well-being, and perhaps even susceptibility to disease, they maintain that to claim that attitude can achieve actual healing is to confuse health-building with the elimination of disease. This second position sees that positive mental attitudes seem to be conducive to good health, but at best have preventive rather than curative value. (This is usually the strongest link that doctors of CONVENTIONAL MEDICINE will accept, and many would not go this far.)

The third position, which sees the link between mind and body as relatively weak, is to consider attitude important only in so far as it helps the patient to deal with illness. As Milton said, 'It is not miserable to be blind; it is miserable to be incapable of enduring blindness.' A positive attitude is then simply part of the coping strategy – albeit an important one – when faced with disease.

ATTITUDINAL HEALING In attitudinal healing one is induced to achieve self-healing, both psychologically and physically, by changing one's attitude to the disease and one's feelings about it. The technique was developed by, among others, Jerry Jampolsky.

AUDITING In DIANETICS people can clear themselves of the painful effects of traumatic memories, preserved as ENGRAMS in the mind, by repeatedly reliving the original experiences which created the engrams. This process is called auditing. When one has successfully erased all such engrams one has achieved the status of a *clear*.

AURA The aura goes by a variety of other names, depending on the different theories about its nature or how it can be detected. They include life-field, bioplasmic field, electromagnetic field, electrostatic field, energy body, or (in KIRLIAN PHOTOGRAPHY) corona discharge. The word 'aura' (from the Greek for 'breeze') is the least scientific but still the most frequently used term for what all who claim awareness of it describe as an energy field surrounding the body. It is usually seen as a mist, haze, glow or oval of light, of varying colours and intensity at different distances from the body. The colours are said to change according to health and mood and depend also on aspects of the individual's character and intellectual development. Gaps and other abnormalities in the aura reflect physical conditions, such as disease, the presence of a tumour or the absence of an appendix. 'If, for example, a certain organ is diseased it will not emit an aura of the same brightness as that emitted by the rest of the body.'[7]

Few people claim to be able to see auras, and since those who do are mostly clairvoyants with paranormal sensibility, it has always been possible to argue that what they see does not have objective reality, being simply their way of describing an intuitive diagnostic process. But since the discovery of Kirlian photography and studies of the effects of strong electromagnetic fields (from power lines) on the human body, it has been accepted that there actually is an electromagnetic field, however slight, around the body.

In classical times Plutarch described the movements of the aura's different colours as an indication of the soul's passions and vices. Paracelsus wrote that 'the vital force is not enclosed in man but radiates within and around him like a luminous sphere.' One of the first people to try to investigate the aura scientifically was the German chemist (and inventor of creosote), Karl von Reichenbach (1788–1869). To distinguish the radiation from electricity and magnetism he gave it a new name: *od*, or ODIC FORCE. A century later, Wilhelm Reich (1897–1957) also claimed to have discovered a non-electromagnetic force which was detectable as emanations around the body and which he called ORGONE. Neither of these theories were taken seriously by scientists generally. The same fate befell Harold Burr's concept of a life-field in the 1930s, although he was one of the first to measure (in millivolts) the weak electric field surrounding living organisms.

Meanwhile some people still kept seeing auras. Dr Walter J. Kilner (1847–1920) of St Thomas' Hospital, London, devised a special screen – two layers of glass with a solution of dicyanin between them, through which he claimed most people were able to see auras. A later researcher, Oscar Bagnall, working with an improved dye, pinacyanol, suggested that the Kilner screen sensitizes the eyes so that they are temporarily able to see a little into the ultra-violet waveband.

Most people who see the aura, whether clairvoyantly or as a more palpable 'luminous mist', subscribe to the view that it represents the life-energy which underlies the life of the body. The first part of the aura, closest to the body, which some see with a darker gap between the body and rays of light at right angles to the skin, is sometimes called the etheric body. Oscar Bagnall, as a scientific researcher, refers to it simply as 'the inside aura'. The etheric body is said to draw in *prana* (in the Indian tradition) or CH'I (Chinese) from the atmosphere and from anything that is ingested and to distribute it through the body. It is the source of all physical vitality, absorbing and transmitting energy through the whole system. Disease manifests in the etheric body before it attacks the physical, and for this reason some systems of medicine such as ACUPUNCTURE work directly on this 'energy body' and only indirectly on the physical organism. Some proponents of AROMATHERAPY make a distinction between the use of herbs in herbalism and the essences which they use, referring to the 'ethereal nature' of essential oils, which bear the 'personality' of the plant. Such aromatherapists would probably hold that the oils act upon the etheric body. Similar views are held by people prescribing BACH FLOWER REMEDIES and VIBRATIONAL THERAPIES.

The second part of the aura, extending to a distance of a foot or more from the body, represents the visible part of what occultists call the astral body. Bagnall calls it 'the outer haze'. It vibrates and changes constantly, reflecting the emotions and desires of the individual; in an emotionally balanced person it should be bright. Bagnall writes that general debility tends to dim the haze. 'A person who is "run-down" will probably have a dull haze. If the degree of run-down-ness amounts to a "nervous breakdown", the haze may extend – spread out, as it were – becoming very indistinct and having no definite distal boundary.' The astral level is one step further removed from the physical than the etheric, but since it underlies the etheric in the same way that the etheric underlies the physical, illness may be indicated here long before physical symptoms manifest themselves. So psychological trauma, which can result in physical disease up to two years later, would register here first.

Beyond this level the aura becomes increasingly tenuous. A third section, more or less oval in shape, surrounds the other 'bodies'; it is usually a pale yellow colour and is said to reflect the individual's intellectual development. Beyond this some may see a pale green band in the aura, representing the higher mind or soul, and at the aura's outermost edge shines the light of the essence or spirit.

AURA-SOMA THERAPY Auro-soma therapy is a VIBRATIONAL THERAPY that according to its creator, Vicky Wall (1918–1991), acts directly on the AURA. Born in London, the seventh child of a seventh child, and the daughter of a deeply religious man who had a knowledge of herbal medicine, she was naturally psychic from an early age, although she did not make use of her ability to see auras until she went blind later in life. She developed aura-soma via inspiration and practical experience when she realized that the oils she was producing as herbal remedies for massage were having a healing effect through their colour. Aura-soma is a form of COLOUR THERAPY using coloured oils that consist of herbal extracts and essential oils. A wide range of colours is used, each bottle being divided into two colours. The appropriate combination can have a healing effect either by being massaged into the skin or even by simply being looked at by the patient.

The bottles of coloured oils are also important in diagnosis. First a choice of colours is made by the patient on the basis of personal preference, and this is an indication to the therapist of the individual's character, constitution, strengths and weaknesses. 'Instinctively each of us chooses the colour of our aura and intuitively knows what our body needs.'[175] When the patient shakes the bottle, the therapist interprets the cloudiness or otherwise of the mixture and the way in which the two colours separate again as an indication of the individual's current state of health. 'A healthy person produces bubbles that readily settle – though not *too* readily – to re-form the two layers. An unhealthy person, or someone lacking in harmony, produces a cloudy effect that takes some time to clear.'[175] The therapist may then shake the bottle over different areas of the body and watch the bubbles in the oils for further diagnostic information.

Much of the theory behind the choice of colours used in treatment is consistent both with the general characteristics associated with each colour and with the system which relates each CHAKRA to one of the seven colours of the rainbow, starting with red for the base chakra and going up to violet for the crown, with the addition of magenta as 'the highest colour'. There are further refinements with particular combinations of colours: for example, royal blue over gold is recommended at times when great mental effort and clear thinking are required; purple over magenta assists in recovery and renewal following illness or an operation; Vicky Wall calls the yellow over pink combination 'begin again oil' or the 'rebirth bottle', helpful with hormonal imbalances, especially at menopause. There is also a general 'rescue remedy' consisting of blue over purple.

AURICULOTHERAPY Auriculotherapy is an alternative name for ear ACUPUNCTURE. There are more than 120 acupuncture points on each ear relating to every part of the body. Usually these are used in combination with other points on the main MERIDIANS, but an 'auriculotherapist' would restrict treatment to points on the ears.

AUTO-ALLERGY See AUTO-IMMUNITY.

AUTOGENIC TRAINING/AUTOGENIC THERAPY/AUTO-GENICS Autogenic training is a deep-relaxation technique developed by a German psychiatrist, Johannes H. Schultz, in 1932, and named by one of his students, Wolfgang Luthe. 'Autogenic' means 'self-generated' or 'generated from within', and autogenics trains the individual in a kind of self-hypnosis, a successor to Oskar Vogt's AUTOHYPNOSIS. The autogenic state is not a hypnotic trance, although in some respects it is similar. It is a means of training the mind to influence the body. In developing autogenics Schultz drew on his knowledge of both HYPNOSIS and YOGA.

A state of deep relaxation is achieved by systematically following a series of attention-focusing exercises. Schultz described these as 'rational physiological exercises designed to produce a general psychobiological reorganization in the subject, which enables him to manifest all the phenomena otherwise obtainable through hypnosis'.[120] Schultz also referred to 'the paradox of self-induced passivity': too strong an effort or purposive volition immediately interrupts the movement toward deep relaxation. Through Schultz's method,

42

individuals learn to abandon themselves to an ongoing organismic process rather than exercising conscious will. The absence of conscious control allows the body to return to a state of equilibrium which is otherwise unattainable. This state is believed to enhance one's natural recuperative and self-healing powers: it is particularly helpful when treating psychosomatic conditions and in reducing the effects of stress, and it may also make self-anaesthetization possible (even to the extent of blocking pain during dental drilling).

Although the final stages of autogenic training involve MEDITATION, the general procedure is different from most other forms of meditation in that it begins with exercises designed to induce distinct physical sensations, leading to relaxation of a purely physical nature. Unusual states of consciousness and spontaneous visualization of symbolic images and the possibility of internal problem-solving come much later. There are six standard exercises for achieving total physical relaxation, after which more specific procedures can be learned to deal with functional and physiological disorders. All such exercises consist of verbal formulae which one is eventually able to use alone, addressing oneself, and only after one has mastered these physically oriented exercises can one move on to the meditative exercises.

The six physically oriented exercises in the standard series focus on different parts of the body in turn, with the intention of evoking particular sensations. These are: first, a feeling of heaviness in the limbs; second, a feeling of warmth in the limbs; third, regularity of the heart beat; fourth, natural, regular breathing; fifth, a feeling of warmth in the upper abdomen; and sixth, a feeling of coolness in the forehead.

There are also six stages in the sequence of meditative exercises. The first stage aims again at physical relaxation, with the eyeballs rolling upward and inward, as if looking at the centre of the forehead. This eye movement is seen in hypnotic subjects and apparently induces more ALPHA RHYTHMS in the brain. (It is also a common pose in the depiction of mystics in art.) The second stage involves the visualization of uniform colour in the mental visual field. In the third stage an object is visualized against this field of uniform colour. In the fourth stage, visualization continues but with abstract concepts such as justice, freedom, happiness. In the fifth stage one visualizes oneself in particular environments, such as on a mountain top or flying, and one becomes an active participant in the imagery. In the sixth stage other individuals are introduced into the scenes being visualized. After progressing through these six stages one is in a very deep meditative state, and one can then introduce personal questions which receive answers from one's unconscious, often leading to insights in a way that resembles the led meditations of practical PSYCHOSYNTHESIS.

In this final stage the danger is, as some have pointed out, that unwelcome images or memories may also be evoked from the unconscious, and the individual is provided with no method of dealing with such disturbing material. 'Autogenic training provides no adequate system for interpreting and analysing repressed subject material, and when such phenomena occur they can be extremely disconcerting and disturbing. Often a great deal of psychotherapy is required to help people work through such highly charged psychic material and come to see its significance without becoming severely disoriented.'[139]

AUTOHYPNOSIS The term 'autohypnosis' was coined by the brain physiologist Oskar Vogt, who discovered that certain of his patients were able to put themselves into a hypnotic trance. It has since been suggested that all cases of hypnosis are in fact examples of SELF-HYPNOSIS.

AUTO-IMMUNITY Auto-immunity, also known as auto-allergy, is a mysterious condition in which the body rejects its own cells. The normal immune response involves the recognition of foreign 'invader' cells and molecules as alien and the production of antibodies against them. In an auto-immune disorder antibodies are produced against certain of one's own cells. These 'auto-antibodies' have been found in cases of ulcerative colitis, in which the mucous membranes of the colon are apparently attacked by the immune system. In some cases of anaemia it seems that auto-antibodies attack red blood cells. It is thought that the damage to the pancreas in diabetics may be auto-allergic, and the same kind of self-inflicted damage is suspected in other diseases such as multiple sclerosis, arthritis, and Addison's disease.

In the absence of any physiological mechanism to explain what causes auto-immunity, the field is perhaps more open than most to psychological speculation. The existence of an auto-allergic personality has been surmised. G. F. Solomon studied female arthritics and their healthy sisters and compared their psychological profiles. What the arthritics seemed to have in common was renunciation or loss of independence: they were more likely to be compliant, subservient, masochistic, restless, depressed and repressed.[1] All these characteristics would be described by Maslow as 'general metapathologies', and there are similarities with what has come to be called the CANCER PERSONALITY.

AUTOKINETIC EFFECT When people are asked to look at a stationary spot of light in an otherwise dark environment, the light appears to move. This is called the autokinetic effect. It has been found that people who report more changes of direction in the movement of this spot are more susceptible than average to HYPNOSIS.[231]

AUTONOMIC NERVOUS SYSTEM Autonomic physiological functions are those over which one does not normally have voluntary control, such as skin temperature, heart beat and blood pressure. Conscious control over the autonomic (involuntary) nervous system was thought to be an impossibility (except by masters of yoga) until the 1960s, when through BIOFEEDBACK it was shown that people can learn to regulate processes such as heart rate, blood pressure, brain wave activity, skin temperature and 'involuntary' muscle contractions. Establishing voluntary regulation of a biological function involves the use of internal psychological states, and some people maintain that there is no such thing as training in, for example, brain wave control: the training is only possible in the inducement of certain subjective states, which somehow, through subjective feelings, focused attention and thought, evoke a related physiological response.

The autonomic nervous system consists of two separate and complementary systems – the SYMPATHETIC and the PARASYMPATHETIC NERVOUS SYSTEM. The sympathetic nervous system controls the FIGHT-OR-FLIGHT RESPONSE, and the parasympathetic the so-called RELAXATION RESPONSE. It has been suggested that EMOTIONS are an individual's recognition of the body's automatic (autonomic) reactions, but the fact that these reactions can be evoked by artificially and deliberately inducing emotions, by imagining them, suggests that the emotions can come first.

AUTONOMOUS v. IDENTIFIED PERSONALITIES The American sociologist Gordon Moss believes that the way individuals react to STRESS is determined by their psychosocial attitude, and he has described two types of personality to accord with two types of attitude he has identified: the 'autonomous' and the 'identified' personalities. The autonomous person regards uncertainty as an unavoidable fact of life; genuine security can only be achieved through independence and self-sufficiency. Autonomous individuals develop their own individual moral codes; they formulate their own expectations rather than have them imposed by a group; and they are more socially and geographically mobile. People with so-called identified personalities take their peer group's beliefs and goals as their own. They are ill-equipped to cope when the values of the group are threatened; and any major social change may reduce both the cohesion of the group and its potential to support the identified individual.[132]

AUTO-SUGGESTION Auto-suggestion is a form of self-hypnosis devised by Emile Coué (1857–1926), a French pharmacist and hypnotherapist. Coué himself avoided the terms 'hypnosis' and 'hypnotist' and referred to the phenomenon as auto-suggestion (i.e. self-induced) even when the subject was following the instructions of a hypnotist.

Coué's attention was first drawn to a customer of his apothecary who had apparently been cured of a long-standing illness by a new medicine which later turned out to be little more than coloured water. This example of the as yet undocumented PLACEBO EFFECT prompted him to investigate further the role of the mind in curing illness. Observing Liébault and Bernheim's work in Nancy in treating patients with hypnosis, he concluded that too much importance was being given to hypnosis as *hetero-suggestion*, the inducing of ideas and actions in the patient by the hypnotist. Whilst not disagreeing with the Nancy school's fundamental theories about hypnosis, he believed that the hypnotist would be unable to induce anything in the mind of the patient without the patient's own *auto-suggestion*.

Picking up on ideas first expressed by Alexandre Bertrand in the 1820s, Coué further stressed the key role played by the imagination of the hypnotic subject rather than the will. For example, the will to live or the will to get better may be utterly defeated by the patient's fear (in their imagination) that they might not. As Coué said, 'When the will and the imagination are at war, the imagination invariably wins the day.' A demonstration of this used by Coué in his arguments was the fact that by imagining a favourite dish we can make our mouths water, yet we cannot simply will ourselves to salivate. The same phenomenon was recognized with even greater effect a few generations later by cinema managers showing the film *Lawrence of Arabia* with its scenes of parched and weary characters wandering about the desert: they noticed a significant increase in sales of cold drinks and ice creams. The imagination is enormously powerful.

Coué referred to the practice of auto-suggestion as 'the education of the imagination', a process in which the will must not intrude. He drew on the teachings of YOGA and the importance it attaches to passive concentration (i.e. concentration without the will). He referred to his 'mantra' – 'Every day, in every way, I am getting better and better' – as an incantation (or AFFIRMATION) and definitely not a command, the aim of which is in part to clear the mind of worries and fears and then to allow the message to seep through into the unconscious. He was one of the first to draw attention (in the West) to the self-defeating effect of exercising the will, the so-called LAW OF REVERSED EFFECT: the harder one tries, the harder the task becomes.

Coué actually practised conventional hypnosis on his patients (after determining whether they were sufficiently 'suggestible'), although he never referred to it as such. The mantra was the additional prescription, to be repeated for a few minutes twice a day between sessions as a renewal of the original suggestion. This routine was recommended by Coué's foremost disciple, Charles Baudouin, who also suggested that when a particular part of the body required treatment it was effective to 'pass the hand rapidly over the affected part', apparently in imitation of the early Mesmerists and 'magnetizers', except that one could perform this on oneself. Such movements, Baudouin explained, 'aid the fixation, the materialization, of our thoughts'.

The 'fixation' of our thoughts referred to by Baudouin is encouraged in other therapeutic mental techniques such as VISUALIZATION and the inner GAME, where attention and emotion also come into play. Although Coué can hardly be said to have founded a school or even established a system, his insights have been incorporated into many subsequent psychological therapies such as AUTOGENIC TRAINING and SILVA MIND CONTROL.

AVOGADRO LIMIT In HOMOEOPATHY and ANTHROPOSOPHICAL MEDICINE remedies are prepared by a process of progressive dilution or ATTENUATION which increases the remedy's potency. At a POTENTIZATION of 12c (diluted in the ratio of one in a hundred 12 times) or 23d (diluted in the ratio of one in ten 23 times) it is unlikely that a single molecule remains in the remedy. This degree of dilution is called the Avogadro limit. The fact that homoeopathic remedies are often prescribed at a potentization of 30c, well beyond the Avogadro limit, represents the main obstacle for the acceptance of homoeopathy by CONVENTIONAL MEDICINE. (Amedeo Avogadro [1776–1856] was an Italian scientist who first formulated the law that equal volumes of gases at the same temperature and the same pressure contain equal numbers of molecules.)

AWARENESS THERAPY Before GESTALT THERAPY became so called it was sometimes known as 'awareness therapy'.

AWARENESS THROUGH MOVEMENT An alternative term for the FELDENKRAIS SYSTEM.

AYURVEDA/AYURVEDIC MEDICINE Ayurveda can be translated as 'science of life' (*ayur* means 'life', *veda* means 'knowledge'; the *Vedas* are the Hindu scriptures, sacred knowledge). It is arguably the oldest known system of medicine, originating in ancient India. By about 500 BC it was being taught at the university of Benares, where the *Samhita* or encyclopedia of medicine was written. Pythagoras is thought to have taken most of his ideas from India, and ancient Greek medical authorities from Hippocrates onwards use many terms of Indian origin, suggesting that western medicine stands in a direct line of descent from ancient India.

Like the ancient Chinese system of medicine to which it also probably gave rise, Ayurvedic medicine makes use of energy points (*marmas*), PULSE DIAGNOSIS and HERBAL remedies, although it seems to have abandoned ACUPUNCTURE fairly early on. Both systems were founded on the belief that the fundamental energies in the universe have their counterparts in the human being and that any imbalance in these energies manifests as disease. In place of the two Chinese forces of *yin* and *yang* Ayurveda has three forces (*doshas* – the system being referred to as the *Tridosha*): these three forces are *vata*, *pitta* and *kapha*, usually translated as wind, fire and mucus. Despite their number they are comparable to the four HUMOURS in the western tradition. They are the bodily manifestations of three of the five universal elements – Earth, Air, Ether, Fire and Water.

ELEMENT	DOSHA	responsible for
Air (+ Ether)	*vata* – wind	respiration, movement
Fire (+ Earth)	*pitta* – bile	heat, digestion, circulation
Water (+ Earth)	*kapha* – mucus/phlegm	secretions, brain, growth, structure

Herbal remedies play an important part in Ayurvedic medicine and they have their effect through the essence of the plant. As in HOMOEOPATHY and the BACH FLOWER REMEDIES, remedies have to be stored in darkness because exposure to sunlight alters this essence, thus changing the effect of the remedy. The Sanskrit word for essence is *rasa*, which also means 'taste', and as in other traditional herbal systems the taste of a herb is held to be indicative of its properties. In Ayurveda there are six basic essences: sweet, sour, salty, pungent, bitter and astringent, and they affect the levels of the *doshas* in the body. For example, half of them (sour, salty and pungent) cause heat, thus increasing *pitta*, and the other half have a cooling effect, decreasing *pitta*.

Ayurvedic medicine lays great emphasis on food, teaching that some foods (such as meat and spices) elevate mood, leading to an aggressive state of mind, whilst others (dairy produce and fatty foods) depress mood, inducing a more passive mental state; a third group (beans, rice and vegetables) helps to produce a clear, balanced, integrated state of mind. Treatment involves prescribing the right food for the patient's condition, according to constitution and season whether or not physical illness has manifested.

Much of Ayurveda is concerned with maintaining health rather than treating disease. The continued harmony of body, mind, spirit and environment is achieved by observing proper diet, exercise, and habits, practising meditation, and maintaining psychological well-being by self-acceptance and love in accordance with the teachings of yoga. All this keeps the immune system strong. An important part of recognizing what constitutes the right diet and general lifestyle is an analysis of the particular individual's constitution (*prakruti*). There are seven basic constitutional types, each being a different mixture of the three *doshas*. Knowing where one's natural weaknesses lie, one can bolster the relevant *dosha* with appropriate food, exercise and behaviour. For example, occasional fasting can benefit *kapha*-dominant types, enabling them to purge themselves of their surplus 'mucus', but it would be inapporiate for *vata*-types who need more regular food to help them to stay grounded.

As well as the allied disciplines of yoga and meditation, Ayurveda makes use of a range of therapies including AROMATHERAPY, VISUALIZATION, MUSIC THERAPY and MASSAGE. In India, astrological readings may also be consulted in the course of a medical diagnosis.

B

B-NEEDS Short for Being-needs. See NEEDS.

BACH FLOWER REMEDIES After qualifying as a doctor in 1913, Edward Bach (1880–1936) practised as a pathologist and bacteriologist, before turning to HOMOEOPATHY. For several years he worked in the laboratories of the Royal London Homoeopathic Hospital, developing medications for chronic complaints such as intestinal toxaemia. While preparing and administering seven new remedies, he noticed that patients who benefited from the same remedies shared the same mental state and emotional difficulties, irrespective of their various physical conditions. He came to the conclusion that the natural extension of the homoeopathic practice of treating the patient rather than the symptoms was to prescribe remedies based on the patient's temperament and emotional condition, which he increasingly believed lay at the root of all illness. As he was later to write, 'Nothing in nature can hurt us when we are happy and in harmony, on the contrary all nature is there for our use and our enjoyment. It is only when we allow doubt and depression, indecision or fear to creep in that we are sensitive to outside influences. It is, therefore, the real cause behind the disease, which is of the utmost importance: the mental state of the patient himself, not the condition of his body.'[86] 'Behind all disease lie our fears, our anxieties, our greed, our likes and our dislikes. Let us seek these out and heal them, and with the healing of them will go the disease from which we suffer.' (From the Introduction to *The Twelve Healers and other Remedies*, added October 1936.)[86]

In 1930 Bach gave up work in London and went to live in the country. He had already started using his intuition in treating his patients and he now became so sensitive that he could experience a particular mental or emotional state simply by holding his hand over a flower. He started experiencing, quite out of the blue, strange unpleasant emotions and negative states of mind, which made him search for the plant which would provide a remedy. He would hold his hand over one flower after another until he found the right one; he would know that he had found it because his peace of mind would immediately be restored. Between 1929 and 1936 Bach discovered thirty-eight healing herbs in this way, all but three of them being blossom or wild flowers of the countryside.

The remedies are prepared in a special way. Originally Bach collected dew from the flowers, but this proved far too time-consuming. For the twenty remedies which are flower-based, the heads of the flowers are placed on the surface of spring water in a bowl and left in the sunshine for three hours. In this time the water becomes impregnated with the healing properties of the plant, and it is then preserved in brandy to produce the mother tincture, the flowers themselves being discarded. Most of the other eighteen remedies are prepared from the twigs and blossom of trees or shrubs; these are boiled in spring water for half an hour and left to cool, after which the same procedure is followed to prepare the mother tincture. As a treatment a few drops of the mother tincture are added to pure water, which can then be sipped at intervals during the day or can be added to other drinks.

The thirty-eight remedies fall into seven groups, according to the type of negative mental or emotional state which they treat: fear; uncertainty and indecision; loneliness; lack of interest in the present; over-sensitivity to ideas and influences; despondency and despair; over-care for the welfare of others. Within each of these groups finer distinctions are made. There are, for example, five types of fear, each of which has its own remedy.

Extreme fear, panic, terror, emergency	Rock Rose
Fear of known things (illness, accidents, crime, the dark)	Mimulus
Fear of the unknown, inexplicable dread, apprehension	Aspen
Fear of mental collapse and uncontrolled temper	Cherry Plum
Excessive fear or anxiety for others	Red Chestnut

Some remedies are called 'type remedies' because they are prescribed for specific personality types: for example, oak is for fighters, people who do not give up in adversity; agrimony is for those who hide their worries behind a brave and cheerful face. Other remedies are for particular states of mind, which can afflict any personality, and they are commonly called 'helper remedies' or 'mood remedies'. Finally there is the famous 'RESCUE REMEDY', a combination of five remedies to be used in cases of bad news, accident, and any situation evoking panic, sorrow, shock or terror.

Bach Flower Remedies are prepared from plants that grow in Britain, even when used to treat people in other parts of the world. Some people have suggested that nature provides what is required for our health in whatever part of the world we live, so in the 1970s an American, Richard Katz, decided to emulate Bach by developing remedies from local plants in his native California. Others have developed their own remedies according to Bach's principles with more specific aims in mind such as 'Changing Habits' or even 'For Kids of Divorce'. However, Edward Bach's own original thirty-eight remedies are still by far the most widely used flower remedies.

In lectures such as *Ye Suffer from Yourselves*, given at Southport in February 1931, Edward Bach discussed in detail his views on the nature of DISEASE and the theory behind homoeopathy. He saw the validity of the idea that 'like cures like' but did not agree that diseases should be treated in this way, for diseases are themselves examples of like treating like. 'It is obviously fundamentally wrong to say that "like cures like" . . . Like may strengthen like, like may repel like, but in the true healing sense like cannot cure like.' 'It is disease itself which is "like curing like": because the disease is the result of wrong activity. It is the natural consequence of disharmony between our bodies and our Souls: it is "like curing like" because it is the very disease itself which hinders and prevents our carrying our wrong actions too far, and at the same time it is a lesson to teach us to correct our ways, and harmonise our lives with the dictates of our Soul.'[86] This is very similar to the ANTHROPOSOPHICAL view of disease. Bach believed that the flower remedies helped to restore our awareness of inner peace and wholeness, thus energizing our self-healing powers and removing the disease.

Other flower treatments are EXULTATION OF FLOWERS and VITA FLORUM.

BACK SHU POINTS See SHU POINTS.

BAREFOOT SHIATSU In amma, an ancient form of Chinese massage which was incorporated into SHIATSU, the practitioner could use various parts of the body other than the hands to apply pressure – knees and even feet. In treating the back, for example, the practitioner could stand on the patient's sacrum and use the other foot to massage the side of the spine and shoulder-blades. Similar techniques were used in the West by BONE-SETTERS.

BASIC NEEDS/THEORY OF BASIC NEEDS See NEEDS.

BATES EYE METHOD William Horatio Bates (1860–1931) was an American eye doctor, born in New Jersey, who pioneered new methods of improving sight without lenses and of healing eye conditions without surgery. Although he spent his early career as part of the medical establishment, he found virtually no sympathy for his new insights among his colleagues, who preferred to toe the line of orthodoxy rather than question its basic assumptions. For example, Bates showed that with his method presbyopia (declining sight with age) could be checked. He also believed that prescribing lenses for astigmatism was likely to do more harm than good: when treating patients, he found that astigmatism could appear, disappear and change its form. Orthodox ophthalmologists disputed both these claims. 'The fact is that, except in rare cases, man is not a reasoning being. He is dominated by authority, and when the facts are not in accord with the view imposed by authority, so much the worse for the facts. They may, and indeed must, win in the long run; but in the meantime the world gropes needlessly in darkness and endures much suffering that might have been avoided.'[9]

The success of the Bates method was brought to the attention of the British public after Bates's death by Aldous Huxley, whose eyesight had been failing persistently and disastrously until he worked with Bates. 'Within a couple of months I was reading without spectacles. And what was better still, I was reading without strain and fatigue.'[90] After Bates's death, his work was continued in America by Margaret Darst Corbett (1890–1961), whose husband's poor vision (and general health) had been restored with the help of the Bates method. She also trained teachers in the method, fighting and winning many legal battles against the ophthalmology establishment in the process. The Bates Association has long been established in the USA, Britain and India. Practitioners are not usually qualified ophthalmologists, which is not surprising given the basic incompatibility between the medical establishment's emphasis on structural abnormality and Bates's view of poor eyesight as a functional disturbance.

The basic discoveries Bates made about sight are: that normal sight is naturally variable; that defective sight can get better as well as worse; that poor sight and eye disease are intimately related; that eyesight is an indication of mental, emotional and physical health. 'We see very largely with the mind and only partly with the eyes.'[9] By this Bates meant that our sight is affected by states of mind, emotions, preoccupations, memory and imagination, as well as by the way we actually use our eyes. So the main faculties which the

Bates method of re-education encourages the patient to develop are relaxation in seeing, awareness (and avoidance) of the strain to see, acceptance of what is seen, attention to and conscious perception of what is seen, and use of the memory and imagination in seeing.

Poor eyesight may be initiated by mental or emotional disturbance, but when psychological well-being is restored it does not follow that perfect sight will also be restored, for the habits of misuse have already been established. Bates's ideas of abnormal function have much in common with the theories of his contemporary, F. M. Alexander, originator of the ALEXANDER TECHNIQUE. For both of them, at the root of any problem (of the musculo-skeletal structure of the eye) lay habitual misuse. The key to both the Bates method and the Alexander Technique is that correct and efficient use of the eye or body means using it (or letting it work) the way it works when it is relaxed.

Good vision means seeing central details vividly and the periphery less clearly. The most sensitive part of the retina, the part which sees with greatest acuity, is the central point, the fovea centralis, but it sees only a very small portion of the visual field at any one time, so we must constantly shift our point of focus from one detail to another. Bates believed this movement, stimulating the fovea centralis, which he referred to as central fixation, was the crucial factor in normal sight. Staring prevents this movement, as does strain or even trying hard to see clearly – the Bates equivalent of Alexander's END-GAINING. Bates claimed that strain was not caused by poor eyesight but the reverse. He also discovered that accommodation – varying the focus to look at objects at different distances – is achieved not so much by changing the shape of the lens as by changing the shape of the eye itself, a procedure which is controlled by muscles external to the eye. It is in the use of these muscles that people are re-educated by the Bates method. (It is interesting to note that because of the relation between neck, face and eye muscles, people learning the Alexander Technique have sometimes been known to experience improved eyesight – lending support to Bates's theory.) Patients are taught to use their eyes in a relaxed and easy manner similar in principle to the way the Alexander Technique teaches the use of the body. As with the Alexander Technique, this right use is not something to be strived for; one learns (or relearns) how to let it happen naturally.

Although eye-tests with an ophthalmologist often result in the patient straining to see, trying to 'get it right' and thus not using the eyes naturally and efficiently, Bates discovered that regular practice with a test card can actually improve eyesight. This is attributed to the feedback that the card gives, plus the relaxed state of attentiveness and acceptance that sight is variable which regular use of the card instils, in contrast to the tension and anxious strain which blight performance in tests with the ophthalmologist. Using memory and imagination when looking at known letters and numbers at a distance is another way of ridding oneself of the tendency to strain.

Other exercises which form a significant part of the Bates method are SUNNING (letting sunlight play on the closed eyes), PALMING (covering the eyes with the palms of the hands, releasing tension and relaxing the eye muscles), splashing the eyes alternately with cold and warm water, shifting attention (to avoid staring), blinking (which also among other things helps to conquer staring), swaying or swinging (becoming more aware of parallax), scanning for practice in near and far focusing (to strengthen the muscles responsible for changing the shape of the eye), and remembering and imagining (e.g. visualizing colours while palming).

Wearing glasses is, needless to say, unnatural and counter-productive. Whilst granting clear vision, glasses make people move the eyes less freely, encouraging staring. They make people expect to see everything in the visual field with equal clarity, which is not natural and tends to make the eyes 'lazy'. This interference with the natural variability of sight and the free movement of the eyes was described by Bates as 'wrong' behaviour being rewarded. Furthermore, if poor sight is symptomatic of emotional or mental disturbance, correcting vision with glasses amounts to suppressing a symptom while disregarding its cause. In any case, corrective lenses never improve the eyes and may invite further deterioration by encouraging them to adopt a habit of abnormal behaviour. In some cases the emotional factors may include an unconscious element of not wanting to see clearly, and the individual may get into a vicious cycle of rapidly failing sight: as soon as the optician prescribes stronger lenses the patient's eyes deteriorate further in accordance with the unconscious refusal to see clearly. In such cases Bates method practitioners such as Peter Mansfield suggest working on the emotional aspect with BACH FLOWER REMEDIES or KINESIOLOGY.[122]

BATHS See HYDROTHERAPY.

BEE VENOM THERAPY Medicated bee venom therapy was developed by one family in Austria and is practised now uniquely by

Julia Owen, a descendant of the originators of the treatment. She has treated a wide range of conditions including arthritis, asthma, eczema, deafness and blindness. The bees, which have been fed on selected medicaments, are pinched behind the head and then placed on the patient, in whom they implant their sting before dying. As with many alternative therapies treatment can only be effective after other medication has been eliminated from the body – a detoxification process – and there may be an initial adverse reaction, comparable to the HEALING CRISIS in HOMOEOPATHY.

BEHAVIOURAL MEDICINE Dr Herbert Benson of the Harvard Medical School was one of the first researchers to recognize and measure the physiological effects of MEDITATION in the 1960s. He became convinced that meditation (particularly the type promoted as transcendental meditation) was a form of therapy, and he referred to its therapeutic effect as the 'relaxation response' (also the title of his book on the subject[11]), which was the opposite of the FIGHT-OR-FLIGHT RESPONSE. He went on to study monks from India and Tibet, and considered to what extent health might be affected by thoughts and lifestyle. He referred to this aspect of health maintenance as behavioural medicine. The choice of adjective seems to ally Benson with the BEHAVIOURIST tradition, even though his ideas are a far cry from those of Watson and Skinner, and he was always keen to demystify what might seem unscientific, claiming, for example, that the word 'bananas' would be just as effective as any TM mantra. The value of his work lies in the evidence he produced for showing that the mind and body affect each other.

BEHAVIOURAL OPTOMETRY Behavioural optometry is a specialized branch of optometry which recognizes that posture, general health and the environment can affect eyesight. It derives in part from the work of Wilhelm Reich (e.g. his concept of ARMOURING) and William Bates, pioneer of the BATES METHOD. Treatment involves eye exercises and the use of training lenses, i.e. lenses that are weaker than normally prescribed full compensatory lenses would be. Raymond Gottlieb, behavioural optometrist and founder of the Eye Gym in Los Angeles, has specialized in devising ways of enhancing children's vision. He believes that the school environment and teaching methods can actually encourage myopia. 'Our perceptual abilities function best when we know that we can handle the environment successfully. But if we expect the environment to overwhelm us, our sensory integration will fragment and our perceptual fields will shrink.'[208]

BEHAVIOURISM/BEHAVIOURIST Behaviourism, the orthodox version of psychology for much of the twentieth century, was the result of the attempt to make psychology scientific by excluding consideration of intangibles such as mental states, emotions and consciousness. Its main concern was therefore overt behaviour rather than subjective states and hypothetical internal motivations. Its founding father was the American psychologist, John Watson, who built on Ivan Pavlov's ideas of conditioning and seemed to deny individuals all sense of autonomy in the pre-eminence which he conferred on nurture over nature. 'Give me a dozen healthy infants, well formed, and my own specified world to bring them up in, and I'll guarantee to take any one at random and train him to become any type of specialist I may select – doctor, lawyer, artist, merchant, chief, and, yes, even beggar-man and thief, regardless of his talents, penchants, tendencies, abilities, vocations, and race of his ancestors.'[176]

In behaviourism's heyday it was very difficult to obtain an academic post in the field of psychology in the West without behaviourist credentials, but not all psychologists and philosophers subscribed to the theory. The philosopher C. D. Broad referred to it scathingly as 'one of those systems so innately silly that they could only have been devised by very learned men.'

What behaviourism persistently ignored was the purposefulness of human beings, our 'remarkable capacity for forming novel kinds of purpose. One of the most striking things about us is that we are highly prolific "intention generators".' It has often been pointed out that the behaviourist 'school of thought', which tried to explain human behaviour without recourse to any notion of intention or purpose, was actually driven by a very determined purpose on the part of the psychologists themselves, whose passionate aim it was to be 'scientific' in a manner modelled upon the activity of the physicist.[32]

It was as a direct reaction against behaviourism that psychologists like Abraham Maslow developed the so-called 'third force' in psychology (the first having been Freud, and the second the behaviourists), which became better known as HUMANISTIC PSYCHOLOGY.

BEING COGNITION/BEING VALUES/B-VALUES See VALUES.

BEING-NEEDS See NEEDS.

BEREAVEMENT Widowers show an increased rate of death from coronary disease, suggesting that bereavement is bad for the heart. This was probably recognized thousands of years ago. The Book of Ecclesiasticus, Chapter 38, gives the following advice to the bereaved: 'Make bitter weeping, and make passionate wailing . . . for one day or two . . . and then be comforted of thy sorrow. For of sorrow cometh death, and sorrow of heart will bow down the strength . . . Give not thy heart unto sorrow: put it away . . . him thou shalt not profit, and thou wilt hurt thyself.'

Studies of bereavement reveal a process of realization which may involve different stages: a) shock, disbelief and denial, followed by b) an intense preoccupation with and longing for the lost person, moving through c) a period of depression, dejection and hopelessness, with finally d) a period of acceptance and resolution.[137] All change involves loss and loss needs to be mourned. Studies of mourning have strengthened the view that acceptance of the sadness associated with any loss is a very necessary part of the maturing process of the individual.

BIAN Stone Age instruments called *bian* have been found in China and are thought to have been used as primitive needles in ACUPUNCTURE. By the time bronze needles were used, the system of acupuncture was already well developed.

BICAMERAL NATURE OF THE BRAIN Gustav Fechner (1801–87) believed that the separation of the two halves of the brain would result in two independent streams of consciousness, two minds. The two halves of the cerebral cortex are linked by a bundle of nerve fibres called the corpus callosum. In the 1950s surgeons started to treat people who suffered from severe epilepsy by severing this link, an operation known as *commisurotomy*. Working on such patients with researchers into epilepsy at the University of Chicago and the California Institute of Technology, the American neurologist, Roger Sperry, proved that the brain functions asymmetrically. Testing these 'split-brain' subjects, Sperry found that when presented with an object in one hand they could not identify a similar object with the other hand by touch alone. Objects seen and recognized by the right hemisphere (shown to the left eye) could not be described by the left hemisphere, which controls language, although words shown briefly to the right hemisphere (via the left eye) were appreciated and matched with objects even though a verbal description by the subject still proved impossible. Fechner had not been far out.

In further experiments anaesthetizing one hemisphere enabled researchers to investigate the faculties of the other hemisphere in isolation. From this research it was discovered that the left hemisphere governs logical, abstract thought, whilst the right governs concrete, imaginal thought; the left deals with verbal information, the right with spacial details. The left hemisphere has long been associated with speech functions, but more recent investigations show that both hemispheres are necessary for effective communication.

With only the left hemisphere active, people become both more articulate and more talkative, but speak in monotones, and their understanding of other people's intonation is severely impaired. For example, they cannot distinguish between male and female voices, and they cannot recognize emotional changes in the voice, such as anger or sympathy. Their own emotional state, however, is decidedly happier and more optimistic, presumably because of the absence of any distracting perception of other people's emotions. Verbal memory improves, but visual memory is impaired, such that it is impossible to identify what is missing in a picture or recognize places. When only the right hemisphere is active, the reverse happens: visual memory improves whereas verbal memory deteriorates. People recognize familiar objects easily but cannot name them; they use a much smaller vocabulary and are less inclined to speak at all; and in terms of emotional state they become much more negative.

The result of all this research is the simple, if somewhat over-simplified theory that people tend to have one hemisphere dominant, and that right-hemisphere dominant people are more imaginative and artistic, and left-hemisphere dominant more logical and abstract (almost a version of C. P. Snow's two cultures: arts versus science). But when people have undergone brain surgery to remove a complete hemisphere (*hemispherectomy*), they have soon reacquired the temporarily lost faculties by using their remaining hemisphere. For example, a man who lost the left half of his brain regained his powers of speech almost immediately, even though initially he could only curse and swear. This suggests to some that both halves of the brain have equal potential and that specialization occurs for efficiency rather than by necessity.[66]

LEFT-HANDEDNESS is a related issue. It is understandable that we may have developed into a predominantly right-handed species because the left hemisphere is more dominant in our general way of thinking, but this does not explain the anomalies. And would it not have been more economical of nature to distribute responsibilities – language to one hemisphere and manual dexterity to the other? Not if language itself grew out of a communication system in which gesture played a key part.

Some people were surprised when it was first noticed that mothers tended to hold their babies on the left, and had done so for as long as there had been portraits depicting mother and child. This is not a sign of left-handedness. One could maintain that this habit leaves the right hand free for other things, but wouldn't a mother prefer to hold her offspring with the hand over which she has better control? It used to be thought this holding position on the left was so that the baby could better hear the comforting sound of the mother's heartbeat. A more recent theory remembers that whilst the left hemisphere deals with facts, the right specialises more in emotional information: there is better monitoring of the baby's emotional state by the right hemisphere via the mother's left eye and similarly better communication from the mother to the child via the left side of her face.

Julian Jaynes devised a simple test to show the laterality of emotional (or non-verbal) perception: people are shown line drawings of two faces and are asked to say which is happier. The two drawings are mirror images of each other, with one half of the face smiling and the other frowning. Eighty per cent of right-handed people choose the face with the left side smiling. This side of the visual field is, of course, processed by the right hemisphere. Just over half of left-handers choose the other face, suggesting that their hemispheric control over verbal and non-verbal perception is reversed, with speech (and handedness) in the right hemisphere and spatial and emotional control in the left.[95]

But each step of the theory seems to be rendered grossly oversimplified by further research. Later experiments in which the recognition of emotions was measured with an EEG has shown that emotions like anger and sadness involve the right hemisphere more than the left, while emotions like happiness involve the left hemisphere: the right hemisphere recognizes sadness faster, the left happiness. This has interesting implications involving the FIGHT-OR-FLIGHT RESPONSE. 'If running were controlled by one specific neural system, it would make more sense to put emotions that are associated with running and moving the arms, fighting or fleeing in the same area of the brain. The current general understanding is that the right hemisphere's control over the large muscle systems allows us to move quickly and to avoid trouble, while the left hemisphere's control over the small muscle system allows us to approach things we are happy about.'[135]

Another aspect of the left/right dichotomy is that since the left-brain is typically so preoccupied with detail, it is the right-brain that enables us to appreciate 'the whole picture'. (It is interesting that we use the word 'picture' in this expression, since the right-brain deals more with visual information.) Colin Wilson maintains that the meaning of what we say as well as its emotional content originates in the right hemisphere: 'As I write these words, the meanings of what I intend to say emerge from my right brain, and my left catches them and clothes them in words.'[184] This extends in Wilson's opinion to appreciating MEANING in a deeper sense. According to this view, an essential task of the right-brain is to supply 'reality', as perceived flatly and analysed rather drily by the left-brain, with the added dimension of meaning. In our customary state of mild stress (or 'generalized hypertension' as Colin Wilson calls it), our left-brain preoccupation with detail prevents this from happening, but RELAXATION enables us to register this 'meaningfulness' as it is appreciated by our right-brain. 'When we are thoroughly relaxed – perhaps on holiday – the right is treated as an equal partner, and we are suddenly surprised to notice that reality can be so pleasant and rich.'[184]

There has been a tendency in recent years for people to go overboard for the right brain, almost to the extent of adopting a 'right-brain good, left-brain bad' attitude, denigrating in particular the linguistic and analytical functions of the left. An English scholar, Hugh Sykes Davies, complains that verbal skills, far from dominating contemporary society, are actually degenerating. As Colin Blakemore says, 'All this fiery rhetoric seems to me to be based on a curious assumption that the two hemispheres of a normal man are as divided as those of Sperry's patients.'[18] 'What we should be trying to achieve for ourselves and our brains is not the pampering of one hemisphere to the neglect of the other (whether right or left), or their independent development, but the marriage and harmony of the two.' He notes that the areas of perception and thought controlled by the right hemisphere are not easily amenable to conventional formal education, which addresses the linguistic, factual and analytical aptitude of the left hemisphere. This does not mean that we should change our educational practices. On the contrary.

'To ignore the special role and the particular educational needs of the dominant hemisphere, and to encourage the minor side to take charge, may produce deleterious consequences in behaviour.'[18]

BIER'S HYPERAEMIC TREATMENT A German physician, August Bier (1861–1949), developed a method of stimulating the blood to flow to a specific part of the body by surrounding the appropriate area with hot air. The treatment was particularly effective in treating conditions such as arthritis, sciatica and varicose veins.

BIOCARDS In the 1930s a Swiss mathematician and engineer, Hans Frueh, designed and produced biocards on which one could plot one's own BIORHYTHMS. He also invented the first mechanical device for calculating these cycles: with it one could see the status of one's biorhythms for any particular day.

BIOCHEMICS The term 'biochemics' was coined by Wilhelm H. Schuessler (1821–98), a German doctor and practising homoeopath, who focused his attention on the inorganic chemicals that make up 5 per cent of the body. He isolated twelve of these minerals, which he referred to as *tissue salts*, and studied their role in the correct functioning of cells, identifying the health problems of patients who were deficient in them. His system is based on five simple principles:

If cell activity is normal there is no disease.
Cell activity is normal if cell nutrition is normal.
The human body needs both organic and inorganic (mineral) substances as cell nutrients.
Mineral deficiency impairs the cell's ability to assimilate and utilize organic nutrients.
Supplying deficient nutrients (in readily assimilable form) revitalizes cells and metabolism.

The twelve tissue salts identified by Schuessler are calcium fluoride, calcium phosphate, calcium sulphate, iron phosphate, potassium chloride, potassium phosphate, potassium sulphate, magnesium phosphate, sodium chloride, sodium phosphate, sodium sulphate, and silica (silicon dioxide). Remedies are prepared in a similar way in one respect to homoeopathic remedies: the salts are usually added in a potency of 6x, one part being mixed with nine parts of lactose and the process repeated six times. Such micro-doses can pass readily into the bloodstream via the mucous lining of the mouth, throat and digestive tract. In other respects the treatment is not at all HOMOEOPATHIC, since it is based on the 'isopathic' idea of administering the very substance which is deemed deficient.

BIOCURRENTS Biocurrents were a form of BIOENERGY postulated by Albert Abrams when he developed RADIONICS.

BIO-CURVES/BIO-CYCLES Alternative terms for BIORHYTHMS.

BIODYNAMIC AGRICULTURE Biodynamic agriculture is a way of getting plants to absorb particular metals so that they can be taken as remedies in ANTHROPOSOPHICAL MEDICINE. Minerals are first added to plants by being mixed in with the fertilized soil, those plants then being composted to fertilize a second crop, which are also composted to fertilize the third seeding. It is the third crop from which 'vegetabilized metal' remedies are derived, such as gold through primrose, copper through camomile, lead through aconite. Plant material used to encourage the building-up processes of the body are gathered in spring rather than autumn, the latter being a more appropriate time for harvesting those intended to have a catabolic effect.

BIODYNAMIC PSYCHOLOGY See BODY-ORIENTED PSYCHO-THERAPY.

BIODYNAMIC PSYCHOTHERAPY Biodynamic psychotherapy is a neo-Reichian therapy developed by the Norwegian psychologist and physiotherapist, Gerda Boyesen. In biodynamic psychology the therapist 'works with both body and mind, with the focus on the body's psychological defences, which are anchored in muscle tension (muscle armour). Massage and breathing techniques are employed in order to help patients to get in touch with their own feelings.'[88] Central to the task of dealing with body ARMOURING is the concept of PSYCHO-PERISTALSIS, the process by which the somatic effects of the emotions are released and cleared by the operation of the digestive system.

BIODYNAMOMETER Albert Abrams (1863–1924) originally called his diagnostic 'black box' a Biodynamometer. It was designed to measure the electromagnetic radiation from a patient. (See ABRAMS BOX.)

BIOELECTROMAGNETICS By the mid-nineteenth century it had been proved that nerves operated electrically. In 1924 Hans Berger discovered electromagnetic BRAIN WAVES. In 1969 David Cohen detected a magnetic field set up by the brain up to a few inches around the head. Electricity is used when the brain receives messages from the nerves and when it computes information. Each time the heart contracts it sends out a wave of between one and three cycles per second (which can be measured by the ECG), and that electrical activity creates a magnetic field around the heart (which can be measured by a magnetocardiograph). The whole body in fact acts as a very weak radio transmitter. The body's electromagnetic field can also be adversely affected by electromagnetic activity in the environment, as shown by those who study GEOBIOLOGY and BIOENTRAINMENT.

Dr Solco W. Tromp of the Biometeorological Research Centre in Leiden has claimed that people leave behind a measurable 'electrostatic aura' when they have been in a room. His work has found that incidents of suicide in Holland cluster around periods when there is a sudden change in the weather.[170] Others have found correlations between such weather changes and heart disease, between solar activity peaks, geomagnetic agitation and heart failure, and conversely between a reduction in heart failure cases and a period of relatively calm sunspot activity.[144]

BIOENERGETICS Bioenergetics is a particular form of somatic psychotherapy developed from the ideas behind REICHIAN THERAPY by Alexander Lowen, ex-patient and pupil of Wilhelm Reich. Chronic muscular tensions are seen as the result of suppressed feelings. For example, retracted shoulders reflect suppressed anger, raised shoulders reflect fear, square shoulders suggest 'shouldering' responsibility and bowed shoulders shouldering a burden. By working directly on the body these feelings can be released, with a liberating effect on mind as well as body. Bioenergetic exercises focus on three main areas: grounding, breathing and character structure. In *grounding* one is encouraged to adopt a specific stance, being aware of one's contact with the ground, such that one becomes more aware of one's personal identity and feels emotionally secure. Any irregularities in *breathing*, caused by the inhibiting effect of muscular tension, are eradicated by special exercises such as having to breathe in a stressful position. In *character structure* there are five types of muscular pattern, each associated with particular emotions: the fear of falling apart ('schizoid'), the fear of isolation or abandonment ('oral'), the fear of failure ('psychopathic'), inadequacy in asserting rights or needs ('masochistic'), and the fear of emotional heartbreak ('rigid'). Each pattern is treated by confronting the particular problems and developing self-awareness psychologically and kinaesthetically.

BIOENERGY According to Wilhelm Reich (1897–1957) disease results from blockages in the balanced flow of energy through the organism. He called this life-force ORGONE, a concept which has antecedents in Reichenbach's OD and in various designations of a LIFE-FORCE such as the eastern PRANA and CH'I. Reich's successors rejected much of the original Orgone Theory, but this energy, which mediates between mind and body, still plays a large part in REICHIAN THERAPY and is more commonly referred to as bioenergy, Alexander Lowen's preferred term. Gerda Boyesen, who developed what she calls biodynamic psychotherapy, has defined bioenergy as 'life-energy of cosmic origin in man'.[88]

BIOENTRAINMENT Bioentrainment refers to 'the process by which living beings become locked on to cycles, rhythms or waves from outside their body limits.'[144] In one sense inner bioentrainment is a necessary part of physiological functioning. For example, if the heart cells do not keep in step with each other the result is fibrillation and an erratic heart-beat. But Guy Playfair considers bioentrainment particularly in the context of the body's electromagnetic field (BIOELECTROMAGNETICS) and the effect of 'electromagnetic pollution'. There are, however, other instances of bioentrainment: CIRCADIAN RHYTHMS have clearly affected the human body and in terms of evolution menstruation is probably linked with the lunar cycle.

Bioentrainment is responsible for causing epileptic seizures when people susceptible to them are exposed to strobe lights flashing at ten cycles per second, the dominant BRAIN WAVE pattern of someone in a slightly dissociated state. These alpha waves can also be induced in normal people while driving down tree-lined roads when the sun is low and casts the tree's shadows across the field of view at a regular rate, depending on the driver's speed.

By ascertaining the individual brain-wave pattern of an individual while asleep, it has been possible to induce sleep by transmitting those patterns through electrodes attached to the person's scalp. Even radio waves transmitted at a distance have, it is claimed, been effective sleep inducers – *radiosleep*, as Playfair and Hill call it.[144]

BIOFEEDBACK/BIOFEEDBACK TRAINING The word 'feedback' first gained currency among pioneers in radio around 1900. The mathematician Norbert Wiener defined it as 'a method of controlling a system by reinserting into it the results of its past performance'. Biofeedback is simply feedback about the body, as might be obtained by weighing oneself on the bathroom scales or taking one's temperature, but the term was not commonly used until the development of various new kinds of sensitive monitoring equipment which made it possible to receive information about internal processes and body functions of which one is normally not aware. Biofeedback training is the procedure by which one can use the continuous flow of such information in order to control the processes being monitored. This may be a therapeutic tool to help the individual to overcome certain health problems, or it may also be used as a short cut to meditation and an aid to achieving certain so-called altered STATES OF CONSCIOUSNESS.

Biofeedback training is based on the principle that any biological function which can be monitored and amplified by electronic instrumentation and fed back to a person through any of the five senses can be regulated by that individual. The information is typically conveyed in the form of moving needles, flashing or dimming lights, bleeps or steady tones. During biofeedback training a person is not told to relax such and such a muscle or lower blood pressure, but rather to concentrate on obtaining whatever signals on the monitoring equipment indicate that the desired internal state has been achieved. Exactly how one does this is still not known. Until the evidence of biofeedback training proved otherwise, most scientists denied that these processes could be brought under conscious control at all (even though certain people such as yogis have claimed these abilities for centuries).

The AUTONOMIC NERVOUS SYSTEM regulates internal processes and responses which were traditionally regarded as involuntary: temperature, heartbeat, blood pressure, the endocrine system, secretions in the digestive system – they were all thought to be beyond voluntary control. That was until Neal Miller, Professor of Psychology at the Rockefeller University, New York, trained rats to 'blush' in one ear at a time (i.e. raise its temperature by increasing the flow of blood). If rats could be taught to do it by operant-conditioning, humans could perhaps also learn how to gain similar control over so-called involuntary processes. In experiments, people who were told that they had varied the temperature of a fingertip by a fraction of a degree were able gradually to increase that variation. By practice with relevant feedback people can learn to control a range of body processes including hand-warming, blood pressure, stomach acidity, scrotal heating (which can result in a reduced sperm count), and peristaltic activity (to overcome constipation or diarrhoea).

The range of equipment used to provide biofeedback includes various types of thermometer (usually to measure skin temperature – an indicator of blood flow), the ESR meter (to measure electrical resistance of the skin – an indicator of stress level), the electromyograph or EMG (to measure muscle activity), and the electro-encephalograph or EEG (to measure brain waves).

The electromyograph was used in the early days of biofeedback to make people aware of slight movements in their vocal tract when reading; this subvocalization slowed down reading considerably and had proved both undetectable and insurmountable before the EMG came on the scene. By monitoring the frontalis muscles with the EMG, sufferers from migraine have learned to control their attacks. Using biofeedback in this way helps to avoid the feedback loop, which could otherwise make a problem worse: while the problem is still small, an individual can alter the gradual progression towards more severe symptoms.

A specific type of muscle feedback is provided by the cardio-tachometer, which monitors heartbeat. Using biofeedback signals from this device a patient can learn to regulate heartbeat, even to the extent that the onset of dangerous irregularities (premature ventricular contractions) can eventually be detected without the monitoring equipment and action can be taken to restore regularity.

Muscle feedback can help to induce relaxation and has been used to wean people off tranquilizers. Respiration is an indicator of anxiety level, so feedback about respiration can also be used to induce relaxation. While in a deeply relaxed state a person can stop the cerebral chatter, listen more clearly to stimuli of every kind (including suggestions) without preconceptions, and gain easier access to the unconscious. Apart from its usefulness in conjunction with psychotherapy, this aid to relaxation can be used in self-programming activities and sleep-learning.

Electrical skin resistance varies according to how tense or relaxed we are; it is an indication of our state of arousal. The FIGHT-OR-FLIGHT RESPONSE brings the sympathetic nervous system into action to enable the body to face immediate danger: heartrate goes up;

blood pressure increases, directing blood away from the skin and organs and into the muscles; muscle tension increases; the digestive system closes down; and the cortisone level in the blood increases. At the same time the slower-acting parasympathetic nervous system is triggered to reverse these effects, in order to bring about a more relaxed state in which further action can be considered calmly once the immediate danger has been evaded instinctively. Much of the STRESS in modern life stems from the fact that the initial fight-or-flight response is not fully discharged, leaving the individual in a semi-permanent state of partial tension and preventing the parasympathetic system from achieving its proper effect. Blood flow to the skin affects electrical resistance and with biofeedback from an ESR meter one can learn to control the relaxing influence of the parasympathetic system. This can work both ways: over-aroused (stressed) people can become more calm and relaxed, whilst under-aroused people can become more alert. The Relaxometer is an ESR meter which has been marketed so that people can learn to control their state of arousal as they wish.

Perhaps the most important discovery made in work on biofeedback training, and a basic principle of its effectiveness, is that 'every change in the physiological state is accompanied by an appropriate change in the mental emotional state, conscious or unconscious, and conversely, every change in the mental emotional state, conscious or unconscious, is accompanied by an appropriate change in the physiological state.'[139] It is not just a matter of gaining control over unconscious physiological processes: those processes can also affect our mental state. For example, when lowering heart rate and blood pressure together, people consistently and spontaneously report feelings of relaxation and calmness; the two physiological changes brought about a psychological change which did not occur when only one of the physiological changes occurred. So biofeedback enables people 'to understand and utilize the link between their personal psychological and physiological processes'.[139] The medical establishment has been slow to appreciate the extent to which many illnesses contain a psychosomatic element, but biofeedback research has not only brought to light evidence of such mind/body interactions, it also provides a means by which many such illnesses might be prevented before they take hold.

Gaining control over brain wave activity is perhaps the most direct way of affecting one's mental state. Insomniacs were some of the first people to be trained to produce specific brain wave patterns. First they learned to relax with EMG feedback from the frontalis muscle, then with EEG feedback they learned to produce the brain waves associated with the onset of sleep. Epileptics have learned to avoid or reduce seizures by inducing brain wave activity which is characteristic of immobility. Many people can reduce the perception of pain by producing alpha brain waves.

When Joe Kamiya, a neuropsychiatrist working in Chicago, first trained people to reproduce alpha brain waves he was surprised how many of them (although not all) reported a sense of pleasure and well-being. Alpha rhythms are typical of a relaxed mental state (just as higher electrical skin resistance accompanies a relaxed physical state). Most people do find this pleasurable, but some seem to find the production of alpha rhythms an upsetting experience; perhaps 'forcibly' reducing their state of arousal causes anxiety and apprehension. In any EEG biofeedback training the individual has to find out the personal significance of specific brain rhythms by monitoring subjective experiences and then choose which to encourage in the light of these findings.

Many people take up brain wave biofeedback training in order to facilitate meditation. The Mind Mirror is an EEG machine designed to show the activity of each hemisphere, so that the user can synchronize the activity of both, such synchronization being a common characteristic of meditation. By combining EEG and ESR biofeedback, researchers have shown that different types of meditation are related to different physiological states. The simplest form of meditation produces alpha and theta brain rhythms and high electrical skin resistance (relaxed body and relaxed mind). But Zen meditation adds to this beta rhythms, i.e. a relaxed body and an aroused mind. (The reverse conditions – aroused body and relaxed mind – seem to be typical of a mediumistic trance.)

Biofeedback has been used in conjunction with REICHIAN patterning, BIOENERGETICS, the ALEXANDER TECHNIQUE and AUTOGENIC TRAINING.

BIOFUNCTIONAL THERAPIES An alternative term for BODY-ORIENTED PSYCHOTHERAPY.

BIOKINESTHESIOLOGY Biokinesthesiology is a system of body energetics which uses muscle testing as a means of understanding an individual's inner state. Typically the subject extends an arm, flexes it and is then posed pertinent questions by the practitioner, who simultaneously pulls on the arm. The degree of resistance or release in the arm is interpreted as giving more accurate information than the individual could ever give verbally – the body's own answer to the questions put. (See also APPLIED KINESIOLOGY.)

BIOMAGNETICS Biomagnetics is a technique used by some osteopaths and acupuncturists to provide spinal and pelvic alignment by passing magnets over acupuncture MERIDIANS. It was developed primarily in Japan.

BIOMATE A device marketed in Britain which enables one to calculate one's BIORHYTHMS.

BION A unit of ORGONE energy.

BIOPHILIA Freud postulated the existence of two opposing and balancing drives in life: Eros or the life instinct, and the death instinct. The life instinct seeks to combine organic substances into ever larger unities, whilst the death instinct tries to separate and break down living structure. He believed that both were of necessity present in every human being and in constant struggle with each other. Erich Fromm (1900–80) modified this in his assessment of human psychology, seeing a spectrum of psychological types ranging from the totally life-affirming to the largely destructive, few people, if any, being wholly one or the other. He named the two impulses *biophilia* and *necrophilia*. In Freud's concept both tendencies have equal rank; in Fromm, biophilia is understood as a 'biologically normal impulse' while necrophilia is understood as 'a psychopathological phenomenon'. 'Destructiveness is not parallel to, but the alternative to biophilia . . . Necrophilia grows as the development of biophilia is stunted. Man is biologically endowed with the capacity for biophilia, but psychologically he has the potential for necrophilia as an alternative solution.'[56]

'Biophilia is the passionate love of life and of all that is alive; it is the wish to further growth, whether in a person, a plant, an idea, or a social group. The biophilous person prefers to construct rather than to retain. He wants to be more rather than to have more . . . He sees the whole rather than only the parts, structures rather than summations. He wants to mould and influence by love, reason, and example; not by force, by cutting things apart, by the bureaucratic manner of administering people as if they were things. Because he enjoys life and all its manifestations he is not a passionate consumer of newly packaged "excitement". Biophilic ethics have their own principle of good and evil. Good is all that serves life; evil is all that serves death. Good is reverence for life, all that enhances life, growth, unfoldment. Evil is all that stifles life, narrows it down, cuts it into pieces.'[56] There are similarities here with the views of humanistic psychologists on GROWTH and GROWTH MOTIVATION, although Fromm did not see himself as belonging to that 'school' of psychology at all. (As is often the case with Fromm, he shows the links between Freud's insights and those of others who would largely reject what they think Freud stands for, but whose theories would probably have been impossible without his pioneering work. See also TRANSTHERAPEUTIC ANALYSIS.)

BIORHYTHMS (also known as bio-curves and bio-cycles). The energies in the human body are said to fluctuate in three cycles: a 23-day physical cycle, a 28-day emotional cycle, and a 33-day intellectual cycle. Knowledge of these cycles, it is claimed, enables one to predict human behaviour in terms of 'good' and 'bad' days at any time of a person's life. Each cycle has a positive or active phase and a negative or passive, recuperative phase, and the days when this polarity changes are generally regarded as critical. The cycles are usually represented as curves on a graph, each line rising to a peak then falling, crossing the baseline into the negative phase, and falling to a trough before rising and again crossing the baseline to start a new positive phase. Each cycle is said to start at birth with the beginning of the positive phase (i.e. rising from the mid-point), so provided one's date of birth is known the status of the three biorhythms can be calculated for any day of one's life.

Two of these biorhythms were first postulated by Wilhelm Fliess in *The Rhythm of Life: Foundations of an exact Biology* (1887). Fliess had studied under Freud and was a nose and throat specialist in Berlin, later becoming President of the German Academy of Sciences. His system was based on the belief that besides the 28-day female 'lunar' sexual cycle there was also a 23-day male 'solar' sexual cycle. He maintained that everyone was basically bisexual, and he used the supposed interaction of these two cycles to explain almost every aspect of human life from episodes of exceptional creativity to the dates of illnesses and death.

Fliess's findings were supported by the work of another researcher, Hermann Swoboda (1873–1963), also a former student of Freud's and professor of psychology at the University of Vienna. He recorded periodic changes in pain and swelling, especially of unexplained inflammations, and observed the course taken by fevers and the frequency of asthma attacks. He found recurrences in cycles of 23 and 28 days. He published his findings in 1904 in *The Periods of Human Life (in their psychological and biological significance)* and elaborated his ideas in *Studies on the basis of Psychology* the following year. In 1909 he devised a slide rule and provided an instruction booklet entitled *The Critical Days of Man* so that people could calculate their own cycles.

The third intellectual biorhythm was not identified until the 1920s when Alfred Tetschler, a Swiss teacher of engineering working in Innsbruck, noticed that the academic performance of his students varied according to a 33-day cycle. From then on biorhythms were taken more seriously in Switzerland than anywhere else. Hans Schwing earned his doctorate in natural science at the Swiss Federal Institute of Technology in Zurich with a treatise on biorhythms. With the help of government statistics and data from insurance companies he analysed deaths from natural causes and in accidents. He calculated that serious accidents were five times more likely to occur on a critical day. Considering natural death, he took only the physical and emotional cycles into account and found that death was eleven times more likely to occur on these critical days. In another study of famous people the mortality rate increased nearly forty times on double critical days, i.e. when two curves cross the baseline on the same day (regardless of whether the change is from positive to negative or negative to positive).

Biorhythms were taken up in Japan in 1965 as a result of George S. Thommen's *Is This Your Day?*[235] being sent to a professor of physiology at the Tokyo Institute of Public Health. Accidents with buses and taxis were found to predominate on the drivers' critical days to such an extent that countermeasures were taken and the accident rate was reduced drastically over a period of years. But similar studies of road accidents undertaken by the British Transport and Road Research Laboratory found no correlation at all between accidents and drivers' biorhythms. According to an inquiry by the NATO Advisory Group for Aerospace Research and Development, there is no evidence that such cycles exist.[211]

Researchers have differing views on which relationships between the three rhythms are most critical. Some maintain that a day when two curves cross in the opposite direction is more critical than when a curve crosses the baseline; others pay more attention to which rhythms are in the positive or negative phase, whilst others consider whether they are rising or falling to be more significant, or whether they are close to a peak or trough, which could cause a dangerous 'spin' period when the curve changes direction. As Bernard Gittelson writes, 'Unfortunately, at its present stage of development biorhythmic interpretation depends too much on the experience and wisdom of the analyst and too little on a generally, widely accepted classification or typology of rhythmic positions and combinations. Unless experienced analysts can come together and agree at least on the terms of biorhythmic interpretation, the theory will be open to the same charges levelled against astrology: that the leeway for interpretation is so wide as to eliminate the theory's claim to accurate predictions.'[63]

Despite the differing views on which relationships might be most critical, the majority of research into biorhythms has been devoted to studying the days when curves cross the baseline. For example, Harold R. Willis, a Professor of Psychology at Southern State College, USA, investigated the records of patients who had died in one hospital during 1973 and discovered that half the deaths had occurred on these critical days. The physical curve crosses the baseline every eleven and a half days, the emotional cycle every fourteen days and the intellectual cycle every sixteen and a half days. This means that roughly 20 per cent of days are critical, about six days a month on average. On physically critical days it is said people are more likely to have accidents or catch cold; on emotionally critical days quarrels or a sense of frustration or depression are more likely to develop, and some schizophrenics become more violent; and when the intellectual cycle is at its critical point we are more likely to suffer from bad judgment, and have difficulty in learning, remembering and expressing ourselves clearly.

Some proponents of biorhythms maintain that different people react in different ways to the various phases and critical days and that one needs to discover one's personal pattern from experience. One golfer, for example, discovered that performance improved when the physical cycle was in its passive phase: in the positive, active phase, when there was supposedly more physical energy available, he seemed to try too hard and concluded that this detracted from other important aspects of performance such as concentration and a more relaxed swing. In other sports too, whilst the active phase of the physical cycle may generally be suitable for training, in competition the best time in the cycle for success will vary according to the individual's temperament.

The plausibility of biorhythms as presently described is doubted by most medical authorities. There is ample evidence that the actual LUNAR CYCLE can affect human behaviour patterns, but this would seem to be at variance with the notion of an internal 28-day emotional biorhythm which supposedly has similar effects. Does one override the other? CIRCADIAN RHYTHMS undoubtedly exist but these are easily maintained by other daily patterns both internal and external (such as sleeping and waking, night and day). There is no obvious way of maintaining the longer cycles of 23, 28 and 33 days, which it could be argued will easily slip out of synchronization. Given that the duration of the menstrual cycle can vary erratically, why should biorhythms of comparable duration be apparently so fixed? If we do have biorhythms of this order of duration, it seems far more likely that they would be more flexible than their proponents claim.

BIOSYNTHESIS Biosynthesis is a school of bodywork, based on bioenergetics and REICHIAN THERAPY but with greater emphasis on the spiritual dimension, developed by David Boadella. 'The central concept in biosynthesis is that there are three fundamental energetic currents or lifestreams flowing in the body, associated with the cellular germ-layers (ectoderm, endoderm and mesoderm) in the fertilised egg out of which the distinctive organ systems are formed. These streams express themselves as a flow of movement throughout the muscle pathways; a flow of perceptions, thoughts and images through the neuro-sensory system; and a flow of emotional life in the core of the body through the deep organs of the trunk. Stress before birth or during infancy and in later life breaks up the integration of these three streams. In biosynthesis the therapeutic re-integration works with breath-release and emotional *centring*; with re-toning the muscles and the *grounding* of posture; and the *facing* and shaping of experience through eye-contact and voice communication.'[20]

BIRTH See NATURAL BIRTH TECHNIQUES, PRIMAL THERAPY, RE-BIRTHING.

BLACK BOX A common alternative name for the ABRAMS BOX developed by Albert Abrams in his work with RADIONICS.

BLINDSIGHT Injuries to the visual cortex in the brain can result in small areas of the visual field being masked from conscious perception, even though unconscious responses to what is detected in those areas can still be made. In other words we can react to what we see without knowing that we have seen it. The phenomenon is known as blindsight.

BLUSHING Blushing (in fair-skinned people) is one of the most obvious PSYCHOSOMATIC effects (the kind studied in transactional PSYCHOPHYSIOLOGY). The physiological effect of reducing the temperature of the blood by pushing more of it to the body's outer surface where it cools faster occurs in all humans. The reddening of the skin is an inevitable side-effect in light-skinned people. But why should the blood need such extra cooling? What has heated it up in the first place, or what has suggested to the brain that it will heat up unless countermeasures are taken?

The threat seems to be one not of excess physical heat but of emotional exposure. As a signal to others of our self-consciousness, blushing betrays the fact that we are in emotional turmoil; it is an immediate signal to others of our strong feelings, which in turn brings those feelings to our own awareness, so that we can deal with them rather than deny them. Perhaps there is a risk of the body overheating as a result of the suppression of action: we feel hamstrung, as when the FIGHT-OR-FLIGHT RESPONSE is frustrated, resulting in STRESS.

BODY ARMOUR See ARMOURING.

BODY AWARENESS THERAPIES See BODYWORK.

BODY LANGUAGE In one sense the term 'body language' can refer to the use of the body as a means of self-expression, as in DANCE THERAPY, EUTONY or EURHYTHMY. It can also refer to the way in which emotional attitudes have become ingrained in muscular patterns, an aspect of BIOENERGETICS and other BODY-ORIENTED PSYCHOTHERAPIES, a fact reflected in certain verbal expressions (such as 'stiff-necked', 'tight-lipped', 'tight-fisted'). More often the term 'body language' is used of a wider range of physical attitudes and movements with which we communicate – usually unconsciously – mental and emotional attitudes. As Freud said in recognition of this unconscious body language, 'If his lips are silent he chatters with his finger-tips; betrayal oozes out of every pore.' In some forms of PSYCHOTHERAPY the therapist may exploit the patient's body language as a means of self-confrontation, by drawing their attention to the unconscious signals they are giving and challenging them to recognize their true feelings.

Body language has received a popular airing in recent years, to the extent that one can learn how to use the body to make a good impression when first meeting someone one wants to get to know better or when being interviewed for a job, and how to 'read' the true reactions of others regardless of what they actually say. Verbal subterfuge is thus rendered less effective: rubbing the earlobe is said to be a sign of uncertainty, suggesting that the ear-toucher has little faith in what is being said, whilst someone who is concealing the truth is quite likely to stroke or scratch the nose. (When children lie they tend to cover their mouths with their hands, and nose-touching in adults is thought by some to be a modification of this more 'instinctive' gesture.)

Lecturers learn that if their audience sit with feet tucked under their chairs, this is a sign of keen interest, whilst boredom is indicated by legs stretched straight forward and feet under the chair in front. Crossing the legs and folding the arms are defensive gestures, expressing the desire to protect oneself, but these actions seem to have other effects. Students who followed the instruction to adopt such a posture throughout a lecture were found to have absorbed less information than those who had been instructed to refrain from crossing their legs and folding their arms and to maintain an 'open' posture. Something about adopting a defensive posture actually inhibits the reception or retention of new information, presumably a relic from the times when if defending oneself physically all one's mental powers were directed towards remembering what one had learned in the past (about the behaviour of one's attacker, the possible ways of countering such an attack) rather than taking in new information.

The intriguing aspect of such research is that deliberately assuming a particular physical position actually evokes the mental or emotional responses with which it is associated. This is particularly true of quite basic emotions and facial movements such as the evocation of happiness through SMILING. Our unconscious recognition of this ability to influence mood and emotional attitude through physical demeanour is reflected in our language, in expressions such as 'shrug it off', 'stiff upper lip', 'grit your teeth' and 'chin up'.

BODY-ORIENTED PSYCHOTHERAPY Body-oriented psychotherapies treat body and mind as inseparable: body types and physical behaviour patterns are an integral part of personality and reflect psychological states. So, for example, a stooped or cramped posture can indicate that an individual 'feels small', and psychological repression has its somatic counterpart in visceral tension. The link between the emotions and the digestive system is evidenced in our capacity to dissolve nervous tension via metabolic action – a natural process known as *psychoperistalsis*, which in healthy individuals prevents stress and tension from becoming chronic and which receives special attention in Gerda Boyesen's BIODYNAMIC PSYCHOTHERAPY. What body-oriented psychotherapies exploit is the fact that the influence of the MIND on the body can apparently work in reverse: bring the body back into balance and you help to restore mental harmony too.

The first to develop a truly somatic psychotherapy was Wilhelm Reich, whose VEGETOTHERAPY developed into the REICHIAN THERAPY which is practised to this day. Stanley Keleman, whose work and writings continue to elucidate and develop Reich's ideas, founded the Center for Energetic Studies in Berkeley, California, where psychologists from other schools gain insight into body-oriented psychology.[109] RADIX is one of several neo-Reichian therapies, but the most popular offshoot of Reichian therapy is probably BIOENERGETICS, developed by Reich's most famous successor, Alexander Lowen, who founded the Institute for Bioenergetic Analysis in New York with John Pierrakos and William Walling. Pierrakos went on to develop his own Core Energetic Therapy, with greater emphasis on the spiritual aspect of the therapy,[14] and Ron Kurtz has added something of eastern spiritual philosophy to his own brand of non-confrontational Reichian therapy to create his HAKOMI THERAPY.

BODY-TYPES There are traditionally three body-types, known as ectomorph, endomorph and mesomorph. In modern times they have been compared with three temperamental components which have similar characteristics: cerebrotonia, viscerotonia and somatotonia, respectively. The mesomorph (somatotonic) is muscle-oriented, the sort of person who enjoys active sport, has great stamina and dynamism and is quite assertive. The plumper endomorph (viscerotonic) is more placid and more sensitive, someone who senses atmospheres and responds 'viscerally', with 'gut reactions', and who is adaptable, sociable and a lover of comfort. The nervous, cerebral ectomorph (cerebrotonic) is recognizably sharper and more linear in outward appearance, someone who enjoys observing, analysing and commenting. Although the notion of a relationship between body-build and personality has not been accepted scientifically, there is statistical evidence that schizophrenic patients are predominantly ectomorphic and delinquent boys in detention centres tend (perhaps not surprisingly) to be mesomorphic. A similar type of personality analysis is performed according to facial characteristics (see FACIAL DIAGNOSIS) and the shape of the skull (see PHRENOLOGY).

BODYWORK The general term 'bodywork' covers a wide range of physical therapies ranging from the 'purely physical' such as OSTEOPATHY, CHIROPRACTIC and SHIATSU, to those such as the ALEXANDER TECHNIQUE which may bring psychological dividends, and to others (sometimes referred to as BODY-ORIENTED PSYCHO-THERAPY), including REICHIAN THERAPY, BIOSYNTHESIS, ROLFING, HELLERWORK and TRAGER WORK, in which the physical technique is intended as a means of achieving psychological well-being through some sort of cathartic release, and MARTIAL ARTS, in which physical benefits are brought about to a great extent by a special type of mental concentration.

BONE-SETTER In most communities there have usually been people, often itinerant, skilled in the art of resetting dislocated bones. The skill was often passed on from father to son – there were no manuals to learn from, and bone-setters seemed to operate almost by instinct. They generally had no medical training whatsoever, and a British government survey in 1910 described them as largely 'illiterate and unlearned' and expressed surprise at the considerable amount of public confidence they enjoyed.

The bone-setter's skill is formalized now in OSTEOPATHY and CHIRO-PRACTIC, but before these new therapies were established in Britain one notable bone-setter at the time of the First World War, Herbert Barker, achieved such fame, treating influential figures such as Lord William Cecil, Admiral Kerr, Major General Sir William Hamilton and H. G. Wells, that he was eventually awarded a knighthood. In 1936 he was even offered facilities at St Thomas' Hospital, London, and he continued to treat famous personages such as the Duke of Kent, John Galsworthy and the heavyweight boxer Georges Carpentier.

Bone-setters such as Sir Herbert Barker never claimed to do more than manipulate in order to rectify dislocations and did not maintain, as many osteopaths and chiropractors do, that such maladjustments are the root cause of other medical conditions.

BO-SHIN In traditional Chinese medicine bo-shin is a method of diagnosis based on analysis of the FACE. Various parts of the face are associated with specific systems in the body, the area above the eyes for example with the nervous system, the mouth and chin area with the digestive system. In the ear the Chinese see a reflection of the whole body, and this notion is exploited in AURICULOTHERAPY.

BRAIN (See also BICAMERAL NATURE OF THE BRAIN and BRAIN WAVES.) For Aristotle the higher faculties of reason had their seat in the heart and the emotions in the liver. His reasoning was simple: life depended on blood, for when blood was lost, life ended; so the source of life must be the heart, where blood seemed to originate. Aristotle therefore believed that the heart was the seat of the soul and of reason. Other civilizations (Sumerians and Assyrians) attributed these functions to the liver for the same reasons. The brain's role in Aristotle's view was merely to cool the blood, using nasal mucus as a coolant fluid. (It is worth noting that even William Harvey, who discovered the circulation of the blood in the seventeenth century, thought that the blood was the medium of mental processes.)

Later Greeks did come to associate the brain with mental activity. Galen of Pergamum (c. 130–201) identified four ventricles in the brain: in the first pair of ventricles sensory analysis took place (*sensus communis*); images were then passed to the middle ventricle, the seat of reason, thought and judgment; and the last ventricle housed the memory. Galen's work was preserved and passed on to posterity by the eleventh-century Persian scholar, Avicenna, and the first to challenge this particular theory was Leonardo. He took wax casts of the ventricles and found that many nerves from sense organs reached the area near the middle ventricle (in fact the thalamus), so what had been the seat of reason and thought (*ratio, cognatio*) now became also the *sensus communis* from which we have perhaps derived 'common sense'.

As we now understand it, the primary job of the brain is to ensure survival, not simply by planning and calculation, but more importantly by mobilizing the organism to respond quickly to changes, discontinuities and upsets in the environment, events which might represent threats. This is accomplished with such mechanisms as the FIGHT-OR-FLIGHT RESPONSE and the release of ENDORPHINS to relieve pain. Through a network of nerves reaching all areas of the body, the brain is able to control precisely the timing of the release of many biochemicals and the appropriate quantity. Some people maintain that the discovery of the chemical nature of the brain has made it less justifiable to claim that there are any distinctions between brain and body, mind and brain. 'Knowing that the brain is more a pharmacy than a computer focuses our attention on the important role of the intrinsic healing systems of the brain.'[135] And: 'To understand health is to understand the central role of the brain in maintaining the resistance of the body.'[135] This is the area of PSYCHOSOMATIC medicine. But it has been shown through experiments with BIOFEEDBACK, AUTOSUGGESTION and CREATIVE VISUALIZATION that the mind can somehow induce the brain to produce certain chemicals, suggesting that the mind as we understand it cannot be an effect of the brain's chemical activity.

BRAIN RHYTHMS/BRAIN WAVES A young German soldier, Hans Berger (1873–1941), fell off his horse when it stumbled down an embankment. He was not seriously injured, but later that day he received a telegram from his father asking if all was well: his sister had had a feeling that he was in danger. As a result of this suspected telepathy Berger decided to study psychiatry (rather than astronomy) and he set out to prove that the brain produced electrical impulses as part of the thinking process, impulses which might also be responsible for thought transference. His equipment was not sensitive by modern standards, but in 1924 he did record electrical signals from the head of his son, at a rate of about ten cycles per second. Berger called this the alpha rhythm. He later discovered that this rhythm disappeared when the subject opened his eyes or performed mental tasks.

Brain waves are now measured by the electro-encephalogram (EEG), an essential tool in BIOFEEDBACK. Four frequency bands have been classified.

Type	Frequency (cycles per second)	Associated activities
delta	0.5–3.5	sleep
theta	4–7	dozing; drifting towards sleep; deep meditation
alpha	8–12	relaxed wakefulness; meditation
beta	13–22	thinking; focusing on the external world

When a brain wave pattern is predominantly beta (a high-frequency, low-amplitude pattern of 13 cycles per second and above), the person is in a state of normal waking consciousness. If the beta activity is extremely high, it is possible that the person is in a state of hyperactivation. The alpha state is typical of relaxed states, especially with the eyes closed, and in meditation (as in YOGA), but the frequency increases towards beta if visual imagery is introduced. As a state of meditation becomes deeper, so the brain wave frequency decreases towards theta. Theta frequencies are slower than those associated with relaxation, but not as slow as those in deep sleep; they occur when one is drifting towards sleep or just waking; this is when hypnagogic imagery may occur, in the transition phase between lower alpha to upper theta.

Brain waves change when a person is under HYPNOSIS. When we smell a flower there is normally no change in the EEG, but if told under hypnosis to smell a flower, the EEG registers a distinct reaction.[178]

BREAST-FEEDING Women who have not breast-fed are statistically more likely to develop breast cancer, and it is often supposed that there is probably a causal connection in physiological terms. But rather than the earlier practice causing the later condition, both situations may be the result of other factors: because of early experiences in their own lives, these women might not have it in their psychological make-up to nurse. Research has suggested that typically a cancer patient is likely to have suffered severe emotional disturbance in early childhood up to the age of fifteen.

BREATHING Breath control and deep breathing are important elements in many therapies such as BIOENERGETICS, REICHIAN THERAPY, PRIMAL THERAPY and RELAXATION THERAPY. In older systems, such as MAZDAZNAN and PRANAYAMA (a branch of YOGA based on breathing and meditation), deep rhythmic breathing is central to maintaining health.

All proponents of therapeutic breathing exercises agree that most people do not breathe deeply enough, failing to use the diaphragm efficiently and thus taking in only a limited supply of air. Deeper breaths immediately provide a greater supply of oxygen to the blood with all the benefits to the rest of the body that accrue from receiving fully oxygenated blood.

BUDO Budo is a Japanese term for MARTIAL ARTS.

BUILDING BIOLOGY The modern office environment in which many people work is believed to be the cause of the so-called SICK

BUILDING SYNDROME, which has given rise to building biology, the study of the effect of buildings on their human occupants.

BURN-OUT Burn-out is the emotional and physical exhaustion seen originally in patients, but now applied to many professional groups. Stages of burn-out include a period of initial enthusiasm followed by stagnation, frustration and apathy, and at different points in this downward spiral the casualties show different sets of symptoms. See also general ADAPTATION RESPONSE.

BUSHIDO Meaning literally 'the way' (*do*) 'of the warrior' (*bushi*), bushido is the Japanese code of honour which finds expression in martial arts (*budo*) and meditation.

BUTTERFLIES Having 'butterflies in the stomach' is the way we feel when the body's FIGHT-OR-FLIGHT mechanism starts to operate, initiating many changes in body chemistry. The feeling originates mainly from the fact that blood is drained away from non-essential activities such as digestion, so that it can flow more efficiently to the limb muscles. We also start to sweat more and the hair muscles make hair stand more erect to increase the body's cooling mechanism.

CADUCEUS In GREEK mythology, Hermes (Mercury) carried a staff with two serpents entwined around it. This caduceus was also depicted in the temples of Asclepius, where serpents were worshipped. Throughout the ancient world the staff and serpents had many symbolic associations; today the caduceus is primarily a symbol for healing.

CANCER PERSONALITY The notion that certain character traits seem to make a person more susceptible to cancer has been developed particularly by doctors in the USA.

In the 1960s researchers recognized that 'Most patients with malignancies appear to have the following characteristics: 1) maternal domination; 2) immature sexual adjustment; 3) inability to express hostility; 4) inability to accept loss of a significant object; and 5) pre-neoplastic feelings of hopelessness, helplessness and despair.'[201]

The research was continued in the 1970s by Carl Simonton and Stephanie Matthews, pioneers of the use of VISUALIZATION in the treatment of cancer, who came to similar conclusions. The negative personality characteristics they identified in typical cancer patients are '1) a great tendency to hold resentment and a marked inability to forgive; 2) a tendency towards self-pity; 3) a poor ability to develop and maintain meaningful, long-term relationships; 4) a very poor self-image.'[210]

Caroline Thomas carried out a long-term study of medical students at Johns Hopkins Hospital to establish possible links between personality and health. Those who went on to develop cancer had been identified as low-key, non-aggressive characters with repressed EMOTIONS and pronounced loneliness.[26] Lawrence LeShan found connections between cancer and loss, especially the loss of a significant relationship for which no substitute can be found: widows in all age groups show higher cancer mortality than both married and single women, and 'the less satisfactory the marital status, the earlier the patient manifests cancer and dies from it.'

Men who later developed cancer scored significantly worse on a 'closeness to parents' scale, and this consequence from their early life must have been reflected in other aspects of their relationships. In fact an unbalanced approach to relationships generally has been linked with cancer, as has an ambivalent attitude towards life. Cancer patients typically have relatively few intellectual interests.

The general conclusions from three decades of research suggest that the cancer personality has a tendency to be passive in relationships and an inability or unwillingness to express emotions – deferring to a partner and 'being nice', also exhibiting perhaps industriousness, perfectionism, conventionality and defensiveness. Perhaps surprisingly, the cancer personality is not likely to suffer from depression. Cancer patients are typically 'copers': they are not the sort of people who go to pieces in the face of stress, but rather the kind who hold themselves together too well. The less fatalistic and the more aggressive they are, the better their chance of recovering; of smokers, those who get lung cancer tend to be less assertive than those who do not. LeShan sees a spiritual as well as a psychological similarity between people who get cancer. They have, he thinks, a Cartesian mechanistic view of the world which leaves them badly equipped to fight this particular battle. 'Perceiving the cosmos as uncaring and unconcerned, the typical cancer patient does not conceive any MEANING beyond the human being and his particular relationship.'[117] One group of Americans with a much lower incidence of cancer than the average are Seventh-Day Adventists. It is impossible to determine which aspect of their lives is the crucial factor in maintaining health – their diet, which is mostly lacto-vegetarian, or their steadfast commitment to life and their own principles.

CAPOEIRA Capoeira is a type of MARTIAL ART practised in Brazil.

CATHARSIS The Greek term 'catharsis', meaning 'purification' or 'purging', was applied to the purging of the emotions when fear or pity were evoked in the audience of dramatic tragedy. Such catharsis was recognized as having therapeutic value even though the emotions were aroused by events witnessed rather than experienced, events affecting others rather than oneself. Catharsis came to be used in psychoanalysis as applying to the beneficial effect of arousing personal emotions that had been repressed. Josef Breuer was the first to use what he called the 'cathartic method': memories which he thought lay at the root of a patient's hysterical symptoms were evoked under hypnosis, the effect being to defuse their power even though the patient did not confront them consciously. (Freud tried this method in 1889 but abandoned it in favour of developing psychoanalysis, which aimed at conscious insight.) Jung was referring to a fully conscious form of catharsis when he said, 'The goal of the cathartic method is full confessional – not merely the intellectual recognition of the facts with the head, but the confirmation by the heart and the actual release of suppressed emotions.' Such catharsis may take an extreme form in certain therapies such as PRIMAL THERAPY. In many therapies the body, as well as the heart and mind, are also involved, as when body ARMOUR which has built up around 'embodied' emotions is successfully broken by the techniques of REICHIAN THERAPY and other BODY-ORIENTED PSYCHOTHERAPIES.

CATHEXIS See REPARENTING.

CAUSALGIA Traumatic damage to nerves, originating for example from a bullet wound, can result in stabbing pains being felt for months after the injury, even though the nerves which would normally be relaying the pain signals to the brain no longer exist. In these circumstances it appears that the brain interprets the absence of such signals as signifying new injury and hence tremendous pain. The condition seems to be related to PHANTOM LIMB PAIN. When the central nervous system finds itself incomplete it manufactures severe pain in the area where there is an absence of sensory input.

CELLULAR MEMORY In REICHIAN THERAPY and DEEP TISSUE MUSCLE THERAPY cellular memory refers to the notion that negative emotions and fears are preserved in the body at a deep muscular level. One of the consequences of this is that the human organism protects itself from the outside world by creating its own body ARMOUR, beneath which the fears and traumas are trapped until released by deep tissue massage or some other kind of BODYWORK. The psychological release felt by students of the ALEXANDER TECHNIQUE might be explained in a similar way.

The notion that organs or areas of the body have memory is also found in the rationale behind the occurrence of so-called FLARE-UPS and HEALING CRISES during certain cancer therapies. If a cancer patient has had surgery prior to embarking on a 'natural therapy' such as the GERSON DIET, there is likely to be a re-opening of the wound caused by that surgery before it heals again once and for all.

CENTESIMAL In the POTENTIZATION or DYNAMIZATION of homoeopathic and anthroposophical remedies the number of times a dilution has been made in the ratio of one in a hundred is referred to as so many centesimal.

CENTRING Centring usually refers to any method of calming oneself, physically, mentally and emotionally, often as a preparation for some mental exercise of concentration, MEDITATION or VISUALIZATION.

CERVICAL SEGMENT In REICHIAN THERAPY the body is considered to be divided into seven areas or segments. The cervical segment includes the muscles of the neck, throat and tongue, and the emotions which are thought to cause problems in this area are sadness and fear. Therapy to release blockages and break down the body ARMOUR in this segment includes tongue exercises and a great deal of strenuous shouting. As with all Reichian-type BIOENERGETIC systems which see a link between the emotions and the functional efficiency of the body, our language provides clues to some of the connections: it is not surprising that the child's fear of a parent who typically uses the threat 'I'll cut your throat' or 'I'll throttle you' often results in problems in the cervical segment later in life, and concealing the fear of insecurity with expressions like 'I'll manage to keep my head above water somehow' is not surprisingly often accompanied by a stiff neck.

CHAKRAS Chakras (from the Sanskrit for 'wheel'), also referred to as 'centres', are focal points for receiving and distributing the LIFE-FORCE around the body and filtering incoming energies from the environment. They may be overactive or underactive, just as the points treated in ACUPUNCTURE sometimes need calming or stimulating. Different spiritual disciplines talk of five, six or seven major chakras, lying along the central vertical axis of the body, with many minor centres in other positions. AYURVEDA teaches that there are seven major chakras lying along the central NADI and twenty-one minor chakras (palms, elbows, etc.). Most therapies which include treatment of the chakras adopt this scheme of seven, five being rooted on the spine although penetrating through the body to the front. The seven chakras are the base (at the base of the spine), sacral (sex organs), solar plexus, heart (or chest), throat, brow (third eye) and crown.

The various chakras are associated with specific aspects of the personality and with parts of the endocrine system. The solar plexus chakra, for example, is regarded as the centre of emotional life, and if overactive may result in strain on the pancreas, indicating the possible onset of diabetes (which can follow emotional shock). An underactive solar plexus, on the other hand, suggests someone who represses deep feelings, and has often been seen in cancer patients (see CANCER PERSONALITY). Chakras are used diagnostically, sometimes with a PENDULUM, by practitioners of VIBRATIONAL THERAPIES such as RADIONICS, COLOUR THERAPY or CRYSTAL HEALING, and by healers who are sensitive to the AURA in that they either see its colours or feel it when using their hands in healing. Vibrational therapies also treat the chakras, and if successfully applied can forestall illness before it manifests in the physical body.

CHANTING Chanting is used in a variety of therapeutic ways. At its most basic it can be regarded as a form of self-expression in the same way as ART THERAPY and certain kinds of MUSIC THERAPY. Many chanting workshops emphasize the idea that everyone can sing and help the participants to lose their inhibitions and find their true voice. Sometimes chanting of this kind is combined with movement in the manner of DANCE THERAPY.

Chanting is also used as an aid to achieving a different state of consciousness, often as an adjunct to BREATHING exercises and MEDITATION. Intoning a continuous note can be an effective way of controlling the slow release of breath. Chanting in this context may also involve the chanting of specific phrases or syllables, such as the mantras that are used in YOGA and AYURVEDIC MEDICINE. It is sometimes claimed that sounds produced in this way have a direct effect on the CHAKRAS. This is often said of *toning*, the singing of one note, often the note for which one feels a strong affinity, one's own tone. An American healer, Laurel Elizabeth Keyes, has developed a meditative technique which involves singing the tone one feels emerging from the earth and coming up through one's feet (rather than originating in the mind). This may be combined with VISUALIZATION and the effect is said to be cleansing and healing, releasing tensions and blockages.

CHEIROGNOMY/CHEIROMANCY Alternative spellings of chirognomy and chiromancy. See PALMISTRY.

CHELATION THERAPY In chelation therapy a mixture of minerals, vitamins and enzymes is infused slowly into the patient's bloodstream with the aim of eliminating heavy metals and other toxic substances. In the case of people with coronary disease, for whom this treatment is most often recommended as a painless alternative to drastic surgery, calcium is one of the minerals to be disposed of in this way instead of being deposited on the walls of 'hardening' arteries. Chelation therapy is also used as a preventive measure.

CH'I The modern spelling of the Chinese *ch'i* (pronounced as 'chee' as in 'cheese') is Qi, but most people still use the former version. It has no exact translation in European languages, being rendered variously as 'LIFE-FORCE', 'vital energy', or even 'matter-energy', but it has much closer equivalents in India (*prana*), Japan (*ki*) and Tibet (*rlun*). The same word is seen in the name of the martial art, Ch'i Kung, now more often spelt QI GONG (but not in T'AI CHI CH'UAN where *chi* means 'ultimate'). Western science is sceptical of the existence of ch'i.

In ACUPUNCTURE and ACUPRESSURE treatment involves affecting the flow of ch'i through the meridians around the body, as does the system of body movements known as LOHAN KUNG. Some western therapies, such as APPLIED KINESIOLOGY and POLARITY THERAPY, have taken over the notion of ch'i energy.

Ch'i is not just another ingredient in the body and cannot even be compared to physical blood. Without ch'i the body would not exist, except as an odd assortment of inorganic chemicals. It can be defined as that which differentiates life from death, and the animate from the inanimate. As one ancient Chinese authority, Wang Chong (27–97), wrote: 'Ch'i produces the human body just as water becomes ice. As water freezes into ice, so ch'i coagulates to form the human body. When ice melts, it becomes water. When a person dies, he or she becomes spirit again. It is called spirit, just as melted ice changes its name to water.' There is disagreement even among Chinese acupuncturists as to whether or to what extent ch'i has a physical reality that the practitioner can sense: some maintain that they can actually alter it, directing it in the manner of so-called QI GONG masters.

There are three types of ch'i in the body: original ch'i, which is inherited from one's parents, and which gradually gets used up; nutritional ch'i, which is extracted from food; and air ch'i, which is extracted from the air we breathe. DISEASE is seen as the struggle between ch'i and pathogenic factors, internal and external, which disturb the body because of its imbalances. When in a state of perfect balance the vitality of the body, its ch'i, is resistant to all everyday pathogens.

CHIAOS All MERIDIANS either start or end at the hands or feet. They can be grouped in pairs according to the quality of energy they conduct. These pairs consist of one meridian on the arm and one on the leg and are known as *chiaos*.

CH'I KUNG The former spelling of QI GONG.

CHILD See INNER CHILD.

CHINESE BALLS Hollow iron balls, small enough to be held comfortably in the palm of the hands and rolled around, are used to aid relaxation. The pressure of the balls on the palms stimulates ACUPUNCTURE points, thereby improving circulation and resulting in a general calming effect.

CHINESE MEDICINE See ACUPRESSURE, ACUPUNCTURE, CH'I,

MERIDIANS, CHIAOS, JING MU, QI GONG, ANMA, BO-SHIN, CUPPING, DISEASE, ELEMENTS, EMOTIONS, GINSENG, HERBALISM, HOLISM, SYMPTOMATIC ACUPUNCTURE.

CHIROGNOMY/CHIROLOGY/CHIROMANCY See PALMISTRY.

CHIROPRACTIC The manipulative therapy known as chiropractic was founded in America by Daniel David Palmer (1845–1913), who started off as a student of Andrew Taylor Still, the founder of OSTEOPATHY, but disagreed with him and left to form his own school of manipulative therapy which he called chiropractic. He claimed to have developed his own technique independently, by following a hunch and treating a man's deafness by administering a sharp thrust (of the kind described by Hippocrates) to a lump in his neck. The two aspects of that first treatment, the neck and the thrust, are the trademarks of chiropractic and distinguish it from osteopathy.

Chiropractors believe that sections of the spine can become displaced and that chiropractic manipulation puts them back, whereas osteopaths, whilst allowing for minor misalignments, regard jamming and locking as more common conditions. Chiropractors also use X-rays more often than osteopaths, which they say help in the diagnosis of misaligned bones. Osteopaths lay greater emphasis on overall posture than chiropractors, who tend to concentrate on the local mechanics of a specific section of the spine (and hence criticize osteopaths for being non-specific). (See also LESION.)

Chiropractic technique is more direct than osteopathy in that thrusts are always administered precisely at the point where adjustment is required, whilst osteopaths often use leverage from other parts of the body to effect realignment, e.g. by twisting a limb. Chiropractors divide themselves into 'straights' and 'mixers': the straights are the more fundamentalist practitioners who believe that the spine alone should be treated, whereas the mixers allow for other types of treatment such as heat treatment and the use of corsets, although they would usually not go so far as to admit the use of drugs or surgery.

Just as osteopaths were once generally regarded as quacks and charlatans by the medical establishment, so chiropractors have often been held in similarly low esteem by osteopaths, particularly since osteopaths have gradually achieved greater respectability.

CHROMOTHERAPY Chromotherapy is an alternative name for

the type of COLOUR THERAPY in which balance and harmony are restored by bathing the body or part of it in light of specific colours.

CHRONOBIOLOGY Another term for the study of BIORHYTHMS.

CIRCADIAN RHYTHMS (Latin *circa*, 'about', and *dies*, 'day'.) It is a commonplace that many physiological processes and states such as metabolism, sleep patterns and variation in body temperature show daily periodicity. What is less well known and not fully understood is the fact that certain aspects of the body's strength also vary markedly during the 24-hour cycle: half of all heart attacks suffered by people being monitored in two coronary care units in Boston and New York occurred either between 8 a.m. and 10 a.m. or between 8 p.m. and 10 p.m., suggesting a diurnal fluctuation in physical resilience.

CLAY THERAPY In some parts of the world people are buried up to the neck in the earth as treatment for a wide range of illnesses. Some have thought the success of this therapy is due to higher than usual concentrations of radiation in the soil. Others have put it down to the mineral composition of the clay, which includes silica, iron, calcium, magnesium and zinc. Clay was used for medicinal purposes, internally as well as externally, in ancient civilizations in Egypt, China and America. Today clay is dug up from sixty metres below the surface near clean rivers (in Argiletz in northern France, for example). It must never include sand or gravel. Used as a face mask it absorbs impurities from the skin; as a compress or poultice it offers pain relief; and taken internally with water, it is claimed, it strengthens the immune system, helps to neutralize and dispose of toxins and alleviates a variety of problems ranging from headaches to hyperactivity.

CLEAR In Scientology and DIANETICS a clear is a perfect individual.

CLIENT-CENTRED THERAPY The notion of client-centred non-directive counselling is associated primarily with Carl Rogers (1901–87), who is sometimes said to have rediscovered the humane value of psychotherapy. Rogers insisted that three conditions were essential to successful therapy: 1) the therapist's GENUINENESS or CONGRUENCE (being a 'real person' in dealings with the client);

2) *empathy*, empathic understanding, appreciating the client's perception of the world ('To sense the client's inner world of private personal meanings as if they were your own, but without ever losing the "as if" quality, this is empathy.'[149]); 3) *positive regard* ('It means that he cares for his client in a non-possessive way, as a person with potentialities'[149]), which includes acceptance – 'I accept you as you are' – and as far as possible non-evaluative – i.e. *unconditional* positive regard ('This is an outgoing, positive feeling without reservations and without evaluations. It means *not* making judgments.').

However, some have seen an internal contradiction here: the enforced attitude of understanding and acceptance which the therapist is expected to show is in fact often the very opposite of genuineness. Rarely is one fortunate enough to find a therapist (such as Rogers) in whom such understanding and acceptance are truly genuine. The second and third conditions are actually essential ingredients in what amounts to a well-intentioned subterfuge on the part of the therapist. The crux of Rogers's theories is that owing to the pressures to conform to the ideals of family and society we repress our true feelings and stifle our innate creativity. As in other types of HUMANISTIC PSYCHOLOGY, Rogers believed in the need for human beings to seek to express love and creativity as a means of fulfilling their potential. But we modify our behaviour, concealing or distorting the expression of our true feelings, according to what is expected of us, so as to gain affection from our family and acceptance from society – what Rogers called *conditional positive regard*. It is the therapist's task to convince the client that it is safe to express one's true feelings. In other words the therapist has to be someone who cares whatever one does, and hence adopts an attitude of *unconditional positive regard*.

In some respects the therapist adopts the role of a caring friend, but friends can be fickle, whereas the therapist always likes you and must always be genuine and non-defensive. This is too much for people like Jeffrey Masson: 'Reading Rogers is such a bland experience that I found myself recalling the old adage that psychotherapy is the process whereby the bland teach the unbland to be bland. This reaction points to something lacking in Rogers and his writings, and that is sensitivity to people's real suffering . . . Rogers clearly believed that "troubles", as he called them, came from within, not from the real world.'[128]

In other words, this type of client-centred therapy is unlikely to be of much help for people who have real problems. In fact some would say it could even do harm: on the one hand some people may end up more guilt-ridden than before if they are encouraged to believe that it is through their own complicity that they are unable to express their true feelings, rather than recognizing the damage that others might have inflicted on them; at the other extreme, people with distorted, violent feelings may be inappropriately encouraged in the belief that such feelings are 'all right'. But for the ordinary 'averagely neurotic' individual with an aptitude for verbalizing, Rogerian therapy can be rewarding and might well result in increased insight.

CLINICAL ECOLOGY Clinical ecology is the study of environmental factors in illness, focusing in particular on food allergies (natural foodstuffs as well as additives) and nutritional deficiencies, both of which have been linked to forms of mental illness.

CLINICAL TRIALS See TRIALS.

CNIDIAN SCHOOL Cnidos, or Cnidus, was an ancient Greek city at the southwest tip of Asia Minor, renowned for its medical school, which was opposed to the more widely accepted Hippocratic school of medicine. Whilst the followers of Hippocrates believed that mankind was a product of the environment, and that diseases arose from natural external causes (and were not inflicted by the gods), the Cnidian school taught that disease was caused by internal factors. Cnidian medical opinion maintained that these pathogens had to be hunted and destroyed, whilst the Hippocratic view was that since disease was nature's way of countering adverse influences and re-establishing balance, the physician's task was to aid nature.

It is interesting that the contemporary division between conventional and alternative medicine, far from being a rerun of this ancient disagreement, takes the same issues but groups them together differently. The conventional view is closer to the Hippocratic in its focusing on external causes, but has lost sight of the notion that disease is a natural way of rebalancing and adopts the Cnidian strategy of trying to seek out the pathogens and destroy them. The attitude of alternative medicine often focuses more on internal causes, like the Cnidian school, but tends to accept disease as 'nature's way' with which the physician should cooperate, as taught by the Hippocratic school.

CO-COUNSELLING Co-counselling is a form of counselling in which the relationship between client and therapist is reversible.

It is not simply CLIENT-CENTRED, but client-directed: the client remains in control and avoids the dependent roles of child or victim which may be adopted in long-term PSYCHOTHERAPY. It also has the advantage of avoiding the financial cost of psychotherapy. The basic idea of mutual therapy was mooted as early as 1932 by Sandor Ferenczi (1873–1933), a Hungarian-born medical doctor who became a colleague of Freud's. In a private diary written towards the end of his life (but not published until 1985), Ferenczi discusses the possibility of mutual analysis, in which the patient and the analyst take it in turns on the couch, the analyst being analysed by the patient.

In the early 1950s in Seattle, Harvey Jackins, a mathematics graduate and former labour organizer (trade union representative), helped a friend, Charlie, who had lost his job and split up with his wife, just by being there and listening while he poured his heart out and cried. Charlie eventually recovered, and Jackins developed his theory of co-counselling. Although Charlie's cathartic experience might have encouraged Jackins to emphasize the overt expression of feelings in a way that became all too common in the 1960s and 70s, Jackins in fact always stressed the importance of intelligence and rationality in co-counselling. He saw the release of tension indicated by tears, trembling, perspiration, laughter, or yawning as 'discharge' – a means of disrupting old patterns and re-evaluating them, rather than a 'restimulation' in the terms of DIANETICS. The usual therapeutic pattern is that of accessing the distress of the INNER CHILD, the cathartic release of pain with insight, and reintegration, followed by celebration and affirmation. The aim is awareness and 'zestfulness' – the natural feeling of a human being.

The basic therapeutic skill in co-counselling is listening without analytic interpretation, judgment, criticism, advice or sympathy. It is non-authoritarian and optimistic, based on supportive and mutual appreciation rather than mere acknowledgment. The best is assumed about each individual in an atmosphere of love, cooperation and enthusiasm. One technique used is that of *validation*: the client is not allowed to complain about feeling a failure, but must say instead, 'I am a success.' Another technique is *repetition*: the client may be encouraged to repeat a phrase about childhood experience again and again until breakdown and 'discharge' occur.

Co-counsellors learn such techniques by following an initial sixteen-week programme. They continue to attend their group of between fifteen and twenty people for as long as they like, but the main aim is that pairs of co-counsellors should meet once a week, taking it in turns to counsel each other. While the one in the client role carries on a monologue, the counsellor never passes judgment or interprets, never reacts emotionally or interrupts, must never seem indifferent and must always be courteous. People in this relationship are not expected to meet socially outside their counselling activities.

If the co-counselling sessions seem to be going nowhere one can change co-counsellors, although this in itself may be disadvantageous since it could encourage avoidance of going into difficult areas. The obvious risk is that any meeting of co-counsellors becomes a mutual admiration society (Rosen has called it 'mutual massage'[151]), and outsiders have characterized so-called 'discharging' as mere bragging. On the other hand there is also something very impersonal about the system, despite, or perhaps because of, its insistent emphasis on 'the inherent natural human being'. Because one's 'distress pattern' is regarded as not really part of oneself, but something which can be thrown off like a snake's skin, there is usually no real understanding of how the pattern arose in the first place – no insight.

Co-counselling can lead people into a rather unreal world in which they are listened to without question or criticism, and praise, whether deserved or not, is always guaranteed. No one ever tells others what to do (except that under no circumstances are they allowed to mix co-counselling with any other therapies), and they are assured that they are all geniuses inside. Does this prepare people for the real world? Rosen describes co-counselling as 'a comfortable refuge for the disappointed'.[151] It is comforting to be told that you are all right really and you need not work on trying to understand how you got the way you are. (REALITY THERAPY operates in a way which places even less emphasis on the past, but lays enormous emphasis on individual responsibility, which may seem lacking in co-counselling.) The illusion is maintained that co-counsellors are virtually a species apart; they are, in Jackin's words, 'inhabitants of a rational island of humans whom they are helping to pull up out of the sea of irrationality in which people and civilization are struggling'.

COGNITIVE THERAPY The cognitive approach to PSYCHO-THERAPY is based on the principle that the way we view the world and make sense of it reflects the conditioning we have undergone through past experiences, and that we constantly process information in organized ways, such as when planning and solving problems. In cognitive therapy people are encouraged to adopt a new point of view and revise the way they feel about themselves and the situations they find themselves in (for example by talking to themselves in more positive, constructive ways). In this way people can change their behaviour. RATIONAL EMOTIVE THERAPY is a variant of cognitive therapy.

COLONIC IRRIGATION Colonic irrigation is a form of cleansing used in HYDROTHERAPY.

COLOUR BREATHING Colour breathing is a form of COLOUR THERAPY which involves the VISUALIZATION of particular colours combined with BREATHING exercises while in a mild state of MEDITATION. Typically the subject evokes positive feelings of happiness and well-being while visualizing beams of coloured light entering through the solar plexus with each inward breath and spreading throughout the body. The choice of colour will depend on the individual's condition or character. With the outward breath, toxins are visualized leaving the body. Colour breathing is related to PRANAYAMA and certain ancient breathing exercises in YOGA.

COLOUR THERAPY Research has shown that colours have different effects on the nervous system. Although the perception of colour is a very subjective experience, it is possible to make generalizations which have implications for colour therapy. The most basic subdivision of colours is into two 'temperature groups': warm colours such as red, orange and yellow are seen as advancing and aggressive, and cool colours such as blue, green and violet are seen as receding and passive. (In China the warm colours would be classified as YANG and the cool colours as YIN.) This distinction can be seen in the fact that a wall painted red appears to be closer than the same wall painted blue, so red rooms look smaller than they are and a red ceiling has a claustrophobic effect; and there are more dented wings on blue cars than on red ones because a parking space between two blue cars seems wider to the motorist trying to get between them.

Red is the first colour one notices. The stimulating effect of red can be put to good use in certain workshops and factories where monotonous actions would otherwise induce weariness much more quickly. Football teams who wear red seem to stand a better chance of winning than those wearing other colours. Red excites, even raising the pulse rate. A study at the New England State Hospital showed that being bathed in red light for half an hour caused the heart rate to increase and blood pressure to rise, whilst blue light resulted in a drop in blood pressure. The Department of Animal Behaviour at Cambridge University has noted the same effect in animals, with red light also apparently lowering the pain threshold.

Blue is the most calming colour of all, reducing tension and inducing relaxation, even to the extent of reducing one's breathing rate. It is thought to help in asthmatic conditions. Blue generally has the opposite effect to that of red; for example, blue objects appear to be larger than they really are. Blue and turquoise are commonly used in the decor of places of healing because of their calming effect. In surveys of public opinion, blue also turns out to be the most popular colour – which perhaps says something about our stressful age. Red is the next most popular colour, but is only half as popular as blue, and the most disliked colour of all is yellow.

An excess of yellow in one's environment can result in a loss of anchorage, a feeling of insecurity, lack of focus and a loss of any sense of purpose. Nervousness and uncertainty increase with too much yellow, and irrational, even irresponsible behaviour may result. At the Institute of Contemporary Arts in London in 1970 an exhibition of intellectual toys and games was held in three differently coloured rooms – black, green and yellow. In the yellow room the exhibits were continually being broken or stolen by visitors, but there was no such trouble in the other rooms. This has led some people to suggest that the choice of yellowish sodium lights for street lighting might be inappropriate, as it could increase the likelihood of crime.

Orange is a joyful colour, not overstimulating as red can be and without the strong sense of detachment that yellow can induce. Green is a relaxing, balancing colour; the green worn by surgeons in the operating theatre promotes a sense of calm. But green is also rather dead; green light is unpleasant and seems to stultify growth. Add a little blue to green to produce turquoise and the effect is much more refreshing, soothing and calming, offsetting the effects of too much red. Pink can also have a calming effect: when police cells were painted pink the result was (albeit temporarily) a much more docile group of detainees.

Advertisers exploit the psychological effects of colour. In one study a new washing powder in a yellow carton was thought to be too strong, and in a blue carton too weak; people preferred the powder from a carton coloured blue *and* yellow. Experiments on the PLACEBO EFFECT have shown that the effectiveness of placebos varies according to the colour of the pill taken, and that different colours are more effective to counter different symptoms.

One of the leading authorities on colour healing, Theo Gimbel, believes that red is not only invigorating, but in excess can induce violence. He suspects that some of the violence of football fans can be attributed to the fact that matches are often watched under strong sodium vapour lamps which have a high level of red light. Cricket, he notes, which has a reputation for being very calm, is always watched in daylight, which has a high blue content.[62]

Gimbel's father, Max Gimbel-Seiling, worked with Rudolf Steiner in Munich between 1912 and 1925, and much of his understanding of colour is strongly influenced by ANTHROPOSOPHY. His theory includes associations between colours and the CHAKRAS, and each vertebra is assigned both a colour and a musical tone. Colour healing is seen as a VIBRATIONAL THERAPY which acts on the subtle energy-body or AURA. This aspect of colour healing is demonstrated most clearly in AURA-SOMA THERAPY.

It is thought that each chakra is stimulated by its corresponding colour. Red stimulates the base chakra, and has an uplifting effect, increasing willpower and courage and helping the individual to over-come depression and inertia. Orange works on the second chakra, the spleen, and gives both physical and mental stimulation. Yellow, acting on the third chakra, the solar plexus, also stimulates the mind and its reasoning powers. Green, controlling the heart centre, has a soothing effect on the nerves, and is regarded as the harmonizer and balancer, neutralizing imbalances such as the malignant cells in cancer. Blue, the colour of the throat centre, which controls self-expression, can alleviate fevers, helping the body to combat infection when temperature rises. Indigo, the colour associated with the brow chakra and the pineal gland, is believed to help in anaesthesia and the control of pain. Violet, linked to the crown chakra and the pituitary gland, is the healing colour par excellence: it is said to be beneficial in mental and nervous diseases, helping in all forms of neurosis and having a tranquilizing effect on the whole nervous system.

Dinshah Ghadiali was the first authority on colour healing to write a definitive work on the subject, *The Spectro Chrometry Encyclopaedia* (1933). In this three-volume study Ghadiali explains that colours represent chemical potencies (just as each element burns with a particular colour), and that the addition of a chemical with an inappropriate colour destroys the balance of the body. He believes that for each organism there is a particular colour that stimulates and another that inhibits, and that each organ or system within the body responds to its own colours (which might not be the same as for the body as a whole). Colour can cure because each organ has its own vibration and therefore responds to a specific colour. For Ghadiali the three primary colours are red, green and violet. Red stimulates liver activity. Violet stimulates the spleen. Green (midway between red and violet in the spectrum) activates the pituitary gland, which controls the activity of all the other glands. Blue is the colour most associated with healing, turquoise relaxes the nervous system, and orange works as an anti-depressant.

Some colour therapists have their own range of colours for the treatment of specific organs or conditions, and maintain that each individual healer should work out their own method. Others believe that each person has their own soul colour and treatment with that particular colour might be the most effective whatever the ailment. Musical tones are sometimes said to be associated with specific colours and music therapy is sometimes combined with colour therapy. CRYSTAL HEALING has also been allied to colour therapy by some healers, seven principal gems being linked to the seven colours of the rainbow.

The usual way in which colours are used therapeutically is by bathing the patient in light shone through a filter of a particular colour. Some practitioners may hold coloured material such as card over specific areas of the body, or recommend that clothes of certain colours are worn. Others train their clients in the VISUALIZATION of specific colours, as in COLOUR BREATHING: the desired colour is visualized and the patient 'breathes in' air of that colour.[25] Colour therapists may also prescribe foods of the desired colour and drinking water which has absorbed sunlight filtered through a coloured screen.

COMPLEMENTARY MEDICINE Therapies which are not recognized as orthodox by the western medical establishment are sometimes described as complementary if it is felt that they can be used alongside CONVENTIONAL MEDICINE. OSTEOPATHY, which is already accepted as part of mainstream medicine in the USA, falls more easily into this category than most other ALTERNATIVE THERAPIES. Since conventional medicine is based entirely on ALLOPATHIC principles, it is difficult to see how HOMOEOPATHY could be described as complementary.

CONCENTRATION One's ability to concentrate is affected less by the presence of distractions than by one's subjective attitude towards such potential distractions. In one experiment two groups of people were exposed to distracting background noises while performing a task; one group had a button with which they were told they could cut out the noises if they wanted to, and the other group had no such button. The group with the control button performed much more efficiently than the group without it, even though they never actually used it. Another conclusion one could draw from this is that tolerance increases with perceived ability to control, or conversely that powerlessness generates intolerance.

CONCENTRATION THERAPY Concentration therapy was an early form of what eventually became GESTALT THERAPY.

CONFRONTATION THERAPY Confrontation therapy is any type of psychotherapy in which the patient is confronted with the analyst's version of what is going on in the patient's mind, thus invalidating the patient's own view. Sandor Ferenczi was the first analyst to consider that a psychoanalytic interpretation of what the patient says can actually be an act of aggression, challenging the patient's perception of reality. In spite of Ferenczi's misgivings, the analyst's taste for interpretation soon became a prerogative and indeed a basic principle of therapy. In *Against Therapy*, Jeffrey Masson drew attention to the early but soon forgotten doubts among psychoanalysts. As Dorothy Rowe writes in the introduction to Masson's book, 'Someone who confronts another person is convinced that he is in possession of the truth and that the other person is wrong and must be made to see the error of his ways . . . In the final analysis, power is the right to have your definition of reality prevail over all other people's definition of reality.'[128] This debate has had far-reaching consequences in the ANTI-PSYCHIATRY movement. CLIENT-CENTRED THERAPY is an attempt to escape the dangers of confrontation, although Masson has been equally dismissive of such efforts.

CONGESTION In systems of medicine which are based on a notion of energy flow around the body – a LIFE-FORCE such as CH'I or *prana* – sickness is deemed to be due to congestion, i.e. a blockage or imbalance in the harmonious flow of that life-force.

CONGRUENCE/CONGRUENT PERSONALITY Carl Rogers talks of the congruent and incongruent personality. Someone who is congruent is seen by others as a real person; you are congruent if you present yourself to others as you really are. 'Each of us knows individuals whom we somehow trust because we sense that they are being what they are, that we are dealing with the person himself, not with a polite or professional front.' Rogers adds that this is an essential quality in a therapist. 'It is this quality of congruence which we sense that research has found to be associated with successful therapy. The more genuine and congruent the therapist in the relationship, the more probability there is that change in personality in the client will occur.'[149] Congruence is equally important in teachers.

CONNECTED BREATH CYCLE In connected breathing there is no pause between inhaling and exhaling. Breathing in, out and in again without holding the breath at all causes hyperventilation, and this is used in REBIRTHING to release emotional blockages and allow subconscious traumas to resurface so that they can be made conscious and overcome.

CONSCIOUSNESS See STATES OF CONSCIOUSNESS.

CONSTRUCT THEORY See PERSONAL CONSTRUCT THERAPY.

CONTACT ASSIST In DIANETICS one may be encouraged to repeat actions which caused an injury as an aid to healing, rather in the manner of 'laying a ghost'. This 'contact assist' is said to 'blow off' the unpleasant body sensations, remove any unconscious reasons for precipitating or prolonging the condition and reduce the predisposition for further injury.

CONVENTIONAL MEDICINE In his now famous address to the British Medical Association conference Prince Charles characterized conventional medicine with these words, 'The whole imposing edifice of modern medicine, for all its breathtaking successes, is like the celebrated Tower of Pisa – slightly off-balance.' He reminded his audience that 'Human nature is such that we are frequently prevented from seeing that what is taken for today's unorthodoxy is probably to be tomorrow's convention,' implying that some ALTERNATIVE THERAPIES would probably find their way into the mainstream before long.

The basic problem is that, as Michael Polyani has pointed out, 'it is the normal practice of scientists to ignore evidence which appears incompatible with the accepted system of scientific knowledge.'[145]

The one aspect of this 'accepted system' which is most antagonistic to alternative medicine is that if something cannot be explained, if the mechanism is not understood, then the therapy is regarded as at best suspect and is usually abandoned as worthless. This is not simply a twentieth-century phenomenon. A sixteenth-century surgeon at St Bartholomew's Hospital, William Clowes, treated burns with different plant remedies depending on the degree of injury and stage of treatment. But there was no explanation for the remedy, so it was abandoned. Two hundred years later burns were being treated with lead lotions, which led to death from toxic absorption, and in the two world wars picric acid and tannic acid were used with terrible consequences. Only four hundred years after the time of William Clowes did 'medical science' discover the active ingredients in his effective plant remedies. This demonstrates the danger in saying that until we have an explanation which accords with current scientific thinking we should not accept the remedy.

The current system of medical science is based on several assumptions which are seldom if ever challenged in conventional medicine.

If you are not sick you are well.
Health and sickness are dependent on external factors.
The germ theory is fact.
Health can be restored by taking a particular drug.

In this last assumption we can see that modern medicine with its tendency to produce IATROGENIC DISEASES has probably become too inclined to resort to drugs at the least provocation. The body recognizes a natural substance as friendly, uses what it needs and passes the rest away, but artificial drugs are identified by the body as foreign and treated in the same way as invading bacteria even if administered for therapeutic purposes. Many drugs are discovered as a result of investigations into herbal remedies among non-industrialized societies. For example, the contraceptive pill is derived from Mexican yams. Side-effects in modern medicines are the result of using isolated active constituents rather than a whole natural plant as would be used in HERBALISM. Although drugs are undoubtedly sometimes necessary, it would be safer to regard them as a last resort. The really important and more fundamental question, which is seldom asked, is: What habits of life have made the use of drugs necessary?

Ivan Illich sees this problem as one for society as a whole, not just for the medical establishment, although it is the medical establishment that has conditioned us to behave in the way we do. In our 'intensely industrialized society, people are conditioned to *get* things rather than *to do* them; they are trained to value what can be purchased rather than what they themselves can create . . . Healing ceases to be considered the task for the sick. It first becomes the duty of the individual body repairman, and then soon changes from a personal service into the output of an anonymous agency . . . and it becomes increasingly difficult to care for one's own health.'[91]

Given the increasing evidence against the general applicability of the so-called GERM THEORY, it is surprising that it still has such a hold on conventional medicine. Pasteur is reported to have voiced his doubts about the validity of the germ theory with his dying breath, but the idea of a single cause for each illness is evidently too attractive for people to abandon easily. Even Lister, when President of the Royal Society, became so obsessed by the idea of bacterial contamination that he insisted on attributing scurvy to 'ptomaine poisoning'. The result was that Scott took sterilized rather than vitamin-rich foods on his expedition to the South Pole in 1911.

Although there is now more emphasis on life-style and behaviour as contributory factors in disease, especially since the work on STRESS by Hans Selye, these factors are still seen as external causes. There is now also growing evidence of the way the chemicals produced by the brain affect the functioning of the body, but the influence of the mind on the body both consciously (as in BIOFEED-BACK for example) and unconsciously (in physical conditions that are worked on and resolved in BODY-ORIENTED PSYCHOTHERAPY) is still largely ignored by conventional medicine.

Because of the medical establishment's emphasis on pathology and mortality there is virtually no systematic information on longevity, spontaneous remission, or people who enjoy good health and die beneficently. In fact there is no clear notion of what constitutes good health. 'Determining the parameters of health by examining pathology is rather like peering through the wrong end of a telescope.'[139]

Medical students are still taught that medicine is, by and large, about the body and its functions; that the body is made up of bits and pieces which are studied as separate and distinct entities. They are still taught about the mind as a separate entity from the body. They are still taught that treatment comes either in the form of a prescription or a surgical operation. They receive little or no training in communication skills and leave medical school with an understanding of disease but no knowledge of health. 'When they eventually go on to the wards, they meet patients who are ill, but also who are anxious, frightened, depressed, angry, and at times, rude and difficult. They see patients in pain, in tears, and witness the last breath of a human being as he struggles for his life. The instruction they get is not on how to handle these difficult human situations. Rather, they are asked about the state of the patient's liver or the latest blood test . . . As the students struggle, not only with having to amass a new set of knowledge, they are overwhelmed with feelings they do not understand. Even worse, they may stop feeling altogether as a protection from these difficulties.'[143]

CORPSE POSE The common name for the SHAVASANA pose in hatha YOGA.

CORRECTIVE EMOTIONAL EXPERIENCE Some psychotherapists try to make up for the emotional deficits in their patient's past by enacting a role which others (mother, father, lover, etc.) have fulfilled inadequately. If, for example, someone was treated over-indulgently as a child, the therapist would err on the side of strictness rather than reproduce that indulgent attitude. Franz Alexander coined the term 'corrective emotional experience' for this approach, which is considered heretical by classical Freudians. Its origins can be traced back to one of the earliest splits in PSYCHOANALYSIS, when Freud's colleague Sandor Ferenczi broke the general taboo on touching and hugged patients to make up for the lack of emotional nurturing in their early lives. He also argued that as an analyst he should ideally have only one patient, for whom he should be available at all times of the day or night. Ferenczi was not typical of early Freudians. In his private diary (not published until 1985) he stated his belief that 'No analysis can succeed in which we do not succeed in really loving the patient . . . It demonstrates a weakness in the psychic organization of the analyst if he treats more kindly a patient he finds sympathetic than one he does not.'

COUEISM Emile Coué (1857–1926) gave his name to the practice of AUTOSUGGESTION which he developed in the 1880s. The simple methods of Couéism owe almost as much to YOGA as they do to Coué's own observations. The mantra he invented to promote health and well-being – 'Every day, in every way, I am getting better and better' – was often misunderstood as a means of willing oneself better, rather than of immobilizing the will and allowing the mind

103

to influence the body through the power of the imagination. Coué did not invent a system or technique so much as offer advice in accordance with his theory that the imagination plays the key role in influencing the way the mind affects the course of a disease. His ideas have been incorporated into many psychological therapies, such as AUTOGENIC TRAINING and SILVA MIND CONTROL.

COUNSELLING The term 'counselling' covers various kinds of talking therapy ranging from simple advice and encouragement to something approaching full-blown PSYCHOTHERAPY. The usual distinction made between counselling and psychotherapy is that counselling is likely to be less wide-ranging, focusing on a particular issue (the reason for seeking counselling, such as bereavement), and to go on for a limited period of time. This may be referred to as 'crisis counselling'. Counselling as a more general therapy is usually understood as being the sort of CLIENT-CENTRED THERAPY which Carl Rogers developed. In both crisis counselling and client-centred therapy the counsellor is seen as 'receptive', a sounding board and a support. The client can voice thoughts and feelings without fear of criticism, while the counsellor encourages confidence and self-esteem. A slightly more active approach may be adopted by counsellors in therapies such as PSYCHOSYNTHESIS, although even here the direction if any will ultimately come from the client under the guidance of the counsellor.

COUNTER-TRANSFERENCE In psychoanalysis, just as TRANS-FERENCE may cause the patient to react to the analyst as if to someone from the past, so counter-transference refers to the analyst's similar reactions to the patient. Although it originally referred to the distortions and inappropriate reactions caused by the analyst's own past, the term is also used to cover all the analyst's emotional reactions to the patient. These may sometimes be deliberately (even if unconsciously) evoked by the patient. Whilst Freud regarded counter-transference as a sign that the analyst's own analysis had been inadequate, Jung conceded that it did not come just from the analyst but was an unconscious response to the influence of the patient.

CRANIAL OSTEOPATHY The skull (cranium) is not absolutely rigid: it consists of several interlocking bones which allow very slight movement. The previously unsuspected motility of the twenty-two component bones and associated membranes was discovered in 1899 by William G. Sutherland while he was training as an osteopath. He concluded that this slight freedom of movement in the skull allowed the brain to pulse rhythmically, an idea which he was able to confirm by touch. Through experimentation and refining his own sense of touch he developed a system of diagnosis by feeling abnormalities in the cranial pulse. Conversely, a cranial osteopath treats patients by applying slight, virtually imperceptible pressure to specific areas of the skull. Cranial osteopathy is regarded as an effective method of treating symptoms such as deafness, sinusitis and lower back pain, as well as more obvious conditions such as migraine and head injuries.

CREATIVE VISUALIZATION See VISUALIZATION.

CRYSTAL HEALING The fact that crystal therapy is often referred to as crystal healing points to a close association with spiritual or etheric HEALING. Crystals are said to focus the healing energy or LIFE-FORCE. The choice of crystal may depend on which CHAKRA the healer considers needs treating, or whether positive or negative energy is required, but many healers use the same crystal in all circumstances, most frequently clear rock crystal. The preparation of the healing crystal involves cleansing by soaking for several days in salt water, some people recommending the addition of cider vinegar. The crystal is then 'activated' and 'programmed' by meditation and affirmations.

Crystal healing has also been allied to COLOUR THERAPY by some healers, seven principal gems being linked to the seven colours of the rainbow. In one unusual form of treatment with gems, the patient's photograph is exposed to a rotating disc set with gems. Since the presence of the patient is not required this has been called *teletherapy*.

CUPPING 1) Cupping is an age-old method of treating a variety of swellings, aches and pains by creating a partial vacuum against the skin, intended to draw blood to the surface. It was widely used by the ancient Egyptians, Greeks, Romans and Chinese (in conjunction with ACUPUNCTURE) and by native North Americans. It is still used in many Mediterranean cultures.

In its simplest form part of an animal's horn would be placed against the skin and the air gently sucked out from the pointed end. More commonly a lighted taper is placed in a cup or glass to create a vacuum, and as the taper is withdrawn the cup is quickly placed on the skin. Instead of a taper a piece of cotton wool impregnated with methylated spirits can be burned in the cup. The patient feels a slight sucking sensation as the partial vacuum caused by the removal of the oxygen holds the cup against the skin; the flesh is drawn into the cup and blood flows into the small blood vessels. This is intended to disperse local congestion associated with the common cold, asthma, pleurisy, rheumatism, arthritis, backache, and muscular injury.

2) In massage, cupping is a technique of striking the body with the cupped hand. The effect is again to bring blood to the surface.

CYBERPHYSIOLOGY Cyberphysiology is a generic term to cover all the various strategies which enable one to control some aspect of body processes, whether by BIOFEEDBACK, SELF-HYPNOSIS, AUTOGENIC TRAINING, MEDITATION, VISUALIZATION, or even the PLACEBO EFFECT. It also includes the mental 'psyching up' which coaches put athletes through before events in which they must perform at their peak.

CYCLES See BIORHYTHMS and CIRCADIAN RHYTHMS.

CYMATICS Cymatics (from the Greek *kyma* meaning 'wave') is the study of the effects of SOUND waves on physical matter. In the eighteenth century, Ernst Chladni, a German physicist and musician, mounted a thin metal plate on a violin and placed very fine sand on the plate. When a note was played on the violin the sand took up a particular geometric pattern, similar to organic shapes. A Swiss scientist, Hans Jenny, continued this research in the twentieth century, photographing the patterns emerging from sand, iron filings, water, mercury and other liquids. The forms produced in this way resemble the growth patterns of living organisms. He also invented a device called a tonoscope which translates sound into three-dimensional images: the sound of the letter O produces a spherical pattern. Some people speculate that these effects have a bearing on the practice of CHANTING – the syllable Om being the most widely used sound in that respect – and on the therapeutic value of MUSIC, as well as on the whole area of VIBRATIONAL THERA-PIES, but nothing approaching a coherent theory has yet emerged.

D-NEEDS See DEFICIENCY MOTIVATION and NEEDS.

DANCE THERAPY Throughout history, from animistic shamans to the whirling dervishes, dancing has often been associated with religious ritual and used as a preliminary to falling into trance. With African witch doctors the trance might also be part of a healing ritual, but the dancing was more likely to be performed by the healer than the patient. In medieval Christian Europe dancing manias were sometimes seen as divinely inspired and had their own patron saint in St Vitus, but little distinction was made between general hysteria and epileptic fits. One of the first westerners to recommend dancing as a controlled therapeutic activity was Rudolph Laban (1879–1959), who emigrated from Germany to Britain at the outbreak of the First World War, and taught dancing as an adjunct to psychotherapy as a means of restoring mental health.

As with other 'creative' therapies used in conjunction with psychotherapy (e.g. ART THERAPY and DREAM THERAPY) dance and movement can also be used diagnostically: the therapist can analyse the patient's movements and thereby get an idea of the individual's self-image and general psychological condition. The development of a clearer self-image and individual identity is one of the things that dance therapy can help with, for example by working initially with kinaesthetic sensations. Through dance, people are able to express themselves non-verbally with a dynamic form of BODY LANGUAGE, sometimes leading to an emotional release through CATHARSIS, and they can also dramatize polarities within the personality, acting out SUB-PERSONALITIES, all of which helps them to feel more 'together' and in control.

Although often practised in groups, dance therapy has more to do with self-expression and self-awareness than with interpersonal behaviour. The psychological benefits accruing from physical activity and co-ordination in dance are reminiscent of the effects of EURHYTHMY and other BODYWORK therapies such as the ALEXANDER TECHNIQUE. Some of the reasons such physical awareness and exertion might lead to greater psychological well-being are explained by

DASEINANALYSE

the theory behind BIOENERGETICS and REICHIAN THERAPY.

DASEINANALYSE See EXISTENTIAL PSYCHIATRY.

DEATH A psychologist at Hatfield Polytechnic, Dr Ben Fletcher, has linked certain occupations with a predisposition for certain causes of death: policemen and telephonists have a higher than average death rate from heart disease, but cancer kills more soldiers and accountants. Does this mean that the environmental factors and psychological stresses associated with certain occupations make one more susceptible to specific fatal diseases? Or are perhaps those who are so susceptible also of a physical and psychological type which makes them more inclined to certain occupations? More surprisingly still, wives, whatever their occupation, showed almost the same 'disease risk-profile' as their husbands, almost as if they were showing solidarity with them. Perhaps the crucial factor is psychological rather than physical or environmental.

The mind certainly seems to have some say in determining *when* we die. It is a commonplace to see dying friends and relatives live just long enough to witness some important family event, apparently willing themselves to stay alive. Perhaps more strikingly it has been shown that the death rate generally rises and falls according to the individual's calendar: Jews tend not to die just before Yom Kippur, and people are statistically less likely to die just before their birthday and more likely to die just afterwards.[108]

The attitude to death adopted by western society is predominantly one of denial. Socrates defined philosophy as 'simply and solely the practice of dying – the practice of death': death was seen then as part of life, indeed the culmination of life. Ancient Greek doctors under the influence of Hippocrates believed it was unethical to treat a patient who was in the grip of a fatal illness, for to do so the doctor pitted himself against nature and challenged the gods. Nowadays doctors seem to wage a constant war against death, almost as if physical immortality were their ultimate goal, and there are more and more complaints about their determination 'officiously to keep alive'.

Ivan Illich has been one of the most outspoken of those who deplore this tendency in modern medicine. 'Traditional cultures confront pain, impairment and death by interpreting them as challenges soliciting a response from the individual under stress; medical civilization turns them into demands made by individuals on the economy, into problems that can be managed or *produced* out of existence.'[91] He refers to the MEDICALIZATION of western society: 'Medicalization constitutes a prolific bureaucratic program based on the denial of each man's need to deal with pain, sickness, and death.'

One way in which society has responded to this is the growth of the *hospice movement*, started in the 1960s by Cicely Saunders (b. 1918). As a nurse she recognized that hospitals were ill-equipped to deal with the needs of the dying. She decided to take further training in medicine and social work with the express intention of opening a hospice for the dying. The St Christopher's Hospice in London, the first of its kind, was founded in 1967. Its purpose was to provide terminal care for the in-patients whilst developing an education and research centre to enable other practitioners to learn the principles of terminal care.

Recognizing patients' psychological needs is paramount in terminal care, and there is now a much greater understanding of the way people come to terms with their own approaching death. Helen Kubler-Ross, who has probably studied these coping strategies more than anyone, has defined five 'stages of dying': 1) denial, 2) rage and anger, 3) bargaining, 4) depression, and 5) acceptance. In some cases a final sixth stage of 'hope' has also been recognized, when death is not only accepted as natural but welcomed, whether as a new beginning or as a rounding off, a final act in which one can still assert one's individuality and celebrate a completed life.

DEATH LAYER In GESTALT THERAPY the 'death layer' is a layer of the personality, also known as the implosive layer.

DECIMAL One of the ways in which the POTENCY of homoeopathic remedies is described is by reference to the number of times the solution has been diluted during preparation in the ratio of one in ten, hence decimal. Remedies are also prepared by repeated dilution in the ratio of one in a hundred, and the potency of these is defined as centesimal. The same POTENTIZATION or DYNAMIZATION process is used in anthroposophical medicine.

DEEP TISSUE MASSAGE/DEEP TISSUE MUSCLE THERAPY
Deep tissue muscle therapy is a form of massage, sometimes also known as rebalancing, which aims to bring the body into its natural posture by adjusting the skeletal system. Muscular shrinkage can be caused by poor diet, stress or emotional factors. Sessions of DTMT can release emotional blockages and result in CATHARSIS, which has

a liberating effect for the patient both physically and psychologically in the same way that ROLFING and REICHIAN THERAPY can penetrate the body ARMOUR.

DEFENCE MECHANISMS Freud conceived the idea of a defence mechanism: when we refuse to acknowledge our violent feelings, fears and anxieties, when we do not face whatever makes us angry, anxious or guilty, we employ defence mechanisms as a way of covering up those feelings. One of the most common defence mechanisms is REPRESSION, pushing the troublesome feeling into the unconscious. DENIAL is similar to repression except that the refusal to face the truth is more of a conscious decision. Another common defence mechanism is *rationalization* – the invention of apparently reasonable explanations for our behaviour to avoid acknowledging our real motives. With *displacement* our feelings are directed away from their real source onto something (or someone) else, as when people who behave subserviently at work, bottling up their anger, take it out on their spouse at home. PROJECTION is another way of redirecting feelings: in this case what one sees as one's own failings are projected onto someone else, who then bears the brunt of the criticisms that one cannot bear to direct at oneself. In *reaction formation* one conceals an undesirable emotional response by behaving unnaturally in the opposite manner.

DEFICIENCY MOTIVATION Abraham Maslow conceived a hierarchy of NEEDS in which deficiency needs are only the first to be satisfied. After physiological needs have been satisfied (food, drink, sex, shelter), the individual is driven primarily by the need for security, order and stability, then by the need for love, affection and a sense of belonging, and then by the need for esteem. Beyond these 'D-needs' Maslow saw 'metaneeds', 'B-needs' or Being-needs coming into play; deficiency motivation is replaced by growth motivation, as experienced fully by SELF-ACTUALIZING individuals – the desire to understand, to grow, to be creative. Being-needs are not usually significant until all deficiency needs have been satisfied, although in acts of heroism one's own individual needs may exceptionally be overruled by the needs of others.

DEFICIENCY NEEDS See NEEDS.

DENIAL If feelings are too painful or unacceptable we may try to block them out: instead of expressing them we deny them.

Emotional responses as diverse as anger and humour may be frowned on by those around us, so we put on an act and hide our true feelings. This is denial.

Denial has had a bad press in recent decades: we are told that we must 'get in touch with our feelings'. But to allow anticipation of threatening situations to intrude into consciousness can cause unnecessary stress, and even if such anticipation is justified, illusions in such circumstances can be of positive benefit. As Ornstein and Sobel point out, 'Whether denial is healthy or not depends on the circumstances and outcome.'[135]

For example, when undergoing surgery patients can adopt one of two possible attitudes: vigilance – wanting to know as much as possible about the operation – or avoidance – showing no interest in what is said about their illness or surgery. In one survey, 'the avoiders seemed to fare better in the post-surgical period than the vigilant. The avoiders were discharged from the hospital sooner and showed less distress . . . extreme vigilance in this pre- and postsurgical setting may be counterproductive since it mobilizes the brain and triggers a stress reaction.' 'Denying the severity of an incapacitating disease may be a helpful first step in coping with it.'[135] Illusion can sometimes allow hope, which is healthy.

DEPRIVATION DWARFISM Deprivation dwarfism occurs when children, in spite of good food and medical care, fail to thrive because they are not held, touched and hugged.

DEPTH PSYCHOLOGY Depth psychology is concerned with plumbing the 'depths' of the UNCONSCIOUS, where, according to Freud, the causes of our neuroses lie hidden until brought to conscious awareness through PSYCHOANALYSIS. In contrast, Viktor Frankl described his own form of psychotherapy (LOGOTHERAPY) as HEIGHT PSYCHOLOGY to point up the difference between it and depth psychology, which in his opinion has a comparatively restricted (and restrictive) focus.

DERMATOGLYPHICS Dermatoglyphics is the study of skin patterns, particularly fingerprints. See PALMISTRY.

DESPAIR See CANCER PERSONALITY.

DETOXIFICATION Many diets (such as the GERSON DIET, used controversially in the treatment of cancer) are based on organic food only, which allows the body to get rid of all the accumulated chemicals that have been absorbed through eating artificially fertilized and processed foods. Since such chemicals are regarded as toxins, this is known as a detoxification process.

DIAGNOSIS There are many different methods of diagnosis used in ALTERNATIVE MEDICINE. Traditional Chinese medicine uses PULSE DIAGNOSIS (*setsu-shin*) as well as the patient's general appearance – posture, eyes, skin colour, etc. (*bo-shin*) and voice quality (*bunshin*). SHIATSU also uses pulse diagnosis, and pressure points are used both for treatment and diagnosis in its western equivalent, REFLEXOLOGY. IRIDOLOGY is the western version of eye diagnosis. A unique form of diagnosis in RADIONICS uses the ABRAMS BOX. Some people claim to be able to make diagnoses by reading a person's AURA, just as others see health conditions in KIRLIAN PHOTOGRAPHS of an individual's hands. Various kinds of personality diagnosis are possible by analysing a person's choice of colour, as in the LÜSCHER COLOUR TEST and AURA-SOMA THERAPY.

DIAGNOSTIC WITNESS In RADIONICS, radiesthesia or DOWSING and related practices a sample of a patient's blood, diseased tissue, or in some instances even a photograph, may be used in the process of diagnosis. The object or specimen which represents the patient in this way is known as the diagnostic witness.

DIANETICS In 1950 Lafayette Ronald Hubbard (1911–86) published *Dianetics: The Modern Science of Mental Health*, which claimed to break new ground in the understanding of the human mind and how it works. According to dianetics the mind is real, although separate from the body, and is superior to the brain. The person is superior to the mind and can therefore correct anything in it that needs correcting. All the pain associated with traumatic events is imprinted in our minds in the form of ENGRAMS, which keep being reimposed by the experience of similar situations, but which can be removed by *auditing*. This involves repeatedly reliving the original painful experience until one is *clear*.

Dianetics recognizes that there are various levels of awareness, and teaches one how to raise the level of one's awareness so that one can become conscious of the source of troubles in the mind. Dianetics was further developed into the 'religion' of Scientology and volunteers or 'ministers' are trained to help people to grow in awareness and overcome the difficulties apparently imposed by their minds, and to confront and deal with the physical difficulties which face them. An action which helps a person to do this is called an *assist*. One form of assist is a *contact assist*, which involves re-enacting as exactly as possible the experience which caused the initial damage. This is appropriate when actual physical injury has occurred, and whilst it is not a substitute for medical treatment it is seen as helping the healing process. Another form of assist is *location processing*, through which individuals are encouraged to observe themselves in the same way that they look at objects in the external world, so that they get a clearer impression of what and where they really are.

DIAPHRAGMATIC SEGMENT In REICHIAN THERAPY the body is divided into seven areas. One of these is known as the diaphragmatic segment and includes the diaphragm, stomach, pancreas, solar plexus, gall bladder, liver, duodenum, kidneys and the muscles of the lower thoracic vertebrae. Fear can become locked in this area in the manner of BODY ARMOUR, causing sensations such as 'knots in the stomach' and pathological conditions such as stomach ulcers, diabetes and liver ailments.

DIATHERMY Diathermy is a type of ELECTROTHERAPY which uses short-wave electric currents or radio microwaves.

In short-wave diathermy currents of about 27,000,000 cycles per second are passed through the affected area of the body between two electrodes, which are separated from the skin either with pads or just air to avoid burning. Injuries are treated in this way both in alternative clinics and in hospital physiotherapy departments, but diathermy's popularity as a treatment for sports injuries has given way to PULSED HIGH FREQUENCY THERAPY.

In microwave diathermy just one electrode is used to radiate the relevant part of the body with radio waves at around 3,000,000,000 cycles per second. The thermal effect is greater than that of infra-red rays, although less than that of short-wave diathermy.

DICYANIN SCREEN Also known after its inventor as the Kilner screen, the dicyanin screen is intended to enable the viewer to see the human AURA. It consists of two pieces of glass, between which is poured a solution of dicyanin – coal-tar dye – to give an indigo-violet tint. The person being viewed usually wears a black silk robe to facilitate vision of the aura.

DIETARY THERAPIES Many diets recommended in alternative medicine are strictly vegan or vegetarian, including large amounts of raw foods and juices, little if any sugar and salt, sometimes with vitamin and mineral supplements. The so-called Guelphe fast consists of nothing but liquid foods – fruit juices, vegetable juices and broths. Some diets may consist of one food alone, such as the GRAPE CURE. Some, like the GERSON DIET, may include liquidized liver as well as fruit and vegetable juices. Although certain diets of this kind often figure in the search for effective cancer treatments, it is also argued that they are not appropriate for cancer patients because they are low in calories and many are expensive and difficult to prepare. Furthermore the resultant weight loss and physical weakness can lead to depression and thence to feelings of guilt if the diet cannot be followed, and anger if it has no positive effect. Various diets of this kind are also associated with alternative treatments for multiple sclerosis, and in conjunction with exercise programmes with the treatment of osteoporosis, another condition which cannot be successfully treated by mainstream medicine.

DIRECT ANALYSIS/DIRECT ANALYTIC THERAPY Direct analysis is the name given to a particular brand of CONFRONTATION THERAPY developed and practised by John Nathaniel Rosen until he surrendered his licence in 1983 after numerous complaints by former patients. The analyst spends many hours with psychotic or schizophrenic patients, entering into their delusional system, then confronting them with the irrationality of their delusions and forcing them to face reality. This could involve actually threatening a patient with a knife and saying, 'All right, I'll cut you up.' In *Direct Analysis: Selected Papers*, Rosen writes, 'Sometimes when I have the patient pinned to the floor, I say, "I can castrate you. I can kill you, I can eat you. I can do whatever I want to you, but I am not going to do it." '[150] Describing Rosen and his work, Jeffrey Masson says, 'One gets the feeling of a dangerous and violent guru who has lost control of himself but not of his peers.'[128] Although this was confrontation therapy in a most extreme form, Masson seems to regard it as an inevitable result of the principles on which PSYCHOTHERAPY is based.

DISIDENTIFICATION See PSYCHOSYNTHESIS.

DISEASE The orthodox view of disease today is probably more mechanistic than at any time in history. According to this view disease occurs when the mechanism of the body fails to work properly, just as machines sometimes break down, and to cure disease all we need to do is fix the appropriate part. Reductionist science helps us to understand the biochemistry of the body and hence how to fix the body when it goes wrong. The mind has no place in this diagnosis. Even the body as a whole is regarded as much less important than the individual parts.

This is how George Engel described the situation in the magazine *Science* in 1977: 'The dominant model of diseases today is biomedical, with molecular biology its basic scientific discipline. It assumes disease to be fully accounted for by deviations from the norm of measurable biological (somatic) variables. It leaves no room within its framework for the social, psychological and behavioural dimensions of illness. The biomedical model not only requires that disease be dealt with as an entity independent of social behaviour, it also demands that behavioural aberrations be explained on the basis of disordered somatic (biochemical or neurophysiological) processes. Thus the biomedical model embraces both reductionism, the philosophic view that complex phenomena are ultimately derived from a single primary principle, and mind-body dualism, the doctrine that separates the mental from the somatic.'[198]

Modern science both reduces and oversimplifies. Just as in physics there is a belief that one unified theory will (eventually) explain the whole cosmos, so in medicine disease is seen as the result of infection or trauma, in which there is a single cause for a diagnosed disorder, and it is generally thought that ultimately we shall find that single cause for each disease and be able to reverse it. The orthodox view says little about why we fall ill: although environmental factors and diet are increasingly being considered as factors, the GERM THEORY still reigns supreme and little attention is paid to the fact that the majority of people at any one time do not succumb to the ever-present germs. Hans Selye, the pioneer STRESS researcher, has considered this and asks the question: 'If microbes are ever present, yet do not cause disease until stress intrudes, what is the cause of the disease – the microbe or the stress?' But such either-or thinking leads nowhere – which is why conventional medicine finds itself at something of an impasse.

At the other end of the spectrum, from the viewpoint of HOLISTIC medicine, disease is seen as a sign that something is wrong with your life. As Jung said, 'When an inner situation is not made conscious, it appears outside as fate.' So disease strikes because the 'inner situation' demands it, rather like Groddeck's notion of the IT. Another big difference between the mainstream and the alternative attitude to disease is that for the latter it is potentially regenerative, not inherently degenerative. According to Jung, primitive peoples saw illness not as weakness of the conscious mind, but as strength of the unconscious mind.

Edward Bach (creator of the BACH FLOWER REMEDIES) expresses the same idea in a more spiritual vein: 'Disease is solely and purely corrective: it is neither vindictive nor cruel: but it is the means adopted by our own Souls to point out to us our faults: to prevent our making greater errors: to hinder us from doing more harm: and to bring us back to that path of Truth and Light from which we should never have strayed.'[6] And: 'Disease is the result of interference: interfering with someone else or allowing ourselves to be interfered with.'[86]

All alternative therapies tend to see disease as a process of healing: it is less a sign that something is wrong than that something is already being put right. Symptoms are evidence that the self-healing process is under way. This attitude was originally part of standard medical opinion. Hippocrates saw disease as made up of two elements: suffering (*pathos*) and the regenerative healing attempts of the body (*ponos*) and he believed that the physician should primarily search for, facilitate and try to understand *ponos*. When one of the four HUMOURS was in excess, certain self-healing processes of the body automatically went into action. It was the physician's job to cooperate with these processes. Hippocrates also recognized the importance of other factors: the physician could not simply intervene and cure disease by tinkering with the body; the patient's attitude was also important, as was the influence of the environment.

These three factors in the origins of disease were also recognized by the Chinese. In Chinese medical theory disease is seen as the struggle between CH'I and pathogenic factors which are able to disturb the body only because of its imbalances (rather like the imbalances in the humours in Greek medicine). These imbalances, which can be regarded as more responsible for 'causing' the disease than the pathogens themselves, are the result of three types of factors: hereditary, internal and external. There are seven internal factors, the seven moods, and six or seven external factors in the interaction between the body and the environment. In addition to any hereditary factor the balance of energy can be affected internally by an excess of anger, joy, anxiety, worry (or obsession), fear, horror and grief (sorrow); externally the possible environmental factors are identified as cold, heat, dryness, dampness, wind and fire (and humidity as a seventh in some authorities).

Sir William Osler (1849–1919) probably recognized that medicine was becoming too obsessed with pathology when he said that it was more important to know about the patient than about the disease: 'Don't tell me what type of disease the patient has, tell me what type of patient has the disease.' In the nineteenth century sickness was still personal; and disease entities were largely theoretical. Ivan Illich likens the arrival of clinical entities on the medical scene to the Copernican revolution in astronomy. As he says, 'Man was catapulted and estranged from the centre of his universe . . . Before sickness came to be perceived primarily as an organic or behavioural abnormality, he who got sick could still find in the eyes of the doctor a reflection of his own anguish and some recognition of the uniqueness of his suffering . . . Now . . . his sickness is taken from him and turned into the raw material for an institutional enterprise. His condition is interpreted according to a set of abstract rules in a language he cannot understand.'[91]

This depersonalization of disease has been recognized by others, such as Lawrence LeShan: 'If your illness or your disease does not fit the textbook requirements, or if you do not respond to medical intervention in the way the physicians think that you should . . . you threaten to make the physician think about you as an individual and to relate to you as a total person, not just as a disease or a broken machine. As he has not been trained to do this, and – indeed – has been trained to do the opposite, this can be very upsetting to him.'[116]

The objectification of disease as some definable entity which many different people have, rather than a condition which as patients we each make uniquely our own, has resulted in the concept of a so-called 'undifferentiated' (or FUNCTIONAL) illness, a type of illness that has no specific diagnosis. Detailed medical tests on patients suffering from such a condition almost invariably show them to be healthy, and the general practitioner is often left with a patient who is unwell but cannot be given a firm diagnosis. Conversely, diseases as specific entities may be present without illness, illness being the subjective state as perceived by the patient. Since one can be ill without an identifiable disease, and diseased without being ill, this has implications for our definition of HEALTH, which should perhaps be seen, not as the total absence of disease nor even as the absence of illness, but as the harmonious integration of all body systems.

117

As long ago as 1957 it was estimated that one third of patients with chronic symptoms have no organic disease and that another third exhibit symptoms unrelated to their organic condition.[180] Yet mainstream medicine still takes little if any account of the mental or subjective aspects of physiological disease. In fact the physician's own subjective attitude is more likely to affect diagnosis and treatment than the patient's: in one study a questionnaire was given to doctors about their own health, including their weight; some weeks later they were asked to complete another questionnaire about obesity; nearly all the doctors defined an obese person as one who weighed slightly more than they did themselves.

There are some signs that a wider holistic view is being taken by some conventional doctors. As Lawrence LeShan puts it, 'Cells or organs do not get cancer. People get cancer. If we wish to cure the disease, we must treat people, not cells or organs.'[116] David Smithers, a British oncologist, seems to support such a view: 'Cancer is no more a disease of cells than a traffic jam is a disease of cars . . . A traffic jam is due to a failure in normal relationships between driven cars and their environment.'

But the so-called MEDICALIZATION of society, whilst depriving patients of their unique status as suffering individuals, has also had the effect of narrowing down what is generally considered to be good HEALTH, to the extent that people may be too ready to regard themselves as ill. The boundary between sickness and health does vary from culture to culture. In Hispanic societies in America, for example, a common ailment is *susto*, described as a failure of the spirit, usually brought on by fear or shock and characterized by a feeling of weakness and a tendency to fall to the ground. It has no true equivalent in other western societies. But western medicine seems to have gone further than any other system in encouraging people to regard any slight deviation from the norm as pathological. For example, diarrhoea may result from the natural tendency to eliminate under stress, but people are inclined to regard such perfectly normal stress reactions as abnormal, which aggravates rather than alleviates the stress.

In Ivan Illich's terms this has resulted in a 'morbid' society. 'In a morbid society the belief prevails that defined and diagnosed ill-health is infinitely preferable to any other form of negative label or to no label at all . . . More and more people subconsciously know that they are sick and tired of their jobs and of their leisure passivities, but they want to hear the lie that physical illness relieves them of social and political responsibilities.'[91] Illich seems to be accusing people of not taking charge of their own ill-health, of being accomplices to the medical establishment's expropriation of disease. The increasing popularity of ALTERNATIVE THERAPIES may be a sign that more and more people *are* taking responsibility for their health.

DISPLACEMENT Failing to accept that we are as we are can result in psychological discomfort which causes us to displace our own unacceptable feelings by blaming or attacking others. This displacement is usually supported by PROJECTION of our own unacceptable character traits onto others.

DISTAL POINTS In ACUPUNCTURE points may be treated which are close to the site of the problem, but very often points will be used which are near the opposite end of the meridian being treated. These are known as distal points. They are generally on the hand, wrist, lower arm, foot or lower leg, since all twelve meridians terminate either in the hands or feet. There are also points on the ears which relate to every part of the body, and a particular branch of acupuncture, AURICULOTHERAPY, specializes in this treatment.

DISTANT HEALING Healing at a distance, without the need for the patient to be present, is recognized as feasible in certain alternative therapies such as REIKI and RADIONICS.

DISTILLATION Essential oils for use in AROMATHERAPY are prepared either by distillation or by ENFLEURAGE. Before the discovery of distillation in about 1000 AD, reputedly by Avicenna, AROMATIC OILS were prepared by infusion.

DO In the USA a Doctor of Osteopathy (DO after the name) is recognized as of equal status to a medical doctor (MD). But the similarity in training and subsequently in general practice tends to blur the distinctions between them, and OSTEOPATHY is seen by many as becoming too closely allied to ALLOPATHIC MEDICINE.

DO-IN Meaning literally 'self-stimulation', do-in is a form of SHIATSU which by pressing ACUPOINTS one can practise on oneself. It also includes movement, stretching and breathing exercises.

DOCTRINE OF CONTRARIES The doctrine of contraries is

a traditional description of what we now refer to as the ALLO-PATHIC methods of modern medicine. According to this doctrine, when there is a deviation from the norm in the body's processes we should apply counteractive measures, for example deliberately trying to cool someone with a fever or administering a laxative as a remedy for constipation. This view, which has held sway in orthodox medicine certainly for the last two centuries in the West, ignores the fact that many symptoms are evidence that the restitutive self-healing powers of the body have been put into effect and that suppressing them will probably simply delay the healing process.

DOGMA/DOGMATIC The dogmatic attitude of many practitioners in mainstream CONVENTIONAL MEDICINE when faced with the claims of ALTERNATIVE THERAPIES is not a new phenomenon. In ancient Greece, whose language has given us the term, the sons and son-in-law of HIPPOCRATES formed a society with the aim of protecting patients from the harmful effects of new medicines. It was their view that Hippocrates had said the last word on all medical matters and that new treatments were not needed.

DOSHA AYURVEDIC MEDICINE is based on three HUMOURS known as *doshas* (Sanskrit). The system itself, sometimes called *Tridosha*, forms the basis of diagnosis and treatment, all disease seen as being caused by an imbalance of these three forces.

DOUBLE-BLIND In clinical TRIALS one group of patients receives treatment with the medication being tested whilst another receives a neutral substance such as saline solution or chalk pills. The patients do not know to which group they have been assigned (randomly) or even that there are two such groups, all assuming that they are receiving the new drug, hence the 'blind' designation. The double-blind refers to the fact that the administrators of the treatment should also be ignorant of whether they are dispensing the 'real thing' or not, since it has been shown that negative expectations can also be fulfilled (the so-called NOCEBO response) in patients who apparently detect their doctor's ideas unconsciously. In a triple-blind trial the evaluators of the treatment are also ignorant of the distribution of patients in the two groups, to avoid the risk of their subjectivity affecting the results.

In Britain the first randomized trial conducted according to the double-blind technique was the British Medical Research Council's streptomycin trial in 1947. The first such trial in America had been in 1931.

DOUCHE See HYDROTHERAPY.

DOWSING Dowsing with a PENDULUM is used diagnostically in RADIONICS and several other therapies where subtle energies are considered to be involved, such as AROMATHERAPY, CRYSTAL HEALING and HOMOEOPATHY. The pendulum may be held over different areas of the body to locate the source of the problem, or in the case of a hollow pendulum containing a DIAGNOSTIC WITNESS it can be held over an anatomical diagram. Some practitioners may use a pendulum simply to confirm a diagnosis they have reached by other means, using their own code of swings to answer Yes/No questions.

DREAMING/DREAMS To our conscious mind, dreaming cannot but be a mysterious phenomenon. It is worth drawing a distinction between dreams and dreaming: dreaming is what happens in repetitive cycles during SLEEP, irrespective of our ability to remember; dreams are our waking memories of this mental activity or some small part of it. It is impossible even to assess how closely the two resemble each other, how accurate the memories are, since recall is necessarily a conscious activity (and the brief history of psychotherapy to date is testimony to the fact that it is extremely difficult for the conscious mind even to begin to understand the unconscious).

There is no generally accepted theory to explain why we dream. Throughout history debate has ranged across a wide spectrum of opinions, from the view that dreams are meaningless or somatic in origin, the result of physiological processes, to the idea that dreams can bring insight of some kind, whether from the gods or the unconscious. So whilst the citizens of ancient Rome followed the practice of 'incubation' – sleeping in temples with the express purpose of being granted a dream which the priests would then interpret, the arch sceptic Cicero held that 'Dreams are not entitled to any credit or respect whatever.' Thomas Hobbes was of the somatic school: 'Dreams are caused by the distemper of some of the inward parts of the body; divers distempers must needs cause different dreams.' (*Leviathan*).

The somatic view grew in respectability and scientific credibility during the eighteenth and nineteenth centuries (even though many individual scientists still recorded and took note of their own dreams, regarding them as valuable in some way). It was Freud who reaffirmed the older concept that dreams are both meaningful and significant. But although he described dreams as 'the royal road to the unconscious', he saw them as coming from the irrational part of our psyche, the id and our unconscious strivings. He deduced that one of the functions of sleep is to defuse our inner sense of frustration by allowing us to have the satisfaction of seeing our desires fulfilled – dreams as wish-fulfilment, often concealing from us the true nature of those wishes. Jung had a very different view of the UNCONSCIOUS and saw dreams as revelations of unconscious wisdom. Others like Erich Fromm have taken the view that we experience both types of dream, rational and irrational, purposeful and purposeless.

Meanwhile, the essentially somatic (as opposed to psychic or psychological) explanation has fragmented into a variety of theories, some spilling over into the mental arena in the sense that the mind is regarded as a mechanism. Dreams are seen as the mental side effect of processing information gathered during the day (the computer theory), or as the information being discarded during some such process (the rubbish theory), or as the result of random firings of neurones in the brain in the absence of external stimuli (the materialist theory), or as unconscious attempts to prepare for the future by trying out various scenarios that might present themselves (the rehearsal theory).

Dreams in babies have been linked with sudden infant death (SID) syndrome. Following dramatic evidence from New Zealand, cot deaths in the UK were halved to 456 in 1992 by encouraging mothers not to put their babies to sleep face down. Dr George Christos, a theoretical physicist at Curtin University in Western Australia (departing temporarily from his usual domain) has suggested that babies sleeping face down in a position which is reminiscent of the foetal position are more likely to dream of being back in the womb. It is known that during REM sleep, when dreams occur, the brain is practically disconnected from most of the muscles of the rest of the body except for the heart and lungs. Dr Christos suggests that the brain might 'forget' that the control of breathing is still vital, and he cites evidence from Stanford University which showed that people dreaming of swimming underwater actually held their breath. In addition to the existing advice to avoid putting babies to sleep face down, Dr Christos suggests they could sleep with a teat in their mouth to remind them of their post-foetal status.

DREAM INTERPRETATION/DREAM THERAPY/DREAM WORK 'All myths and all dreams have one thing in common, they are all "written" in the same language, *symbolic language*.'[55] So writes Erich Fromm in *The Forgotten Language*, and he goes on to say that 'Symbolic language is a language in which inner experiences, feelings and thoughts are expressed as if they were sensory experiences, events in the outer world.' Whatever the 'school' of psychology, the notion that dream images and events 'stand for' something else prevails throughout psychotherapy and lies at the root of the notion that dreams need interpreting if we are to understand them.

Freudian analysts interpret dreams as a means of defusing unconscious drives to which it would be unacceptable to allow free rein in waking life; they therefore represent a means of gaining access to the unconscious, even though they seem designed to conceal the truth about ourselves. For Jungian therapists dreams represent a more constructive intervention of the unconscious, pointing the individual towards greater wholeness and INDIVIDU-ATION; ARCHETYPES present themselves as dream images, as do different aspects of the psyche such as the ANIMUS/ANIMA and the SHADOW. Dream work or 'nonclinical dream therapy' has greater affinity with Jung's view of dreams than with Freud's, and is based on the assumption that dreams are designed to reveal rather than conceal the unconscious. Montague Ullman stresses the honesty in the 'self-healing machinery' of our dreams: 'While we are asleep and dreaming, our self-healing machinery propels us into a realm where feelings are displayed honestly. They shape images that may frighten or delight us, but that is not their intent. Their intent is simply to tell it like it is.'[173]

Ullman has broadened the concept of dream therapy to include working with dreams without such overt interpretation and without the need for a trained therapist, adopting the principle of 'deprofessionalizing the dream'. He considers that the important aspect of dream work is not interpretation so much as appreciation, and in group dream therapy members of the group in turn give a commentary on and appreciation of the dream just related by one of their number as if it were their own dream. The one who actually had the dream then has a wide range of associations and ways of understanding the dream on which to base a personal appreciation, without having to disclose its 'real' meaning to the others. As Deborah Jay Hillman puts it, 'The dreamer is, in effect, using the group as an instrument as he explores the dream's metaphorical references in his life.'[172]

Dream work is a dynamic process when compared with the static or passive response the dreamer makes when given an interpretation by an analyst. Most types of 'nonclinical' dream work are experiential, rather than didactic or intellectual, and involve developing an active relationship with dreams – learning to recall dreams, keeping a dream journal, sharing dreams with others, and being able to re-enter the dream and to experience it again from a waking perspective. The images evoked in a dream can be reworked in a variety of ways: as well as being written down, they can be drawn or modelled (ART THERAPY), incorporated in SAND-PLAY, or acted out in the 'dialoguing' technique of GESTALT therapy.

DRIVES Freud saw the individual driven by certain needs, such as the pleasure principle, the strongest motivating force being the libido (the sex-drive), with its negative counterpart, the supposed death-instinct. Other psychologists saw the hunger for love (Reich) and the need for self-respect (Adler) as significant. Abraham Maslow absorbed and transformed these drives in his hierarchy of NEEDS.

DROWN'S STICK PAD In RADIONICS an early diagnostic instrument was a rubber diaphragm stretched over a metal plate, developed by Ruth Drown. This replaced the abdomen of a healthy individual in the circuit originally devised by Albert Abrams, which also included the variable resistance box, known as the 'black box' or ABRAMS BOX, and a sample from the patient (DIAGNOSTIC WITNESS). By stroking the rubber lightly with the fingers while altering the resistance and noting the resistance when the rubber stuck to the fingers (hence 'stick pad'), the practitioner was able to diagnose different disease conditions, each of which was associated with a particular resistance.

DRY RUN SURGERY Before undergoing surgery in which HYPNOSIS will be used to induce anaesthesia, the patient may go through a 'dry run' of the operation. The mock operation includes all preparations, sponging with alcohol in the area where the incision will be made, a light stroke with an instrument from the surgeon with his accompanying commentary that the incision is being made and that the patient will feel no discomfort, and with the hypnotist's constant encouragements to relax. Such dry run surgery may be repeated several times before the real operation takes place to ensure that the patient is able to relax totally under such extraordinary conditions.

DYNAMIC PHYSIOTHERAPY An alternative term for BIODY-NAMIC PSYCHOTHERAPY.

DYNAMIZATION In ANTHROPOSOPHICAL MEDICINE dynamization is the equivalent of POTENTIZATION in HOMOEOPATHY and refers to the process of preparing a remedy from a raw material. The material is added to an inert substance in the proportion of 1 part in 10 and succussed at least a hundred times, which produces the first decimal potency, abbreviated to 1x or 1D. The whole process is repeated, diluting again by a factor of ten to produce the second decimal potency, 2x or 2D. This may be continued up to the thirtieth decimal potency. (At a molecular level no part of the raw material is present at potencies above 23x.) It is unusual for potencies of more than 30x to be administered, although one exception is belladonna, used in a potency of 60x when treating various psychic disturbances. It is claimed that succussions release the essential nature of the material and imprint its energies on the inert dilutants.

DYSPONESIS Dr George B. Whatmore, a physician in Seattle, Washington, coined the term 'dysponesis' (*dys*, wrong, faulty; *ponos*, effort, energy) to refer to the way in which people defeat themselves unwittingly by misdirecting their energy. In some ways this is reminiscent of Alexander's concept of END-GAINING, but Whatmore is more concerned with physiological changes within the body. For example, before performing in public people may increase their heart-rate and flood the system with adrenalin; if this becomes a habitual pattern the increased blood pressure and persistent hormonal imbalances can lead to pathological tissue deformity. Dr Whatmore's theory holds that many psychosomatic conditions such as impotence and exaggerated fear are dysponetic patterns. He also maintains that psychotherapy is of little value in treating such conditions; the answer, he believes, lies in BIOFEEDBACK. 'Misplaced efforts are capable of producing a variety of functional disturbances within the organism. Biofeedback instrumentation is designed to discover dysponetic functioning in specific systems and then help people adjust the faulty functioning before it develops into a chronic symptom or severe disorder.'[232]

DYSTONIC PATTERNS Maintaining a posture of tension, with part of the body permanently braced, hunched, twisted or collapsed, leads to patterns of imbalance in the muscles, which seem incapable of returning to their natural state. These dystonic patterns can be counteracted by certain BODYWORK therapies such as the ALEXANDER TECHNIQUE and REICHIAN THERAPY.

E METER The RELAXOMETER is a galvanic resistance machine which is used as a BIOFEEDBACK device. Attached to the fingertips, it gives an indication of one's level of tension by measuring skin resistance and emitting an auditory signal ranging from a low buzz to a high whine. The E meter as used by scientologists (see DIANETICS) is a similar machine which, however, gives no feedback to the subject, the auditory signal being replaced by a needle on a scale which only the observer can see. The subject is therefore to some extent 'an open book' to the observer, who decides what if anything to disclose concerning the subject's internal state.

ECTOMORPH See BODY-TYPES.

EFFLEURAGE Not to be confused with ENFLEURAGE, effleurage is a method of massage, originating in SWEDISH MASSAGE and often used in AROMATHERAPY. Long, slow, gentle strokes are made with the whole hand, usually in the direction of the heart. The pressure may be varied: light strokes are intended to have an effect on the nervous system, whilst deeper strokes affect the muscles and circulation.

EFFORT TRAINING Effort training is Dr George B. Whatmore's term for his treatment of people with DYSPONESIS – functional problems deriving from a misdirection of energy. This phenomenon can be seen in a very simple form when one worries about a problem so much that one is unable to concentrate on trying to solve it. With the help of BIOFEEDBACK, Dr Whatmore trained his patients to redirect their energy properly and escape from dysponetic patterns such as exaggerated fears, chronic depression or impotence.

EGO In most systems of psychology the ego (Latin for 'I') is that part of ourselves with which we consciously identify: the ego is who we think we are – our subjective identity. For Freud the ego, working according to the exigencies of the Reality Principle, seeks to mediate between the drives of the ID, serving the Pleasure Principle, and the dictates of the inner conscience or SUPEREGO. Although we are more conscious of our ego identity than of any other part of our psyche, much of ego behaviour is unconscious – ego DEFENCE MECHANISMS, for example. For Jung, too, the ego mediates both between the psyche and the environment and between the conscious and unconscious elements of the psyche, but more than that it constructs a PERSONA behind which it can hide, gives rise to a SHADOW, and determines the psychological life of the individual by its relationship with the SELF.

EGO FUNCTIONS The four modes of behaviour or faculties which Jung called ego functions are four ways in which human beings consciously try 'to understand and adapt themselves to the world and whatever happens to them'.[101] They are an essential part of Jung's analysis of PSYCHOLOGICAL TYPES. Having first established the basic attitudinal distinction – EXTRAVERT/INTROVERT – Jung set about looking for further basic characteristics 'which might serve the purpose of giving some order to the apparently limitless variations in human individuality'[99] and he found two more pairs of opposites: thinking/feeling and sensation/intuition. Thinking and feeling are considered to be rational and discriminating, whilst sensation and intuition are non-rational means of perception. Thinking gives meaning and understanding, and feeling (which is not simply emotion) gives value; sensation is perception through the senses, and intuition is perception through the unconscious. 'Sensation establishes what is essentially given, thinking enables us to recognize its meaning, feeling tells us its value, and finally intuition points to the possibilities of the whence and whither that lie within the immediate facts.'[101]

ELECTRO-ACUPUNCTURE ACUPUNCTURE points can be stimulated electrically as well as with needles. The most common form of electro-acupuncture treatment is with a TRANSCUTANEOUS ELECTRICAL NERVE STIMULATION (TENS) machine, which is used in the control of pain. It has been shown that this treatment triggers an increase in the brain's production of ENDORPHINS.

ELECTROMYOGRAM (EMG) An electromyogram is an electronic instrument which measures muscle activity, used in (electromyographic) BIOFEEDBACK.

ELECTRO-POLLUTION See ELF.

ELECTROTHERAPY Electrotherapy is an umbrella term for a variety of treatments which use electromagnetic energy either by direct application to the body, or by placing the relevant part of the body in an electromagnetic field; it covers the use of radio waves as well as electricity. The term is also sometimes misleadingly used to include ULTRASONICS.

The Roman physician Scribonius Largus prescribed the application of an electric fish to a patient's head as a cure for headache, and Pliny the Elder recommended the shock from such a fish as a remedy for labour pains. In the eighteenth century it was thought that the physical convulsions of epileptics protected them from madness, and that madness could therefore best be treated by applying physical stress to the patient.[18] The modern equivalent of this is perhaps the controversial though continuing use of electro-convulsive therapy in the treatment of mental illness.

The first modern therapeutic use of electricity was GALVANISM, the application of direct current, developed two hundred years ago and soon followed by FARADISM, in conjunction with which it is still sometimes used. A later development in the use of low frequency currents is INTERFERENTIAL THERAPY. Claims have been made for the therapeutic effect of HIGH FREQUENCY CURRENTS, but even higher frequencies are used in DIATHERMY, including radio waves used in microwave diathermy. High energy radio waves are also used in PULSED HIGH FREQUENCY THERAPY. Another short-wave therapy is Dr Jules Samuels's particular brand of ENDOGENOUS ENDOCRINOTHERAPY.

ELEMENTS In ANTHROPOSOPHICAL MEDICINE the main organs are associated with particular elements: the heart – Fire, the kidneys – Air, the liver – Water, the lungs – Earth. These affinities suggest some treatments. Steiner said, 'If you examine the Earth qualities of plants you will find in them the remedies for diseases which originate in the lungs . . . If you take what circulates in the plant, its juices, you will have the remedy for all disturbances connected with the liver.' It may seem strange that the lungs are linked with Earth rather than Air, but they show their close relationship to the physical world by the fact that through respiration they are in constant contact with the world of matter and are always taking parts of that matter into themselves and making it available to the physical body.

Traditional ACUPUNCTURE treatment is also given in accordance with the relationships between physiological systems and the five elements of Chinese thought, although the only obvious similarity between Chinese and western systems is that the heart is associated with Fire. The Chinese ascribe the kidneys to Water, the spleen to Earth, the lungs to Metal (which is usually regarded as the Chinese equivalent of the western Air) and the liver to Wood – the 'extra' fifth element, of a rather different nature from the other four.

In AYURVEDIC MEDICINE there are also five elements – Earth, Fire, Water, Air and Ether – but these combine in pairs to form three forces (*doshas*), each of which governs different types of physiological activity: Air and Ether govern respiration and movement, Fire and Earth govern temperature, digestion and circulation, and Water and Earth govern growth, secretions and the brain. (These five have also been incorporated in POLARITY THERAPY, in which each element corresponds to one of the main 'centres'.)

Looking at medical authorities through history, from the ancient Ayurvedic and Chinese systems to the ancient Greek and anthroposophical systems, we see a progression in the way elements were associated first with general physiological processes (Ayurvedic), then with systems around an organ (Chinese), and then in the West with individual organs. This may have been partly a result of the greater willingness in the West to dissect the body and investigate organs directly, although it also reflects the increasing objectification of processes that were originally regarded as somewhat ethereal. (See also HUMOURS.)

ELF ELFs are extremely low frequency electromagnetic waves, emitted from electrical equipment such as radios, televisions and computers. Exposure to ELF electromagnetic fields is thought by some to increase the risk of cancer, hormonal changes, disorders of the nervous system, stress and anxiety. The problem is sometimes referred to as electro-pollution. Devices to be worn around the wrist have been marketed which, it is claimed, counteract and neutralize the ELF radiation around the wearer.

ELIXIRS An elixir is a general remedy, a panacea or 'cure-all', and hence a remedy which is also life-enhancing if taken when one is in good health. Medieval alchemists devoted much time to searching for 'the elixir of life', which it was believed would prolong life indefinitely. (The word is thought to come via Arabic – al iksir, the elixir – from the Greek xerion, which was a powder used for treating wounds.)

Most elixirs are herbal remedies (although the alchemists used other substances in their concoctions). One of the oldest and probably the most widely used youth-preserving elixir is the 'man-shaped' root GINSENG, which seems to have superseded its western equivalent, the mandrake. In ANTHROPOSOPHICAL MEDICINE the life-prolonger is Birch-leaf Elixir, which it is recommended can be taken in spring and autumn throughout life to guard against the sclerotic diseases of old age. An alternative to ginseng that has been marketed more recently as a general elixir is royal jelly, and to judge by the claims made for it, it would seem that Evening Primrose Oil is also rapidly acquiring the status of an elixir.

ELIZA Named after the character in *Pygmalion* (and *My Fair Lady*), Eliza is a computer program created by Joseph Weizenbaum, a computer scientist at MIT, who believes in the possibility of artificial intelligence. Eliza imitates a psychoanalyst by simply regurgitating variations of what the patient says. It is usually quite some time before patients realize, if indeed they ever do, that they are not dealing with a live human being at the other end of their computer terminal. Some might think the Eliza program says less about the feasibility of AI than it does about the lack of intelligence required for certain aspects of PSYCHOANALYSIS.

EMANOMETER The emanometer is a British variant of the ABRAMS BOX (the 'black box'), a diagnostic instrument used in RADIONICS. In the early 1920s the British authorities hoped to avoid a repetition of the scandal surrounding the unorthodox activities of Albert Abrams when he had tried to market his box in the USA: they set up an official investigation of the emanometer under Sir Thomas Horder. Much to their surprise, the Horder report concluded that the claims made for the emanometer were accurate, but this vindication was of little use to Abrams himself, who had died before the report came out. The investigation showed that measurements with the device enabled one to distinguish between a homoeopathic remedy and a neutral substance.

EMG Common abbreviation for the ELECTROMYOGRAM, equipment used in electromyographic BIOFEEDBACK.

EMOTIONS Can we control our emotions, or are we controlled by them? With one breath we might tell someone to cheer up or calm down, and with the next maintain that we can't help what we feel. Telling ourselves to cheer up often seems more likely to make us sink further into gloom and depression. As Margaret Donaldson says, 'Those of us who live in twentieth-century Western cultures are heirs to somewhat confused and limited ideas about the possibility of emotional control. On the one hand . . . the belief that we have some power to regulate what we think and how we act but not how we feel has wide currency. We say things like: "I'll go and think it over", or: "I decided to have a think about that"; whereas we do not usually talk about deciding to have an emotion . . . However, it is evident that we do also urge one another to attempt certain kinds of control in ways that imply some belief in the possibility.'[32]

Aristotle recognized the difficulties of controlling the emotions, or making effective use of them: 'It is easy to fly into a passion – anybody can do that – but to be angry with the right person to the right extent and at the right time and with the right object and in the right way – that is not easy, and it is not everyone who can do it.' He also recognized the value of CATHARSIS, which he said cleanses the mind of suppressed emotions, and we often say that 'a good cry' makes you feel better. Why is this? Emotional tears contain more protein than tears induced by irritants, so it has been suggested that emotional crying is an eliminative process whereby tears remove toxic substances from the body.[191] Just as emotional release is beneficial, suppression of the emotions is a hazard to health.

Most traditional systems of medicine link the emotions with the cause of physical disease. According to ancient Chinese medicine, an imbalance of emotions can disturb the functioning of internal organs (and vice versa): an excess of worry can damage the lungs (and since the Chinese do not separate organ and function, that includes the whole respiratory system). Similarly, an excess of HAPPINESS can damage the heart and the circulatory system, anger damages the liver, fear the kidneys and the sexual function, and desire the spleen and the digestive system.

The ancient Greeks believed that DISEASE was caused by imbalances in the four HUMOURS, and cancer was associated with an excess of melancholy. Nowadays cancer is often associated with suppression of emotions, especially the suppression of anger. It has been shown that long-term survivors of cancer express much higher levels of anxiety, hostility, alienation and other negative emotions than short-term survivors. Such people, because of the overt expression of negative emotions even to the doctors treating them, would often be described as 'less well adjusted', but by expressing their negative attitudes they seem to gain strength from them. Some of our idiomatic language suggests that we may have had unconscious insights into this long ago: 'getting something off your chest' may somehow be a protection against lung or breast cancer. (Other slang expressions perhaps reflect the fact that the emotions are also associated with bowel disorders.) Without emotional expression, of course, STRESS increases, and a variety of diseases are associated with the damaging effects of stress, including diabetes, arthritis, multiple sclerosis and Addison's disease, all of which are linked with auto-allergic responses and AUTO-IMMUNITY. HOSTILITY also seems to have an adverse effect on health.

The value of emotional expression (as a means of reducing potentially damaging stress) seems to extend to those who are not suffering from any particular disease: the way we express our feelings seems to influence health and LONGEVITY. 'Lieberman found that the single most successful prediction for long life in aged individuals was how much aggressiveness they expressed and how much anger. Passivity and refusal to express anger may well lead, as many people think, to a biological deterioration or it may heighten the magnitude of the stress that someone experiences. Aggressive behaviour in some circumstances seems to enhance survival.'[135]

Needless to say, positive emotions are also beneficial to health: in one experiment, watching a film of Mother Teresa tending the poor of Calcutta increased the viewers' salivary immunoglobin A (an antibody against viral infection), regardless of whether they liked her or not. Watching comedy programmes on television has the same effect, and Norman Cousins became famous for apparently curing himself with LAUGHTER. So whilst grief and anger can depress the immune system, laughter and empathy strengthen it.[118] HOPE also seems to have a positive effect.

It is clear that certain emotions are intimately bound up with the secretion of certain chemicals, hormones, which in turn have a physiological effect. This can be seen in the FIGHT-OR-FLIGHT response: fear induces the secretion of adrenalin, which causes among other things heart palpitations. (It has been shown that adrenalin itself, injected into the system, does not induce feelings of fear.)

The common link between emotions and hormones is the hypothalamus in the brain: impulses identified with emotions originate in the hypothalamus and then pass to the cortex, where the emotion is 'experienced', and the hypothalamus also regulates the release of hormones. Hormones affect the functioning of the body's cells and organs. So emotions affect physical well-being – for good or ill.

Can we then cultivate the arousal and expression of certain emotions? Paul Ekman thinks we can. In experiments at the University of California he has shown that assuming different facial expressions induces one to feel the associated emotions – smiling eventually makes one feel more cheerful, for example.[155] This was recognized by Charles Darwin in 1872: 'The free expression by outward signs of an emotion intensifies it. Passions can be produced by putting people into appropriate attitudes.'[30] The fact that we experience laughter as 'infectious' may also be an expression of this tendency. At a different mental level we can also induce certain feelings with a simple command, according to the principles of SELF-HYPNOSIS and AUTOGENIC TRAINING.

EMPATHIC UNDERSTANDING/EMPATHY According to Carl Rogers, one of the three essential conditions in CLIENT-CENTRED THERAPY is the therapist's empathy with the client.

EMPIRICAL MEDICINE Samuel Hahnemann, the founder of homoeopathy, believed that the healer must act in accordance with what is actually perceived in nature and the individual patient rather than on the basis of preconceived notions or scientific 'proof'. Such treatment is empirical, born of actual experience rather than previous theory and conjecture. In its medical sense 'empirical' also refers to the anti-Hippocratic school of medicine at Cnidus in Asia Minor: unlike Hippocrates, CNIDEAN MEDICINE regarded disease as originating within the organism itself, which made it all the more necessary that the physician should treat the patient as a unique individual rather than as just another example of an established disease pattern. This empirical attitude (a narrower sense of the word than when it is used in a philosophical context) is part of a HOLISTIC approach to health care.

ENANTIODROMIA Carl Jung took the word 'enantiodromia'

from Heraclitus. Meaning 'spontaneous reversal', it refers to the inherent tendency of any entity to transform into its opposite and is an essential property of all homoeostatic systems. (The most commonly cited everyday example of homoeostasis is a thermostat: to maintain temperature within the desired range it has to be capable both of changing that temperature and of ceasing to change it, allowing the environment to warm up and cool down.)

Within a family it is natural for offspring to compensate in their own lives for the deficiencies of their parents – an example of the family group's enantiodromia. Personal enantiodromia may be experienced as a mid-life crisis, when one suddenly questions all one's previously held values and cherished ambitions. 'At the stroke of noon the descent begins. And the descent means the reversal of all the ideals and values that were cherished in the morning.' Jung saw this mid-life enantiodromia as a change from an extraverted life in society to a more introverted way of life, a spiritual search. He also saw the possibility of enantiodromia in society itself: we may be in need of a cultural shift from youthful exuberance towards more mature wisdom, a change which could be facilitated by the fact that older age-groups predominate in a population, so long as a significant proportion of mature adults are prepared to work towards INDIVIDUATION.

ENCOUNTER GROUPS/ENCOUNTER THERAPY By the 1950s Kurt Lewin's T-GROUP training had become established. The process of learning how to relate to others in the group made people realize that they wanted to learn more about themselves, their 'real selves' rather than the roles to which society made them conform. In encounter groups the emphasis shifts towards personal growth, although the interpersonal element is still very strong and indeed essential to the method. The leader is not an expert who instructs or tells people what to do, but a facilitator who suggests how the members of the group might best take advantage of the situation they are in. Which is not to say that the leader does not take an active role in the group, or that no training is required: a good encounter group leader will probably be trained in several therapies such as GESTALT or BIOENERGETICS. The general approach in encounter groups owes much to the work of Carl Rogers in CLIENT-CENTRED THERAPY.

The encounter group offers its members the opportunity to escape from the constraints of the normal (western) world, in which people seldom express their true feelings and hardly ever touch. The first breaking-the-ice exercise will probably involve touching, which in this instance means touching strangers – one of the great taboos in our culture. In the encounter groups touching helps people to feel safe, so that they are more likely to take risks and voice their innermost thoughts and feelings. Participants may be asked to say what they like or dislike about their own bodies, and to express their feelings about every other member of the group. There may be much cushion-beating when suppressed feelings about close relatives are finally admitted and released. Negative feelings are expressed and owned rather than suppressed and denied, and people are encouraged to 'feel OK' about themselves and their feelings, thus building up their confidence and self-esteem.

END-GAINING End-gaining is a term coined by Alexander, creator of the ALEXANDER TECHNIQUE. It refers to the common tendency people have of focusing too much on the end-result of their actions instead of on the actions themselves. It is akin to the familiar phenomenon of trying so hard that the extra effort becomes an impediment rather than an aid to success. End-gainers are people who are so anxious to achieve something that they never consider whether they are using the right means to achieve it.

In the preface to the 1941 edition of his *The Use of the Self*, Alexander stresses that anyone following the Technique must recognize that 'to "try and get it right" by direct "doing" is to try and reproduce what is known, and cannot lead to the "right", the as yet "unknown".'[2] We worry too much about the end-result instead of focusing on the *how*, what Alexander called the 'means whereby'. As Wilfred Barlow put it, 'When we are concerned with *ends* rather than *means*, our bodies don't function as well. The human organism is built for process-operation, not for end-gaining.'[8]

The same could be said of any activity, physical or mental. Total absorption in what we are doing (as a whole process) leads to success, whereas a preoccupation with the end-result of our efforts often leads to disappointment. Many psychological therapies have realized this (perhaps casting an eye over their shoulder to the teachings of Buddhism and their emphasis on the now). The principle is also recognized in the BATES METHOD of correcting or improving vision: staring hard in an attempt to see more clearly causes strain, which impairs vision. However, being absorbed in the process does not mean focusing attention on the details of what we are doing. As Michael Polyani pointed out, if pianists concentrate on their fingers they play badly; a pianist must attend *from* the fingers *to* the music.[145] This problem has sometimes been linked to the BICAMERAL NATURE OF THE BRAIN, the preoccupation with the detail of what we are doing being a symptom of the excessive dominance of the analytical left-brain. The problem of end-gaining suggests that the right hemisphere, being more concerned with 'the whole picture', should be more involved than it is.

ENDOGENOUS ENDOCRINOTHERAPY As a general umbrella term, endogenous ('from within') endocrinotherapy ('treatment of the glandular system') covers a wide range of therapies which are intended to stimulate or bring into balance the functioning of the endocrine system without actually administering glandular extracts derived from external sources. (The use of such extracts, the 'replacement' method favoured by orthodox medicine, does not encourage the body's own homoeostatic processes, accelerates the atrophy of underfunctioning glands and creates dependency, as well as costing a great number of animal lives.) Among the therapies which aim to affect the endocrine system are HOMOEOPATHY, HERBAL MEDICINE, ACUPUNCTURE and related types of treatment (ACUPRESSURE, SHIATSU, REFLEXOLOGY, etc.), APPLIED KINESI-OLOGY, and even, or perhaps particularly, the seemingly more mystical systems such as AYURVEDIC and ANTHROPOSOPHICAL MEDICINE, and those VIBRATIONAL THERAPIES which aim to treat the CHAKRAS such as COLOUR THERAPY and GEM THERAPY.

As a specific therapy, endogenous endocrinotherapy also refers to a form of ELECTROTHERAPY developed by Dr Jules Samuels in Amsterdam. When a pinch of skin is held so that the blood flow is cut off, the oxygenated blood eventually becomes de-oxygenated and the 'reduction time' during which this happens (usually about twenty-five seconds) is an indicator of both metabolism and hormonal balance. With a spectroscope the variations in this reduction time can be measured more accurately and the therapist can decide which gland needs treatment. The gland is then irradiated with short-wave radiation for a few minutes.

ENDOMORPH See BODY-TYPES.

ENDORPHINS/ENKEPHALINS Why does rubbing ease pain? Rubbing the site of a bump stimulates the release of opioid peptides or painkilling chemicals known as endorphins (from *endo*genous mor*phine*). Morphine, the active ingredient in opium, has long been used as a painkiller; it blocks the brain's reception of pain signals. But endorphins are five to ten times more powerful than morphine. Enkephalins (Greek for 'in the head') are another group of opioid peptides produced in the brain and were discovered and isolated by John Hughes and Hans Kosterlitz at the University of Aberdeen in 1975.

The natural response to pain is withdrawal, a reduction in activity which allows the organism to recuperate. But in some cases this is counterproductive: the organism must act (the FIGHT-OR-FLIGHT RESPONSE), so a temporary block on the awareness of pain can allow appropriate action to be taken, hence the production of endorphins. Endorphins are also released during labour to help both mother and fetus to withstand pain. The production of endorphins is seen to rise when patients receive ELECTRO-ACUPUNCTURE (TRANS-CUTANEOUS ELECTRICAL NERVE STIMULATION) as treatment for pain. But STRESS can deplete the levels of endorphins, aggravating migraines, backache and even the pains of arthritis (though not the disease itself).

Because of their analgesic effect endorphins were artificially synthesized and administered to people in pain. But side effects were the same as with opiates – confused memory, learning difficulties, constipation, depressed appetite – and as well as producing euphoria they were addictive.[17]

ENEMAS See HYDROTHERAPY.

ENERGY See LIFE-FORCE.

ENFLEURAGE Enfleurage is a process of producing oils from flowers, used in aromatherapy. Flower heads are pressed into purified fat, or spread on filters which are placed in oil, and left until all the essential oil from the flowers has been absorbed and they wilt. The flowers are removed and replaced with fresh ones and more oil is absorbed. This is repeated until the fat or oil is saturated with essence from the flowers. Using fat in this method produces a *pommade* – often used as a perfume or ointment. Nowadays the essential oil is extracted from the fat by mixing it with alcohol. The oil dissolves in the alcohol, but the fat doesn't and can be separated. When alcohol containing the oil in solution is heated the alcohol evaporates, leaving the pure oil, which is known as an absolute. Some aromatherapists believe that alcohol destroys the properties of the essences, and therefore use oil initially rather than fat, and then separate the essence by distillation.

ENGRAMS L. Ron Hubbard (1911–86), founder of DIANETICS, claimed that the unborn fetus receives impressions from the outside world, ranging from physical violence suffered by the mother to conversations it 'overhears', and that out of these are formed memory traces in the brain. Borrowing a term from neurophysiology, he called these memory traces engrams.

The orthodox scientific view is that the prenatal brain is incapable of recording memories, since the nerves have not yet developed their myelin sheathing which is a prerequisite for memory formation. Hubbard denied the primary role of myelin in coding memories.

ENKEPHALIN See ENDORPHINS.

ENLIGHTENMENT INTENSIVE An enlightenment intensive is an interactive group experience lasting between three days and a week which blends the reciprocal technique of CO-COUNSELLING with the Zen practice of meditating on a so-called paradoxical question or *koan*. Groups vary enormously in size and are led by a facilitator, but the work is done in pairs or *dyads* with participants changing partners for each exercise. Exercises last for about forty minutes and partners take it in turn to ask each other a question such as 'Who are you?', 'What are you?', 'What is life?', 'What is another?' 'What is meaning?'. After five minutes with one person trying to answer the question, roles are reversed and the answerers become the questioners for five minutes, and so on. Even though strictly speaking the questions are not all koans, the method of progressively finding new ways of answering them enables one to achieve a refreshing state of relaxation and well-being and detach oneself from concern with one's identity while gaining a sense of getting closer to the essential truth and understanding oneself better. Enlightenment intensives are seen as particularly beneficial for people who are facing a crisis in their lives or as follow-up personal GROWTH experiences for those who have participated in other group therapies such as GESTALT.

ENMESHMENT Re-connecting with one's feelings after suffering alienation from them can result in emotional confusion such that one relates to others without clearly set boundaries. This state is known as enmeshment.

ENSTASY Mircea Eliade coined the term 'enstasy' (by analogy with 'ecstasy') to refer to the type of ecstatic ALTERED STATE experienced while being fully aware of one's bodily sensations.

ENVIRONMENT/ENVIRONMENTAL FACTORS It has been shown that hospital patients in a room with a view recover more quickly than those whose windows look out onto a brick wall. A view of trees helps even more, perhaps because of the effect of the COLOUR green. It is easy to see that the environment affects people's mental state as well as their physical well-being, without having to invoke the ideas used in the Chinese art of FENG SHUI or the like; but such ancient systems may simply be a way of understanding influences which we are only just beginning to measure scientifically: we now know that the presence of positive and negative IONS in the atmosphere can have a profound effect on health, as can the presence of a strong electromagnetic field.

The influence of the environment is also felt in life events and changes of circumstances. STRESS often originates from a mismatch between perceived environmental demands and one's perceived ability to adapt to those demands.

ESALEN The Esalen Institute on the Californian coast south of San Francisco was founded in 1961 by Michael Murphy and Richard Price as a centre for workshops (such as ENCOUNTER GROUPS), therapy (such as GESTALT and CLIENT-CENTRED THERAPY) and research in all aspects of the HUMAN POTENTIAL MOVEMENT.

ESSENCES/ESSENTIAL OILS Alternative terms for AROMATIC OILS.

est The acronym for Erhard Seminars Training is always written in the lower case, supposedly because it is unpretentious. Its supporters believe (some would say paradoxically) that the lower case stresses the unpretentious nature of est itself. It is also, of course, Latin for 'it is'. est advertises itself as neither a therapy nor a religion, but as a technique to change people's lives. It was founded in 1971 by Werner Erhard.

Werner Erhard was formerly John Paul Rosenberg, a car salesman. In 1960 he left his wife and four children, changed his name (calling himself after the then Chancellor of West Germany) and started a new life, which however turned out to be not so very different, at least for the first ten years. By 1970 he had remarried, fathered three more children and moved on to selling encyclopaedias, working his way up to vice-president of the organization. Along the way he had become familiar and acquired a certain facility with the ideas of popular psychology and 1960s philosophy, imbued with Scientology, Zen and Taoism. He became a successful instructor of Mind Dynamics, a spiritual discipline established by Alexander Everett, and then decided to go independent and created est.

The essential purpose of the training is that we should accept what is and what we are, however unpalatable that might be, rather than constantly think about what should be and regret what is not. We define ourselves through our past experiences, and too often we evaluate our past as good or bad, when those experiences are no more than our present thoughts about them. Why can't we just be ourselves? We should also accept responsibility for ourselves rather than look for others on whom we can lay the blame. Many of the exercises are designed 'to settle unfinished business', and to recognize that we need not be trying to get anywhere – we are there already. If we regret spending so much money on est just to find out that we know it all already, it doesn't matter, and it doesn't not matter either – it just is. There are elements of Taoism in this approach.

The training can be quite an uncomfortable experience. Over 200 people are closeted in a room for fifteen hours a day (sixty hours spread over two weekends) with few breaks for the body's natural processes of refuelling and elimination, and Erhard's autocratic regime means that no one is allowed to leave the room for any purposes except at the ordained times. (est is sometimes punningly described as 'no-piss training'.)

Erhard has been accused of 'making the mistake of teaching self-awareness as if it ought to exclude other sorts of awareness.' est training participants are almost exclusively white, well-dressed, well-educated, healthy and relatively wealthy. According to Rosen: 'These were still the children of the dream who, having passed through their phase of political activism or maximum material comfort, had run smack into some private emptiness.' So what does the authoritarian Erhard give them? Insults, the opportunity to say that life stinks, and 'freeze-dried Zen'.[151]

ETHERIC BODY See LIFE-FIELD and ANTHROPOSOPHICAL MEDICINE.

ETHERIC HEALING See VIBRATIONAL HEALING.

EUPSYCHIA Utopia (Greek for 'no place') was invented by Sir Thomas More in 1516 as an imaginary and implicitly unattainable ideal state. Although utopianism later came to be used as a description of any political philosophy which believed in an ideal future state of social harmony which might be achieved, Utopia has always had connotations of impracticality. For this reason Abraham Maslow coined a new word, Eupsychia (*eu* – 'good', *psyche* – 'mind'), to refer to 'the culture that would be generated by one thousand SELF-ACTUALIZING people on some sheltered island where they would not be interfered with ... the word "eupsychia" can also be taken another way. It can mean "moving toward psychological health".'[127] The Eupsychian society is one of high SYNERGY, in which the interests of the individual and those of the community are not mutually exclusive or incompatible (as Freud thought inevitable). It creates an environment where people can develop their potential and satisfy their innate psychological NEEDS.

EURHYTHMICS Eurhythmics is a method of expressing the rhythmic aspects of music by physical movement, half dance, half gymnastics, devised by Jaques Dalcroze (1865–1950), a Swiss music teacher, composer and professor of harmony. It is a type of musical rather than body awareness training, designed to develop the ability to respond immediately to changes of rhythm in music.

EURHYTHMY Eurhythmy is an art of movement created by Rudolf Steiner (with the help of Lory Smits, a seventeen-year-old girl) in 1912 as part of anthroposophy (and as a therapy as part of ANTHROPOSOPHICAL MEDICINE), which saw its first public presentation the following year. As with all anthroposophical activities, it embodies the harmonious use and interaction of all elements of the human organism – body, soul and spirit.

The aim of eurhythmy is to express in physical movement the essential content of words and music. As Steiner said, eurhythmy 'expresses the gestures inherent in speech and music'. It enables 'a person or group of people to carry out movements which bring to expression the elements of music and language in visible form, just as the organs of language and song do it in audible form. The human being or group of human beings becomes a larynx.' Speech and music are made visible not in an arbitrary or improvised manner, but in accordance with correspondences between specific types of sound and particular body movements, especially of hands and arms. Certain kinds of movement represent the vowel sounds, for example, and others the consonants. Steiner gave his first lectures on eurhythmy to a group of doctors in 1921, by which time he had developed curative eurhythmy as a therapy, recommending particular movements and exercises for specific ailments, both physical and mental. It has proved particularly effective with children: it is used to treat those with psychiatric disorders and to assist in the natural development of normal children.

It is perhaps worth noting that eurhythmy was developed at about the same time as the ALEXANDER TECHNIQUE and Rudolph Laban's ideas of DANCE THERAPY, with both of which it has much in common, although the philosophy behind it is essentially anthroposophical.

EUTONY Derived from the Greek for 'harmonious' or 'well' (*eu*) and 'tension' (*tonos*), eutony is a method of achieving physical self-awareness through movement and self-observation. Its founder, Gerda Alexander, was involved in dance in the 1920s and 1930s and recognized that in so-called 'free movement' pupils were in fact imitating their teacher rather than experiencing and expressing themselves through their own bodies. The aim of eutony is to instil in individuals sensitivity to their own bodies, from which it is hoped comes greater self-knowledge. It is often used in conjunction with PSYCHOTHERAPY. As with the FELDENKRAIS TECHNIQUE, which has comparable aims and methods, tuition may be one-to-one or in groups, and the emphasis is always on individualized lessons rather than mechanical repetition. If eutony is to be distinguished from other techniques it is perhaps in its insistence on avoiding anything prescriptive: students are guided towards exploring their physical being and achieving self-knowledge in their own way. As Gerda Alexander says, 'When you help the other person by your own will, you invade him and usually make him even more tense. It is very important to begin all treatment with this in mind: What does the other body need?'

EXHAUSTION See ADAPTATION RESPONSE.

EXISTENTIAL PSYCHIATRY/PSYCHOTHERAPY The existential approach to psychotherapy emphasizes the philosophy of existentialism as much as psychological theory. Existentialism focuses on what it regards as 'the givens' of existence – being, death, authenticity, suffering, alienation, responsibility. According to Martin Heidegger, we create for ourselves modes of 'being in the world' which trap us in 'inauthentic existence'. This results in a sense of 'unfreedom' which can be the root cause of neurosis. Through analysis we can acquire a more objective view of our 'world design', and recognize and change what is inauthentic and constricting about it. The Swiss psychologist and student of Jung, Ludwig Binswanger, whose clinic was visited by many famous people including Nijinsky, Martin Buber, Karl Jaspers and Martin Heidegger, maintained that although his *Daseinanalyse* (literally 'existence analysis' or 'being there analysis') could be therapeutic it was not a therapy. Binswanger and the 'Zurich school' always regarded themselves as analytical psychologists. This attitude is reflected in the absence of techniques and recognized strategies on the part of an existential psychotherapist, and in the manner of training. The trainee therapist develops a particular attitude to life, self and others under the guidance of a supervisor, with whom the relationship is almost that of student and guru.

Some of the ideas behind existential psychotherapy are echoed in personal construct theory (e.g. acquiring an objective view of one's 'world design', one's way of viewing the world), but PERSONAL CONSTRUCT THERAPY uses many techniques to help the client achieve this. Another form of existential psychotherapy which is more oriented towards therapy is Victor Frankl's LOGOTHERAPY.

EXPECTATION The expectation that one will recover from an illness is a crucial element in the PLACEBO EFFECT, and anticipating the PAIN one will feel while waiting to have an injection will almost certainly exacerbate that pain when it is actually felt. Mental attitudes of this kind can have a profound effect on aspects of physical performance too, as was shown in an experiment with soldiers going on a long march. All the soldiers in the experiment marched 40 km but with different expectations while doing so. They were divided into four groups: group 1 were told the exact distance they had to cover and were kept informed of their progress; group 2 were told they were doing 'the long march' but the distance was not specified and they were given no information about their progress; group 3 were first told that they were to do 30 km, but at the last moment another 10 km was added; group 4 were told that they would have to do 60 km, but were in fact stopped at 40 km.

The experimenters checked morale, performance (including the number of drop-outs) and stress (measured by levels of two hormones which are believed to rise as stress increases). Group 1, who received the maximum amount of information, fared best of all, and group 2, who had the least information, fared worst and suffered the greatest stress. Group 3 were discouraged when told to do another 10 km but did it. Group 4 were so discouraged that some gave up after only 10 km, and those who finished were more exhausted after 40 km than those in groups 1 and 3.

Expectation is clearly involved in the power of SUGGESTION, which can be surprisingly influential even without HYPNOSIS. Blindfolded children, when told that their arms had been touched with poison ivy, to which they knew they were allergic, reacted according to their expectations, suffering symptoms of swelling, erythema and itching, even though they were actually touched with something perfectly harmless.[23] Perhaps we should take more notice of such negative expectation. Doctors have been shown to exhibit greater fear of death than either healthy or sick people. Since they can easily communicate such anxieties to their patients, Ivan Illich has suggested that when treating people with serious conditions they could be regarded as carriers of 'infectious fright', adversely affecting their patients' chances of recovery.[91]

A particular form of expectation – hope – seems to be beneficial to general health. It has been shown that one of the best predictors of future health is self-rated health. People who rate their health poorly die earlier and have more disease than their counterparts who view themselves as healthy. In a seven-year survey of old people in Manitoba, Canada, 'subjective self-reported health was more accurate in predicting who would die than the objective health measures from physicians.'[192] Does this mean simply that we know ourselves better than doctors can, or is it an indication of the benefits of optimism?

EXPLOSIVE LAYER In GESTALT THERAPY the explosive layer, or life layer, is the highest level of the personality.

EXTERIORIZATION/EXTERNALIZATION See PROJECTION.

EXTEROPSYCHE/EXTEROPSYCHIC In TRANSACTIONAL ANALYSIS the exteropsychic ego state is more commonly referred to as the Parent.

EXTRAVERT/INTROVERT The extravert/introvert distinction was first noted by Dr Furneaux Jordan in 1896. In *Character as Seen in Body and Parentage* he identified 'two generic fundamental biases in character', which he called active and reflective. In *Psychological Types* (1921) Jung discusses Furneaux's ideas and adopts this basic notion, renaming the two types *extravert* and *introvert* (words of his own invention). These types represent two ways of reacting to circumstances, two different attitudes to life. 'There is a whole class of men who at the moment of reaction to a given situation at first draw back a little as if with an unvoiced "No", and only after that are able to react; and there is another class who, in the same situation, come forward with an immediate reaction, apparently confident that their behaviour is obviously right. The former class would therefore be characterized by a certain negative relation to the object, and the latter by a positive one . . . the former class corresponds to the introverted and the second to the extraverted attitude.'[101]

The extravert is typically sociable, confident in new surroundings, enthusiastic, and likes organizations and group activities. When the possibility of conflict arises the extravert either meets others halfway or prefers to argue or to try to alter the situation somehow, rather than withdraw as would the INTROVERT. The disadvantages of an overly extravert attitude are a tendency to need an audience and to play to it, the desire to make a good impression at the risk of appearing superficial; there is consequently a dislike of being alone, and when others express a preference for such a lifestyle it is regarded as abnormal and morbid. Extraverts are also liked more by the world at large than by those who are close to them.

A balanced attitude obviously calls for both extraversion and introversion, but most people find that they develop one side of the equation at the expense of the other, which remains unconscious. It has often been said that in the West we tend to favour the extraverted attitude: terms such as 'outgoing', 'easy-going' and 'well-adjusted' have positive connotations, whilst the introverted attitude has a somewhat negative flavour associated with being self-centred, dreamy and impractical. This bias has been cited to account for the technological superiority of the West, whilst the East, with its material poverty, has shown more concern for spiritual development. This is something of an oversimplification, but so is the division of people into psychological types and Jung recognized this: 'While people may be classed as introverts or extraverts, these distinctions do not cover all the dissimilarities between the individuals in either class.'[101] '. . . being extraverted is therefore a superficial and too general criterion to be really characteristic.'[99] For this reason Jung increased these two basic categories to eight by combining them with the four EGO FUNCTIONS in his theory of PSYCHOLOGICAL TYPES.

EXULTATION OF FLOWERS Exultation of flowers is a general ELIXIR prepared after the manner of the BACH FLOWER REMEDIES but from as many as eighty-four flowers in the one preparation, and only when the flowers are at their peak according to the season and sometimes to the phase of the moon. It was produced and marketed originally by Alick McInnes in 1956 and, since his death in 1975, by Kay McInnes. The intended effect, as in the case of the Bach remedies and other VIBRATIONAL THERAPIES, is on the psyche and on the radiations flowing through the body.

FACE/FACIAL DIAGNOSIS Just as certain personalities and temperaments are associated with certain BODY-TYPES, and other character traits and aptitudes are linked to bumps on the skull in PHRENOLOGY, so the face is also said to reveal information about an individual's constitution and character. In oriental medicine this aspect of diagnosis is part of *bo-shin*, or the art of seeing. All aspects of the face – nose, forehead, cheeks, ears, etc. – are interpreted as part of the YIN/YANG duality. The overall shape of the head can indicate extravert or introvert characteristics: a square, wide jaw with a smaller crown is regarded as typifying an active, perhaps aggressive person, whilst the opposite – a weak jaw with a wide crown – indicates a passive, more thoughtful person. A parallel can be drawn between the eyebrows and the life-line on the hand in PALMISTRY: a strong constitution is shown by long, full eyebrows, whilst short, sparse eyebrows indicate a weak, sickly constitution. The degree of slant in the eyebrows is thought to show whether the individual is prone to anger or is of a peaceable disposition, a fact which is exploited by artists who draw cartoons. Reference is made to facial skin condition, colour and texture when diagnosing a person's state of health, and specific areas of the face are associated with specific organs in the same way that parts of the eye are related to specific organs in IRIDOLOGY. For example, the area between the eyebrows shows the condition of the liver, below the eyes the kidney, and between the eyes and the cheekbones the lungs.

FACTOR S Legendre and Piéron, researchers in neurology, believed

FALSE SELF

that a chemical (Factor S – for sleep) accumulated in the brain of a tired animal, and that if fluid from the brain of a tired animal were injected into the brain of another, the recipient would fall asleep. This sounds rather unlikely, but John Pappenheimer at the Harvard Medical School discovered that cerebral fluid from tired goats, when injected into the brains of rats and rabbits, did enhance their SLEEP.[207]

FALSE FEEDBACK To some extent our emotional experiences are conscious interpretations of unconscious reactions; the inner states which these reactions reflect can be described in terms of physiological changes – muscle tension, blood pressure, secretion of adrenalin, etc. Therefore our emotional experiences depend in some way on the mind's interpretation of these internal signals (see also FEEDBACK LOOP). It is even possible to mislead the mind by giving it false information about the inner state of the body – so-called 'false feedback' – and thus evoke emotions which are not wholly justified. If, for example, people hear a rapid heartbeat which they are led to believe is their own, they experience emotions associated with that heartbeat. In experiments men found pictures of women more attractive when the heartbeat which they thought was their own increased; women found pictures of shocked and grieving people more unpleasant when they thought their own heartbeat increased. In some situations one can take advantage of this phenomenon and acquire more control over emotions: deliberately smiling can have the effect of improving one's mood, making one feel happier. Through BIOFEEDBACK one can also learn to gain control over internal processes which could lead to the experience of certain emotions.

FALSE MEMORY SYNDROME See REPRESSED MEMORY THERAPY.

FALSE SELF According to the psychiatrist R. D. Laing (associated with the ANTIPSYCHIATRY movement), people who are insecure may split themselves into two systems: a system of false selves presented as a mask to the world, and an inner self of authentic experience which is not revealed to others, the TRUE SELF. The family and friends of such individuals, recognizing that they are not relating to the world satisfactorily, then pin labels on the 'sick', 'crazy' person, whose false self will oblige by compliantly behaving in the deviant way appropriate for such labels. Sartre would have called this false self the 'real self'; it deals with the real world, but

147

it is a construct, set between the world of others and the true self.

FARADISM Faradism, named after Michael Faraday, who invented the electromagnetic coils and the Faradic currents the therapy makes use of, was one of the earliest forms of ELECTROTHERAPY (following GALVANISM) and one which still has application today. A Faradic current is a pulsating current of varying frequency and duration, which resembles the natural nerve impulse that activates muscles. In Faradism the current is applied to the body by means of a coil encased in a plastic pad, helping fractured bones to mend, stimulating enervated muscle and relieving the pain of muscle injury, particularly sprained ankles and lower-back pain. Small units, called TRANSCUTANEOUS ELECTRICAL NERVE STIMULATORS, are often used by athletes to relieve aching muscles and joints after long training sessions and competitions.

FEEDBACK LOOP Migraine may be triggered by a variety of factors such as dietary imbalance and psychological stress. The onset of pain induces further tension in anticipation of a migraine attack, which aggravates the pain, increases the tension, and makes the migraine even worse. This vicious circle is known as a feedback loop. The same phenomenon can be seen when STRESS arises out of our refusal to act in accordance with the instinct of the FIGHT-OR-FLIGHT RESPONSE. 'While the subcortex reacts to stress by preparing for fight or flight, the individual consciously restrains himself. Immobility is interpreted by the subcortex as insufficient preparation for fight or flight, and the individual experiences mounting tension in a highly destructive cycle.'[139]

FEELING FUNCTION In Jungian psychology there are four EGO FUNCTIONS, four basic faculties we can use to orient ourselves in the world, one of which we are likely to favour over the other three, depending on our particular PSYCHOLOGICAL TYPE. These four functions are thinking, feeling, intuition and sensation. Although closely allied to the emotions, this concept of feeling is not simply an emotional response, since each of the four functions can lead to emotional responses. Feeling is the faculty we use to know the value of something or someone, and is diametrically opposed and inimical to the thinking function, which is more concerned with data than values.

FEELINGS See EMOTIONS.

FELDENKRAIS METHOD/FELDENKRAIS TECHNIQUE The Feldenkrais Technique is a method of retraining the body through movement and self-awareness to improve both posture and general health, restoring the body to full functional efficiency. It is comparable to the ALEXANDER TECHNIQUE except that it focuses more on movement; it has been described as a western T'AI CHI. Like the Alexander Technique it grew at least in part out of its founder's treatment of his own condition, for which conventional medicine seemed inadequate.

Dr Moshe Feldenkrais (1904–85) was a Russian-born Israeli engineer and atomic physicist who studied and worked in Paris until the invasion of France in 1940 when he escaped to Britain. He was also a keen soccer player and a judo black belt (he opened the first judo school in Europe). When an old knee injury kept flaring up and all the best doctors could do was suggest surgery which had only a 50 per cent chance of success, Feldenkrais decided to study the mechanics of human movement and teach himself to walk without pain. As well as working with F. M. Alexander he studied anatomy, physiology, neurology, psychology, yoga and Gurdjieff's spiritual philosophy.

Feldenkrais devised thousands of exercises to instil self-awareness into his pupils. (As with the Alexander Technique, people undergoing training in the Feldenkrais method are referred to as pupils or students rather than patients or clients.) Some of these exercises are taught to large groups of people (up to 300 in some cases) in Awareness through Movement classes, with the teacher giving verbal instructions as the students go through a sequence of gentle movements. The other component in the method, known as Functional Integration, is a one-to-one technique in which the teacher guides the student non-verbally through touch, gently extending the possibilities of the neuromuscular system which has become chronically restricted simply through habit. Feldenkrais students acquire a new self-image, new perceptions of natural movements such as crawling and walking, awareness of breathing while moving and of the way different parts of the body move in relation to each other.

Basic to the theory behind the Feldenkrais method is the principle that our inner life – our thoughts, emotions and character – is expressed in the way we move: 'Habitual patterns of acting are the somatic structure of what we call personality and character.'[75] If we are made aware of these habitual patterns (which are, of course, unconscious in the ordinary way), and then change them, we can thereby induce psychological change: 'If the neuromuscular system of a widow is depressed, then if she is taught to change the pattern, she will no longer be depressed.'[75] Although there is no place for emotional self-expression or cathartic experience in the Feldenkrais method, because of the relationship between the emotions and the body it does bring psychological as well as physical benefits. As Feldenkrais said, 'posture is one of the best clues . . . to the activity of the brain.'[41]

FENG SHUI (pronounced 'fung shway') Feng shui is the ancient Chinese art of recognizing positive and negative factors in the environment, whether in the landscape (the two characters which make up the term mean 'wind' and 'water'), in cities or inside buildings. Modern feng shui practitioners advise people on the most beneficial arrangement of furnishings in homes and offices, as well as on their siting. The principles of feng shui were laid down in the *Li Shu* or 'Book of Rites', one of the oldest Chinese texts devoted to religion. The life-energy, CH'I, flows through the environment as well as through the body, according to the YIN and YANG qualities of particular features in relationship to each other (hills, rivers, roads, corners, telegraph poles, doors, windows, mirrors, etc.). The attributes of the five elements – wood, fire, earth, metal and water – which are assigned to places also help to determine what activities a particular place is most suitable for. The inability of the modern scientific method either to explain or remedy such phenomena as SICK BUILDING SYNDROME might suggest that we could still learn something of value from the ancient art of feng shui.

FERTILITY/INFERTILITY In these stress-conscious times it is sometimes suggested that like so many other medical conditions infertility is a result of stress. If so, why are rape victims statistically not less but more likely to conceive? It seems unlikely that we have evolved in such a way as to favour the offspring of forcible sex. It has been shown, however, that stress in some women results in irregularity of menstruation.

The average sperm count in American males has steadily decreased over the last two or three generations. People have also noted increased sexual insecurity in men – the degree to which a man's identity is conditional on his positive sexual identity. The implied link between sexual insecurity and infertility has yet to be proved, but there is evidence that men undergoing infertility investigations suffer further decline in their production of sperm, suggesting a vicious circle of a problem being exacerbated by anxiety about it.

Perhaps it would be more useful to consider infertility as a possible defence against becoming a parent. There may be a correlation between one's unconscious assessment of parenting potential (in oneself or one's partner) and the likelihood of conception. In that case it would be more profitable to consider whether and why at some level one member of the infertile couple feels (or fears) that the child might not be well parented. This might involve psychotherapy, but the offspring would almost certainly benefit.

John Harrison, a psychotherapist in Australia, has described just such a case.[81] After undergoing every type of gynaecological test a woman's infertility was described as IDIOPATHIC, meaning the doctors could find no reason for it. In psychotherapy it soon emerged that as a child she had been loved excessively by her father and her mother had been violently jealous of their closeness. As an adult she unconsciously feared that this behaviour pattern would be repeated if she became a mother, and that she would lose the love of her husband if she had a daughter. So her body refused to conceive. (As Groddeck said, 'If you hate your parent, you will fear your own child.'[67]) In this case psychotherapy with John Harrison was successful. Once she recognized that her parents' behaviour pattern need not be repeated in her own married life, the woman's whole personality and physiology changed. Whereas she had been rather girlish in appearance, she developed a more womanly figure. Her hormone balance rectified itself naturally and eventually she conceived normally.

FIGHT-OR-FLIGHT RESPONSE The fight-or-flight mechanism was first described in 1914 by Walter Cannon in *The Wisdom of the Body*. As soon as the mind recognizes a threat it triggers the release of adrenalin and cortisol from the adrenal glands. Glycogen is released from the liver, boosting the level of sugar in the blood and thus putting more energy at the organism's disposal; the pupils of the eyes dilate, giving better vision in dark surroundings; blood pressure and pulse rate increase, getting more oxygen to the brain for quicker thinking; blood retreats from digestive organs and concentrates on getting to the limb muscles; body cooling mechanisms come into action, switching on the sweat glands and activating the hair muscles which make hair stand more erect; and the blood's ability to clot is also enhanced.

When an animal is in danger all these changes increase its ability to cope with the situation, whether by defending itself or running away. The decision whether to fight or flee is made easier by the fact that the brain receives more oxygenated blood so that reactions are speeded up. For modern humans in 'civilized' circumstances, the fact that more rapid thinking is made possible by the enhanced blood supply to the brain is practically the only really beneficial effect of the primitive 'fight-or-flight' response. In other respects it has perhaps outlived its usefulness in a modern human context. It continues to operate, but in situations where the advantages of quick thinking are greatly outweighed by the physiological disadvantages: the mechanism comes into play when we are stuck in traffic jams, frustrated by bureaucracy or confronted by an angry boss. The tuning up, excitation, refuelling and subsequent inactivity of all these circuits result in STRESS. Society decrees that overt physical reactions would be inappropriate and unacceptable, whatever the oppression or sense of frustration we feel. 'Our bodies automatically prepare to flee or fight, but, all too often, neither response is appropriate. Persistent elicitation of this inappropriate response disrupts nearly every bodily system influencing immune disorders, heart disease, gastro-intestinal disease and hypertension.'[135]

The fight response is of two kinds – external and internal. Overuse of the external fight response, typical of the so-called TYPE A PERSONALITY, can result in heart disease. Over-use of the internal fight response, in which the response is given no overt expression, suggesting to the outside world that the individual is in complete control, may result in a tendency to develop gastro-intestinal disease such as ulcers or irritable bowel syndrome.

Fight and flight are not the only two possibilities: a third possible course of action has been proposed, called the *flow response*, the 'stay cool' reaction. But this too can be overdone, resulting in changeable, inconsistent attitudes, the province of the obsessional character who latches onto new, fashionable ideas with a vengeance. Dr Patrick Pietroni has suggested that these three responses can be seen in the three modes of reacting to the threat of nuclear attack during the cold war.[142] The fight response was characteristic of those in power, the armers who fuelled and managed the arms race, the 'better dead than red' brigade. The flight response was demonstrated by the disarmers, whilst the majority probably fell into the flow response group, going along with the view of those in power, perhaps thinking that 'I can't do anything about it' or even 'I'll be dead anyway, so why worry?'

FIRST LAW The so-called First Law of Hippocrates was 'Above all, do no harm', sometimes expressed in Latin as *Primum non nocere*.

FIXATION See SUBLIMATION.

FLARE-UP When people stop orthodox allopathic treatment of a serious condition and start following a different regime (such as the GERSON DIET in the treatment of cancer), there is often a strong initial reaction in the body against the new diet or therapy. This is usually regarded as an essential part of the detoxification process – the body can finally rid itself of all the toxic substances that have been introduced into it in the form of drugs, but it can be extremely worrying for the patient, who suddenly seems to be getting sicker. These so-called flare-ups can recur at intervals during the initial stages of the new treatment. In some cases when cancer patients have had surgery for the removal of cancerous growths, their wounds, which have healed once, may open up again, but the second 'more natural' healing will be more complete.

FLOTATION/FLOATATION THERAPY See SENSORY DEPRIVATION.

FLOW RESPONSE See FIGHT-OR-FLIGHT RESPONSE.

FLOWER MEDICINE/FLOWER REMEDIES See HERBALISM, BACH FLOWER REMEDIES, EXULTATION OF FLOWERS and VITA FLORUM.

FOCUSING In the 1960s researchers at the University of Chicago studying the methods used in PSYCHOTHERAPY found evidence that clients who were in direct contact with their felt experience benefited most from their therapy. Eugene Gendlin coined the term 'focusing' for his way of helping people to become aware of actual experience 'from inside' and as it is happening.

FOGGING Fogging is one of the techniques for responding to manipulative criticism in ASSERTIVENESS TRAINING.

FOLK MEDICINE In the West, folk medicine (also commonly

referred to, except in the USA, as TRADITIONAL MEDICINE) is what modern CONVENTIONAL MEDICINE has largely replaced, although elements of it have sometimes survived in rural areas. It covered a wide spectrum of treatments from HERBALISM – its strongest feature – to practices that bordered on superstition. Although folk medicine is sometimes held in high esteem by proponents of ALTERNATIVE MEDICINE since it used primarily NATURAL REMEDIES, its basic principles were far from HOLISTIC and were in some ways closer to the ALLOPATHIC, symptom-attacking approach of the average modern doctor. People went to their local 'wise woman' or 'cunning man' expecting a remedy (or a concoction of remedies – POLYPHARMACY) which would take away the symptoms of their disease, without giving much thought to underlying causes. With musculo-skeletal problems they would wait for the next visit from the itinerant BONE-SETTER.

The term 'folk medicine' became more prominent in public perception in the 1950s with the publication of a book entitled *Folk Medicine* by an American country doctor, D. C. Jarvis. When he set up his new practice in the state of Vermont he recognized that the local people already had a repertory of treatments, very different from his own and including a certain amount of myth, but some of which were undeniably effective. How else could so many people with 'unsophisticated' health care reach ages well above sixty-five? He noticed also that young children, if left to their own devices, instinctively choose the foods their bodies require, preferring raw vegetables and fruit to sweets, for example. Animals too have an instinct for healing themselves: 'They know unerringly which herbs will cure what ills.'[94] Jarvis concluded that the American pioneers had developed their folk medicine from observing the behaviour of animals.

Jarvis's own recommendations were perhaps less dramatic than the underlying insights of his book, and of course it was his simple prescription for a healthy life that the reading public seized on: drink two teaspoons of honey and two teaspoons of apple cider vinegar in warm water once a day. Jarvis discovered that this was an excellent recipe for avoiding arthritic disorders. He also established the body's need for potassium (present in apple cider vinegar), and investigated the body's acid and alkali reactions to specific foods. He recognized the value of honey both as a sweetener in preference to sugar, providing essential mineral salts, and as a remedy in the treatment of conditions such as hay fever and sinusitis.

FOOT ZONE THERAPY See REFLEXOLOGY.

FORMULA ACUPUNCTURE An alternative term for SYMPTO-MATIC ACUPUNCTURE.

FRONT MU POINTS See MU POINTS.

FRUITARIANISM Fruitarians have a much more restricted diet than other vegetarians, even more restricted than vegans (who exclude dairy products): they eat only uncooked fruit and nuts, maintaining that cooking 'kills' food and destroys its oxygen content. They hold that animals thrive because they eat 'living' food, straight from the growing plant, and therefore so should we. The GERSON DIET contains some elements of fruitarianism (although it includes liver), but even more restricted is Joanna Brandt's GRAPE CURE.

FUNCTIONS See EGO FUNCTIONS and TRANSCENDENT FUNCTION.

FUNCTIONAL ILLNESS A so-called functional illness is an unidentified illness, also referred to as an undifferentiated DISEASE, in which no cause has been found for the symptoms. It has also been called *idiophanic*, characteristic of that particular individual, which suggests that adequate diagnosis and successful treatment probably depend on consideration of many different aspects of that individual, rather than simply the manifest symptoms. In the nineteenth century, women with a generalized functional illness were likely to be diagnosed as suffering from hysteria; alternatively such women were said (by their male doctors) to be suffering from 'the vapours'. Neurasthenia, typified by fatigue and general weakness, is a contemporary example of an illness with no apparent physical cause, although there is probably a strong PSYCHOSOMATIC element involved. The scorn heaped upon people suffering from ME shows the extent to which a medically recognized cause still confers respectability on an illness. This is even apparent in the comments of Michael Baum of the King's College School of Medicine and Dentistry when he says, 'I may choose to describe undifferentiated illness as the somatic manifestation of unhappiness', which for all its recognition of the psychosomatic element sounds belittling and dismissive. His attitude is perhaps made clearer when he goes on to say, 'My own personal prejudice would be to classify "undifferentiated illness" as a spiritual malaise requiring an infusion of spiritual solace rather than exposure to the pseudo-scientific gobble-degook of the acupuncturist.'[177]

Looking at patterns of illness that are prevalent in other contemporaneous cultures we may also find conditions that have no equivalent in our own culture, such as the 'evil eye' or *mal de ojo* in Hispanic societies.

FUNCTIONAL INTEGRATION See FELDENKRAIS METHOD.

GALENIC In the sixteenth century, Galenic physicians favoured the use of HERBAL preparations which would cooperate with the body's natural healing processes. Paracelsus was the most influential of these physicians. The opposing view, held by 'Spagyric' physicians was that chemical preparations could be used to halt or change the development of the disease. The arguments between the two parties have continued to this day, although they are now labelled 'ALTERNATIVE' and 'orthodox' or CONVENTIONAL medicine.

GALVANISM The Italian physiologist, Luigi Galvani (1737–98), gave his name to the galvanometer, the process of galvanizing and medical Galvanism. Born and educated in Bologna, he became professor of anatomy at the university there in 1762. In 1789 he published the results of his now famous experiments with electrical impulses in animal tissue: he had hung a dissected frog by its legs on two brass hooks against an iron trellis and attributed the resultant twitching to innate 'animal electricity'. Although he drew the wrong conclusions – the current was actually produced by the metal contacts – his pioneering research did establish that living things had electrical properties.

Galvanism is a form of ELECTROTHERAPY and refers to the application of direct current (not AC) to the body in one of three ways: medical Galvanism, surgical Galvanism, and iontophoresis. The main use of surgical Galvanism has been the removal of unwanted hair through the caustic effect of the electric current. Medical Galvanism was once a popular treatment for sports injuries: the current improves the circulation of the blood, thereby reducing inflammation by speeding up the reabsorption of the inflammatory fluids.

In the technique of iontophoresis, a piece of gauze impregnated with a solution of the relevant drug is placed between one of the electrodes and the skin. When the current is switched on, ions of the drug tend to migrate towards the opposite electrode, thus introducing the drug into the body and enabling it to reach the site of injury or inflammation requiring treatment. In cosmetic therapy enzymes are introduced in this way to facilitate the dispersal of fat.

GAME-PLAYING LAYER In GESTALT THERAPY the game-playing layer is the lowest level of the personality, also called the phoney layer.

GAMES In TRANSACTIONAL ANALYSIS games are the patterns of behaviour which people follow, adopting a particular role when they find themselves in a particular situation and behaving in a fairly predictable way with an ulterior motive. They derive not just from social programming (as do PASTIMES) but from individual programming. Berne describes a game as 'a recurring set of transactions, often repetitious, superficially plausible, with a concealed motivation; or, more colloquially, a series of moves with a snare, or "gimmick".' Furthermore, 'Every game . . . is basically dishonest', whilst other sequences in transactional analysis (procedures, rituals and pastimes) are 'by definition candid'. The 'pay-off' is a defining characteristic of a game.[12] (See also ASSERTIVENESS TRAINING.)

GATE CONTROL THEORY Ronald Melzack and Patrick Wall put forward a new theory of PAIN in 1965.[216] They suggested that pain signals were transmitted to the brain via a series of gates in the spinal cord, and that closure of the appropriate gate would prevent the pain signal from reaching the brain. One way in which such a gate might be closed was through the well-established process of counter-irritation, e.g. the fluid in a blister, or a change in temperature. According to the theory, stimulation of larger nerve fibres could block off pain impulses from smaller nerve fibres. It is for this reason that ice-packs are used to counteract the effect of a hangover, for the large fibres relay signals about heat, cold and touch, although a further consideration might be that diverting the sufferer's attention from the original painful condition reduces the degree of pain felt. It has also been suggested by some that

GEMS

this is how ACUPUNCTURE works. However, the gate theory of pain has been largely superseded by the discovery of ENDORPHINS and by the fact that these messengers from the brain to the body are released after acupuncture treatment, providing natural long-term pain relief.

GEMS See CRYSTAL HEALING.

GEOBIOLOGY Geobiologists study an area of BIOELECTROMAG-NETICS which focuses on environmental influences on the body's electromagnetic field, and more specifically on 'electromagnetic pollution'. This, they claim, can be caused by radar stations, radio transmitters and high-tension cables, people who live near such sites having suffered a variety of illnesses. Researchers in Germany's 'Verein für Geobiologie' (Geobiology Union) also refer to *geopathic* or *geopathogenic* zones, where there are anomalies in the natural magnetic field. Such anomalies have been held responsible for sickness. In the 1930s Baron von Pohl used DOWSING to detect 'earth radiation' and people with cancer always seemed to live in houses built on these geopathic sites. It has been shown that pigeons can locate food (albeit in an artificial environment) by following magnetic clues, and it is thought that the 'detector' which is exploited in the homing instinct is keratin, present in human skin, hair and nails as well as in birds' feathers.[144]

GEOPATHIC/GEOPATHOGENIC See GEOBIOLOGY.

GERM THEORY Although still referred to as a theory, the notion that most diseases are caused by micro-organisms that invade the body is regarded by mainstream medicine as incontrovertible fact.

The possibility that plagues might be caused by the activity of minute organisms was not proved until Pasteur's time, although the ancients had suspected something along similar lines. Hippocrates believed that rotting food gave off a *miasma* which caused malaria ('malaria' means literally 'bad air'), and by the sixteenth century it was thought that seeds of illness could be conveyed in three ways: by touch, by contact with an object already touched, and by breathing affected air.

Not until the late nineteenth century was modern bacteriology established by Pasteur and Koch, but even then some medical minds regarded the theory as too pat. In 1892 a Bavarian scientist, Max von Pettenkofer, wanting to disprove Robert Koch's claim that

158

cholera was caused by microbes, obtained a sample of the cholera bacillus and drank it. All he suffered was mild diarrhoea.

The question that has still not been fully answered 'scientifically' is, given the general acceptance of the germ theory, why is it that only certain people succumb when exposed to germs? It has been noticed that in cholera epidemics a disproportionate number of young adults are laid low, rather than the weakest members of the community, the young and the old. In normal circumstances the cholera bacterium is killed by the acid secreted in the stomach, but we now know that fear and panic tend to reduce the production of such digestive juices (as in the FIGHT-OR-FLIGHT response). So there may be some justification for claiming that diseases such as cholera, dysentery and typhoid, even though 'caused by' bacilli, are also in part psychosomatic, since they enter the body via the stomach, whose chemistry is easily influenced by mental factors.

There are similar reservations about the germ theory in the matter of the common cold. We do seem to catch it off each other, but when? At the Common Cold Research Unit in Salisbury it was found that certain groups of people were much more likely to develop colds when exposed to the virus: firstly those described by psychologists as introverted, and secondly those who had recently experienced significant changes in their lives such as a new job, retirement, marriage, divorce or bereavement. IMMUNITY can clearly be affected by the mind and by events which other researchers have considered quantitatively when estimating an individual's susceptibility to infection by adding up their recently accumulated LIFE CHANGE UNITS. Hans Selye has pioneered the research into STRESS as one of the prime factors in determining whether a person falls ill: 'If microbes are ever present, yet do not cause disease until stress intrudes, what is the cause of the disease – the microbe or the stress?'[158]

It seems that Pasteur himself was ultimately not convinced that the germ theory told the whole story: his last words were reported to be: 'Bernard is right. The germ is nothing; the terrain everything.' Claude Bernard had written, 'Illnesses hover constantly about us, their seeds blown by the wind, but they do not set in the terrain unless the terrain is ready to receive them.'

GERSON THERAPY/GERSON DIET As a young physician in Germany, Max Gerson (1881–1959) suffered from severe migraine, which did not respond to any of the available orthodox remedies. Noting that the diet of our ape-like ancestors consisted of fresh fruit and raw food, Gerson tried to change his body's chemistry by adopting a similar diet. It apparently cured his migraine and he found it successful in treating other chronic diseases.

In the 1920s Gerson used his diet successfully to treat patients with chronic conditions such as tuberculosis, arthritis and vascular disease, before moving on to cancer. By July 1946 he had recorded such remarkable results that he came close to being granted US government support for research into his dietary cancer therapy, but the orthodox medical lobby won the day.

Gerson's theory was that the diet restores the body's normal chemical balance, reactivates its natural defences and enables it to heal itself. The imbalance which can eventually lead to disease has in his view three main ingredients: a deficiency of potassium (lost in chemical fertilization, food processing and normal cooking), a surfeit of sodium (added in those same processes) and oedema – excessive fluids in body tissue (associated with the accumulation of the excess salts). With the inability of the body to rid itself of the unwanted salts, sodium invades cells, changing their acidity and affecting the production of hormones, vitamins and enzymes. In this condition, Gerson believed, naturally occurring weaker cells are further damaged, and prompted to adopt a fermentative type of metabolism in order to survive, thus becoming cancerous and achieving self-preservation only by destroying neighbouring tissue.[61]

The main feature of the Gerson treatment is an hourly intake of fruit and vegetable juices and a strict adherence to organically grown food. The body's *detoxification process* is further helped by regular enemas and injections of liver juice. Periodically there may be so-called *flare-ups*, in which the body reacts violently against the new diet, or when scars left by past surgery become open wounds which have to heal again.

There are few centres where the Gerson diet is rigorously practised nowadays, but foremost among them must be the clinics run by Gerson's daughter, Charlotte, in Mexico. It was there that for two months in 1981 Beata Bishop, suffering from malignant melanoma and given only six months to live, was treated. On her return to London she continued to follow the strict regime for a further sixteen months, and eventually, fully cured, she described her experience of the treatment and her concurrent psychological development in *A Time to Heal*.[16]

GESTALT THERAPY Gestalt therapy is one of the leading psychotherapies in the field of HUMANISTIC PSYCHOLOGY and the HUMAN

POTENTIAL MOVEMENT, and an early example of non-directive counselling or client-centred therapy. As a therapy it emphasizes awareness arising out of experience rather than analytical understanding, and out of that awareness can come greater personal responsibility. It is not to be confused with Gestalt psychology, from which the therapy derives its name and its initial theoretical basis.

Gestalt psychology was born in Berlin in the 1920s with the coming together of Wolfgang Kohler (1887–1967), Kurt Koffka (1886–1941) and Max Wertheimer (1880–1943). Gestalt therapy was first developed by Frederick (Fritz) S. Perls (1893–1970) and his wife, Laura, in New York in about 1950. They had both been trained as psychoanalysts in pre-war Germany; Laura had also attended lectures by the three leading Gestalt psychologists (Kohler, Koffka and Wertheimer), and Fritz was later supervised by the controversial psychiatrist, Wilhelm Reich (1897–1957). During the 1960s Fritz Perls moved first to California and then to British Columbia. Working with Perls were also Ralph F. Hefferline and Paul Goodman, co-authors with him of *Gestalt Therapy*.[140] The first UK Gestalt Training School was founded in London by Ischa Bloomberg in 1974.

Gestalt psychology was concerned primarily with the psychology of perception and learning. *Gestalt* is German for shape, form, figure or pattern, but in the wider meaning of the term it refers to what is perceived as distinct from the background or field of perception. It is obvious that one cannot exist without the other, and this simple insight reflects the more general maxim of Gestalt psychology, that the whole is greater than the sum of the parts. The Gestalt psychologists recognized that we do not perceive the world atomistically: the mind does not grasp a long series of tiny fragments which it then puts together to form a whole picture; rather it grasps the relation between patterns of fragments, it grasps the whole without needing to build it up out of constituent parts. Similarly, mental processes are seen as wholes that cannot be analysed into smaller components. And according to Gestalt psychology, when we learn something new our whole perception of our environment is affected.

As the founders of Gestalt therapy said: 'The greatest value in the Gestalt approach perhaps lies in the insight that the *whole determines the parts*, which contrasts with the previous assumption that the whole is merely the total sum of its elements. The therapeutic situation, for instance, is more than just a statistical event of a doctor plus a patient. It is a meeting of doctor and patient.

If the doctor is rigid and insensitive to the specific requirements of the ever-changing therapeutic situation, he will not be a good therapist.'[140] Reading between the lines one can perhaps detect an implied criticism of traditional psychoanalytic practice here. The Freudian analyst hardly participates in the encounter with the patient and may stay out of sight while the patient stares at the ceiling; the Gestalt therapist participates actively in the encounter.

Fritz Perls is regarded by many as having replaced stultified psychoanalytic techniques with a truly liberating psychotherapy. In psychoanalysis there is much verbalizing; in Gestalt therapy the emphasis is on experiencing and acting out. Nouns are out and verbs are in. Instead of interpreting dreams as the analyst might, the Gestalt therapist helps the client to reach their deeper meaning by encouraging him to re-experience them, describe them in the present tense and bring everything into the here-and-now. Where the traditional analyst interprets the patient's described experiences according to a system which was very much the property of the analyst, in Gestalt therapy the client works with past experiences by reliving them in the present and describing what is being experienced, with interventions from the therapist only to clarify.

Perls described Gestalt therapy as the psychology of the obvious. Producing a list of observations beginning 'Now I am aware that . . .' helps one to become more aware of one's relationship with the environment. A similar exercise helps the individual to appreciate the distinction between observation and inference: 'I observe that you are smiling; I infer that you are pleased.' Much of Gestalt therapy focuses on training in awareness of this kind. (At one time Perls considered calling the new form of therapy 'awareness therapy' or even 'concentration therapy'.) It is therapeutic because it improves one's contact with oneself and with the environment.

This is one of the first steps in reorganizing our field of awareness, so that we can start to recognize what it is in our own actions that prevents us from getting what we want at any particular moment. We are encouraged to take responsibility for our own feelings. A simple device in this respect is the changing of statements like 'My shoulders are tense' into their responsible version, 'I am tensing my shoulders', and then asking not 'Why?' but 'How am I tensing my shoulders?' In this way greater body-awareness is also achieved as part of the growing awareness of the constant flux of sensations, feelings and relationships.

Much use is made in Gestalt of an empty chair. To clarify splits or polarities in a personality, one places certain feelings that are troublesome or a particular aspect of oneself (or a particular SUB-PERSONALITY as it might be called in PSYCHOSYNTHESIS) in the empty chair and embarks on a dialogue with it. Then one moves over to the empty chair to respond. By externalizing problems in this way they become much more accessible to the individual. Disowned aspects of one's own personality are generally projected onto others with whom normal relations then become impossible. In therapy, instead of talking about people regarded as troublesome in one's life, one again engages in dialogue with them, playing out all the roles, being those troublesome people, and thus re-experiencing and re-owning what one had denied in oneself and projected. Dreams are seen as dramatizations of projection. They represent the unfinished business of the unconscious. So 'dreamwork', re-enacting dream experiences and engaging in dialogues with specific elements of the dream, both animate and inanimate, helps one to re-own and reintegrate those projected fragments of the personality.

Sometimes Perls remodelled existing psychoanalytic concepts in much more accessible ways. 'Repetition-compulsion' became more simply – and more dynamically – 'unfinished business'. ('The patient feels compelled to repeat in daily life everything he cannot bring to a satisfactory conclusion.') Acting out selected aspects of this behaviour again and again enables the individual eventually to perceive a new level of meaning.

Breaking through to new levels, or layers of the personality, is a key aspect of Gestalt. Perls developed a theory of personality layers. The lowest he called the *cliché layer*, where totally unaware people go through life following meaningless formulae or clichés, reacting rather like robots. A little above that in the system is the *game-playing* or *phoney layer* of the personality, where roles are played, perhaps manipulatively, without any real contact being made. If we manage to be more honest and genuine than this we can break through to the *phobic* or *neurotic layer*, where we still resist accepting what we are, building up an elaborate system of shoulds and shouldn'ts which are a distortion of our real feelings. If we break through both the phoney and the phobic layers and become aware of our real feelings and problems, the initial reaction is one of despair. This Perls called the *impasse*. Only by accepting the despair can we break through to the next *implosive* or *death layer*, which may result in a catatonic state, such is the awareness of blocked feelings and the contraction of psychic energy. The final, fifth layer is the *explosive* or *life layer*. Breakthrough to this level is achieved by some form of outburst: grief, anger, joy and orgasm were the four types of explosion identified by Perls, although others have added the shaking and cold sweats which accompany sudden total relief from fear and pain. With the explosion the blocked energies are released and the individual feels free and fulfilled. Only on this level can a person live authentically.

Adult inhibitions are generally seen in Gestalt as unhealthy. For example, as adults we may be irritated by a child who stamps and screams with frustration while waiting for something, and then we marvel at the total transformation in the child's demeanour when it gets what it has been waiting for. 'Far from proving that a child can't wait, it proves precisely that he *can* wait, namely, by jumping with impatience: he has an organic equilibrating technique for the tension; and afterwards, *therefore*, his satisfaction is pure, full, unclouded. It is the adult who cannot wait – he has lost the technique . . . What is the harm in the childish drama? It offends the adult audience because of their repression of the similar tantrum, not because of the sound and fury but because of the unconscious distraction. What is here called maturity is likely neurosis.'[140]

It is easy to see how this might in inexpert hands have led to an ill-defined 'let it all hang out' attitude, particularly in the anti-authoritarian climate of the 1960s. (Stressing the harmful effects of the SUPEREGO also seems typical of that era.) Other Gestalt practitioners have recognized that this therapy is most effective with overly socialized, restrained and rather constricted individuals. Unstable people with vulnerable personalities may be further unbalanced by Gestalt's confronting techniques unless treated with sensitivity, commitment and great patience by an experienced therapist.[40]

There is perhaps an overly naive view in Gestalt that, since the organism has an innate tendency towards health and the full expression of its potential, removing obstacles to growth will naturally result in growth, without any need for discipline or striving or work of any kind. Gestalt has been criticized for undervaluing the intellect, creating self-centred individuals who are insensitive to the dependency needs of others (having overcome them in themselves), ignoring the past and avoiding the significance of the unconscious in successful growth. Much of the criticism that has been directed at the general ethos of the 1960s has been directed even more specifically at Gestalt, and in particular at Fritz Perls. For example, he began group sessions with a Gestalt 'prayer' that reeks of his own time and place:

I do my thing, and you do your thing.
I am not in this world to live up to your expectations.
And you are not in this world to live up to mine.
You are you and I am I,
And if by chance we find each other, it's beautiful.
If not, it can't be helped.

In the words of Jeffrey Masson, arch-critic of psychotherapy: 'Gestalt group-therapy technique depends on a single individual who acts as the leader and superego for the rest of the group. Perls made no bones about arrogating to himself all the privileges and power of a traditional guru. Implicit in this power is the ability to cause great pain and destruction to others, either directly or by causing the group to turn on, attack, and brutalize one of its members. Perls seemed positively to revel in the power he held over the people in his groups.' And further, 'Clearly Perls thought of himself as a guru. He dressed the part and looked the part, with long white beard and hair, beads, sandals, and flowing robes. He behaved that way as well, in the tradition of the Zen master, making paradoxical statements, shocking his listeners with his actions . . . But he was unaware of how his language and his behaviour were dictated by the times in which he lived.'[128]

Nevertheless Gestalt is still the third most practised method of psychotherapy in the USA, and having perhaps freed itself from the more idiosyncratic characterizations deriving from the personality of Perls himself, it is flexible enough to be used in conjunction with other methods such as BIOENERGETICS and the guided imagery of PSYCHOSYNTHESIS. Conversely, many features of Gestalt have been adopted by other therapies. It has contributed more than most to the range of techniques at the disposal of the modern therapist.

GINSENG Ginseng is probably the most well-known general panacea or ELIXIR. The medicinal part of the ginseng plant is the root, which (like the mandrake) is often thought to resemble the human body. Hence its name, which in Chinese means literally 'man-plant'. It grows in China, Korea and Siberia and was known to Chinese medicine as long ago as 3000 BC. Battles were often fought over the territories where it grew, and it was considered to be the property of the emperor. Related varieties grow in Japan, India and Nepal, and another variety is native to North America. Ginseng has long been renowned for its medicinal and rejuvenating properties, and as an aphrodisiac. It is used as a natural tonic, strengthening the body's overall resistance to infection and all stressful conditions. As well as being an anti-stress agent, it also acts as a stimulant to the cerebral cortex and the central nervous system. The root can be sucked as a rapid antidote to fatigue, but it is usually dried and taken either as an infusion or in powdered or tablet form. Doses can be varied and there are no known side effects.

GOSSIP POSTURE In many patients the initial diagnosis made by an osteopath includes recognition of a slightly misshapen spine: instead of being straight the spine has assumed a long, gentle S-curve. This is usually caused by the habit of putting most of one's weight on one leg, rather than distributing it evenly between the two, a lounging attitude typified by leaning against a garden wall; hence its familiar name – the gossip posture.

GRAHAMISM Grahamism was a movement in the USA advocating vegetarianism, bathing, sunlight, fresh air, dress reform, sex hygiene and abstinence from alcohol. It was founded in the early nineteenth century by Sylvester Graham, a Pennsylvanian temperance lecturer.

GRANDFATHER CLAUSE There has been much debate in recent years about the possibility of introducing statutory registration for all alternative practitioners, obliging them to belong to a professional body which would establish and maintain minimum training requirements and enforce an appropriate code of professional conduct. In the event of such a law being introduced, a so-called 'grandfather clause' would allow long-standing practitioners with considerable experience to continue to practise despite a lack of formal qualifications.

GRAPE CURE After reading Upton Sinclair's book *The Fasting Cure*, Johanna Brandt, a Cape Town naturopath who was suffering from cancer, started fasting. With each fast the growth of the cancer was checked, but, as she wrote, 'It seemed to take a new hold whenever I broke the fast – because I took the wrong foods afterwards.'[21] Eventually she found the right food – grapes – and she lived on nothing but grapes for six weeks, effectively destroying the cancer and building new tissue.

GRAPHOLOGY/GRAPHOTHERAPY In the second century BC Chinese philosophers remarked that the quality of the strokes in an individual's calligraphy carried information about that person's temperament. The Romans too speculated about the relationship between handwriting and character. One of the first books on character analysis through handwriting was written by Camillo Baldi in 1622. The term 'graphology', literally the study of writing, was coined much later (as the French *graphologie*), around 1878 by the Abbé Jean Hyppolyte Michon (1806–81). He accepted that handwriting is an expression of the writer's personality and tried to equate specific letter-shapes with certain character traits. This rather over-simplistic view still has popular appeal.

According to popular graphology, for example, a tight-looped 'e' indicates secrecy, and an 'o' that is left open at the top shows a tendency to indiscretion. A 't' with the cross stroke above the vertical and unattached to it comes from a writer who has 'lost touch' with reality, whilst one that is at the right level but unattached and to the right of the vertical is typical of people whose ideas run ahead of their actions. The range of possible positions and styles for the dotting of one's 'i's' has a plethora of interpretations.

More important than any spurious correspondence between features of individual letters and features of character is the overall style of the handwriting, which is determined more by relationships between letters and the whole flow of the script than by the letters themselves. Given that the way in which writing reflects the writer's inner state is more complex and more difficult for the untrained eye to recognize than magazine articles on graphology might suggest, there are certain global aspects of a piece of handwriting which are commonly taken as indications of general personality traits.

Some of these seem blindingly obvious on a practical level: wide margins suggest extravagance and narrow ones economy. Others may seem to derive from verbal associations: angular, spiky writing reflects an angular, spiky character, whilst rounded script indicates a more easy-going disposition. Whether the lines of writing rise or fall as they progress across the page is supposed to show whether the writer is optimistic ('looking up') or pessimistic. The slope of letters is regarded as significant: forward for an extravert, backward for an introvert. The writer who leaves spaces between words that are wide enough for about two letters is someone who characteristically lets others have their say ('allows them space'), whilst a cramped style suggests a more defensive character.

It seems more realistic to try to interpret general characteristics such as the size, angle and connection of letters, the shading of strokes (pressure), or lay-out and spacing, than to home in on minute details of individual letters. Yet even this sort of analysis has still not been validated by scientific evidence. Nevertheless, graphologists are increasingly consulted by employers recruiting staff.

The normal handwriting of a healthy individual has a natural rhythm, which includes fluctuations such as varying letter-size caused by brief tensions. Rigid regularity is in fact unnatural and may indicate excessive tensions in the writer. Despite the lack of scientific evidence to support any theory of graphology, the analysis of handwriting has been used to supplement the diagnosis of emotional maladjustment and psychiatric illnesses, and changes in handwriting are sometimes used to monitor progress (or lack of it) during psychotherapy. It is in this sense that the term *graphotherapy* is commonly used. In the USA there have been studies which trace the changes in stroke quality while patients are suffering from cancer and alcoholism. (It is interesting to note that 'stroke quality' was the key factor in handwriting analysis identified by the Chinese over two millennia ago.) Graphotherapy can also involve making conscious changes in one's writing style in order to invite the corresponding psychological characteristics.

GRAVITONICS Gravitonics is a method of reducing tension in the lumbar region and promoting musculo-skeletal realignment by suspending oneself upside-down from a bar by the legs and performing simple, unstrenuous gymnastic exercises.

GREEK MEDICINE AND MYTHOLOGY In ancient Greece it was Apollo, the Sun god, and his son, Asclepius (Aesculapius), who became identified as the fathers of medicine. Asclepius was snatched from his mother's womb by Apollo and given to Chiron, the centaur, to bring up. Chiron had an incurable wound and was the original ARCHETYPE of the WOUNDED HEALER. It was from him that Asclepius learned his art and skill. He became famous during the Trojan war, as did his two sons Podalirios (father of internal medicine) and Machaon (father of surgery). Asclepius had a large family and his two daughters, Hygeia and Panacea, became associated with hygiene and treatment respectively. The links between the Sun god Apollo, the centaur Chiron, the warrior Asclepius and medicine all help to emphasize the aggressive nature of this branch of human endeavour. (Modern medicine continues in the same tradition, as is betrayed by the language we use: we talk of the 'battle against cancer', of 'fighting disease' with 'the magic bullet', of 'stamping out infection'.)

In spite of this, the most famous physician in ancient Greece,

HIPPOCRATES (c.460–c.377 BC), adopted a much less aggressive attitude to DISEASE, believing that it was the physician's task to encourage and cooperate with the body's natural healing powers – a view held by most practitioners of ALTERNATIVE MEDICINE today. Around the same time, Plato (c.427–347 BC) was preaching the importance of what we now call HOLISM: 'The cure of the part should not be attempted without treatment of the whole. No attempt should be made to cure the body without the soul and if the head and body are to be healthy you must begin by curing the mind, for this is the greatest error of our day in the treatment of the human body that physicians first separate the soul from the body.'

Basic to practically all ancient systems of medicine was the significance of the HUMOURS, which most conventional practitioners would maintain find no parallel in modern medical analysis. The western system of humours was refined and established for centuries to come by Galen (c. 130–201), who also recognized the importance of the EMOTIONS in restoring and maintaining physical health.

Modern medicine still sees itself as in a direct line of descent from Hippocrates, although some of his tenets are not upheld by conventional medicine. He would have disapproved of many of today's interventionist measures, believing that it was the physician's task to assist nature in healing. Interventionism fits in more with the principles of the rival CNIDIAN SCHOOL.

GRINDLER METHOD The Grindler method is a technique of developing one's sensory awareness, a western form of hatha yoga developed in the 1920s in Germany by Elsie Grindler. While lying, sitting, standing or performing very slow movements, one tries to become as conscious as possible of bodily sensations, concentrating on one's breathing and on everything that is going on in the body. Through the development of this KINAESTHESIA one begins to realize how much one has separated oneself from the body, and the parts of the body from each other. The habitual lack of attention to bodily sensations is recognized as an aspect of the fragmentation of the self, and rediscovering the ability to attend in this way and be in one's body results in a greater feeling of both physical and emotional well-being.

GROUNDING Grounding is used in many different types of therapy, and usually refers to establishing an awareness of being focused in the body and rooted in the real world. This may be as a preliminary exercise, as in BIOENERGETICS, or as a rounding-off to refocus

169

attention on physical reality after a mental exercise such as guided imagery in PSYCHOSYNTHESIS.

In BIOSYNTHESIS being grounded means an individual is in a state of physical equilibrium appropriate to the activity involved, particularly with regard to muscle tone: 'The therapeutic work of *grounding* is concerned with establishing a good relationship between the voluntary, semi-voluntary and involuntary modes of movement and with recreating a more appropriate muscle tone. Muscle tone can be unbalanced in two directions. Hypertonus is an excess of tension, more than is required for a particular action; the muscles feel tense, knotted and rigid. Hypotonus is a deficiency of tonus, less than is necessary for a particular action; the muscles feel slack, spongy and over-sluggish.'[20]

GROUP PATHOLOGY See MASS HYSTERIA.

GROUP THERAPY Group therapy was introduced in the USA by Joseph Hersey Pratt (1872–1942). Instead of meeting the therapist alone for a private session, several individuals meet together to share their experiences and feelings. The therapist is generally also present and guides the discussion. The hope is that by interacting with each other on a cognitive and emotional level, they will gain insight, understand themselves better and overcome any psychological problems. Often it is a problem which they have in common, such as bereavement or alcoholism, which forms the basis of the group. In psychiatric institutions group therapy may be used as an aid to teaching patients social skills. (See also ENCOUNTER GROUPS and PSYCHODRAMA.)

GROWING TIP The growing tip refers to the few people at any one time who can be regarded as 'good specimens' of contemporary humanity. Abraham Maslow believed that one could learn a great deal about human nature and human potential by studying a small segment of humanity which he called the 'growing tip', consisting of exceptionally healthy, mature people. He proposed the use of 'good specimens' as examples for studying 'the best capability that the human species has'. These psychologically healthy people were what he called 'SELF-ACTUALIZERS'. 'On the whole I think it fair to say that human history is a record of the ways in which human nature has been sold short. The highest possibilities of human nature have practically always been underrated.'[124]

'If we want to know the possibilities for spiritual growth, value growth, or moral development in human beings, then I maintain that we can learn most by studying our most moral, ethical, or saintly people . . . Even when "good specimens", the saints and sages and great leaders of history, have been available for study, the temptation too often has been to consider them not human but supernaturally endowed.'[124]

Others have since taken up Maslow's call to study such 'good specimens'. Most notable among these is Piero Ferrucci, a leading psychotherapist in PSYCHOSYNTHESIS, whose book *Inevitable Grace* records and reflects on what he calls breakthroughs in the lives of 500 great men and women, experiences which he believes can act as guides for our own self-realization.[43]

GROWTH/PERSONAL GROWTH Personal growth has gone by many names: individuation, personal autonomy, SELF-ACTUALIZ-ATION, self-development, SELF-REALIZATION, even productiveness. There are slight differences between some of these, but they are clearly dealing with the same basic idea. By growth we usually mean the continuing development of character, capacities, talents, creativity and wisdom: the fulfilment of one's potential as a human being. Growth is a process of becoming rather than a state of being, which is why this word is often used in conjunction with the other terms, many of which seem to suggest some sort of end-state. Not until we are nearing the end of life can we feel that such an end-state has been reached in the sense that growth is complete. Abraham Maslow, considering those people who are predominantly 'growth-motivated', believed that the desire for growth does not diminish as growth progresses but actually increases. 'The appetite for growth is whetted rather than allayed by gratification. Growth is, *in itself*, a rewarding and exciting process, e.g. the fulfilling of yearnings and ambitions, the acquisition of admired skills, the steady increase of understanding about people or about the universe, or about oneself; the development of creativeness in whatever field, or, most important, simply the ambition to be a good human being.'[125]

Growth involves being drawn constantly towards new experiences. 'Growth is understanding what we have not yet been able to conceive, feeling what we have never felt, doing what we have never done before. It is daring what we have never dared. It may not, therefore, necessarily be pleasurable. It obliges us to leave our comfort zone, to progress into the unknown.'[42] So the process of healthy growth is 'a never ending series of free choice situations, confronting each individual at every point throughout his life, in which he must choose between the delights of safety and growth, dependence and independence, regression and progression, immaturity and maturity. Safety has both anxieties and delights; growth has both anxieties and delights. We grow forward when the delights of growth and the anxieties of safety are greater than the anxieties of growth and the delights of safety.'[125]

The growth psychologies vary in the degree to which they expect growth to occur automatically, once the obstacles to it have been removed, and to what extent the individual has to apply self-discipline and work towards growth. Maslow, while believing that human beings have an innate tendency towards growth, which he called GROWTH MOTIVATION, also recognized that growth was not automatic. All branches of humanistic psychology have criticized classical Freudian psychology for pathologizing everything and ignoring the individual's natural potential for healthy growth, a view which Maslow described as 'seeing everything through brown-coloured glasses'. But Maslow also recognized a complementary tendency among extreme proponents of the growth school 'to see the world through rose-coloured glasses and generally slide over the problems of pathology, of weakness, of failure to grow'.[125] Maslow saw neurosis as a condition arising out of a failure to grow.

But if growth is natural and instinctive, what prevents it? Maslow believed that rather than being prevented from growing we sometimes of our own volition evade growth, perhaps because of a fear of our own greatness. This he called the Jonah Complex: 'So we often run away from the responsibilities dictated (or rather suggested) by nature, by fate, even sometimes by accident, just as Jonah tried – in vain – to run away from *his* fate.' We are afraid of the power of our own emotions and in any PEAK EXPERIENCE, when we feel that we are truly and fully ourselves, those emotions may reach unprecedented intensity. 'It is partly a justified fear of being torn apart, of losing control, of being shattered and disintegrated, even of being killed by the experience.'[124] Alternatively we may avoid real growth by setting low levels of aspiration, perhaps as a defence against arrogance and sinful pride, the *hubris* of Greek tragedy and of the legends of Prometheus and Faust. These stories demonstrate what happens to those who believe themselves to be as gods. 'You *must* be aware not only of the godlike possibilities within, but also of the existential human limitations.'[124]

GROWTH MOTIVATION 'What a man *can* be, he *must* be.'[126] Abraham Maslow spoke more than most of growth motivation. He was a firm believer in the individual's innate appetite for GROWTH. 'Man demonstrates in his own nature a pressure toward fuller and fuller being, more and more perfect actualization of his humanness in exactly the same naturalistic scientific sense that an acorn may be said to be "pressing toward" being an oak tree.'[125]

According to orthodox behaviourist psychology, human beings naturally seek equilibrium, the reduction of tension, and most behaviour is then defined in tension-reducing terms. Freud had held basically the same view, believing that human behaviour was motivated by the pleasure-pain principle: we constantly seek pleasure and avoid pain. For Abraham Maslow, one of the leading proponents of Third Force or HUMANISTIC PSYCHOLOGY, such tension-reduction theories cannot adequately explain human behaviour. He believed that humans have an innate tendency toward growth and self-actualization. 'If the motivational life consists essentially of a defensive removal of irritating tensions, and if the only end product of tension-reduction is a state of passive waiting for more unwelcome irritations to arise and in their turn, to be dispelled, then how does change or development or movement or direction come about? Why do people improve? Get wiser?'[125]

The effect of tension-reducing behaviours must be relatively short-term, but as Maslow realized, 'Growth motivation may be long-term in character. Most of a lifetime may be involved in becoming a good psychologist or a good artist. All equilibrium or homeostasis or rest theories deal only with short-term episodes, each of which has nothing to do with each other.'[125]

'Growth motives, on the other hand, maintain tension in the interest of distant and often unattainable goals. As such they distinguish human from animal becoming, and adult from infant becoming.'[3]

GUIDED IMAGERY When a VISUALIZATION exercise follows a description or story-line narrated by the therapist (or read from a book) it is called guided imagery. This type of exercise forms an important part of PSYCHOSYNTHESIS.

HAKIM Hakims are practitioners of HERBALISM on the Indian sub-continent and in Islamic communities.

HAKOMI THERAPY Developed by Ron Kurtz as a non-confrontational BIODYNAMIC THERAPY, Hakomi therapy combines the basic elements of REICHIAN THERAPY with a more supportive approach, incorporating ideas from meditation practices and self-directed healing strategies.

HAND HEALING/LAYING ON OF HANDS See THERAPEUTIC TOUCH.

HANDWRITING See GRAPHOLOGY/GRAPHOTHERAPY.

HAPPINESS According to traditional Chinese medicine, an imbalance of the emotions can disturb the functioning of the internal organs (and vice versa). This applies equally to what we might regard as 'positive' as well as 'negative' emotions. Consequently, the Chinese believe that an excess of happiness (or imbalances brought about by 'forced' happiness) can damage the heart and the circulatory system. (One is reminded of professional comedians who die of heart-attacks.). Many ancient systems of medicine with their theories of HUMOURS held similar views.

Perhaps surprisingly, modern research into STRESS to a certain extent supports this notion: certain kinds of happiness may be regarded as life-threatening rather than life-enhancing. Among the list of life-events from which one accumulates 'life change units', producing a total which correlates with one's susceptibility to disease, are many events which one would normally regard as happy: marriage and holidays, for example. Viktor Frankl believes that the 'pursuit of happiness' is actually counter-productive and doomed from the outset, the WILL TO MEANING being the primary motivation in human life.

According to a paper published in the *Journal of Medical Ethics*,[206] happiness, like anxiety, mania and many other departures from the norms of mood and behaviour, should be regarded as a disorder. The author of the article, Richard Bentall, a psychologist at the University of Liverpool, using familiar psychological jargon, proposed to rename happiness a 'major affective disorder (pleasant type)'. Among the reasons for redefining happiness as a psychiatric disorder he cited the fact that like other such disorders happiness is biologically disadvantageous: it tends to increase reckless behaviour and other high-risk activities such as excessive eating and drinking. 'Happy people overestimate the amount of control they have over events . . . They delude themselves into thinking the world is a nicer place than it really is.' In other words, happiness can distort one's perception of the world: depressed people have much more realistic perceptions and are more in touch with reality. Since happiness can lead us to make less objective judgments, it increases the risk we run of finding ourselves in dangerous situations.

This proposed reclassification of happiness was actually a spoof suggestion by Richard Bentall, but it did have a serious purpose. He was questioning the methods used by psychiatrists when deciding what is a psychiatric disorder. He claimed that the only reason we do not classify happiness as a disorder is that we actually like being happy. He was drawing attention to the often overlooked fact that in the supposedly objective, scientific discipline of psychiatry, value judgments play a key role; deciding what is the norm is seldom an objective procedure.

Another example cited by Bentall is that of hearing voices, which psychiatrists generally regard as a sign of schizophrenia. But this is a result of their paying attention only to those people who complain of hearing voices (or who are victimized by friends or family when they talk about their experiences). Although they have not been the object of so much study, many people hear voices and are not distressed by the experience at all; in fact they often regard it as a gift (as of course do most so-called primitive peoples).

These ideas are reminiscent of Thomas Szasz's *The Myth of Mental Illness*, and of R. D. Laing's notion of ANTI-PSYCHIATRY.

HARA According to Japanese tradition the *hara*, situated just below the navel, is the vital centre of the human body. It is a focus of attention in many Japanese practices in bodywork and meditation. Its equivalent in other systems is the solar plexus CHAKRA.

HARDINESS INDUCTION COURSES Hardy people transform problems into opportunities and thereby do not elicit the STRESS responses to life events, which are so damaging to health. To develop this characteristic in an attempt to acquire a certain immunity to stress, Salvatore Maadi and Suzanne Kobasa created their Hardiness Induction Courses. The exercises and activities increase one's sense of control over stress by focusing on both physical and mental sensations when in stressful situations, while encouraging a sense of commitment, control and challenge.

HARP A study of the effect of various alternative therapies on people with AIDS is being conducted at the Bastyr College Research Department in Seattle, Washington. In this Healing AIDS Research Project (HARP) are included therapies such as HERBALISM, HOMOEOPATHY, HYDROTHERAPY, NATUROPATHY, NUTRITION, AUTOGENIC TRAINING, COUNSELLING and PSYCHO-THERAPY.

HATHA YOGA Hatha yoga is one of the six traditional forms of YOGA in ancient Indian teaching. The term 'hatha' is probably a combination of two Sanskrit words, *ha* meaning 'the sun' and *tha* 'the moon', suggesting the uniting of two opposites (rather than a derivation from the root *hath* meaning 'to oppress, control by force', as has also been suggested). Hatha yoga uses physical exercises and postures known as *asanas* (from the Sanskrit root meaning 'to sit'), often in combination with the breathing exercises of PRANAYAMA.

The purpose of the asanas is to promote and maintain both physical suppleness and mind-body harmony. Many go by the names of animals (lizard, cobra, caterpillar, butterfly, cheetah, ostrich, etc.) and they are often used in set sequences: each posture is adopted slowly and smoothly and held for a short time without strain. Initially they feel uncomfortable (much as the behaviour patterns encouraged in the ALEXANDER TECHNIQUE seem unnatural at first), but eventually, as Indian tradition has it, 'The posture becomes perfect when the effort achieving it vanishes.' As Mircea Eliade describes it in *Patanjali and Yoga*, the asana 'gives a rigid stability to the body while at the same time it reduces physical effort to a minimum. Thus one avoids the irritating sensation of fatigue or of the numbness of certain parts of the body; one controls the physiological process; and thus one makes it possible for one's attention to be occupied exclusively with the fluid part of consciousness.'[38] The lotus position is often adopted for meditation, and the 'corpse' pose is used for total relaxation.

HAY DIET An American physician, William Howard Hay (1866–1940) devised a diet for the treatment of digestive problems based on his ideas that acid from fruit and gastric acid produced when we eat protein interfere with the digestion of carbohydrates, and that carbohydrates should therefore not be eaten at the same time as fruit and protein.

HEALERS/HEALING The term 'healing' often refers specifically to the type of therapy practised by spiritual healers, psychic healers, faith healers, and those who treat the 'subtle body' via the AURA, perhaps treating each of the major CHAKRAS in turn. Some seek to distinguish between those healers who actually touch the patient's physical body, as in THERAPEUTIC TOUCH, and those who keep their hands a little distance away from the body in the patient's aura, but such a distinction seems to be far less significant than that between two types of healers who could be described as 'transferrers' and 'channellers'. Some healers maintain that they are transferring some of their own energy or LIFE-FORCE to the patient, whilst others describe themselves simply as channels, attracting and directing this energy towards the patient from God or the cosmos (as in REIKI). 'Transferers' do sometimes eventually succumb to one of the major illnesses they have been treating, suggesting that their own energy has in fact been diminished in some way, whilst the 'channellers' often report feeling invigorated after spending several hours healing.

HEALING CRISIS During HOMOEOPATHIC treatment symptoms may initially get worse before they are alleviated, a situation referred to as a healing crisis. Another sort of healing crisis is sometimes referred to as a FLARE-UP, common in cases where patients have previously had surgery or been treated by ALLOPATHIC medicine and then go on a wholly natural diet to 'detoxify' the body.

HEALTH It is seen as one of the errors of CONVENTIONAL MEDICINE that health is equated simply with the absence of DISEASE. The direct consequence of this is that people think about their health only when they are actually ill. This tendency had already been noticed and warned against many centuries ago: Maimonides wrote, 'He is a great fool who believes he only needs a physician when he is ill.' Alcmaeon, the first Greek to write a medical treatise, practise dissection and recognize that the brain is the central organ in the sensorimotor system, defined health as 'the equal and cooperative

177

mingling of the separate elements in human nature'. In 1946 health was defined in a similar way by the World Health Organization as 'a state of complete physical, mental and social well being'.

The president of the American Medical Association, M. C. Todd, has said, 'Health is not the mere absence of disease, but a positive quality of living.' Lawrence LeShan sees this as one of the key characteristics of the HOLISTIC approach to health: 'It is far more than the absence of disease, it is a *process* of approaching one's fullest, most zestful, and joyful participation in every aspect of one's life.'[116] He has also drawn attention to another aspect of the disease-health dualism: 'The body and physical disease are in the realm of sight and touch . . . health is in the realm of consciousness'[116] – hence, in part, the difficulty in arriving at an objective definition of health. By its nature health is intangible. LeShan points out that today the welfare of a population is considered almost entirely in secular terms. Even the WHO definition 'omits a crucial part of what it means to be human – the spiritual, the deep and basic need to have a meaningful framework for existence'.[116] The fact that this aspect of human life is generally not considered at all as a factor in health means that many conditions are classified as physical illnesses almost by default.

So behaviour that is disapproved of tends to be considered illness requiring treatment rather than crime requiring punishment or sin requiring conversion. 'Alcoholism thus becomes a disease, and the physician's prerogative to treat, even though he does not know the cause and has no reason to suspect that the cause is biological. Further, there is no reason to suspect that he is more effective dealing with it than are the courts or the church, and he is less successful than the peer treatment of AA.'[116] (Crisis COUNSELLING should probably be regarded as part of health care, and there are signs that group practices of general practitioners are increasingly coming round to this view.)

There is much more information available today concerning pathology and disease than there is on health and health maintenance. Or as LeShan puts it, there is more talk of survival – how a person survives when sick – than of 'thrival' – how a person thrives.[116] But for some people the pendulum has swung to the opposite extreme and health is regarded as something that has to be constantly worked at, a preoccupation worthy of Molière's Harpagon. Health is then seen as a task, as Ivan Illich has pointed out. 'Health has ceased to be a native endowment each human being is presumed to possess until proven ill, and has become an ever-receding goal to which one is entitled by virtue of social justice.'⁹¹ Is this really what we mean by health maintenance?

Illich stresses that in a healthy society there should be only occasional medical intervention. 'Healthy people are those who live in healthy homes on a healthy diet in an environment equally fit for birth, growth, work, healing, and dying; they are sustained by a culture that enhances the conscious acceptance of limits to population, of ageing, of incomplete recovery and ever-imminent death.'⁹¹ Illich's definition of health includes a strong element of the ability to adapt, so that ageing, healing when damaged, suffering, and 'the peaceful expectation of death' are all accepted in their own time. So health, rather than designating the absence of sickness, can in a sense be regarded as including sickness. 'To be in good health means . . . to be able to feel alive in pleasure and in pain; it means to cherish but also to risk survival.'⁹¹

HEALTH WATCH Formerly known as 'Quackbusters', Health Watch is a British organization dedicated to assessing and criticizing the methods of ALTERNATIVE MEDICINE and exposing what they regard as worthless or fraudulent. The dropping of their original name suggests that they are perhaps more open now to the possibility that CONVENTIONAL MEDICINE might not have all the answers. As their deputy chairman and vice-president of the Royal College of Pathologists, Professor Vincent Marks, says, 'I think the established international medical profession is recognizing that there are other skills than their own which may help people to lead better lives.'²²⁸

HEART DISEASE See TYPE A PERSONALITY, and RELATIONSHIPS.

HEIGHT PSYCHOLOGY By analogy with the 'depth psychology' of psychoanalysis, Viktor Frankl coined the term 'height psychology' in 1938 to refer to his LOGOTHERAPY. He evidently approved of and repeatedly quoted a comment made by Anatole Broyard in the *New York Times* (26 November 1975): 'If "shrink" is the slang term for the Freudian analyst, then the logotherapist ought to be called the "stretch".'⁴⁵,⁴⁶ As Frankl himself wrote, 'Logotherapy expands not only the concept of man, by including his higher aspirations, but also the visional field of the patient as to potentialities to feed and nurture his will to MEANING. By the same token, logotherapy immunizes the patient against the dehumanizing, mechanistic concept of man on which many a "shrink" is sold – in a word, it makes the patient "shrink-*resistant*".'⁴⁶

HELIOTHERAPY Sunbathing (*helios* is Greek for 'sun') has had a bad press in recent years, but it has a long tradition as an integral part of many cures. The therapeutic effects of the sun's rays are said to be at a maximum in the early morning, and treatment has often been combined with HYDROTHERAPY, with care also being taken to ensure that the patient gets a good dose of negative IONS. Despite the dangers of excessive radiation, ultra-violet light is believed to improve many aspects of health, including resistance to infection, skin condition, muscle tone, calcium and phosphorus metabolism, respiration, blood pressure, endocrine functioning and general metabolism. Sun-lamps are used when there is insufficient natural sunlight. They are particularly effective when treating people for SAD — SEASONAL AFFECTIVE DISORDER.

HELLERWORK Hellerwork is a form of bodywork which combines elements of ROLFING and the ALEXANDER TECHNIQUE. It was developed by Joseph Heller, a former American aerospace engineer, who was trained by Ida Rolf and became president of the Rolf Institute in Boulder, Colorado. He put together a course of eleven ninety-minute sessions of physical re-education, consisting of deep massage and physical exercises intended to encourage better body posture. The focus in these sessions progresses from one part of the body to another: starting with the chest and breathing, the treatment moves on to general body posture, the release of muscle tension in the limbs, pelvis, back and head, and the maintenance of balance. As tensions are released in each area, there are psychological benefits: for example, the individual feels more in tune with and in control of the body, which improves self-assurance. As with rolfing, the treatment encourages the release of both physical and emotional trauma, but in the case of Hellerwork more emphasis is placed on the verbalization of the memories and issues that surface in this way in order to increase self-awareness.

HEMISPHERIC SYNCHRONIZATION Since the discovery of BRAIN RHYTHMS and the BICAMERAL nature of the brain, scientists have used the ELECTRO-ENCEPHALOGRAPH not only to reveal the electrical activity in the brain, but to show people the type of activity in each hemisphere, so that they can try to bring the two into synchronization. This form of BIOFEEDBACK has been exploited by the manufacturers of an encephalograph called the Mind Mirror (Audio Ltd., London). The standard encephalographs used in hospitals help to identify anything that is pathological in the brain rhythms, ignoring what is simply a reflection of mood, but for those who use the Mind Mirror this aspect of mental state is all-important and the subject is shown which rhythms are dominant in each half of the brain. Mind Mirror III can be linked up to a personal computer so that the rhythms can be displayed on a VDU (as opposed to the LCD of the earlier models). It has been claimed by others (e.g. Mentronics Systems) that synchronization in both halves of the brain can be induced by the use of sound played through headphones.

In all these experiments the aim seems to be not simply to make the two halves more alike in their activity so much as to make the left half behave more like the right, reducing the amount of left-brain thinking and achieving a relaxed state of heightened awareness of the kind that is associated with right-brain styles of perception.

HERBAL MEDICINE/HERBALISM Herbal medicine is the use of plant remedies to restore health. In the context of herbalism the word 'herb' is used to cover all plant life, including flowers, trees, ferns and even seaweeds and lichens. The term has a much wider scope of reference here than it has in a strictly botanical sense. The key factor in the use of such remedies is that whatever part of the plant is used, it is used in its biochemical entirety, unlike chemicals that are isolated (even from plants) or synthesized in the laboratory. This means that herbal remedies are chemically much more complex than modern 'orthodox' drugs, and include many proteins, enzymes and trace elements, all of which are regarded as significant. Strictly speaking, herbal remedies do not cure ailments; they do not use ALLOPATHIC means, fighting against whatever germs or toxins have invaded the body. Rather it is believed that they stimulate the body's own reactions against the invader, encouraging the patient's natural recuperative powers by re-establishing the balance of the various elements within the body. Because they do not bombard the body with one artificially concentrated chemical, herbal remedies are generally thought to be free from toxic side effects.

Herbalism must have been the earliest type of medicine practised by humanity. The Chinese *Pen Tsao* (Great Herbal) has been dated at c.3000 BC, and we know from stone and papyrus records that herbal remedies were also being used in Sumer and Egypt in the third millennium BC, but these dates are indicative more of mankind's newfound ability to preserve information in writing than of when we actually started to use medicinal herbs. Plants which we know to have therapeutic properties have been found in the graves of Neanderthal man, who became extinct about 30,000 years ago.

If any form of medical therapy can be said to predate herbalism it is NATUROPATHY: the natural use of whatever nourishment nature provided, including herbs with medicinal properties when required, must originally have been instinctive. Animals naturally seek out the plants they need to restore physical health, and there is no reason to suppose that mankind did not do the same. Once human consciousness developed to the extent that mankind started to rationalize its actions, it no doubt saw what the animals did and followed suit. Eventually a large corpus of such herbal knowledge was accumulated: this formed the 'Great Herbal' of China and the Egyptian Ebers papyrus (1500 BC), and was included in Pliny's *Natural History* (AD 77) and the works of Galen (c.130–201).

In the Middle Ages herbalism became enmeshed in an elaborate system of correspondences between the herbs and the planets and between the herbs and parts of the body. The appearance of a plant was thought to be significant: for example, yellow flowers or roots were deemed good for people with jaundice, and lungwort, shaped like the lungs, was used to treat lung disease. The Swiss alchemist and physician, Paracelsus (1493–1541), was one of the first to formulate the so-called Doctrine of Signatures around such associations. The effect of a herb was then increasingly seen as a result of sympathetic magic or the stars with which it was associated rather than as a result of any properties of the herb itself.

In England, King Henry VIII's herbalist and director of the Royal Gardens at Hampton Court was John Parkinson (1567–1629). His *Theatrum Botanicum*, eventually published in 1640, was the first comprehensive study of plant remedies grouped according to their medicinal properties, a system of classification still used today. It listed 3,800 plants and their applications. Perhaps more famous, although 'tainted' by the preoccupation with astrological corre-spondences, is *The English Physician Enlarged, or the Complete Herbal* (1653) by the astrologer, Nicholas Culpeper (1616–54).

The accretion of magic and astrology became a handicap to herb-alism when it had to start competing with pills and potions made from synthesized drugs or even from naturally occurring but con-centrated, purified extracts. However, in England herbalists had been protected by Act of Parliament during the reign of Henry VIII, and, perhaps also as a result of the popularity of 'folk remedies' in agrarian communities, herbalism always managed to survive even though cut off from the mainstream of medical practice.

In the second half of the nineteenth century herbalism in the United

States had a new lease of life and a greater degree of respectability in the guise of 'physiomedicalism'. But the new doctrine enjoyed only temporary success, since it was based on the theory that the sole cause of sickness was a disturbance of the body's normal equilibrium, denying any effect of micro-organisms. Emetics and colonic cleansing also featured greatly in physiomedical treatments, but the main element in them was the use of herbal remedies to restore 'the life force'.

Meanwhile, in Britain, divisions were growing between herbalists who were primarily dispensers, basically shopkeepers with a side-room for consultations, and those who preferred to see themselves as qualified practitioners. In 1864 the National Institute of Medical Herbalists was founded to train, examine and accredit practitioners. Many less academically minded herbalists were not in sympathy with this method of trying to improve standards, and they set up the rival British Herbalists Union. After all, being able to pass an examination was no guarantee that one would be an effective practitioner. But the demand for recognized qualifications would not go away. Another training centre, the Faculty of Herbal Medicine, was founded in the 1940s, but the split between the traditional and the academic approaches remained. It was to a certain extent inevitable, given the desire for herbalism to be accepted as a medical discipline: 'The price of higher standards was disunity: the price of unity was lower standards.'[92] The disunity was one of the main reasons herbalism did not come under the remit of the National Health Service when it was established in 1948.

It has been suggested that the fact that herbal remedies were never available free on the NHS might have contributed to the next upsurge of interest in herbalism in Britain: the theory is that the PLACEBO EFFECT works more effectively if one has actually paid for the treatment; we value more what we have had to pay for and therefore expect it to work better – an attitude akin, perhaps, to the 'no pain, no gain' idea. But herbalism also enjoyed another revival in America in the 1960s, thanks partly to a book written by an orthodox physician, D. C. Jarvis, who rediscovered folk remedies and proposed a few simple daily prescriptions for maintaining general health.[94] He revived interest in the idea that animals and children instinctively know what is best for them where food is concerned. But with increasing concern over the side effects of allopathic drugs, overprescription of antibiotics, and the realization that a significant number of hospital patients are being treated for conditions actually caused by medical treatment, it is not surprising

183

that interest in herbalism continued to grow through the 1970s[112] and 1980s. (See also BACH FLOWER REMEDIES, GINSENG.)

HETERO-SUGGESTION Emile Coué (1857–1926) believed that the crucial factor in hypnosis was not that the hypnotist was able to influence the mind of the subject willy-nilly – suggestion by 'another' (*hetero*) – but that hypnotic subjects themselves were responsible for the effect in an act of AUTOSUGGESTION. He coined the two words to point out the distinction he wanted to make in his theory of what happens in hypnosis.

HIERARCHY OF NEEDS See NEEDS.

HIGH FREQUENCY CURRENTS High frequency currents are generally considered to be above 100,000 cycles per second, in a range where they have no contracting effect on muscles. But the currents produced by so-called high frequency apparatus used in ELECTROTHERAPY are usually of medium frequency. It has been claimed that treatment with high frequencies stimulates hair growth, although its main value is as a means of cauterization in certain skin conditions. (See also PULSED HIGH FREQUENCY THERAPY.)

HIGH FREQUENCY PHOTOGRAPHY See KIRLIAN PHOTO-GRAPHY.

HIPPOCRATES Hippocrates (c.460–c.377 BC), the most famous physician in antiquity, was born and practised on the Greek island of Cos. On another island, Cnidos, a rival school was set up (the CNIDIAN SCHOOL), but Hippocrates remained the foremost exemplar of GREEK MEDICINE. He gathered together all that was considered to be of value in what was known of medicine in his day and is still regarded as the father of western medicine. The principles of the ethical code which is attributed to him – the Hippocratic Oath – are still followed by medical practitioners today. It contains injunctions against harming patients (including euthanasia) and taking advantage of them, and imposes total confidentiality. 'According to my power and judgment, I will prescribe regimen in order to benefit the sick, and do them no injury or wrong. I will neither give on demand any deadly drug, nor prompt any such course ... Whatsoever house I enter, there will I go for the benefit of the sick, refraining from all wrong-doing ... Whatsoever things I see or hear in my attendance on the sick which ought not to be voiced abroad, I will keep silence thereon.'

HOLISM The word 'holism' was coined by General Smuts in the 1920s (from the Greek *holos*, meaning 'whole') when defining his philosophical belief that the fundamental principle of the cosmos is the creation of self-contained systems, 'wholes'. For Smuts, holism was a 'factor operative towards the making or creating of wholes in the Universe . . . Holism is a factor which underlines the synthetic tendency in the Universe and is the principle which makes for the origin and progress of wholes in the Universe. Wholeness . . . marks the line of evolutionary progress and holism is the inner driving force behind that progress.'[162] This is not quite the same as saying the whole is greater than the sum of the parts, a more common inter-pretation of holism which comes rather from GESTALT psychologists. In current usage 'holism' tends to refer more to an attitude than to a philosophical principle, and 'holistic' means loosely the opposite of REDUCTIONIST – considering a system in its entirety rather than focusing on isolated parts of it.

In medicine the idea behind holism is that the physician considers the whole person – body, mind and spirit – and the whole person within other systems – family, community, culture and environment. To some extent all medical practitioners would probably claim to be holistic (it is interesting to note that the word 'health' also comes from a root meaning 'whole': Old English *hael*), and many object to the way in which alternative practitioners seem to have laid claim to the description. Fairly typical of orthodox sceptics is Michael Baum, of the King's College School of Medicine and Dentistry, London. He complains that 'many complementary therapists have hijacked the idea of holism' and says it is 'sheer nonsense to say that conventional medicine is not holistic in its outlook'.[177] This would seem an extravagant claim to many patients of conventional doctors. Fortunately there is a growing number of people in the medical establishment who recognize that there is something unsatisfactory in the way patients are often treated, and who try to satisfy their own patients' requests for 'holistic treatment' whilst still adopting a realistic view of what 'being holistic' really means. One such is Patrick Pietroni, who makes the same point as Michael Baum but with a more moderate voice: 'It is unfortunate that the term holistic medicine has become almost synonymous with alternative medicine.' He reminds us that 'Holism espouses an approach and does not dictate any particular therapy.'[143]

The need to consider 'the whole person' is not a new idea and has been emphasized by many throughout the history of medicine. At the same time there has also been a tendency towards reductionism. Plato said, 'The cure of the part should not be attempted without treatment of the whole. No attempt should be made to cure the body without the soul, and if the head and body are to be healthy you must begin by curing the mind, for this is the greatest error of our day in the treatment of the human body that physicians first separate the soul from the body.' That error received an enormous boost when Francis Bacon decided to 'put the body on the rack and make it reveal its secrets', and for the next three hundred years western medicine was more or less ruled by reductionist principles. So over two millennia after Plato the same urgings were still necessary, and in 1959 the President of the American Cancer Society echoed Plato in his address to the Society, saying: 'There is solid evidence that the course of disease in general is affected by emotional distress . . . Thus, we as doctors may begin to emphasize treatment of the patient as a whole as well as the disease from which the patient is suffering . . . It is my sincere hope that we can widen the quest to include the distinct possibility that within one's mind is the power capable of exerting forces which can either enhance or inhibit the progress of this disease.'[139]

Unfortunately both factions in the debate include people who seem to use a rather partial definition of holism and to some extent misrepresent their opponents. Michael Baum condemns the holistic theories of his 'complementary colleagues' as 'completely metaphysical', saying that they 'relate to some as yet undiscovered, and for all we know non-existent, "natural life force" ',[177] without giving any credit to the holistic *practices* of alternative practitioners.

On the other side, as Carl Simonton has pointed out, 'A large number of "holistic practitioners" are anti-traditional medicine, quite narrow, and dogmatic in their views. This is not holistic medicine. Holistic medicine includes complete technological medicine.'[159] Lawrence LeShan goes further: 'There is no such thing as a holistic technique or modality. There is only a holistic *attitude* . . . An acupuncturist, a homeopath, or a nutritionist who believes that he has *the* answer and that all that anyone needs is his approach is certainly not holistic.'[116] Patients too who ostensibly subscribe to holistic principles may still expect and prefer a MAGIC BULLET type of treatment – taking a remedy to get rid of the symptoms without worrying too much about whether there might be an all-important emotional factor in the condition.

Since PSYCHOSOMATIC aspects of illness are being increasingly recognized, conventional medicine is having to take note of the holistic approach, for there is no other way of predicting and preventing psychosomatic disorders. If the medical establishment devotes all its energy and resources to treating DISEASE per se, many vital factors may be overlooked. Disease is sometimes simply the way a much larger complex of problems and circumstances manifests itself – its clearest symptom – and only a holistic approach enables the physician to recognize this. Kenneth Pelletier is encouraged in the belief that conventional medicine is adopting a more holistic attitude, and that 'This concept of holistic, preventive health care is one of most important innovations in modern medical research and its clinical applications. It is very important to note, however, that this approach is not critical of or antagonistic to contemporary allopathic medicine.'[139] There does, however, seem to be a risk here that 'holistic' might be interpreted simply as 'eclectic', despite the fact that ALLOPATHIC medicine is actually incompatible with some alternative therapies (which should not therefore be designated as 'complementary').

It has always been a basic principle of Chinese medicine that one treats the patient, not the disease. This means that different people with the same symptoms and the same disease (in western terms) will receive different treatment – a fact which makes CLINICAL TRIALS as understood by conventional medicine virtually impossible. At some level patients need recognition of the fact that their illness is unique in the sense that it is particular to them, but much of what the conventional doctor does indicates precisely the opposite. They are not encouraged to understand their condition, which is often shrouded in the mystery of medical jargon, and are deprived of real involvement in both disease and treatment (the problem of MEDICALIZATION). By way of contrast, patients who attended chiropractors were shown to have developed a better awareness of their condition because they felt that they had a more equal relationship with the therapist.[212] Similarly, when patients need surgery the surgeons often treat them without ever speaking to them, whether through lack of time or through ignorance of how necessary such contact actually is. This criticism extends to general practitioners, who often fail in their pastoral role because they are poor communicators. As Lawrence LeShan points out, the patient should be actively involved in treatment: 'It is relevant that the word "cure" derives from the same root as the word "curiosity". Be "curious" and take your destiny into

HOLISTIC-DYNAMIC PSYCHOLOGY

your own hands. It is a lot safer there than in the hands of strangers.'[116]

LeShan's analogy with the methods of the gardener and the mechanic is an apt description of the way in which medicine seems to be pulled in two directions: 'The gardener deals with the whole – with the organism in an environment. The mechanic fixes nonfunctioning parts.' He suggests that present interest in a more holistic approach 'has developed primarily because of this awareness that technology is not enough'. 'All levels of [the patient's] being are of equal importance in the prevention of disease and the search for health. In the cure of disease, this wider interest also has the purpose of bringing more strongly into play that patient's own self-healing and self-repair.' He also notes that 'What all holistic methods have in common is the underlying hunger, the profound search, for some way to see and respond to the patient as a complete person, not just as a collection of functioning or nonfunctioning organs.'[116]

The basic principles behind the idea of holistic medicine are:

Each individual is unique – body, mind and spirit.
All states of health have a psychosomatic element.
Health maintenance is beyond the scope of pathology alone – one cannot ignore psychosocial aspects of life-style and personal fulfilment.
Illness represents a creative opportunity for the patient to learn more about him/herself.
Patient and doctor share responsibility for the healing process.
The practitioner must also have a high degree of self-knowledge.

And central to all is the fact that, as the French surgeon, biologist and Nobel prize-winner Alexis Carrel said in 1935, each human being is 'an indivisible whole of extreme complexity'.

HOLISTIC-DYNAMIC PSYCHOLOGY This was one of the terms coined by Abraham Maslow to refer to his Third Force Psychology, before it became more generally known as HUMANISTIC PSYCHOLOGY.

HOMOEOPATHY The word homoeopathy (or homeopathy) is made up of two Greek words: *homoios*, meaning 'same' or 'similar', and *pathos*, 'suffering'. The principle of *similia similibus curentur* – 'Let likes be treated with likes' – was present in the writings of Hippocrates and of early Arab physicians, but the first to formulate a coherent doctrine of homoeopathy was Samuel Friedrich Christian Hahnemann (1755–1843).

While studying medicine in Leipzig and Vienna, Hahnemann had supported himself largely through work as a translator of scientific texts, and he continued to do this long after qualifying as a doctor in 1779. While translating Cullen's *Materia Medica*, a standard medical textbook of the time, and when he was dealing specifically with the section on the use of quinine (from cinchona or Peruvian bark) in the treatment of the intermittent fever common in malaria, it occurred to him to find out what effect the drug would have on a healthy subject. So he took quinine himself and discovered that its effect was similar to the symptoms it was used to treat. Further experimentation on himself led to the realization that many drugs commonly used to treat specific symptoms actually induced those symptoms when taken by a healthy person. This became his 'law of similars'. Further 'provings', as he called his tests, using increasingly dilute doses of the drugs on both healthy subjects and sick, led to the second principle of homoeopathy, the 'law of potentiation': the effect of a remedy is inversely proportional to its concentration. In other words, whilst large doses of a drug often aggravate the symptoms, decreasing the amount in a dose increases the drug's potency as medicine.

Hahnemann first published his theory of homoeopathy (the term was also his invention) in a paper in 1796, and after many more years of research and experimentation he described the system of homoeopathic treatment fully in his *Organon of the Rational Art of Healing* (*Organon der Rationallen Heilkunst*, 1810).[68] In this he described disease as 'an aberration from the state of health': an illness was not an entity in itself, capable of being removed from the body; it was rather a condition which showed that the body was already fighting against some imbalance and using its natural recuperative powers to regain health. He recognized that killing a germ which was thought to cause a disease was not enough to effect a cure, since the underlying cause was the patient's prior condition which made the body susceptible to that germ.

In the sixteenth century Paracelsus had also held this view: 'All illness is purgatory – a process of purification'; and a century later Thomas Sydenham, the 'father of British medicine', similarly regarded illness as a form of cure, which physicians should learn to understand rather than eliminate: he described disease as 'no more than a vigorous effort of nature to throw off the morbific matter, and thus recover the patient'. Continuing in this tradition, Hahnemann realized that symptoms needed to be interpreted rather than merely removed. When symptoms did disappear, it would be in reverse order of their appearance, and this was part of a third principle of homoeopathy, the 'law of cure', which states that a cure is effected 'from above downwards; from within outwards; from a more important organ to a less important one'.

As in HERBALISM, prognosis is often more important than diagnosis: if the body is already curing itself and this cure manifests itself to us as disease, then the physician should understand the path that the disease is going to take and try to facilitate rather than prevent it. Hence the logic in the use of 'similars', drugs which in a healthy person would induce the very symptoms that are present in the disease. (This type of reasoning is probably more appropriate than the often cited analogy with vaccination, in which a mild dose of a disease is introduced into the healthy body so that it can produce its own antibodies and thus defend itself against any subsequent invasions by more severe strains of that type of disease.)

The fourth principle of homoeopathy is that of the single remedy, the use of 'simples'. Homoeopathic treatment is with one drug at a time, based on only one naturally occurring substance, derived from plants (as in herbalism), minerals or snake venom. The most obvious reason for this is that the more substances the physician prescribes, or the more compounded the substance is, the more likely the patient is to suffer serious side effects. Again, Paracelsus had been one of the first to propound the benefits of treatment with single simple remedies, against the more popular doctrine of 'polypharmacy' – using a witches' brew of many ingredients.

Initially, it was also as a way to reduce the possibility of unwanted side effects that Hahnemann started diluting his drugs. But it is here, in the so-called law of potentiation, that the principles of homoeopathy seem most at odds with conventional logic, for the more a drug is diluted, the stronger its effect on the patient becomes. Another controversial aspect of a drug's preparation is succussion, the rapid shaking of the diluted solution in a precisely calculated way in order, it is claimed, to transfer the 'energy' associated with the substance to the solution.

For the degree of concentration described as potency 1 (decimal), a grain of the substance to be used as the drug is added to a neutral substance (usually alcohol and water) in the ratio 1:9, and the solution is 'succussed'. One part in ten of this solution is therefore the original substance. Potency 2 would be achieved by repeating the process, using the potency 1 solution as the new 'mother tincture'. Each successive dilution, or attenuation, reduces the presence of the original substance in the solution by a factor of ten, so that in potency 6 the drug is present as one part in a million. Centesimal dilutions are prepared by performing each step in the ratio of 1:99. So potency 2 (centesimal) represents one part in 10,000, and potency 6 one part in 1,000,000,000,000. It can be shown that long before an attenuation of potency 30 is reached (a typical prescription), there are no molecules of the original substance left in a given quantity of the remedy. Hence the importance of succussion and the references to energy: Hahnemann believed that the power of a remedy was in its pattern rather than in its substance, akin to the modern theory of morphogenetic fields. But more important to Hahnemann than any theory was the empirical evidence of his own provings, which orthodox science has still not been able to explain.

Until recently, documented evidence of the success of homoeopathy was more anecdotal than scientific. During the cholera pandemic of the 1830s, for example, in the Homoeopathic Hospital in Golden Square, London, only one sixth of the cholera patients died as opposed to an average of over a half in orthodox hospitals. But no one knows what other variables might have been involved. Testing homoeopathic remedies scientifically has always been problematical. Double-blind tests depend on the assumption that with sufficient subjects one can regard them all as equal or average, whilst homoeopathic treatment requires each patient to be treated as a unique case: one cannot look for a universal remedy for the common cold because everyone catches it for different underlying reasons. Furthermore, orthodox medicine now attributes 30 per cent of many cures to the placebo effect (plus the fact that, given time, most patients get better), and so scientists explain away or rather simply ignore the results of homoeopathic treatment.

However, in recent years many tests have been devised which prove conclusively that homoeopathic remedies work, even if we do not know why or how. Dr David Taylor Reilly was a sceptic when he began researching into the effectiveness of homoeopathic remedies at the Glasgow Royal Infirmary. Despite being impressed by nearly two centuries of documentation testifying to the success of homoeopathy, he toed the orthodox line and attributed that success to suggestion. In 1983 he carried out tests with hay fever sufferers: half took a placebo and half took the homoeopathic remedy (based on the pollen which sparked off the reaction) and they all kept diaries. The positive result in favour of homoeopathy was put down to a badly managed test with too few subjects (about thirty). In 1984 Reilly carried out a TRIPLE BLIND test with five times as many patients, and the homoeopathic remedy proved to be 15 per cent more effective than conventional hay fever treatments. Some of the most convincing tests involve animals, where clearly no placebo effect can be at work. In one case a few monthly drops of a remedy in the drinking troughs of half a herd of cattle reduced the mortality rate of the calves to a very small percentage compared with the other half of the herd which was fed and watered in exactly the same way but without the remedy. Rats given a dose of carbon tetrachloride that would normally cause severe liver damage and death can be protected by the prior administration of 15c potency of carbon tetrachloride which does not contain any material strength and therefore when analysed would simply be pure water.[110]

In 1988 Jacques Benveniste published the results of a series of experiments he performed at the French Medical Research Council in Paris (INSERM) and from which he concluded that water possesses 'memory'. He claimed that an antibody solution, repeatedly diluted (as are homoeopathic remedies) until it contained no molecules of the original antibody, still caused white blood cells to respond as if the antibody were present. Benveniste's work has provoked ridicule from much of the scientific establishment, typified by the reaction of the editor of *Nature* who for many years refused to publish any of his claims.

Homoeopathic philosophy also makes useful distinctions between predisposition, both constitutional and hereditary, and causation in disease; and between *exciting* causes, which 'trigger' a disease process, and *maintaining* causes, which prevent cure although they would be insufficient to excite disease. All this makes the diagnostic process extremely complex for the practitioner, who must delve into the past history of the patient at all levels, including character and emotional history. Homoeopathy was the first modern discipline to insist on the unity of mind and body, and in some respects Hahnemann's own method of treatment anticipated psychotherapy. Not only did he pay close attention to physical symptoms, he also listened to whatever patients had to say about their feelings, both physical and psychological. He was probably the first practitioner to treat 'the whole person' in the way that we understand the phrase today.

Some basic principles in homoeopathy

Disease is a disturbance of 'vital force'.
Symptoms are outward signs of the body's attempt to free itself from disease.
The body is self-healing, so the aim of any treatment is to remove obstacles and stimulate the body's own healing power using the minimum intervention.

A symptom may affect a particular organ, but disease is of the whole.
Suppressing symptoms will not cure disease but will drive it inward
    and make it worse.
To achieve cure one must always work with the totality of symptoms –
    physical, emotional and mental; treating an isolated symptom is likely
    to be suppressive.
The nature and order of appearance of symptoms is the best guide to cure.
In a true cure, symptoms will disappear in the reverse order of their
    appearance.

The status of homoeopathy varies greatly from country to country.
In some countries it is barely tolerated, whilst in others (France
and Germany, for example) it is recognized for reimbursement from
health-insurance schemes. In Britain it is unique among alternative
therapies in having some sort of official status within the medical
establishment: there are six NHS homoeopathic hospitals in the
UK.

HOMOEOPUNCTURE Homoeopuncture is a combination of ACU-
PUNCTURE and HOMOEOPATHY, developed particularly in Sri Lanka.
The needle is dipped into the remedy before pricking the skin, thus
dispensing with oral application.

HOOK-UP See TRAGERWORK.

HOPE Many EMOTIONS affect health for good or ill. Hope is a
particular type of positive EXPECTATION which is often regarded
as having a beneficial effect on health. For the terminally ill, the
hope of living long enough to see a particular event seems to
enable people to delay DEATH until after the date they have been
looking forward to.[108] Conversely, loss of hope saps both the will
to live and the physical strength to survive. 'In informal discussions
physicians often describe some of their patients as having "lost the
will to live" or having "given up hope", somehow suggesting that
hope is vital to survival. Yet hope is virtually ignored as a subject
of medical research . . . Unlike denial, which involves a negation of
reality, hope is an active way of coping with threatening situations
by focusing on the positive.'[135]

HOSPICE MOVEMENT See DEATH.

HOSTILITY Of all the EMOTIONS, hostility is the one which is
thought to be the most destructive characteristic in the TYPE A

PERSONALITY. It has been linked with blood pressure reactivity, the severity of coronary artery disease, and death from all natural causes including coronary heart disease.

HUMAN POTENTIAL MOVEMENT With developments in the 1950s in GESTALT THERAPY and HUMANISTIC PSYCHOLOGY there was a marked shift away from the psychoanalytical concern with patients in need of treatment towards therapeutic techniques aimed at facilitating the personal development of clients. Psychologists and psychiatrists had previously concentrated on the study and treatment of the sick; the new practitioners were more concerned with enhancing the psychological well-being of the normal individual. Healing meant not simply making whole what was broken, but making one feel more whole, more fully oneself and more at one with the whole universe. Traditional psychoanalysis wanted merely to iron out problems and produce a well-adjusted individual, and Abraham Maslow noted that this grey image of adjustment was all that most of us had to model ourselves on. 'Every age has had its model, its ideal. All of these have been given up by our culture; the saint, the hero, the gentleman, the knight, the mystic. About all we have left is the well-adjusted man without problems, a very pale and doubtful substitute.'[125]

The new preoccupation with personal GROWTH – becoming everything one could possibly become, fulfilling one's potential as a human being – spawned many new therapies and therapeutic techniques such as BIOENERGETICS, TRANSACTIONAL ANALYSIS and PSYCHOSYNTHESIS. So-called growth centres started springing up, where practitioners of these therapies held workshops. The most famous of these was probably the ESALEN Institute in Big Sur, California. The 1970s saw a proliferation of such centres, and the notion of a human potential movement was born.

The human potential movement and the 'growth' industry it gave rise to inevitably came in for a great deal of criticism. Typical among the critics is R. D. Rosen, who refers to the 'giddy infatuation with self-actualization', the 'extolment of "liberation" in virtually any form', the 'incontinent narcissism' which comes of over-emphasizing ego psychology 'at the expense of a deeper, psychodynamic critique', the 'narcissism engendered by the idea of just "being oneself" '. For Rosen it is a movement full of 'truisms published as striking revelations', in which 'Keeping up with the Joneses has been transformed into a Wholer-than Thou attitude'.[151]

Erich Fromm is equally dismissive of what he calls 'the great shams' which form 'a kind of spiritual smorgasbord program'. He writes, 'With some dishes of the smorgasbord ... there is nothing the matter with the teaching, my only criticism being the atmosphere in which it is taught. In other endeavours the sham lies in the superficiality of the teaching, especially when it pretends to be based on the insight of the great masters. But perhaps the greatest sham is that what is promised – explicitly or implicitly – is a deep change in personality, while what is given is momentary improvement of symptoms or, at best, stimulation of energy and some relaxation. In essence, these methods are means of feeling better and of becoming better adjusted to society without a basic change in character.'[57]

HUMANISTIC PSYCHOLOGY In 1968 Abraham Maslow (1908–70) wrote: 'Psychology today is torn and riven, and may in fact be said to be three (or more) separate, non-communicating sciences or groups of scientists. First is the behaviouristic, objectivistic, mechanistic, positivistic group. Second is the whole cluster of psychologies that originated in Freud and in psychoanalysis. And third there are the humanistic psychologies, or the "Third Force" as this group has been called, a coalescence into a single philosophy of various splinter groups in psychology.'[124] Maslow's change of emphasis did not mean that he discarded the first two schools of psychology: their theories may have been inadequate but some of their techniques were still useful. Nor did he regard Third Force Psychology as the end of the story. As he went on, 'I am Freudian and I am behaviouristic and I am humanistic, and as a matter of fact I am developing what might be called a fourth psychology of transcendence as well.'[124] Maslow was the first to develop a holistic theory of psychology.

Maslow took issue with the majority of earlier psychologists who had based their theories of human nature more on observations of deviants than on healthy individuals. 'If one is preoccupied with the insane, the neurotic, the psychopath, the criminal, the delinquent, the feeble-minded, one's hopes for the human species become perforce more and more modest, more and more "realistic", more and more scaled down, one expects less and less from people ... It becomes more and more clear that the study of the crippled, stunted, immature, and unhealthy specimens can yield only a cripple psychology and a cripple philosophy.'[126] Instead he believed one should investigate the positive aspects of human behaviour: if one understood mental health one might start to understand mental illness, but not vice versa. 'Freud supplied to us the sick half of psychology and we must now fill it out with the healthy half.'[125]

Basic to Maslow's view of psychology is his concept of the HIERARCHY OF NEEDS, the last of which, SELF-ACTUALIZATION, represents a shift from basic life-sustaining needs, 'D-needs' or deficiency needs, to the meta-needs of life-enhancement, 'B-needs' or Being NEEDS. When psychology is concerned more with pathology, the main aim of psychoanalysis is the adjustment and social integration of the individual. In humanistic psychology the emphasis is on dynamic growth towards fulfilment as a human being, and the individual finding that sense of purpose within. Maslow remarked that a cat apparently has no problem in being a cat; yet human beings often seem to find it quite difficult to discover and satisfactorily attain what it means to be fully human. The fundamental aims of humanistic psychology are self-discovery and self-fulfilment.

Critics of humanistic psychology have sometimes accused it of being too concerned with the narcissistic preoccupations of self-discovery without any reference to the society in which the individual lives. But it is worth noting that whilst psychoanalysis has always been concerned with the adjustment of the individual to society, the values of that society are not usually questioned. It is an important tenet of humanistic psychology, however, that the more fulfilled one is as a human being, the more one recognizes oneself as part of the whole human species; being more truly and more fully human is not therefore just an 'ego-trip': it has a positive effect on society itself because one becomes a more responsible member of that society. Nevertheless Maslow used to have to point out to some of his followers that self-actualization was a description and not a prescription: one could only work towards it by being concerned with something beyond oneself.

Another important part of Maslow's view of psychology was the role of values, particularly those he called Being-values or 'B-VALUES', the values that self-actualizers naturally seek. He believed that 'the ultimate disease of our times is valuelessness', a condition that leads to apathy, amorality, anomie, hopelessness, and renders life apparently meaningless.[123] 'The state of being without a system of values is psychopathogenic. Human beings need a philosophy of life, a religion, or a value system, just as they need sunlight, calcium, and love.'[125]

The more psychologically healthy individuals a society includes, the more stable and successful that society will be. Maslow also considered what kinds of human institutions were conducive to psychological health and growth in the individual, referring to them as EUPSYCHIAN. He found that human-oriented (Eupsychian) institutions and growth towards self-actualization in individuals were in SYNERGIC relation to each other, each encouraging and supporting the other.

There are many therapies which have the common aims of self-discovery and self-fulfilment and come under the general heading of humanistic psychology. The term perhaps has a wider reference now than Maslow's original Third Force psychology, although it remains a holistic psychology. The methods used may include BODYWORK – in recognition of the psychosomatic link – and such techniques as GESTALT, CO-COUNSELLING and ENCOUNTER GROUP therapy. Since humanistic psychology also covers what Maslow called the fourth psychology of transcendence and TRANSPERSONAL PSYCHOLOGY, it also includes systems such as PSYCHOSYNTHESIS.

HUMOUR See HAPPINESS, LAUGHTER and EMOTIONS.

HUMOURS For the ancient Greeks and Romans the world was made out of four elements – earth, air, fire and water – which were in themselves combinations of the four essential qualities – coldness, heat, moisture and dryness. These elements had corresponding fluids or humours in the body: black bile, blood, yellow bile and phlegm, and diseases arose from imbalances in these humours.

Qualities	Element	Humour	Temperament
cold/dry	earth	black bile	melancholic
hot/wet	air	blood	sanguine
hot/dry	fire	yellow bile	choleric
cold/wet	water	phlegm	phlegmatic

Hippocrates wrote in *On the Nature of Man*, 'The body of man has in itself blood, phlegm, yellow bile and black bile; these make up the nature of his body, and through these he feels pain or enjoys health. Now he enjoys the most perfect health when these elements are duly proportioned to one another . . . and when they are perfectly mingled. Pain is felt when one of these elements is in defect or excess, or is isolated in the body without being compounded with all the others.' All ancient systems of medicine held similar views in this respect, even though the number of elements and humours varied from one part of the world to another.

In the West, the system was perfected by Galen (c.130–c.201), whose prestige as the principal medical authority lasted for fifteen hundred years. Each organ was ruled by various qualities, elements and humours, and psychological characteristics were also determined by them – hence the four *temperaments*: melancholic, choleric, sanguine and phlegmatic. A characteristically angry person, for example, was thought to have an excess of bile, and a calm one too much phlegm.

Before the time of Galen, the Pythagorean Philolaus had taught that life was maintained by various spirits flowing through the body. They were of three kinds: vegetative or natural spirits, which were present in all living things; vital spirits, which endowed living creatures with the power of movement and were therefore present in all except plant life; and animal spirits, which only human beings possessed ('animal' is here derived from *anima*, meaning 'soul'). Galen inherited this system and explained further that natural spirits were manufactured by the liver, which also made blood from food; the blood washed around the body like a tide delivering the spirits to all parts of the body via the veins. In the heart, which was seen as something like a furnace, the spirits were charged with an extra quality provided by air from the lungs (the bellows fuelling the fire), transforming them into vital spirits. (Plants had no heart and therefore their sap could never contain vital spirits.) The vital spirits in the blood then passed via the arteries to the brain, where in humans the animal spirits produced reason and consciousness.

Galen recognized that a person's emotions and state of health are inextricably linked. He once noticed that a patient he was called to see, a girl suffering from insomnia, listlessness and fatigue, reacted at the casual mention of a particular dance troupe: she became flushed and her pulse rate increased. Galen experimented by announcing on one day that Morphus was performing, and then checking her pulse. Next day he mentioned that Pylades was dancing and again checked the girl's pulse, which this time was quite disturbed. 'Thus I found out,' Galen wrote, 'that the woman was in love with Pylades.'[17]

For Galen, experiences were one of the main causes of disease since they caused the movement (motion) of humours around the heart (hence 'emotion'). He regarded love, anger and grief as particularly dangerous for the heart, a conclusion which is not very different from that of modern research into heart disease and STRESS.

Other ancient systems of medicine have linked heart problems to HAPPINESS.

Although the system of humours is dismissed by modern science, its basic premise is not too far removed from what we now understand to be the unit of action in the nervous system – chemical transmitter molecules: the four humours have been replaced by hundreds of chemical messengers. Even character traits may be defined to a certain extent by these chemicals: 'Different concentrations of these various neurotransmitters in the brain may well determine temperament, mood and the function of the intrinsic healing systems of the brain.'[135]

Some modern doctors have recognized that in their system of the humours the ancients somehow intuited a simplified version of modern biochemistry. 'Hippocrates anticipated the modern concept of imbalance of homeostasis as a cause of illness in his theory of imbalance of the four humours: blood, phlegm, black bile and yellow bile. If we substitute enzymes, endocrines, immunoglobins and neuropeptides for his humours, the simile is virtually exact. In fact we have now come full circle, but have scientifically definable entities, as opposed to mystical designations, to work with.'[230]

HURRY SICKNESS People with coronary artery disease are often characterized by 'time urgency', excessive devotion to work, excessive hostility, denial of fatigue, competitiveness and a hard-driving nature. This whole pattern is referred to as 'Hurry Sickness'. Rosenman and Friedman called these coronary-prone people TYPE A.[52] Hurry sickness pervades the whole life-style of the Type A personality, even invading leisure time: not a single minute of precious time can be wasted – the Type A person must always be engaged in something constructive.

HVT The high velocity thrust is a particular THRUST used in OSTEOPATHY.

HYDROTHERAPY All forms of treatment involving water, whether taken internally or externally, are referred to as hydrotherapy. Hydrotherapy is a significant part of most examples of NATURE CURE such as the KNEIPP CURE.

Since water is essential for all life, it is natural that wells should have been venerated by primitive man. In ancient times people also recognized the health-giving powers of natural spring water, and Roman baths became an integral part of social life. With the decline of the Roman empire such therapeutic bathing fell into disuse, but the eighteenth century saw the rise of many European spa towns (so called after the original Spa, a resort in Belgium) and it again became fashionable to 'take the waters'. This meant both drinking and bathing in the natural spring water, which contained elements such as sodium, potassium, magnesium, calcium, iron, nitrogen and sulphur. It was thought that bathing enabled the minerals present in the water to be absorbed through the skin, but spa water typically contains more gaseous constituents than solid mineral material. Modern proponents of such treatment have considered that it is as free ions rather than as mineral salts that these elements can best be assimilated and utilized by the body. Because of the different constituents in the water of different springs, certain spa towns acquired a reputation for treating specific conditions: e.g. Baden Baden for respiratory and gynaecological problems, Vichy and Marienbad for the digestive system. Therapeutic immersion in spa waters is less fashionable nowadays, but natural spring water is bottled and transported for consumption in ever greater quantities and forms an essential ingredient in a *naturopath*'s diet.

Other types of hydrotherapy exploit the fact that water can easily be used to apply heat (or cold) and pressure to the body. Douches exploit the effects on the body of hot or cold water under pressure and have a further advantage in that a specific part of the body, such as sprained or arthritic joints, can be treated with directional jets and sprays. With any external water treatment the application of heat temporarily draws blood to the surface of the skin, whilst cold water initially drives the blood away from the surface. Alternating the two can have a beneficial effect on circulation: a common pattern of such treatment would be two to three minutes in a bath of hot water followed by half a minute in cold. Short immersions or sprays of cold water alone have an invigorating effect: cold baths and cold wraps may be used to treat colds and fevers. Hot baths on the other hand are enervating, but they increase the efficiency of the sweat glands and with open pores the skin absorbs whatever preparation has been added to the water.

Sweating also enables the body to get rid of waste matter, and this is one of the main benefits of steam treatments. In the Russian bath and the Finnish sauna, profuse sweating is induced by sitting in a room where hot steam is generated (or in a cubicle where it is piped); after about fifteen minutes the bather plunges into cold water (or snow). Steam cabinets are used in the same way. The Turkish bath differs in that perspiration is induced by dry heat rather than steam. The full treatment is usually rounded off with massage and rubbing and scraping the skin to remove all that has been sweated out through the pores.

Cleansing is also an integral aspect of internal forms of hydrotherapy, the main ones being inhalation, colonic irrigation and enemas. Catarrh in the sinuses and throat can be loosened by inhalations of steam, and various herbal extracts such as friar's balsam, lupulin and stromonium (thorn apple) are often added to the water. An enema involves injecting water into the rectum so that when it is evacuated it cleanses the bowel of any residual faecal matter. This is often necessary before abdominal surgery or X-ray investigations of the large intestine, but it is also an important part of many dietary programmes (such as the GERSON DIET), particularly if fasting is involved, since with a change in the usual digestive flow waste may easily get lodged in the folds of the rectum. Colonic irrigation extends the enema cleansing into a much larger area of the colon, so much so that the lactobacillus communis which resides there, and on which we depend for the digestion of cellulose, often gets washed out too, necessitating the addition of goats' milk yoghurt and more fibre to the diet. Colonic irrigation is unsuitable for people with diverticulitis and certain kinds of colitis, but it often forms part of a general therapeutic regime, particularly where dietary changes are involved. It also loomed large in many of the prescriptions recommended by Edgar Cayce in his psychic readings.

HYPERACTIVE Hyperactive children have been redefined by Lawrence LeShan as 'children who aren't school adjusted'. He remarks that administering drugs to such children is reminiscent of the practice of the Jivaro people of South America ('one of the most hostile and aggressive societies ever discovered'), who force-feed children who consistently misbehave with datura, a powerful hallucinogen, in the hope that it will encourage them to mend their ways.[116]

HYPERTONUS See GROUNDING.

HYPNOANALYSIS Hypnoanalysis is a form of HYPNOTHERAPY in which the therapist (or analyst) uses hypnosis to communicate directly with the patient's unconscious and gain access to repressed memories. Freud rejected this bypassing of the patient's conscious mind as too easy, believing that only through conscious recall in PSYCHOANALYSIS could true insight be obtained.

201

HYPNOSIS/HYPNOTISM It was a Scottish surgeon, James Braid, who coined the word 'hypnotism', a shortened version of his earlier coinage, 'neur-hypnotism' (literally 'nerve sleep'), to replace MESMERISM, which had too many associations with an outdated theory. In his book *Neurypnology* (1843) Braid advanced a theory of hypnotism which dispensed with the supposed external influences of 'animal magnetism' involved in mesmerism and proposed a physiological explanation of the phenomenon: *staring fixation*. Staring at an object for a long time induced fatigue in the eyelid muscles which led to more general exhaustion in the nerve centres and then to greater suggestibility. Later Braid moved away from this physiological explanation and adopted a more psychological approach with his concept of *monoideism*: focusing on a single idea, or a single train of thought, could make some people more open to suggestion.

Throughout the history of hypnotism there has been little agreement on what hypnosis actually is: whether it is physiological or behavioural; whether the hypnotic subject is in a trance or manifesting a particular psychological attitude. Hypnosis is often regarded as a separate state of consciousness which is neither sleeping nor waking, but which is characterized by a relaxed, lethargic appearance and the loss of personal initiative – a trance state in which one is highly susceptible to the suggestions of the hypnotist. But there is another view according to which hypnosis is not a different state of consciousness at all but simply a heightened attitude of strong motivation and positive expectation, such that the individual is actually more willing to carry out the suggestions of the hypnotist.

One should not read too much into the apparent similarity between hypnosis and sleep, for the initial instructions by the hypnotist invariably include many suggestions that the subject is feeling drowsy, cannot keep the eyes open, etc. In fact there is evidence for supposing that hypnosis is definitely not a state of consciousness like sleeping or dreaming: when told to behave as if alert or relaxed, hypnotized subjects follow the instruction exactly and the alert or relaxed state is manifested. And during hypnosis there are no delta BRAIN-WAVES, which are characteristic of sleep. But the initial sleep-inducing instructions do have a purpose: for physiological reasons they help hypnotic subjects to believe and put their faith in the hypnotist. Turning the eyes upwards when the lids are already closed makes it impossible to open them again without first bringing the upward gaze down, so the hypnotist's suggestion that one's eyelids are stuck together is a fair reflection of the actual situation. (The eyelids may open very slightly, revealing only the whites of the eyes.)

Essential requirements in successful hypnosis are intensity of attention and absence of counter-suggestion; emotion also helps, as does imagination, but not necessarily the will. Emile Coué said, 'In the conflict between the will and the imagination, the force of the imagination is in direct ratio to the square of the will.' In other words the imagination will always win. In fact the efforts of the will can be seen as counter-productive, giving rise to the law of reversed effect (i.e. the harder you try the more difficult it becomes, as in Alexander's concept of END-GAINING). Ainsley Meares, an Australian psychiatrist, has suggested that hypnosis is an atavistic process, characteristic of a more primitive mind. Before we acquired a brain cortex, he suggests, the mind operated by conditioning and suggestion alone. By overruling the ego in the cortex the hypnotist causes the subject to regress to this primitive state.

It is possible to exaggerate the importance of the hypnotist in all this. Some have suggested that all examples of hypnosis are actually examples of *self-hypnosis*: '. . . hypnosis is achieved by the person himself as opposed to being achieved by the hypnotist. There is only auto- and never hetero-hypnosis. What the person expects to happen – does happen.'[47]

Perhaps more important than the heightened suggestibility is the hypnotized person's capacity for demonstrating many abilities which are not possible in the normal state. Two distinct levels of hypnosis have been identified. The first stage is sometimes called the *lethargic state*; people can be anaesthetized hypnotically in this lethargic state and still carry on a conversation with the dentist or surgeon operating on them. The next stage, which cuts off the intellect, is referred to as the *somnambulist state*.

As well as raising their PAIN threshold, hypnotized subjects can alter skin and body temperature and increase their powers of memory and recall. Skin reactions can be induced as well as suppressed: if told that they are being touched by a stinging nettle or a hot coal, hypnotized subjects show the appropriate physiological response (which may also explain the phenomenon of STIGMATA). People can also divide their awareness under hypnosis: whilst reporting an absence of pain as suggested under hypnosis, when told that part of their consciousness will nevertheless be aware of the pain the 'hidden observer' is able to indicate recognition of pain by raising a finger.[83]

As with the power of SUGGESTION, the ability to affect our own physiology when under hypnosis is exploited in curing many skin conditions: warts, acne, psoriasis, and neurodermatoses are often treated effectively by hypnosis, and even one famous case of icthyosis. In 1950 an anaesthetist attending the unsuccessful skin transplant operation of a boy whose whole body was covered in black warts and horny skin decided to try hypnosis and told the boy while under hypnosis that the warts on his left arm would disappear. After a few days they did. Informing the surgeon of his success, the enterprising anaesthetist, who had not known the full details of the boy's condition, was told that his ichthyosiform erythrodermia was incurable, and subsequent attempts to use hypnosis, although successful, were less than 100 per cent effective. The use of hypnosis, or HYPNOTHERAPY, in the treatment of physical diseases is still relatively unusual, although it is used in combination with VISUALIZATION. On the other hand, a fairly wide range of psychological conditions are treated in this way.

HYPNOTHERAPY The use of hypnosis to treat psychological conditions was recognized and exploited by Josef Breuer, an older colleague of Freud's. He discovered that certain symptoms were the consequence of painful memories and repressed emotions, hidden to normal consciousness, but that if these were verbalized by the patient spontaneously under hypnosis the symptoms would disappear. Breuer's discoveries were absorbed by Freud in his concept of the UNCONSCIOUS, but he rejected the use of hypnosis for therapeutic purposes, considering that it allowed too easy access to the repressed memories and too rapid suppression of the symptoms. The 'cure' was consequently (in Freud's opinion) less permanent, less thorough, and more a result of the patient's desire to satisfy the hypnotist. Instead of using hypnosis to treat his patients, Freud developed PSYCHOANALYSIS.

The pioneer of modern hypnotherapy was Milton H. Erickson (1901–80), who saw no disadvantage in eliminating symptoms quickly and without INSIGHT. The very title of one book about hypnotherapy, *Changing Individuals*,[70] shows how low a priority the patient's insight can be. Originally it was not the aim of an analyst to change people, but to help people understand themselves. This aspect of all kinds of psychotherapy has been attacked by Jeffrey Masson: 'The therapist is no longer a consultant but a people changer who fails if the case fails.'[128]

Nevertheless a wide range of conditions are treated successfully with hypnotherapy. These include phobias, compulsions, obsessions, general anxiety, and habits such as overeating, smoking and drinking alcohol, although in the case of unwanted habits there must also be a strong motivation on the part of the patient to eliminate them. Most hypnotherapists reject the idea of simply inserting a new instruction into the patient's mind, such as 'You will never want to smoke again.' Hypnotherapy should be more concerned not with putting something into the patient's mind but with taking something out, finding the root cause for the compulsion, phobia or obsession and removing the troublesome subconscious memory which is causing problems in the patient's life. For example, treating someone's agoraphobia simply by implanting the suggestion that they will no longer be afraid of open spaces would result in the agoraphobia being replaced by some other 'irrational' fear, since its root cause would remain untouched.[69]

HYPOTHALAMUS The hypothalamus is that part of the brain which controls hunger, thirst, shivering, temperature regulation, blood sugar levels and many EMOTIONS. It also controls the pituitary, the key organ in the endocrine system, responsible for regulating the secretion by other glands of many chemicals which ensure the harmonious functioning of the body's cells and organs. Surgical removal of the hypothalamus or of certain parts of it leads to suppression of the immune system response.

HYPOTONUS See GROUNDING.

HYSTERIA See MASS HYSTERIA and FUNCTIONAL ILLNESS.

IATROGENIC DISEASES/IATROGENESIS In 1975 Ivan Illich could write, 'The disabling impact of professional control over medicine has reached the proportions of an epidemic.' He brought a medical term into lay language, naming this epidemic *iatrogenesis* (from *iatros*, Greek for 'physician', and *genesis*, 'origin'). In *Medical Nemesis: The Expropriation of Health* (republished as *Limits to Medicine*)[91] he draws attention to the fact that there is no direct relationship between medical progress and improvements in health and life expectancy, which are more a consequence of better social conditions (diet, hygiene, etc.) than of the effectiveness of doctors. In fact an increasing number of people are ill as a direct result of the intervention of doctors; their illness is iatrogenic – caused by doctors. These physician-generated conditions result from surgical misadventures, drug reactions, false diagnoses and hospital-acquired infections. They are the result of *clinical* iatrogenesis. Illich showed that at the time he was writing 15 per cent of all hospital admissions were the result of medically induced disease, and 7 per cent resulted in some compensatable injury. This problem has continued to grow since Illich's book was published. One study at Boston University Medical Center found that 36 per cent of patients admitted to the hospital suffered from one or more complications as a side effect of medical care. In 9 per cent of patients the iatrogenic illnesses were serious, and they contributed to the death of 2 per cent of the patients.[220]

Illich identifies three types or three degrees of iatrogenesis: clinical, social and cultural. 'Iatrogenesis is clinical when pain, sickness, and death result from medical care; it is social when health policies reinforce an industrial organization that generates ill-health; it is cultural and symbolic when medically sponsored behaviour and delusions restrict the vital autonomy of people by undermining their competence in growing up, caring for each other, and ageing, or when medical intervention cripples personal responses to pain, disability, impairment, anguish, and death.'[91]

In any society 'oriented towards open-ended enrichment', in Illich's words, 'people come to believe that in health care, as in all other fields of endeavour, technology can be used to change the human condition according to almost any design. Penicillin and DDT, consequently, are viewed as the hors d'oeuvres preceding an era of free lunches. The sickness resulting from each successive course of miracle foods is dealt with by serving still another course of drugs.' Thus *social* iatrogenesis increases everyone's dependence on the medical establishment, generating new needs and the overconsumption of drugs; it lowers our level of tolerance for pain, reduces the validity of self-care, and increases 'hospitalization' of people who were formerly cared for at home; and it mystifies and distorts people's perception of their own bodies in unintelligible jargon. Illich even complains about the preoccupation with preventive medicine in the guise of regular check-ups. 'People are turned into patients without being sick,' he claims. This 'medicalization of prevention . . . tends to transform personal responsibility for my future into my management by some agency', a phenomenon which Illich says is a major symptom of social iatrogenesis. Finally there is what Illich calls 'the death-dance around the terminal patient', in which the patient is even further deprived of autonomy.

All this leads to a situation in society in which people no longer appreciate sickness, pain and death as a natural meaningful part of life. *Cultural* iatrogenesis 'sets in when the medical enterprise saps the will of people to suffer their reality'. Medicine has 'undermined the ability of individuals to face their reality, to express their own values, and to accept inevitable and often irremediable pain and impairment, decline, and death'. This inevitably means that life is greatly diminished, and since the activities of the medical establishment seem to support the belief that pain and suffering are meaningless and encourage the vain hope that they can be conquered if one surrenders oneself to the doctors, the fact that pain and suffering persist actually increases the psychic pain of those who, having been told that they are powerless, see that the doctors are powerless too.

One of the consequences of iatrogenesis which was not yet so apparent when Illich wrote *Medical Nemesis* has been its contribution to the increased demand for ALTERNATIVE MEDICINE. Part of the attraction of alternative medicine is that in some respects it re-empowers the individual: in addition to providing an obvious opportunity for the exercise of choice, most alternative systems of medicine also invite the individual to take some responsibility for self-healing. Patients become clients and healing becomes a cooperative venture. Furthermore most alternative systems tend to regard pain and illness as more meaningful, compared with the warlike stance adopted by conventional medicine: pain and illness belong to the individual again, and they can often be seen as opportunities for personal growth.

ID In psychoanalysis the Id (Latin for 'that') refers to the instinctive impulses of the individual: the drives which appear to be outside the control of the EGO but which nevertheless come from within oneself. The term had been used by Nietzsche but was introduced by Freud, who perhaps preferred the Latin form partly to distinguish it from its main antecedent, Groddeck's notion of the IT.

IDENTIFIED PERSONALITY See AUTONOMOUS V. IDENTIFIED PERSONALITIES.

IDIOPATHIC An illness is described by doctors as idiopathic when it conforms to no recognized pattern; the patient's suffering (*pathos*) is individual (*idio-*) and cannot be treated as an example of a generalized condition. In practice this label is used when doctors are at a loss to know how to treat someone's condition. Alternative therapists would maintain that all patients should be regarded as unique individuals in any case. Ivan Illich has written at length against the tendency of modern medicine to expropriate a person's DISEASE, diminishing the value of the individual's suffering through the objectification and MEDICALIZATION of a personal process.

ILLNESS 'Illness' and 'disease' often seem almost synonymous in everyday use: 'illness' is simply seen as a more general or perhaps a less serious condition than 'disease'. But it is possible to make a useful distinction between the two: a DISEASE is what the doctors diagnose in a patient; the illness is what the patient experiences. Lawrence LeShan's definition of a patient is instructive here: 'A patient is a person with a disease (a dysfunction of processes), an illness (how he feels), and a life-style. All three come together in a pattern before he visits the doctor.' He also notes that 'With the medicalization of . . . society, the physician now has the power to legitimize one's "illness" (the feeling of being sick) by conceding that one actually has a disease. He also has the power to deny this legitimacy.'[116] The implication here is that the uniqueness of the individual's suffering, and hence also the personal reasons for it, tend to be ignored when doctors pay so much attention to the disease, treating it rather than the patient and the illness.

ILLUSION By and large illusions are frowned upon, especially other people's, and it is generally regarded as wrong to sustain people in their illusions. The popular belief is that CONFRONTATION with REALITY is far healthier: we have to 'face up to the facts'. But evidence suggests that illusion can actually lend increased strength to the PLACEBO EFFECT: in cases of serious illness illusion can sometimes allow for HOPE to be maintained, which is healthy. Perhaps too often a medical prognosis appears to give equal significance to facts and implications, overlooking the fact that implications are ambiguous, and apparently underlining the possibility of a negative outcome. These implications, which in many cases will remain unfulfilled, can do much damage by destroying a patient's hope: even though they are often expressed as statistical probabilities (or rather 'improbabilities'), the mind cannot but focus on the possibility, indeed likelihood, of a negative outcome. The usefulness of illusion in such circumstances is that a patient's hope will not be undermined by these negative implications.

IMAGERY/IMAGINATION See VISUALIZATION.

IMMUNITY/IMMUNIZATION We tend to regard immunization as one of the achievements of modern western medicine, but this ignores the fact that similar methods of protecting oneself from infectious diseases were practised long before our 'scientific' approach held sway. It must have been recognized by the earliest civilizations that certain diseases can only be contracted once in a lifetime, and that this initial contact with the disease presumably endowed the patient with subsequent immunity. Inoculation against smallpox, using actual smallpox pus, was practised in China as far back as the eleventh century. By the early eighteenth century British travellers to Constantinople were coming into regular contact with inoculation, to such an extent that Princess Caroline, wife of the future George II, had two of her own daughters inoculated in 1722, at a time when doctors considered the practice to be superstitious nonsense.

Not until 1796 did Edward Jenner bestow scientific respectability on the practice. He had noticed that milkmaids were never as pockmarked as the rest of the community and surmised that their exposure to cowpox might confer immunity to smallpox. He proved his theory by infecting patients with pus from infected cows (*vacca* is Latin for 'cow', hence vaccination), which did in fact render them immune to infection from smallpox.

The more we learn about the immune system, the more evident it becomes that in most situations the protection from disease which we call our immunity is not as black-and-white as might be suggested by concentrating on specific diseases like smallpox, polio and tuberculosis. In general terms it is not a question of whether we are immune or not, but of the degree to which our defences against infection are effective: immunity varies and can be influenced both beneficially and adversely by a range of factors, internal and external. The GERM THEORY is increasingly seen as a gross oversimplification of how and why people succumb to DISEASE, and as medical researchers learn more about how the human organism resists ever-present germs, they are looking more into what makes it drop its natural defences.

A prime candidate for chief culprit in this scenario has been

STRESS, and since the 1960s it has been possible to calculate, albeit rather informally and unscientifically, the risk of succumbing to serious illness according to a tally of LIFE CHANGE UNITS. Now that immunity can actually be measured scientifically some of these ideas are receiving confirmation: Stephen Schliefer at Mount Sinai in New York found that two months after being bereaved widowers had depressed immunity as compared with their immune response just before bereavement. It has also been shown that death from tuberculosis and pneumonia is more likely to occur in people who have recently experienced divorce or separation from their spouse.

None of this would come as a surprise to anyone brought up in any traditional system of medicine in which disease was attributed to disharmony brought about by an imbalance in the HUMOURS. A practitioner of traditional ACUPUNCTURE should also be skilled in recognizing imbalance before it manifests as physical illness, so that countermeasures can be taken. (It was for this reason that Chinese physicians were traditionally paid only so long as the 'patient' was in good health; payment ceased whenever illness intervened.) Researchers are now discovering that the EMOTIONS affect the immune system. For example, one of the best predictors of diminished effectiveness of the immune response is loneliness. The physiological link between emotions and the immune system is the HYPOTHALAMUS and hormones. Although there are many more hormones than there were humours and the chain of physiological events is much more complex than that suggested by the notion of mere 'imbalance', the similarity between ancient and modern medical theories in this area is still quite striking. The hypothalamus, as well as being concerned with the emotions, regulates the release of hormones from the pituitary gland, which in turn controls the activity of the other glands in the endocrine system, including the thymus, which produces T-cells (T-lymphocytes), the key agents in the immune system. So we have the following sequence: emotions, hypothalamus, pituitary gland, hormone secretion, thymus, T-cell production, immune response.

Although the PSYCHOSOMATIC element in health is far from being fully understood, it is now undeniable that the mind, presumably as with the emotions via the hypothalamus, can affect the immune system, as experiments with HYPNOSIS have shown. And the power of SUGGESTION is a significant factor in the principles of SELF-HEALING. This area of medicine is now referred to as PSYCHOIMMUNITY.

IMPLOSIVE LAYER In GESTALT THERAPY the implosive layer is the layer of the personality which lies above the so-called impasse that separates it from the lower phoney and phobic layers. Only by conquering the despair of the impasse can one reach the implosive layer, and thence move on to the final explosive or life layer.

INCONGRUENCE/INCONGRUENT PERSONALITY Carl Rogers writes, 'One of the things which offends us about radio and television commercials is that it is often perfectly evident from the tone of voice that the announcer is "putting on", playing a role, saying something he doesn't feel. This is an example of incongruence.'[149] Rogers rated CONGRUENCE or genuineness as a high priority, even a prerequisite, in a therapist.

INDIVIDUATION In Jungian psychology individuation is the process by which one gradually becomes more aware of oneself as an individual – unique and whole. Jung said, 'I use the term "individuation" to denote the process by which a person becomes a psychological "in-dividual", that is, a separate, indivisible unity or "whole".'[97] It is more noticeably the concern of the second half of life. The individuated person (or more accurately, the individuating person, since the process is never complete) has greater awareness of SELF – self-realization – healing the rift between the conscious and the unconscious. 'Conscious and unconscious do not make a whole when one of them is suppressed and injured by the other.'[97] Jung described individuation as 'an expression of that biological process – simple or complicated as the case may be – by which every living thing becomes what it is destined to become from the very beginning'. This is not the same as individualism: being individualistic implies the arrogant assertion of the EGO – being too ego-centred. In the individuation process the ego encounters the Self and recognizes its relationship with the Self without ever being wholly identified with it, although the process will probably be punctuated with occasional experiences of INFLATION, perhaps alternating with ALIENATION – examples of situations in which the ego's relationship with the Self goes awry.

The individuation process is often described as a journey, and it is represented as such in many myths. One encounters and has to deal with many ARCHETYPES along the way, assimilating the SHADOW, for example, and following a script which is written and directed by the Self, for the goal throughout life is manifestation of the Self and the realization of one's full humanity. As Anthony Stevens writes, 'The great paradox of the whole process is that in realizing one's full humanity one is, at the same time, actualizing one's unique individuality. To individuate in the full Jungian meaning of the term, is to defy the tyranny of received opinion, to disengage from the banal symbols of mass culture and to confront the primordial symbols in the collective unconscious – in one's own unique way. Only thus does one become in-dividual, a separate, indivisible unity or "whole".'163

INFERTILITY See FERTILITY.

INFLATION Inflation is the term used by Jungian analysts to refer to the attitude which accompanies identification of the EGO with the SELF or with a powerful ARCHETYPE from the collective unconscious. The small ego arrogates to itself qualities of the much larger Self, thus becoming 'inflated', and is deluded into thinking itself all-powerful, all-knowing and all-wise. In Greek tragedy hubris was the supreme example of inflation. Our image of God is a reflection of the Self, and the inflation resulting from ego-Self identity can manifest as a Messiah complex. But it would be wrong to associate inflation only with Greek heroes and crazed individuals who set up cults, for we all go through the condition periodically to a greater or lesser degree in the process of INDIVIDUATION.

'We are born in a state of inflation. In earliest infancy, no ego or consciousness exists. All is in the unconscious. The latent ego is in complete identification with the Self. The Self is born, but the ego is made; and in the beginning all is Self.'35 The child experiences itself as the centre of the universe. Childish irresponsibility in an adult can be an indication of inflation.

In mythology the primeval state of oneness with the Self is reflected in the Garden of Eden scenario, before the birth of the ego and consciousness, represented by the Fall. When the ego is born it feels itself alienated from the world around it – driven out from the Garden of Eden. Inflation and ALIENATION may alternate while the ego finds a meaningful relationship with the Self.

INHALATION See BREATHING, PRANAYAMA and HYDROTHERAPY.

INNER CHILD The Child is one of the three ego states in TRANS-ACTIONAL ANALYSIS (also referred to as 'archaeopsychic' or 'regressive'). In REPARENTING, people revert to behaving as if they were children as part of the treatment for any condition which is seen as having its roots in a lack of adequate parental nurturing during childhood. Ever since Freud decided that our psychology is conditioned to the extent of becoming virtually fixed by our experiences as a child, most forms of PSYCHOTHERAPY spend a great deal of time digging up childhood memories and 'dealing with them', which usually involves some kind of cathartic ABREACTION. Mainstream psychiatry has seized on this 'repressed memory therapy', uncovering stories not just of parental neglect but of childhood abuse. To some extent this has resulted in a backlash in the 1990s, many wishing they could recover the relative peace of mind that their instinctive forgetfulness had enabled them to achieve until the therapists started probing.

James Hillman criticizes the current preoccupation with what therapy calls the inner child for other reasons. He sees it as disempowering: 'By emphasizing the child archetype, by making our therapeutic hour rituals of evoking childhood and reconstructing childhood, we're blocking ourselves from political life ... So *of course* our politics are in disarray and nobody's voting – we're disempowering ourselves through therapy.'[84]

INOCULATION See IMMUNITY.

INSIGHT In early German psychiatry, the term *Krankheitseinsicht*, which came to be translated as 'insight', was used to refer to the patient's recognition of his or her own illness. A patient was considered to have improved as soon as he, or more often she, said, 'I am sick' – just as prisoners who admit their guilt are more likely to get remission of their sentences. In other words, a patient's progress and cure was conditional on acceptance of society's definition of illness. As Jeffrey Masson has pointed out, 'What the German nineteenth-century physician defined as "sick" would probably today be called "independent". "MORAL INSANITY" was the term most often applied to a young woman who did not accept her subordinate role in society. The same criteria are at work in today's psychiatric institutions, where a patient cannot be released until willing to admit that the reason for being there is a good one.'[128] This is a view shared by others, such as R. D. Laing and supporters of the ANTIPSYCHIATRY movement.

INSOMNIA In a lecture in 1920 Rudolf Steiner predicted an epidemic of insomnia in the second half of the twentieth century. Insomnia, he maintained, derives from fear of and denial of the world of the spirit. In deep sleep the ego and astral body are said to withdraw from the physical/etheric complex, and by avoiding sleep the insomniac attempts to prevent recognition of the reality of the spirit world.

INTENTION/INTENTIONALITY The idea that we do things with intent was relegated to the status of an illusion by BEHAV-IOURISTS. Intentionality is an aspect of minds, not brains and reflexes, and both common sense and introspection suggest that we 'make our minds up' and choose our intentions freely. But the extent to which we have conscious control over our intentions was put in doubt by Freud with his analysis of mistakes and slips of the tongue. In Groddeck's view the IT seems to have priority over any intentions we might think we have, deciding for example when we fall ill and what 'accidents' befall us. Jung was also of the opinion that whatever we did not face in our psyche would confront us somehow in the external world; for him it was the SELF that took charge. Despite all this the practical effects of AUTOSUGGESTION, AUTOGENIC THERAPY, SILVA MIND CONTROL and even POSITIVE THINKING and AFFIRMATIONS suggest that we do have consider-able control over our intentions, and BIOFEEDBACK research has revealed mental powers over the body which had previously only been associated with YOGA.

INTERFERENTIAL THERAPY (sometimes mistakenly referred to as 'inferential' therapy) Interferential therapy is a form of ELECTROTHERAPY in which two separate currents of slightly differ-ent medium frequencies are applied to the body through electrodes, such that where they 'interfere' with each other a very low frequency rhythm is produced. This is said to control pain and to improve circulation of both blood and lymph, in addition to the usual effects of electrotherapy – the toning and exercising of damaged muscles. The direct application of a current of such low frequency would meet with such skin resistance that the intensity would have to be increased greatly for the effects to be felt by the underlying tissues; the interferential method overcomes this problem.

INTERPERSONAL APPROACH In classical PSYCHOANALYSIS the analyst is someone who observes, analyses and gives the patient 'interpretations'. An interpersonal analyst participates more in the relationship. One way in which this might be demonstrated is in their attitude to TRANSFERENCE: instead of assuming that a patient's anger is directed at someone from the patient's childhood rather than at the analyst, the interpersonal analyst will try to understand to what extent the patient's perception of such feelings might be accurate. Interpersonal psychoanalysis also acknowledges that the patient is not as passive as classical Freudians would maintain: character is not so fixed, not determined solely by childhood experiences, and development is affected by interaction with others.

INTROJECTION When someone important to us voices opinions, judgments or criticism, we may introject those opinions, embrace them as our own, and accept the person's PROJECTIONS onto us as true. If a parent projects feelings of inferiority onto a child, criticizing it as worthless, the child may introject these criticisms and come to believe them. Positive feelings may also be introjected, resulting sometimes in individuals having great difficulty later in life in living up to their own expectations of themselves.

INTROSPECTION Introspection was banned by the BEHAVIOURISTS and mistrusted by the Freudians, but out of Jung's own introspective analysis of himself he developed a deep understanding of the human psyche and a whole system of analytical psychology. Introspection is essential to all branches of HUMANISTIC PSYCHOLOGY. Only through introspection can one discover and deal with one's SUBPERSONALITIES, for example, and most forms of DREAMWORK are introspection par excellence. It is because of introspective elements that humanistic psychology has sometimes been criticized for being too narcissistic, the ultimate 'ego-trip', but understanding how one's own psyche works can lead to greater understanding of others and of how to deal with the world. Nevertheless there is a danger that the real world can get forgotten in the fascination with one's own inner life; hence the importance of GROUNDING after any session involving fantasy and imagination.

INTROVERT The difference in attitude to life shown by the extravert and the introvert is probably the most well-known aspect of Jung's theory of PSYCHOLOGICAL TYPES. The introvert typically lacks confidence with other people and tends to be unsociable, being clumsy in social situations, feeling lost in large gatherings and preferring reflection to activity. Introverted people do not respect conventionality as much as extraverts do, valuing their own judgment above the generally accepted opinion. Their qualities are more apparent to their own small group of intimate friends than to the world at large and they tend to be loyal and sympathetic. The tendency for extraverts to need to impress others seems a waste of time to the introvert, but the extravert is the one who usually 'gets on' in life.

INTUITION Intuition is one of the four EGO FUNCTIONS in Jungian psychology, the other three being thinking, feeling and sensation. Jung regarded these as the four basic ways in which we can know something, each of us tending to favour one over all the others, an idea which is central to his theory of PSYCHOLOGICAL TYPES.

In BICAMERAL BRAIN theory intuition is associated with the right hemisphere of the brain, the area which also controls spatial perception and our understanding of global concepts. The fact that language and logic seem to be manipulated primarily by the left hemisphere has been seen as explaining why intuitive notions are sometimes difficult to express and explain.

IONIZATION THERAPY Most people would agree that mountain air, sea breezes, fountains and waterfalls have a positive effect on our mood and sense of well-being. This is thought to be a result of the negatively charged ions in the atmosphere, contrasting with the positively charged ions in stuffy atmospheres, city fogs, the atmospheric conditions before a storm, and certain hot winds such as the foehn in central Europe and many other 'winds of ill repute' which seem to induce irritability and headaches. Air ionization therapy involves producing negatively charged air particles artificially for the benefit of people breathing the air.

The Greek word *ion* means 'going', and was first applied by Michael Faraday in about 1834 to the part of a molecule that passed from one electrode to another in electrolysis. An ion is an atom or group of atoms which has lost or gained one or more of its electrons, thus giving it a positive or negative charge. Electrons themselves have a negative charge, so ions with surplus electrons are negative, and those that have lost electrons are positive, attracting other atoms to them. When a positive ion meets a neutral ion it produces a negative ion. Electrons are knocked off atoms and transferred to and fro in situations where friction occurs, caused typically by (fresh) wind, breaking waves or falling water. (Ionization is also caused by radiation, and the ionosphere is that part of the atmosphere in which gas atoms and molecules are stripped of their outer electrons by short-wave [ultra-violet] radiation from the sun.)

It is the negative ions in the air that seems to be therapeutic. It has been shown that they stimulate plant growth, whilst inhibiting or even destroying the growth of bacteria and fungi. In animals the main effect seems to be to stimulate glandular activity, e.g. increasing brain serotonin, a neurotransmitter associated with relaxed moods. Rats raised in a negatively ionized atmosphere developed a cerebral cortex 9 per cent larger than those in non-ionized atmospheres.

Air stripped of negative ions has the reverse effect, causing plants to wilt and die, and increasing the rate of death among humans from bacterial pneumonia and influenza; people who breathe such air over a long period suffer a loss of mental and physical efficiency. Although the physiological effects of breathing negative ions is not fully understood, it is known that ions are present in plant and animal cells and play an important part in a variety of processes such as muscle contraction, nerve impulse conduction and the activation of enzymes.

Much activity in modern life is carried out in air that has been depleted of negative ions: polluted city air, air that is circulated through air conditioning systems, and the air in environments containing a great deal of electronic equipment (e.g. VDU screens) and artificial fibres (e.g. in office carpets, which are often observed to create a lot of static electricity). It was in such environments that the first artificial 'ionizers' (air-ion generators) were used in the 1950s, but it was not until the 1970s that documented evidence of the beneficial effects of such gadgets was published. Some office workers even refused to participate in one such controlled study because it would have involved half of them having to work with their ionizers switched off.[221] A surfeit of positive ions in the atmosphere may be one of the key factors in the phenomenon of SICK BUILDING SYNDROME.

Although many people notice no difference at all when breathing air treated by ionizers, others insist that they feel better generally and those who suffer from certain conditions such as migraine, hay fever and asthma are likely to report an alleviation of their symptoms. Trials carried out by the Human Biology and Health Department of the University of Surrey suggested that mental alertness and efficiency are also affected by ions in the atmosphere. In experiments with a battery of standard tests, people's performance naturally fluctuated during the day, rising in the morning and falling in the evening; in a positively charged atmosphere the decline set in earlier and was more pronounced, whereas in a negatively charged atmosphere the standard of performance was maintained throughout the day.

IONS See IONIZATION THERAPY.

IONTOPHORESIS See GALVANISM.

IRIDOLOGY/IRIS DIAGNOSIS Iridology is not a therapy in itself but a diagnostic tool used by certain NATUROPATHS and practitioners of other therapies such as HERBALISM, HOMOEOPATHY and ACUPUNCTURE. It is the technique of diagnosing a person's state of health, both physical and mental, by studying the appearance of the iris. The theory behind this is that it is in the eyes that the nervous system 'comes to the surface'. Iridologists believe that the nerve filaments of the iris are linked to every organ in the body (for which there is as yet no anatomical evidence), and therefore receive impressions from the whole nervous system: not only is the individual's present condition revealed in the iris but also past conditions and future tendencies.

Although markings in the eyes have been referred to by physicians down the ages and were mentioned by Hippocrates, the modern theory of iridology was first propounded by two people independently of each other in the nineteenth century: a Hungarian surgeon, Ignatz von Peczely, and a Swedish homoeopath, Nils Liljequist. The modern map of iris zones also owes much to the early iridologist Pastor Felks (1856–1926) and more recently to Bernard Jensen in America. Dr Jensen's map divides the iris both radially into segments and into circular zones around the centre, so that there are ninety-six areas, each relating to a particular organ or physiological function. The right eye relates to the right side of the body and the left eye to the left side.

In diagnosis 'attention is given to the purity and brightness of the colouring. In a state of good health, the colours are bright and clear; in ill health, or a toxic condition, the colours are defiled and dull.'[96] As well as changes in colour there may be white or black marks such as dots, rings or radiating lines. In general white marks indicate inflammation and overstimulation and sometimes accompany the healing process, whilst darker markings relate to reduced function and understimulation.

IRLEN LENSES/IRLEN SYNDROME While Helen Irlen was working as director of an educational learning disability programme in Long Beach, California, and investigating the reading difficulties of adults who were highly motivated and of above average intelligence, she discovered that the apparent movement of the print on the page that they complained about was often eliminated by covering the page with a sheet of coloured plastic. Different people found different coloured overlays most helpful in stopping the distortions. The implication is that some people are hypersensitive to specific wavelengths of light and that this sensitivity causes sight problems that are most acute when looking at patterns with a high degree of contrast – e.g. print on paper. Using overlays or tinted lenses to exclude just the wavelengths to which one is sensitive overcomes the problem. Treatment has focused largely on children, who are often wrongly (in Helen Irlen's opinion) diagnosed as suffering from dyslexia. She estimates that in the UK between 12 and 15 per cent of children are affected by the condition.[229] If this is so, one is prompted to wonder whether such a large proportion have always been so affected or whether it is a relatively new phenomenon. If the latter, what are the possible causes? A lack of sunlight? (See LIGHT THERAPY.) An increase in the use of artificial lighting, or in television and computer screens? (See BIOELECTROMAGNETICS.)

ISCADOR Iscador is a remedy used in ANTHROPOSOPHICAL MEDI-CINE, derived from mistletoe. Mistletoe grows parasitically, drawing all its nutrients from the host tree, and is therefore regarded as uniquely independent of terrestrial and cosmic influences. Because of this, as a remedy it strengthens the patient's sense of individuality and independence and is often used in conjunction with treatments for cancer (although it is not in itself a remedy for cancer). Its effect seems to be to initiate an immunological response by 'reminding the body who its enemies are', as an anthroposophist has expressed it, and its use has been accompanied by an increase in lymphocytes.[23]

IT In *The Book of the It*,[67] described by Lawrence Durrell as 'that neglected masterpiece', the maverick German psychoanalyst Georg Groddeck (1866–1934) refers to the unconscious – 'the sum total of an individual human being, physical, mental and spiritual, the organism with all its forces' – as the 'It' (*das Es* in German). 'The universe which is man, I conceive of as a self unknown and forever unknowable, and I call this the "It" as the most indefinite term available without either emotional or intellectual associations.' Both the body and the mind are creations of this It. For Groddeck the It is far more important than the EGO; it is the real personality, whilst the ego is simply 'a mask devised by the It to hide itself from the curiosity of mankind'. 'The It animates the man; it is the power which makes him act, think, grow, become sick or sound, the power, in brief, which animates him.' Groddeck does not claim that the It actually exists; it is merely a way of seeing, a convenient rule-of-thumb method for attacking the real under its many masks.

According to Groddeck, 'Health and sickness are among the It's forms of expression.' 'Disease is a vital expression of the human organism.' 'Man creates his own illnesses for a definite purpose.' Groddeck regards illness as basically an escape mechanism, a means of avoiding reality without feeling guilty by reverting to a kind of childhood. This 'flight into illness' enables an individual to put off dealing with inner conflicts, often by repressing them to such an extent that they never become conscious.

Like Freud's unconscious, the It can use symptoms of illness to indicate – often by means of linguistic associations – what the real problem might be. One's attitude to a person one finds particularly objectionable might be the root cause of a pain in the neck; one type of back pain (when on one's feet) might indicate a situation in which there is someone or something that one simply can't stand, whilst another type of back pain (whilst lying down) might indicate a sense of being under attack and a refusal to take such behaviour lying down.

As well as having a profound influence on Freud's notion of the ID and on the methods of REICHIAN THERAPY, Groddeck is often regarded as the father of PSYCHOSOMATIC medicine.

JIN SHIN/JIN SHIN DO Jin Shin is a form of ACUPRESSURE, which uses a pattern of gently held acupoints on selected meridians to balance the body's energy system. Fewer points are used than in SHIATSU, but they are held for much longer – anything from one to five minutes. During treatment the patient is encouraged to adopt a meditative state to facilitate the balancing of energies.

JING (Formerly spelt 'ching') In traditional Chinese medicine, *jing* is the essence inherited from parents, which determines our basic constitution and our ability to grow and develop.

JING MU *Jing mu* is the principle in traditional Chinese medicine by which the qualities of an animal are imparted to a person who ingests part of it. For example, it is believed that eating the powdered bones of a tiger gives strength and that a tiger's penis increases virility.

JUNGIAN PSYCHOLOGY See EGO, SELF, SHADOW, PERSONA, ANImUS/ANIMA, ARCHETYPE, INDIVIDUATION, EGO FUNCTIONS, EXTRAVERT/INTROVERT, TRANSCENDENT FUNCTION, UNCONSCIOUS, ANAGOGIC INTERPRETATION, ANALYTICAL PSYCHOLOGY, DREAMS, ENANTIODROMIA, METANOIA.

KAPHA One of the three humours (*doshas*) in AYURVEDIC MEDICINE, translated as mucus or phlegm and associated with the element of water.

KARATE See MARTIAL ARTS.

KI *Ki* is the Japanese equivalent of the Chinese *Qi* or CH'I.

KINAESTHESIA Kinaesthesia (from the Greek for 'to move' and 'sensation') is the sense we have of the movement of our own body. The word was used by Alexander in the expression 'debauched kinaesthesia' to refer to our unreliable feelings and faulty sensory awareness of the body. He taught that habit and perception shape each other in such a way that an act that is familiar, no matter how great the misuse involved, is likely to feel right, whereas an unfamiliar act is likely to feel wrong even if the use is good. This is why the movements taught by the ALEXANDER TECHNIQUE, which is a way of re-educating people both in the use of their bodies and ultimately in their kinaesthetic sense, will at first seem unnatural and uncomfortable.

KINE In his *Introduction to Kinesics* in 1952, Ray Birdwhistell introduced the term 'kine' to refer to the smallest measurement of BODY LANGUAGE, such as a wink or a shoulder shrug. He also developed a notational system of symbols or hieroglyphs for recording such body movements.[15]

KINESICS Kinesics is the study of BODY LANGUAGE, non-verbal communication through behavioural patterns which include gestures, facial expression, posture and movement. (See also PROXEMICS.)

KINESIOLOGY Kinesiology (from the Greek for 'to move') means the study of human movement, relating anatomy and mechanics. In this sense all MANIPULATIVE and POSTURAL THERAPIES are based on kinesiology, but the word is more often used in the sense of APPLIED KINESIOLOGY, also sometimes called 'touch for health'. In this therapy touch is used less for its physical effect than as a means of transmitting or arousing healing forces in the manner of ACUPUNCTURE or SHIATSU.

KIRLIAN DIAGNOSIS/KIRLIAN PHOTOGRAPHY There have been many claims and counter-claims surrounding the form of electro-photography known as Kirlian photography, named after its inventors, Semyon and Valentina Kirlian. The method used nowadays, in which the object to be photographed is placed directly on sensitised paper which in turn is in contact with a negative electrode, is a gross simplification of the technique used by the Kirlians in the 1930s. This increases the potential influence of variables such as atmospheric composition, humidity and pressure, making the photographs extremely difficult to interpret. When photographed in this way inanimate objects also display a 'corona discharge', so it would seem doubtful that the presence of this alone represents evidence of a SUBTLE ENERGY or LIFE-FORCE permeating and surrounding the body.

However, when studying the corona of the same piece of living tissue (or organic matter) under different conditions one can see variations which suggest that the condition of the organism is somehow reflected in the electromagnetic field which surrounds it. There is not only a marked difference between the corona around a leaf taken from a healthy plant and that of one taken from a diseased plant, but the corona of a leaf also changes as that leaf dies and decays. Perhaps most intriguingly, when seeds or bread are simply touched by a healer the corona around them becomes much more energetic, suggesting that electromagnetic energy can perhaps be transferred from one person to another. Something similar may be happening when the coronas around the fingers of a married couple photographed on the same plate seem to merge, whilst those of strangers appear to repel each other.

It is known that ACUPUNCTURE points coincide with points of

low electrical skin resistance, and when photographed with Kirlian photography they have been shown to change both in disease and following acupuncture treatment.[217] This suggests that it could be the acupuncture points and MERIDIANS that determine the significant changes in the electromagnetic field around people and animals as revealed in Kirlian photographs. Traditional Chinese medicine maintains that any imbalance in the so-called ENERGY BODY is present and detectable before disease actually manifests in the physical body. This fits in neatly with the use of Kirlian photographs as a diagnostic tool and with such claims that with them one can detect the onset of cancerous growths. However, they do not show whether the cancer is likely to progress or simply wither away, and the anxiety caused by such information at such an early stage may even exacerbate the problem.

Not only does the corona around the hand change according to one's state of health, but it also reflects changes in mood and mental activity. After just fifteen minutes of yoga exercises the corona is stronger and more complete, whilst no such effects are produced by standard gymnastic exercises. States of RELAXATION induced by HYPNOSIS, MEDITATION and acupuncture seem to produce wider and more brilliant coronas. Comparable changes in coronas have been reported after a PSYCHOTHERAPY session in which the individual was made more self-confident and aware of their creative strengths. Equally, more clearly defined breaks in a corona could suggest new problems that are being brought to consciousness and need dealing with. It has been suggested that Kirlian photography can be used to keep a check on the progress of people in psychotherapy, a claim that has also been made for PALMISTRY.

KNEIPP CURE Father Sebastian Kneipp (1821–97), a dominican priest from Wörishofen in Bavaria, became famous throughout Europe for his invigorating regime of ice-cold plunges, physical exercise, herbal teas, sunshine and fresh air. He discovered the efficacy of this therapy or 'NATURE CURE' by restoring and improving his own health when suffering from a serious lung condition which was then considered fatal. Against the advice of his doctors, who recommended avoiding sunlight and staying in bed, he took daily ice-cold baths followed by physical exercise, such as walking barefoot through snow, on wet grass or in a cold stream. Exercise in the intense cold of the ice or water causes blood to flow to the limbs which both warms the limbs and improves circulation. Kneipp maintained that the purpose of HYDROTHERAPY was threefold: 'to dissolve the germs of diseased matter contained in the blood; to remove the diseased matter from the system; to restore the purified blood to its proper circulation; to strengthen the weakened constitution and render it fit for renewed exertion.' The Kneipp cure attracted 20,000 patients annually to the village of Wörishofen during Father Kneipp's lifetime and is still practised in Germany, Austria and Switzerland.

KUNG FU See MARTIAL ARTS.

KYPHI The ancient Egyptians used a mixture of AROMATIC OILS known as *kyphi*. Used in the form of solid incense, it was burned at sunset as an offering to Ra: as the smoke rose heavenwards, so did the prayers to Ra. Our word 'perfume' – from the Latin *per fumum*, meaning 'through smoke' – probably has its origin in a comparable practice. The fumes may also have had a soporific and narcotic effect. The Greek historian, Plutarch, wrote of kyphi that 'Its aromatic substances lull to sleep, allay anxieties, and brighten dreams.'

KYPHOTIC The round-shouldered, hunched posture common to many people who spend much of their working lives sitting at a desk is known as kyphotic (from the Greek *kuphosis*, meaning humpback). Much of the ALEXANDER TECHNIQUE is devoted to rectifying this condition, which commonly results from a dropping forward of the middle of the neck and a pulling back of the head, resulting in tension of the muscles which go up into the back of the skull. In BIOENERGETICS a variation of this condition has been called the 'dowager's' or 'widow's hump' – 'produced by the pileup of blocked anger'[119] at just that point in the body where anger is shown in animals by raising the hackles and erecting the hair along the spine. 'Its occurrence in older women,' writes Alexander Lowen, 'indicates that it represents the gradual piling up of unexpressed anger as a result of a lifetime's frustration ... I should make it clear that what is blocked is the physical expression of anger in hitting, not its verbal expression. Some dowagers or widows are noted for their sharp tongues.'[119]

L-FIELD See LIFE-FIELD.

LABELLING THEORY Labels tend to be self-perpetuating. In an experiment led by David Rosenhan of Stanford University, eight people pretended that they had been hearing voices and reported to a mental hospital describing their 'condition'. Diagnosed as schizophrenic they were admitted to hospital, whereupon they behaved perfectly normally, giving accurate accounts of their lives to the medical staff. They were 'treated' for between seven and fifty-two days and in no case was the original diagnosis revised. Rosenhan concluded that once they had been 'labelled' as schizophrenic, all subsequent behaviour was seen to support that classification. Thomas Szasz refers to this as the *social reaction theory*, and it has been incorporated and extended in R. D. Laing's ANTIPSYCHIATRY.

LATERAL THINKING Edward de Bono, inventor, researcher and founder-director of the Institute for Cognitive Studies in Cambridge, first published his ideas on thinking as a creative skill in 1967 in *The Use of Lateral Thinking*. He suggested that thinking is not related to knowledge and IQ, and that logic as a characteristic of 'vertical thinking' is restrictive where creative thinking is concerned. He coined the term 'lateral thinking' to refer to the technique of thinking about problems from different angles and exploring alternatives, instead of making instant judgments and using logic to back them up. Vertical thinking and tunnel vision go hand in hand. Lateral thinking involves being open to possibilities and finding (or creating) unexpected connections. It resembles both insight and humour, but differs from them according to de Bono in that thinking can be taught. His suggestion that children should be taught how to think was thought preposterous when he first made it, but thinking now has a place on the curriculum in many schools. It has been found that children with low IQs can be excellent problem-solvers using lateral thinking.

One of the techniques of lateral thinking is to tackle a problem by taking a word at random and trying to find connections or relationships between the problem and the word. While working on these connections, which can be quite absurd, the thinker often achieves unexpected insight which helps to solve the problem. The knack lies in finding a method that will enable the ideas to flow.

There is an interesting parallel between the way we tend to use the mind and the way we tend to use (or misuse) the body. Much of the restrictive effect of logic and vertical thinking is the result of habit, as are the common problems associated with bad posture. Edward de Bono's courses on thinking are a kind of ALEXANDER TECHNIQUE for the mind.

LAUGHTER Laughter as defined by eminent psychologists and philosophers such as Freud, Kant and Herbert Spencer is essentially a means of discharging surplus tension or mental excitation. There are many different types of laughter, each with a specific effect. As we know that laughter is linked to feeling good, it seems that laughter must serve some deep therapeutic purpose.

In monkeys something approaching laughter is a display of aggression, and in humans too derisive laughter can be aggressive, especially when one group laughs at another. Some anthropologists on the other hand suggest that laughter is close to tears (hysterical laughter can, after all, turn to tears) and believe that it is induced by surprise or shock which is not really threatening. When we laugh, we may perform up to twelve separate gestures, fifteen facial muscles contract, and many physiological changes take place: breathing deepens and quickens, blood pressure is reduced, blood vessels close to the skin expand and improve circulation (an effect sometimes noticed as blushing), making us feel warmer. A further effect of all this (perhaps significant to the therapeutic benefits of laughter) is an increase in the level of oxygen in the blood, which helps natural healing and resistance to infection; and the production and release of pain-killing endorphins is stimulated.

Norman Cousins became famous for curing himself of an 'incurable' illness. In 1964 he contracted ankylosing spondylitis, a crippling and extremely painful disease in which the spine becomes increasingly immobile. He felt that being in hospital seemed to exacerbate his condition rather than improve it, so since the medical authorities said there was nothing they could do to cure him anyway, he decided to take charge of his treatment himself. He left the hospital, took a room in a hotel (no doubt already cheered by the financial saving) and hired as many comedy films as he could. He discovered that laughter actually acted as an anaesthetic: ten minutes of hearty laughing provided at least two hours of pain relief. His only 'medication' during this cure was vitamin C in massive doses. Having cured himself of his crippled condition, Cousins proceeded to gather further evidence for his firm belief that his recovery was due to laughter and published his story in 1978 as *Anatomy of an Illness, as Perceived by the Patient.*[29] He continued to give lectures on his cure until his death in 1990.

Cousins's book was greeted with scorn by the medical establishment but some researchers have come to accept his view. Their research has widened to cover SMILING, HAPPINESS and mood and the EMOTIONS generally. In a paper published in the *Journal of the Royal College of General Practitioners* in 1985 it was stated that laughter definitely had positive medical effects: 'When we laugh we secrete hormones that stimulate the heart and act as natural painkillers. Stress is reduced. Calories are burned off and digestion is improved.'[209] In France a movement known as *jovialisme* has been set up to promote laughter – referred to as 'stationary jogging' – as a therapy. Laughter therapy rooms for cancer patients have been set up in South Africa.

LAW OF CURE The nineteenth-century homoeopath Constantine Hering defined the Law of Cure as consisting of four ways in which symptoms disappear as the patient is restored to health. Symptoms disappear from interior to exterior (i.e. the surface symptoms last), from the more vital to the less vital (again the most superficial last), from above downwards (which can be understood as from mental to physical) and in reverse order of their appearance.

LAW OF POTENTIATION/POTENTIZATION Hahnemann, founder of HOMOEOPATHY, discovered from his 'provings' that if a remedy was diluted it became more effective, more potent. This Law of Potentiation is one of the fundamental principles of homoeopathy.

LAW OF REVERSED EFFECT Many people have pointed out that the harder one tries, the harder a task seems to become – the so-called 'Law of Reversed Effect'. Emile Coué recognized this in the context of AUTOSUGGESTION, where he believed the crucial role was played by the imagination and not the will. In the ALEXANDER TECHNIQUE the problem is known as END-GAINING, and to overcome it one focuses not on what one is trying to achieve but on what one

227

is actually doing at any particular moment – the means rather than the end. Similar problems are confronted in the BATES METHOD of improving eyesight: Bates recognized that vision is further impaired by the strain induced by screwing up the eyes in a vain attempt to see better. It seems we sometimes have to 'trick' the mind into not trying, distracting it somehow so that what we are doing just happens. Ideally, we should stop thinking about the results of our activity and become totally absorbed in the activity itself.

All 'mind control' therapies stress the importance of 'relaxing into' a form of concentration rather than deliberately concentrating and exerting all one's will-power. This has always been characteristic of eastern mental disciplines such as YOGA and of MARTIAL ARTS such as T'AI CHI, but it has taken longer to become generally recognized in the West.

LAW OF SIMILARS The main axiom of HOMOEOPATHY is that one should treat like with like: the substance prescribed as treatment is selected initially because of its tendency to produce the same symptoms as the disease being treated. This is the 'law of similars'.

LCU See LIFE CHANGE UNITS.

LEFT-BRAIN/RIGHT-BRAIN See BICAMERAL NATURE OF THE BRAIN.

LEFT-HANDEDNESS/LEFT-HANDERS According to current esti- mates there are nine million left-handed people in the UK (ap- proximately one in seven), and thirty million in the USA. These estimates are probably more accurate now than at any time in the past. In 1860 only 2 per cent of the British population were said to be left-handed. By the 1950s this estimate had risen to 7 per cent, and in 1980 the general view was that around 10 per cent of the population were naturally left-handed although many had 'suppressed' the tendency.[19] Recent American surveys suggest that left-handers constitute between 15 and 20 per cent of the popula- tion. It sometimes appears that left-handedness is on the increase, although from most statistics in the past it has been impossible to discern how many natural left-handers had been coerced into becoming right-handed. Although the pressures to change have been reduced, it is impossible to say when, if ever, they will have been totally eliminated, so we cannot predict when the statistics will show the true incidence of innate left-handedness, or whether the incidence is actually rising. (When such authors as Diane Paul declare categorically that 'There is no doubt that left-handers are increasing', they are referring to declared practice and habit rather than innate tendency.[138])

People like to associate being left-handed with the outstanding qualities of certain historical figures – Alexander the Great, Charlemagne, Joan of Arc, Nelson; great actors – Charlie Chaplin, Greta Garbo; and particularly famous artists and men of genius such as Picasso, Einstein, Holbein, Michelangelo and of course the 'patron saint of left-handers', Leonardo da Vinci. Whether being left-handed actually has anything to do with genius is a moot point: one could also add the infamous to this list of greats, such as the Boston Strangler and Jack the Ripper. It has been suggested that being made to feel different as a child is a significant factor in the development of genius,[166] in which case left-handedness is just one of many possible factors that could lead to a sense of being an 'outsider'.

Since the BICAMERAL NATURE OF THE BRAIN was discovered in the 1950s, people have tried to find links between handedness and specific mental aptitudes. The fact that most people are right-handed (and the right hand is governed by the left hemisphere) is seen as being intimately bound up with the dominance of all left-brain functions in modern (western) civilization with its emphasis on logic, analysis and reductionist techniques. Our technological society is seen as a product of left-brain thinking, the right brain being more active in artistic pursuits and mysticism.

If an artistically untrained (right-handed) person draws a sketch of a familiar object the result is often not very successful. Betty Edwards says this is because we know too much about the object and try to put that knowledge in the drawing. But if a right-handed person starts trying to draw with the left hand the success rate is quite surprising – much greater than if one were to start trying to write with the left hand. The right brain appreciates shape much better and can therefore instruct the left hand to produce a much more accurate sketch than the right.[36]

Does this explain why so many great artists have been left-handed? Perhaps, although the same could be said of many great scientists. It may be that a truly effective brain is one in which neither hemisphere is wholly subjugated by the other. (Many of the early nuclear physicists had a mystical streak which suggested highly active and well-coordinated right brain functions.) According to the art historian Kenneth Clark, the nerves of Leonardo's eye and brain were 'supernormal', enabling him to draw and describe the rapid movements of a bird's wings, which were indiscernible to other people and which could not be verified until the invention of slow-motion filming techniques.

Although the link between left-handedness and artistic ability suggests that the right hemisphere is dominant for motor skills in left-handers, they tend to have the same left/right distinction for verbal and non-verbal information as the majority. This applies to 70 per cent of left-handers, with half of the remainder having 'mixed dominance' and the other half the reverse of the norm. (One way to identify which hemisphere controls a person's speech is by monitoring their gestures: research has shown that the hand used most for gesture when speaking is usually the one governed by the hemisphere which controls speech.) The lack of a constant pattern may explain why language difficulties are sometimes but not always associated with being left-handed. Cyril Burt found that nearly 12 per cent of left-handers had stammered at some time in their lives, as opposed to only 3 per cent of right-handers. Most people seem to believe that stammering results from excessive interference of the left hemisphere with right hemisphere functions, so when control of writing is wrested from the right brain (in left-handers) and imposed on the left, speech (also governed already in most left-handers by the left hemisphere) suffers. But other researchers believe there is no connection between stammering and left-handedness *per se*, although speech impediments may arise as a result of other people's behaviour around a child who is left-handed. Some maintain that speech and language disabilities appear disproportionately in left-handers only *after* they have been forced to use the right hand against their natural inclination. Such pressures result in general nervousness which is reflected in all modes of communication.

How long has humanity been predominantly right-handed? Neolithic flint tools were apparently suitable for both left-handed and right-handed use, indicating that stone-age people were probably ambidextrous. Stone-age tools did not need to be specifically right- or left-handed, but the more advanced bronze-age tools could not be used interchangeably. The present dominance of right-handedness seems to have emerged during the Bronze Age, when tools were made with cutting edges that were suitable for right-handers only. One possible reason for preferring the right hand for such tools is linked with the development of warfare. An old theory put forward by Thomas Carlyle (1795–1881), himself by nature left-handed, was that in battle people protected themselves – and particularly the heart – with shields held in the left hand. This meant that the right hand, in which the weapon was held, *had* to become more 'dextrous'.

There are many unanswered questions regarding left-handedness. Why do left-handers have higher rates of immune disorders and migraine head-aches? Why are there more left-handed men in the world than left-handed women? Why is there a greater than average chance of a third child being left-handed? Why are pro-portionately more left-handed children born to older mothers? Why do left-handers have more learning disorders? The reasons for left-handedness itself are still not understood, so it will be a long time before any of these questions are answered.

LEPROSY It has been suggested that an unknown proportion of people described in the past as lepers were misdiagnosed, or alternatively that the term 'leper' (meaning literally 'scaly', from Greek *lepis*, 'a scale') was more freely and less specifically applied than today. The numerous accounts of 'miraculous' cures of lepers might have something to do with the possibility that many were in fact suffering from psoriasis, a condition much more open to PSY-CHOSOMATIC influence. In some ways psoriasis is an imitation of leprosy; it certainly engenders (or perhaps reflects) similar feelings of separation and shame in the sufferer.

LESION A lesion is an injury or the structural change in the body resulting from an injury, but the word is used more loosely by manipulators such as osteopaths and chiropractors when referring to any misalignment in the spine or joints which needs adjusting, such as the locking together of two vertebrae. In this sense a lesion has been described as 'a condition of impaired mobility in an intervertebral joint'.[164] Some osteopaths prefer the term 'derangement', which is equally vague; chiropractors tend to talk about 'SUBLUXATIONS', a slight shift in position of one vertebra in relation to the next. The vagueness of such terms in the eyes of conventional medicine makes it difficult for orthodox doctors and practitioners of osteopathy and chiropractic to communicate with each other. (A similar situation arises out of the use of terms like MIASM in homoeopathy and radionics.)

LIBIDO According to Freudian psychology, libido is the vital energy arising out of the ID and seeking gratification. Although usually associated with the sex drive it includes other aspects of instinctive urges, all of which are positive in the sense that they promote life. Freud also recognized that negative energies also reside in the id: the term 'mortido' has since been coined to refer to these destructive drives. (See also SUBLIMATION.)

LIE-DETECTORS Lie-detectors depend on the fact that most people find telling lies stressful, and their effectiveness is one of the most tangible proofs of the way in which the mind can affect the body. The mind is aware of being in a stressful situation and the body reacts automatically to this STRESS. Most people cannot consciously control these reactions, which include changes in heart beat, blood flow and skin resistance. The rare instances when individuals have succeeded in duping a lie-detector point to the fact that even what are normally regarded as automatic physiological responses can with practice be brought under conscious control (although in the case of a pathological liar, stress may not be experienced at all).

LIFE CHANGE UNITS In the 1960s psychologists asked people how much adjustment they felt was required for specific events in their lives, compared with marriage, which was given an arbitrary rating of fifty Life Change Units. On the Holmes-Rahe SOCIAL READJUSTMENT RATING SCALE (1967) the death of a spouse was set at 100 LCUs (Life Change Units). The significant discovery from this research was that STRESS is felt as a result of positive events such as marriage, holidays and promotion, as well as negative events such as divorce, bereavement and losing one's job. Another discovery was that cultural factors are involved in the degree of stress associated with such life events, with people in America, Europe and Japan reporting quite different ratings for some of them.

LIFE EXPECTANCY See LONGEVITY.

LIFE-FAILURE In *The Farther Reaches of Human Nature*,[124] Abraham Maslow describes an illustration in an old psychology textbook. It showed 'a line of babies, pink, sweet, delightful, innocent, lovable' and a row of passengers in a train, 'glum, grey, sullen, sour', and the caption underneath read simply, 'What happened?' Maslow's answer to the question would be 'life-failure'. He regards neurosis as a failure of personal growth. When all one's deficiency NEEDS are met, growth motivation takes over as the driving force in one's life. 'We have, all of us, an impulse to improve ourselves, an impulse toward actualizing more of our potentialities, toward

SELF-ACTUALIZATION, or full humanness or human fulfilment.' But sometimes we are blocked, or rather we block ourselves, we fear our own greatness and destiny, we run away from responsibility and from our talents. This is what Maslow calls the Jonah complex. He says we need to be sensitive to our 'inner voices'. 'Getting along with one's inner world may be as important as social competence or reality competence.' Much of HUMANISTIC PSYCHOLOGY and therapies such as PSYCHOSYNTHESIS are aimed at conquering this sense of life-failure by enabling us to reconnect with these inner impulses which have been stifled.

LIFE-FIELD/LIFE-FORCE One of the main ideas that underpin most complementary therapies is that of a biological energy, which in the case of traditional Chinese medicine is called CH'I, in AYURVEDIC MEDICINE *prana*, and in POLARITY THERAPY positive and negative energy. The homoeopath, herbalist, naturopath, acupuncturist and to some extent the osteopath all view the manipulation of this indefinable vital force as the essential factor in successful therapy. It was also a key factor in the medicine of the native American tradition, north and south, appearing as *huaca* to the Incas, *wakan* to the Sioux, and *orenda* to the Iroquois. It has been rediscovered in various forms on the fringes of western medicine, as Reichenbach's OD and as Wilhelm Reich's ORGONE and its lesser manifestation in neo-Reichian therapies, BIOENERGY.

The life-force flows around the body along pathways (or MERIDIANS) and disease results from blockages in this flow. Just as the blood flows around the body, this subtle energy is regarded as flowing around the energy-body, sometimes called the *etheric body*. According to many esoteric systems (such as anthroposophical medicine) the etheric body contains the formative forces that underlie and shape all animate matter. Harold Saxton Burr has referred to this 'organizing field' as the *life-field* (L-field), and it has been suggested that this is what is revealed in KIRLIAN PHOTOGRAPHY. Hernani Andrade, director of the Institute of Psycho-biophysics in São Paulo, has also proposed that the body tissues are organized by a biomagnetic field, which is not a product of the body but shapes the body in the way that patterns of iron filings can be seen to be shaped by an external magnetic field.[187] In its 'visual' form this energy-body is often referred to as the AURA. It is via the aura that most types of spiritual healing, such as REIKI, have their effect, concentrating particularly on the CHAKRAS (focal points for receiving and distributing the subtle energies and filtering incoming energies from the environment), and all VIBRATIONAL THERAPIES work at this level.

There is no general agreement as to whether the life-force is electromagnetic or not. It can be shown that the human body is surrounded by an electromagnetic field, and Burr's research into the L-field was based on this, but Reich maintained that orgone was not electromagnetic, and most practitioners working in the vibrational therapies would consider that this subtle energy is as yet undetectable with the technology so far developed by science.

LIFE LAYER The life layer is the highest layer of the personality in GESTALT THERAPY, the level of heightened awareness.

LIFE-STYLE In recent decades the research into the effects of STRESS have convinced many people that the way we live is responsible for many of our health problems. 'The message is disseminated that something called "life-style" is the culprit. The "new germs" of today are bad habits such as smoking, risk factors such as broad changes in "life events", and extreme psychological reactions to environmental disruptions such as job loss or divorce.'[135] These life events are given numerical values (LIFE CHANGE UNITS) so that an individual's chances of falling ill can be assessed. On the other hand, some researchers have concluded that 'Knowing whether a person smokes, has high blood pressure, or elevated cholesterol does very little to predict who will have a heart attack . . . 86 percent of those who had the very highest risk for heart attacks did not have a heart attack over the ten years of study.'[205] Other studies have shown that the best predictor for heart disease in people under fifty was none of those familiar physical risk factors, nor a 'life event', but job dissatisfaction.[233] The notion of life-style alone omits consideration of PERSONALITY traits and ATTITUDE, which seem to be at least as important, if not more so, in assessing an individual's resistance or susceptibility to certain diseases.

LIGHT THERAPY Light therapy is the standard treatment (apart from anti-depressants and psychotherapy) for the type of depression which has become known as SAD, 'seasonal affective disorder', sometimes called the winter blues. It is seasonal in that it occurs in the northern hemisphere from September or October to March, and particularly in the winter months when daylight is at its shortest. SAD has only acquired recognized status in recent years, and the first study of SAD and light therapy was not published until

1984, despite the fact that something of the phenomenon and the treatment was known to the ancients. Hippocrates wrote, 'It is chiefly the changes of seasons which produce disease', and the second century physician Aretaeus recommended that 'Lethargics are to be laid in the light and exposed to the rays of the sun, for the disease is gloom.' Treatment of SAD with light therapy (not to be confused with chromotherapy, which uses light of specific colours and is more commonly referred to as COLOUR THERAPY) involves sitting in full-spectrum fluorescent light for three hours before dawn and three hours after dusk.

Mood (along with many vital functions such as sleep, temperature control, hunger and sex drive) is regulated by the hypothalamus, which is linked directly by nerve fibres to the retina. It is thought that low levels of serotonin in the hypothalamus cause depression, and serotonin is at its lowest in the hypothalamus in winter. The synthesis of serotonin is also enhanced by eating carbohydrates, which may explain why some people try to cheer themselves up by eating chocolates, sweets and starches, in an instinctive attempt to increase serotonin in the brain. Reduced levels of dopamine have also been suggested as a factor in SAD, and dopamine is released in response to light.[152]

In the winter of 1968–69 there was a very bad flu epidemic in the USA. Five per cent of the population of the county of Sarasota in Florida went down with the virus, but in one particular establishment not a single member of staff took sick leave during the whole period of the epidemic. The employer concerned was the Obrig laboratories. As the manufacturer of contact lenses, Obrig was particularly interested in the effects of good lighting. They had designed their building with special plastic window-panes that transmitted ultra-violet light in all office and factory areas, enabling the staff to enjoy full-spectrum light as if they were outdoors. John Ott of the Environment Health and Light Institute in Sarasota put the Obrig workers' immunity down to the therapeutic effects of natural, undiluted light. (He also showed that mice under pink fluorescent light lived less than half as long as mice under full-spectrum sunlight.)[144]

The human menstrual cycle probably evolved in synchronization with the lunar cycle. It is thought that ovulation probably occurred at the time of the full moon when vigilance to defend oneself was less of a preoccupation. As a result of this idea, women with menstrual irregularities were advised to sleep with the light on for four nights from the fourteenth to the seventeenth night of their cycle, which would then regularize itself immediately. It has been suggested that this could also be an effective method of birth control since one could more reliably guarantee the menstrual rhythm. It has also been suggested that girls menstruate at an earlier age nowadays because they spend more time in artificial light than previous generations did.

LOCATION PROCESSING In DIANETICS, location processing is a technique of becoming more aware of what and where one is by self-observation.

LOGOTHERAPY Logotherapy is a form of EXISTENTIAL PSYCHO-THERAPY developed by Viktor Frankl, whose experiences in concentration camps during the Second World War convinced him that our mental and even physical health depend largely on a sense of purpose and meaning. 'A literal translation of the term "logotherapy" is "therapy through meaning" . . . The notion of *therapy through meaning* is the very reverse of the traditional conceptualization of PSYCHOTHERAPY, which could rather be formulated as *meaning through therapy*.'[46] In this 'meaning-centred (psycho-)therapy', Freud's pleasure principle is replaced as the basic human motivating force by the 'will-to-meaning', and the frustration of this 'will-to-meaning' is regarded as the root cause of neurosis. Frankl takes (Freudian) psychoanalysts to task for 'their own hidden motivation, their unconscious desire to devalue, debase and depreciate what is genuine, what is genuinely human, in man'.[46] If psychoanalysis succeeds in eliminating a neurosis, all too often it leaves only a void in its place, because 'depth psychology' does not recognize the importance of meaning. (Hence Frankl's coining of the term 'HEIGHT PSYCHOLOGY' to refer to his own kind of therapy.)

In this, Frankl may appear to come close to Kurt Goldstein's concept of SELF-ACTUALIZATION and Abraham Maslow's ideas about VALUES and valuelessness (although Maslow's hierarchy of NEEDS includes a much wider range of motivations). On the other hand Frankl sees self-transcendence as the motivating factor within the will-to-meaning, rather than self-actualization, which is the 'unintended effect' of successfully transcending self. He also regards other humanistic therapies as inadequate: 'the ENCOUNTER GROUP movement and SENSITIVITY TRAINING boil down to reactions to social and emotional alienation respectively. Yet the reaction to a problem must not be confused with a solution to the problem . . . The properly conceived encounter group not only indulges in the self-expression of the individual members but also promotes their self-transcendence.'[46] So in logotherapy, analysis does not focus on the unconscious but on discovering one's life purpose and on going beyond the self.

LOHAN KUNG Lohan kung (lohan gong) is an ancient Chinese healing system based on body movements which have the purpose of activating the flow of CH'I through the body and restoring physical and mental balance. These basic movements, known as the Eighteen Lohan Hands, are said to have been discovered by an Indian monk, Bodhidharma, known to the Chinese as Ta Mo, who developed them initially to counteract the fatigue and pains induced by long periods of meditation in inhospitable conditions in a cave. The technique survives in the continuing practice of QI GONG and has influenced MARTIAL ARTS such as T'AI CHI CHUAN and AIKIDO.

LONGEVITY Francis Bacon was probably one of the first to consider the prolongation of life as a new task for physicians. He divided medicine into three offices: 'First the preservation of health, second, the cure of disease, and third, the prolongation of life', describing the third as 'the most noble of all'. The same could be said of modern medicine, although the ranking order may have changed: longevity seems to be the major preoccupation today, at least in the West. On the basis of the capacity for cell renewal in each organ, it has been estimated that physiologically the human body should be capable of living for between 100 and 150 years.

In the United States today, there are only about three 100-year-olds per 100,000 people. In some other, more primitive parts of the world (such as Abkhasia in Georgia and Hunza in Kashmir), there are as many as forty to sixty centenarians per 100,000. Why is this? Are people in such societies under less stress? No: if anything, the stresses and responsibilities of the elders in those communities increase with age. Perhaps there is a clue here. We tend to regard STRESS as life-threatening, forgetting that boredom and lack of MEANING may be even more harmful. The various groups of people who live longer than average include business leaders who don't retire, orchestra conductors, successful artists, women listed in *Who's Who*, nuns, and Mormons. In this context remaining active and being dedicated to one's occupation seem to be significant factors – probably more significant than the advances of modern medicine.

In the seventeenth century, Edmond Halley, the English astronomer, made some of the first actuarial tables of life expectancy. He estimated that in 1687 a sixty-year-old could be expected to live another 12.09 years. Two hundred years later this had risen to 12.2 years, and in 1950 it was 15.7. In other words modern medicine has added very little to the lifespan of a sixty-year-old. Fewer people die young, but old people do not live much longer than they ever did, and social factors have probably extended life more than medical factors.

One relatively recent development is the longer life expectancy of women as compared with men: before the industrial age men consistently outlived women. This was due to a variety of factors: the high incidence of death of women in childbirth, the fact that men tended to get more regular physical exercise, working hard on the land, with no such thing as idle retirement and fewer time pressures. It has been suggested that the gap between the life expectancy of men and women may start to diminish as more women are absorbed into the modern workforce and are subject to all the associated pressures. The implication is that life-style is probably the most significant factor in determining lifespan.

LUCID SLEEP See ARTIFICIAL SOMNAMBULISM.

LÜSCHER COLOUR TEST Max Lüscher was a professor of psychology at the Institute of Psychodiagnostic Medicine, Basle. He believed that colours have emotional value and that a person's colour preferences reveal basic personality traits. For example, a strong liking for red is characteristic of an extravert with a strong will, whilst those who dislike red are usually more withdrawn. People who choose black often prove to be potential suicides, and those with grey as first or second choice often seem to lack confidence and show feelings of inadequacy. Preferences can also reveal potential health problems. People who choose red or yellow over other colours seem to be more susceptible to heart trouble, whilst those who choose brown tend to block their feelings and may become cancer patients. (See CANCER PERSONALITY.) In the famous Lüscher test eight colours are used – orange-red, bright yellow, green, dark blue, violet, brown, grey and black, and the subject arranges them in order of preference, twice. The interpretation is made according to the combination of the two sequences. A longer Lüscher test uses seventy-three cards of twenty-five colours and shapes, requiring forty-three different selections to be made. Although Lüscher's pioneering work on our emotional reactions to colour was of enormous importance, it has little to say directly about

COLOUR THERAPY, since the colours used in this test are rather drab when compared with the more vibrant colours which are regarded as having therapeutic value.

LYMPHATIC ROSARY In IRIDOLOGY the appearance of a ring of white beads around the rim of the iris is known as the lymphatic rosary and is said to indicate reduced pituitary and thyroid function. It is also often present in cases of obesity. Treatment usually involves the use of herbs which act upon the lymph system, such as fenugreek.

MACROBIOTICS 'Macrobiotics' (from the Greek *macro*, 'big', and *bios*, 'life') originally meant 'the science of prolonging life'. More recently the term was applied by the Japanese philosopher George Ohsawa to his nutritional system to reflect the idea that with an appropriate diet one can enjoy a fuller life. As with most systems of alternative medicine, macrobiotics is used both as a therapy to treat people when they are sick and as a preventive measure to maintain good health. Ohsawa developed his ideas on nutrition from his studies of Indian, Chinese and Japanese philosophy and used his understanding of diet to cure his own tuberculosis. In the 1950s he took macrobiotics to Europe and America, where he continued to expound the system until his death in 1966.

According to oriental medicine, all foods have YIN or YANG characteristics, and a macrobiotic diet aims at providing the right balance of these polar energies. What is appropriate in any given situation depends on the state of the individual, the life-style, the environment and the weather. Each of these will tend to be more yin or more yang, indicating whether more yin or yang energy should be supplied in the diet. For example, physically active people (yang) will tend to need more yang food. But in environmental terms the complementary energy is required: in a hot, dry environment (which is yang) yin foods should be eaten. Yin foods are, in fact, those that grow in a yang environment, which is why a macrobiotic diet consists largely of what is in season and growing locally.

Yin and yang growth cycles follow a seasonal cycle. In winter (when the climate is cold and damp, i.e. yin) vegetal energy descends into the root system of plants, and as the leaves dry the plant becomes more yang; food which grows at this time tends to be drier and can be kept for a long time without spoiling (e.g. root vegetables). In summer (which is yang) plants are more watery and can provide the cooling effect needed in hot weather.

YIN FOODS	YANG FOODS
grow taller above the ground	grow below the ground
are softer and juicier e.g. fruit and leaves	are drier, harder and shorter e.g. roots, stems and seeds
grow in a hot dry climate (yang)	grow in a cold wet climate (yin)
tend to be hot and aromatic	tend to be salty and sour
cause an acid reaction in the body	cause an alkaline reaction in the body

Although certain foods are largely avoided because they are too yin (e.g. sugar) or too yang (e.g. meat, poultry and eggs), it is clear from the above that most foods are a mixture of yin and yang. Moreover, the same food may provide the required yin energy for one individual whilst being predominantly yang for another. Changes in the yin/yang quality of food can be brought about by cooking: cooking quickly and adding salt increases the yin, whilst slow cooking makes food more yang. Other factors, such as colour and texture, may also be considered when determining the quality of particular foods.

The process of diagnosing the right diet for a particular person in particular circumstances is long and complicated, and oversimplification and generalization led to several unfortunate cases of malnutrition in the USA. As is so often the case, Ohsawa was never as obsessive or as prescriptive as some of his followers. 'Go and make your own macrobiotics,' he said; 'I have only described the way that was suitable for me.' Since Ohsawa's death his work has been continued by Michio Kushi, director of the East-West Foundation, which has branches in London, Paris, Boston and Amsterdam.

MAGIC BULLET The so-called magic bullet approach to disease and medicine refers to the medical establishment's tendency to search for one simple cure for any disease. The fact that in some cases one particular drug does knock out a disease (e.g. penicillin as a cure for syphilis) has lent disproportionate support to the notion that such a magic bullet can be found for each and every disease. One effect of this faith in single cures has been a similar over-emphasis on single causes in CONVENTIONAL MEDICINE. The focus on pathology ignores psychological and social factors in the development, course and resolution of diseases. In agriculture it was recognized long ago that disease resistance can be fostered by providing livestock with particular environments, but our medical advisers seem to have lagged behind in this understanding.

It should be recognized, for example, that people are healthier today not simply because they receive better treatment when ill, but because they tend not to become ill in the first place. What has lowered the death rate and increased LONGEVITY over the last hundred years or so is not so much the improvements in medical treatment as the decline in deaths from the infectious diseases of youth, which was largely a result of social changes. Life expectancy at age 45 has actually changed very little over the past century. Moreover, deaths and disease from common infections were already in decline long before IMMUNIZATIONS and antibiotics came on the scene. The death rate from tuberculosis, for example, was reduced by 97 per cent in the century *before* streptomycin was first employed.

Belief in the myth of the magic bullet has also distorted the general understanding of what constitutes 'health care'. It has been suggested that it would be more appropriate to refer to modern health-care systems as 'disease care' systems, since they are concerned with the sick. It should be recognized that the relationship between this disease care and the health of the general population is extremely tenuous. 'Providing more and more medical care does not necessarily produce healthier people.' (In fact, because of IATROGEN- IC DISEASES one could claim the reverse.) 'A healthy population is one that does not get sick in the first place, rather than one that gets sick and then is returned to health by medical care. There is more to be gained by a thorough study of how organisms avoid illness than there is from the study of disease agents alone.'[143] It is unfortunate that the rise in interest in preventive medicine has coincided with a rapid increase in the cost of the 'magic bullets' we are so fond of and a consequent shortage of funds for preventive treatment which would not have obvious and immediate results.

One should be careful not to lay too much of the blame for this on the medical establishment alone: the general public does seem to demand 'magic bullets'. And even when people take up systems of ALTERNATIVE MEDICINE they often adopt a similar approach: adherents of HERBAL MEDICINE, for example, may use a particular remedy such as evening primrose oil as if it were just such a magic bullet, and most of us are much keener to look for a 'quick fix' than we are to investigate why we got sick in the first place. Although it is HOLISTIC MEDICINE which is generally seen as the antithesis of the magic bullet approach, it might be more accurate to regard its antithesis as the cultivation of a sense of responsibility for one's own state of health.

MAGNETISM/MAGNET THERAPY/MAGNETIC HEALING See MESMERISM and BIOMAGNETICS.

MAGNETOGEOMETRIC POTENCY SIMULATOR See POTENCY SIMULATOR.

MAINLINE MEDICINE See CONVENTIONAL MEDICINE.

MANIPULATION/MANIPULATIVE THERAPY In most parts of the world one can find the equivalent of old-style BONE-SETTERS, which suggests that manipulation is one of the oldest types of treatment we have. Manipulative therapies range from the purely mechanical such as SWEDISH MASSAGE, OSTEOPATHY and CHIROPRACTIC to the BODY-ORIENTED PSYCHOTHERAPIES such as REICHIAN THERAPY, ROLFING and APPLIED KINESIOLOGY, with a few which start out as purely physical but may also be beneficial psychologically, such as the ALEXANDER TECHNIQUE and the FELDENKRAIS TECHNIQUE. Manipulation of a more insubstantial nature is involved in energy-based systems of medicine and therapies such as ACUPUNCTURE, QI GONG and POLARITY THERAPY, in which the therapist tries to influence the flow of CH'I, *prana* or the life force through the body. (See also REFLEXOLOGY, ACUPRESSURE, SHIATSU, METAMORPHIC TECHNIQUE.)

MANTRA A mantra (Sanskrit) is a phrase, word or sound which is repeated either aloud or silently in certain types of MEDITATION. A general practitioner in London, Dr Chandra Patel, teaches simple mantra-meditation to patients with high blood pressure, obesity and tobacco addiction, for whom he claims it has beneficial effects.[17] In mantra YOGA the effects of meditation are thought to be enhanced by the sound vibrations produced by CHANTING: the vibrations are said to have a direct influence on the etheric body or LIFE-FIELD via the CHAKRAS.

MARASMUS Infants sometimes die as a result of inadequate mothering, insufficient touching and a lack of affection – DEPRIVATION

DWARFISM. Their illness has been called 'marasmus' (by Margaret Ribble) or 'anaclitic depression' (by René Spitz) and manifests as an inability to develop and a susceptibility to a variety of life-threatening diseases because of a collapse of the body's defences. This is clear evidence that the immune system is affected by the EMOTIONS.

MARMA *Marmas* are energy points in AYURVEDIC MEDICINE, used in massage in the manner of ACUPRESSURE POINTS, but not needled as in ACUPUNCTURE.

MARTIAL ARTS Chinese martial arts (*wu-shu*) are of two types: *nei chai*, 'inner family', and *wai chai*, 'outer family'. Those disciplines in the inner family are Taoist-inspired, whilst those of the outer family originate outside China, usually in India.

The Taoist-inspired disciplines aim to cultivate vital energy and economy of strength, rather than physical strength and endurance. They emphasize the principles of relaxing and sinking; the movements are slow and fluid, and they are performed meditatively. The aim is both to build health and to cultivate peace of mind. The prime example of this inner group is T'AI-CHI.

AIKIDO, which was developed in the 1920s, also belongs to this group; although practised with a partner it is not competitive (*ai* means 'unite' or 'harmonize'). Both t'ai-chi and aikido stress the idea of 'non-doing'. Other martial arts in this group are QI GONG (or Chi Gung), sometimes translated as 'kinesiatrics', a form of healing through muscular movement, and *xing-yi* or 'mind boxing'.

The outer group of martial arts emphasize muscular strength, conditioning and endurance. Kung fu (meaning 'task', 'work' or 'exercise') belongs to this group, as do its Japanese derivatives, karate (which means 'Chinese hands' or 'empty hand'), jujitsu and judo, all of which owe much to Chinese wrestling techniques. In kendo, another Japanese martial art, similar principles to those of sword-fighting are applied, although it is now usually practised with swords made of bamboo, and in ninjutsu the combatants are fully armed. The generic term for martial arts in Japan is *budo*.

MASS HYSTERIA In July 1982 at an annual jazz festival in Hollinwell, England, there was a sudden unexplained outbreak of nausea, vomiting, abdominal pain, burning eyes and a metallic taste in the mouth among children. Food poisoning was immediately ruled out since there had been no communal eating. Crop-spraying was considered as a possible cause, but there had been none. A leak from a chemical plant was suggested, but that suspicion also proved unfounded (and even if there had been such a leak, the wind had been in the wrong direction). The only explanation was mass hysteria.

In this instance 500 people were treated either at the site or in hospital, some being detained overnight, and several victims were still unconscious two hours after the onset of the illness. The conditions were typical for such incidents: a warm day, an emotionally charged atmosphere, and a concentration of young females marching and blowing musical instruments with the risk of hyperventilation. Once an individual member of such a group exhibits the symptoms, others begin to suffer in the same way and the group seems to behave as one organism. If this sounds far-fetched, we need only remind ourselves of the infectiousness of yawns to recognize that group behaviour is still far from being fully understood.

MASSAGE Massage is used for its mechanical effect on the body in MANIPULATIVE THERAPIES such as SWEDISH MASSAGE, OSTEO-PATHY, CHIROPRACTIC and the ALEXANDER TECHNIQUE, but it also forms an integral part of many bodywork therapies which have a psychological component such as REICHIAN THERAPY, ROLFING and DEEP TISSUE MUSCLE THERAPY. In POLARITY THERAPY and energy-based systems such as ACUPRESSURE and SHIATSU it is also used as a means of affecting the flow of CH'I, and in AROMATHERAPY it is one method by which the skin is encouraged to absorb the essential oils. As a therapy in itself, massage in oriental medicine is inseparable from the notion of stimulating the energy flow in the body, relieving fatigue and stiffness, for example. In the West, massage is geared more towards working on the muscles, joints and nerves: gentle pressure with the fingertips is used to suppress nerve function, and heavier pressure to stimulate.

MAZDAZNAN Meaning 'Master Thought', Mazdaznan is a way of life derived mainly from Zarathustrian teachings, adapted for the West by Otoman Zar-Adusht Ha'nish (1844–1936). In 1902 he founded the Mazdaznan Association with the main objective of teaching people how to develop physical, mental and spiritual balance. Deep rhythmical breathing forms an important part of the discipline, sometimes in combination with singing to activate particular glands. The recommended diet is lacto-vegetarian and in illness only naturopathic remedies are used. Great emphasis is laid on understanding oneself, knowing one's strengths and weaknesses and recognizing how one's 'type' needs to be taken into consideration when making choices.

MEANING Many writers on health matters have recognized the importance of meaning for both mental and physical well-being. 'Make no mistake about it, a sense of having a place in the larger scheme of things, as all our history shows, is a real and basic human need. We cannot ignore and starve this need and expect to escape unscathed any more than if we ignore the needs of our body or our mind.'[116] A lack of meaning has been linked with the so-called CANCER PERSONALITY. Jung saw the first half of life (up to the age of forty) as the time when we explore and come to terms with the external world, whilst in the second half of life, from forty onwards, we are more concerned with exploring the inner world, seeking answers to questions such as 'Who am I?' and 'What is the purpose of life?' Jung felt that the problems brought to him by people over the age of forty were essentially spiritual. Considering his experiences in concentration camps in the Second World War, and trying to fathom what it was that enabled some to survive against all odds, Viktor Frankl decided that the crucial factor was a sense of meaning. For him the 'will to meaning' is the most fundamental motivation in human beings and he has made it the basis of his LOGOTHERAPY. All HUMANISTIC PSYCHOLOGY tends to regard a sense of purpose (meaningfulness) as a key area for consideration, whilst classical PSYCHOANALYSIS has regarded such matters as out of bounds.

MECHANO-THERAPY It was as 'mechano-therapy' that OSTEOPA-THY was first described in the *British Medical Journal* in a surprisingly favourable article by Alexander Bryce in 1910. The accompanying editorial suggested that the medical fraternity should not dismiss out of hand therapies such as 'the higher bone-setting'. Such open-mindedness was both untypical and short-lived.

MEDICALIZATION The percentage of births at home in the UK declined from 33 per cent in 1961 to 3 per cent in 1976. This is an example of 'medicalization' as identified (and decried) by Ivan Illich: what were formerly regarded as inalienable natural processes are now handed over to medical professionals, since we are deemed incapable of handling them ourselves. 'Even pregnancy is – in practice – generally regarded as a nine-month self-limiting illness, often requiring surgery at the end.' A similar fate has overtaken the way we handle death, with more and more people dying in hospital rather than at home. 'Medicalization has gone so far that we no longer even believe in our ability to die alone or in the warmth of the company of our loved ones.'[91]

There are two aspects to this general trend. Not only are natural processes such as birth and death diminished and devalued, in that those undergoing them are regarded as sick, but illness in general is considered to be an aberration requiring treatment rather than evidence of the body's healthy self-regulating system. Instead of supporting the body in its efforts, CONVENTIONAL MEDICINE intervenes with ALLOPATHIC drugs which can only be prescribed by experts who, according to Illich, have usurped our rights over our own natural functions. In this sense medicalization has contributed enormously to the destruction of the individual's sense of responsibility for his or her body. 'Medicalization constitutes a prolific bureaucratic program based on the denial of each man's need to deal with pain, sickness, and death.'[91] With the abandonment of a sense of responsibility for one's own physical and psychological condition comes the expectation that the experts in whose hands one has placed oneself will be able to put everything right (hence the MAGIC BULLET approach). 'Traditional cultures confront pain, impairment and death by interpreting them as challenges soliciting a response from the individual under stress; medical civilization turns them into demands made by individuals on the economy, into problems that can be managed or *produced* out of existence.'[91]

MEDITATION In physiological terms, meditation is a state of relaxation in which the body reacts in ways which are the opposite in virtually all respects to the FIGHT-OR-FLIGHT RESPONSE. In this non-aroused state the pulse slows down, blood pressure and breathing rate are reduced, metabolism decreases, there are changes in the concentrations of oxygen and carbon dioxide in the blood (less oxygen is consumed and less carbon dioxide eliminated), there is an increase in blood flow to the fingers and toes and an increase in electrical skin resistance. There are also alterations in the brain wave pattern: there is often an increase in alpha rhythms and a synchronization of brain waves between left and right hemispheres.

The meditative state does not resemble a hypnotic trance, and the state of mental arousal varies according to the type of meditation. In some forms, such as TRANSCENDENTAL MEDITATION (TM), the aim is to still the mind. When the incessant activity of the mind is stilled, meditators experience that aspect of their being which is prior to and distinct from their thoughts and from attention itself. It is this state which has been called transcendental awareness, cosmic consciousness, satori. But some forms of meditation, such as kriya yoga, kundalini yoga and karma yoga, involve high arousal and extremely active mental involvement.

According to Zen Buddhists there are at least seven types of meditation: 1) through BREATHING exercises (YOGA, QI GONG); 2) by concentrating the mind on one point; 3) through VISUALIZATION; 4) through mantra yoga (CHANTING, TM); 5) devotional thoughts, religious prayer; 6) by identifying with the mind (in philosophy); 7) through movement (MARTIAL ARTS, T'AI-CHI, QI GONG, YOGA, DANCE). The essence of Buddhist meditation is to achieve optimal awareness of reality, particularly of one's body and one's mind but also of the world. This is sometimes referred to as MINDFULNESS, and this particular type of self-awareness is an important aspect of Fromm's TRANSTHERAPEUTIC PSYCHOANALYSIS.

In the 1960s there was a great deal of research into BIOFEEDBACK, in which it was found that 'a meditative state of deep relaxation is conducive to the establishment of voluntary control by allowing the individual to become aware of subliminal imagery, fantasies and sensations.'[139] Following this and other research into the physiological effects of meditation it was possible by the late 1970s to claim: 'No matter how organic a disease appears to be, there is inevitably an accompaniment of psychological and emotional stress which can aggravate the condition. Although it is highly premature to maintain that meditative or relaxation techniques can cure such disorders, it is certainly clear that such approaches can alleviate or eliminate the attendant anxiety and stress.'[139] On the other hand, conventional medical science even ten years later maintained that there was still no solid body of evidence to support the contention that meditation reduces the physiological effects of stress, and claimed that research had concentrated too much on looking for quick rather than long-term changes in those who meditate regularly.[181]

Someone who meditates regularly becomes more reactive to the environment but also recovers more quickly when a stressful situation has passed. Meditators often find they need less sleep at night. Meditation has been used to treat asthma, phobias, hypertension and other psychosomatic disorders. It also forms an important part of SELF-HEALING. Ainsley Meares believes that meditating to relieve the mind of conscious worries and attain a state he calls mental ataraxis enhances the body's immune system. He uses ATAVISTIC REGRESSION to help patients to empty their minds and attain this state of inner calm.

A beneficial side-effect of meditation in this context is the insight or intuition which it seems to facilitate, as Meir Schneider, a leading exponent of self-healing, has found. 'There came a time when I no longer needed to *search* for new exercises; they would just "come" when I needed them. I would meditate on what I was trying to accomplish while working on myself and inspiration for new exercises would come – exactly the right exercises for my back, my legs, my eyes. This also began to happen with regard to my patients. By attuning myself to them and to their needs, I knew what to do with them.'[157]

MEDULLA/ADRENALIN The adrenal glands are situated near the kidneys; each gland has an outer cortex and an inner medulla (not to be confused with the medulla oblongata in the brain). Stress signals from the SYMPATHETIC NERVOUS SYSTEM cause the adrenal medulla to secrete the hormones adrenalin and noradrenalin (also known in the USA as epinephrine and norepinephrine), which when distributed by the blood cause the body to respond with a jolt and a surge of energy (the 'adrenalin rush') as part of the FIGHT-OR-FLIGHT RESPONSE. This can enable people to perform feats of physical strength that they are not normally capable of, such as lifting a car to save a trapped child. The suggested difference between adrenalin and noradrenalin is that adrenalin is the 'fear hormone' and noradrenalin the 'anger hormone', an indication of the way in which the EMOTIONS are bound up with the chemistry of the body.

MEGAVITAMIN THERAPY In the late 1960s Dr Linus Pauling (1901–94), Nobel prize-winner for chemistry in 1954 and for peace in 1962, developed a theory that many illnesses and psychiatric disorders were a result of imbalanced biochemistry caused by vitamin deficiency. Some of the first conditions to be treated in this way were mental illnesses, and Pauling called his approach 'orthomolecular psychiatry', which he defined as 'the treatment of mental disease by the provision of the optimum molecular environment for the mind, especially the optimum concentration of substances normally present in the body.' Treatment consists of large doses of vitamins, much greater than originally thought beneficial, depending on the condition and the individual patient; Pauling believed that certain individuals need specific vitamins in much larger doses than average. He also expressed the view that 'it is possible by rather simple means, essentially nutritional, to increase the length of life expectancy for young and middle-aged people . . . by about twenty years.'

The treatment of schizophrenia with large doses of vitamin B3 (supplementing conventional psychotherapy and electroconvulsive therapy) was pioneered by Osmond and Hoffer. Large doses of vitamin C were used by Pauling and others in the treatment of cancer, and this approach has been adopted in certain alternative cancer clinics such as the Bristol Cancer Help Centre (usually in combination with mineral supplements). The use of vitamin C as a prophylactic against the common cold, one of Pauling's first areas of research, is perhaps the most widely used example of megavitamin therapy.

MELANCHOLY Melancholic was one of the four classical TEM-PERAMENTS as described by Galen (c.130–201). He also observed that melancholic women were more likely to suffer from cancer than sanguine women, an early version of modern speculation on what constitutes the so-called CANCER PERSONALITY.

MENTAL SCIENCE Also known as the Science of Health and Happiness, Mental Science was developed as part of the philosophical movement known as New Thought as a way of using the mind to effect changes in character and even external circumstances. Phineas Parkhurst Quimby (1802–66), a clockmaker, founded New Thought and developed his mental science as a method of AUTOSUGGESTION from the principles of MESMERISM. Mental science is the precursor of later self-help and self-improvement programmes such as POSITIVE THINKING.

MENTASTICS See TRAGERWORK.

MERIDIANS In Chinese medicine the pathways along which CH'I flows are called meridians. ACUPUNCTURE points lie along these meridians and they are also used in ACUPRESSURE, REFLEXOLOGY and SHIATSU, which is sometimes used in conjunction with AROMA-THERAPY.

MESMERISM Mesmerism was what we now know as HYPNO-SIS, although the change of name became necessary because of the paraphernalia surrounding the process and the theories of 'animal magnetism' with which the Viennese physician Franz Anton Mesmer (1734–1815) embellished his technique. In 1774, Mesmer demonstrated mesmerism. Patients sat around a tub of water containing metal bottles of water which Mesmer had magnetized, thus creating a magnetic field. Each patient held an iron rod attached to one of the bottles, and Mesmer occasionally laid his hands on a patient's body to enhance the effect of 'animal magnetism', his version of the all-pervading vital energy or life-force (akin to the Indian concept of *prana*). Before long a 'mesmeric' state was induced in some of the · patients, who suffered fits or convulsions. Mesmer apparently cured illnesses such as paralysis by stroking the patient's body with a magnet or with gold 'to restore the flow of animal magnetism'.

When acting as Mesmer's assistant the Marquis de Puységur treated a patient by tying him to a lime tree he had 'magnetized' and passing a magnet over his head. When told to untie himself the patient obeyed instructions without opening his eyes and Puységur realized that he was in some sort of trance, which he referred to as 'artificial somnambulism'. All the mesmerist's instructions were carried out without question and with the utmost ease. Mesmer had also recognized this phenomenon but thought it incidental to the convulsive crises which in his opinion were the crucial sign that animal magnetism was flowing through the patient's body and that healing was taking place. But before long people realized that any change in the patient was the result of the mesmerist's suggestions rather than a consequence of the redirection of insubstantial energies.

Mesmerism was a true forerunner of HYPNOTHERAPY: it was the first genuinely effective surgical anaesthesia used in the West and it was used regularly before ether (1846) and chloroform (1847). In 1842 the surgeon W. S. Ward carried out the painless amputation of a leg on a patient hypnotized by mesmerism. The patient was denounced as an impostor and the report was deleted from the Royal Medical and Chirurgical Society's records. Today the Royal Society of Medicine has a section of Medical and Dental Hypnosis. Before the introduction of ether, John Elliotson, who instructed Dickens in the principles of mesmerism, had carried out seventy-six painless operations using mesmeric anaesthesia, which the *Lancet* decried as 'the harlotry which dares to call itself science'.[178]

MESOMORPH See BODY-TYPES.

METAMORPHIC TECHNIQUE Metamorphic technique grew out of Robert St John's prenatal therapy, which was itself based on a particular aspect of REFLEXOLOGY. St John discovered that manipulation of certain reflex points relating to the spine (along a line or MERIDIAN extending from the big toe to the heel) could evoke and release tensions originating in the gestation period. The earliest part of the gestation period is accessed by massaging points that relate to the upper part of the spine, while those relating to lower down the spine correspond to times progressively closer to birth. St John used his prenatal therapy to treat disturbed or handicapped children, also teaching the parents how to use the therapy on their children by massaging each foot and sometimes the hands and the head. (Chinese medicine also taught that certain ACUPOINTS corresponded to the pre-birth period.)

Other practitioners have extended metamorphic technique to the treatment of adults, but according to the principle that rather than treating specific disorders they enable patients to heal themselves. It is a fundamental tenet of the technique that an expectant mother's state of mind can affect the future health of the unborn child. Working on spinal reflex points of the feet, hands and head helps the individual to loosen and escape from the restrictive patterns set up during the gestation period.

METAMOTIVATION In HUMANISTIC PSYCHOLOGY people are regarded as motivated not only by NEEDS but also by VALUES. Abraham Maslow placed the basic needs in a hierarchy with physiological needs at one end of the scale and SELF-ACTUALIZATION needs at the other. Beyond this hierarchy he placed what he called 'growth needs' or 'Being-values' (or 'B-values' in contrast to 'D-needs' – deficiency needs). These are the higher needs or 'metaneeds' by which people are motivated as their basic needs are satisfied. Maslow described this aspect of motivation as metamotivation. Growth needs themselves cannot be placed in a hierarchy. They include concepts such as truth, beauty, goodness, uniqueness, wholeness, perfection, completion, justice, aliveness, richness, meaningfulness, simplicity, effortlessness, playfulness and self-sufficiency.

METANOIA 'Metanoia' is the term psychologists use for spiritual conversion and repentance. In Jungian terms it is when the EGO becomes more aware of the SELF; one realizes that the VALUES of the ego should be brought in line with those of the Self, and accepts that one's life and actions should be governed by the permanent

251

values of the Self rather than the whims of the ego. Erich Fromm would regard metanoia as the realization that one's life should be oriented towards 'being' rather than 'having'.[54]

METAPROGRAMMING Metaprogramming is a term coined by John Lilly to refer to the elimination, manipulation or alteration of our mental 'programmes' – the pre-established beliefs and attitudes which condition our behaviour and our perception of the world.

METAPSYCHOLOGY 'Metapsychology' is the term originally used by Freud to refer to the structure and function of the psyche, analogous to anatomy and physiology in reference to the body. The major difference is that the theories of metapsychology are abstractions rather than observable entities and any such model of the psyche is, as Freud readily admitted, a fiction, an imaginary model which does not represent concrete reality. However, all psychologists seem to develop such a 'map' of the psyche, which they say helps them to understand the workings of the mind. But even their warnings against mistaking the map for the territory conceal the assumption that the mind can usefully be likened to territory. Because we live in space even our abstract language tends to be spatial, so it is not surprising that we represent many systems and processes diagrammatically in spatial terms. What perhaps is surprising is that these representations are nearly always two-dimensional. There are dangers in this. Abstract notions are not only 'reified', but also located in a flat landscape (peopled by cardboard sub-personalities) which further diminishes whatever psychic reality these entities, impulses and complexes may possess. So certain aspects of psychological life become frozen, set in concrete, regarded as being fixed and located 'in' the UNCONSCIOUS MIND rather than having fluidity or resembling 'modes' of consciousness. Despite the undoubted usefulness of maps of the psyche such as Jung's or that proposed in PSYCHOSYNTHESIS, it is remarkable that we still find them so necessary. After all, we use the gears of a car without needing to represent them to ourselves diagrammatically. Perhaps one day we will understand metapsychology without diminishing it to something that can be drawn on the back of an envelope.

MIASM/MIASMA In HOMOEOPATHY, a miasm is a tendency to disease which is usually considered to be inherited. Hahnemann identified five infectious miasmic disorders: psychotic, syphilitic, psoric, cancerous and tubercular. In RADIONICS a miasm is a similar weakness, inherited or acquired, and detectable through DOWSING with a pendulum by a sensitive.

MICROWAVE (DIATHERMY) THERAPY See DIATHERMY.

MIDDLE UNCONSCIOUS See PSYCHOSYNTHESIS.

MIGRAINE The word 'migraine' is a shortening of Greek *hemikrania*, 'half of the skull', a reference to the tendency for the pain to start on one side of the head. Sufferers associate feelings of anxiety, nervous tension, anger or repressed rage with their migraine attacks, suggesting a strong link between the physical condition and the EMOTIONS. Certain PERSONALITY traits are commonly associated with migraine, and in some cases it is important to recognize the SECONDARY GAINS which might accrue with the condition, for example the opportunity for privacy from a demanding family, or the avoidance of another debilitating condition – the OPTIONAL ALLERGY syndrome. With AUTOGENIC TRAINING some patients have been able to alleviate or completely avoid an attack.

MIND The Ancient Egyptians believed that the mind-spirit-soul resided in the bowels and heart. The Sumerians located the mind in the liver. Plato reasoned intuitively that the mind resided in the head, and for Hippocrates the brain was the organ of the mind. Our usual reaction on considering these ancient notions is that the Greeks were right, because the mind *is* the brain. But is it? And why should the mind *be* anywhere? The view that some people are beginning to consider is that the mind is not a *part* of the body at all, but an integrative principle of the *whole*.

Kenneth Pelletier expresses the dilemma well. 'Science describes an evolutionary progression from inorganic matter to non-conscious entities, such as plants and lower animals, and finally to consciousness in animals and man. Consciousness is said to arise spontaneously when animals achieve a certain complexity of brain structure. This is reminiscent of the medieval theories of spontaneous combustion due to "phlogiston", prior to the discovery of the role of oxygen in combustion. Physical matter is considered to be primary, and consciousness is viewed as an epiphenomenon which arises spontaneously at a certain stage of biological evolution. At best this position is an assumption, and at worst it may be a misconception which impedes innovation. In all meditative systems, consciousness is regarded as primary.'[139]

Research into BIOFEEDBACK has shown the extent to which the mind can control physiological processes that were formerly regarded as wholly automatic (the responses of the AUTONOMIC NERVOUS SYSTEM), an ability which those adept in the techniques of MEDITATION (particularly YOGA) had claimed for centuries. Science can now tell us how the brain controls these processes, but not how that control can become voluntary, subject to the will. Research into the links between the EMOTIONS and BODY LANGUAGE has shown surprisingly that the effect can be reversed: not only do certain emotional attitudes result in specific physical postures, gestures or facial expressions; if those physical 'responses' are deliberately adopted, the associated emotion is then induced. Another aspect of this phenomenon had already been noticed in people learning the ALEXANDER TECHNIQUE and in BODY-ORIENTED PSYCHOTHERAPY, where psychological well-being can be induced by bringing the musculoskeletal structure of the physical body back into balance, reversing the processes that have given rise to BODY ARMOURING, for example. Psychological and physical health seem inextricably linked.

The example of improving mental health by means of body-oriented psychotherapies might suggest that the body 'rules' the mind, but the body's structural imbalances in such cases have their origin in mental attitudes, and ultimately it is the (mental) decision to do something about it that enables the individual to escape from the habitual, rigid, debilitating attitudes of both body and mind. The whole area of PSYCHOSOMATIC illness suggests that if one does rule the other, it is the mind that is supreme. Becoming more aware of one's UNCONSCIOUS attitudes and processes is also seen as generally beneficial. It is as if more of the mind then comes under the control of the WILL. Unconscious attitudes and tendencies may have a great deal to do with the conditions which give rise to disease (as suggested by theories about the CANCER PERSONALITY), and changing them can only be achieved if they become conscious. This is an essential part of SELF-HEALING, allowing the body's natural healing powers to go into action. This may be achieved by, as it were, wiping the mental slate clean in certain types of 'passive' MEDITATION and ATAVISTIC REGRESSION, or it may involve more active meditative techniques such as imagery and VISUALIZATION. In either case the will to heal oneself must be there.

Meir Schneider, a leading exponent of self-healing, believes that certain so-called DISEASES are not so much diseases as processes.

'Multiple sclerosis and arthritis are degenerative *processes*, not diseases. Unless the cooperation of the mind is sought in reducing the tension in the body and lessening the overload on the nervous system, the nerves of the multiple sclerosis patient will continue to deteriorate.'[157] It is in such conditions that self-healing and the power of the mind is most effective. Schneider distinguishes between true disease, for which modern medicine is very successful at finding cures, and 'the pathologies which arise from the mind's rigidity', for if suppressed in one form, these 'pathologies' will simply manifest as another disease. 'As long as we fear disease, it will never disappear. I believe that even if we stop vaccinating children against polio, an epidemic would be unlikely to recur – the fear of the threat of polio has gone. It has been transferred to other diseases. It is useless to overcome the fear of a particular disease. It is the fear itself which we must eradicate.'[157]

MIND MODULES Michael Gazzaniga sees the brain as organized into hundreds, maybe thousands, of independent 'mind modules' that continuously absorb and silently respond to what is happening within us. These mind modules cover all aspects of perception, sensing, memory and body functions, absorbing new information from outside and triggering responses as appropriate. Having no language, they express themselves only through behaviour, but one particular mind module, the 'interpreter', is able to interpret the behaviour of the others and informs another, the 'talker', which then verbalizes the interpretation. This is thought to explain why so much of our mental activity is below the threshold of our consciousness.

It is significant that the interpreter works retrospectively, devising a reason for the action triggered by another mind module. This is a reflection of our capacity to hypothesize. So EMOTIONS are the mind modules' way of registering certain automatic physiological responses ('I feel sad because I realize I am crying.'). SUB-PERSONALITIES can also be accommodated in this theory: the fact that many sub-personalities may co-exist in one person is simply a reflection of the notion that different sets of memories are retained by different mind modules. The central 'I' is then seen as the creation of the interpreter module.

MINDFULNESS Mindfulness is a particular type of awareness which overcomes the tendency to behave automatically, as if half-asleep. Many thinkers from Plato to Gurdjieff and Colin Wilson have spoken of the extent to which we live our lives in a somnambulant state, seldom if ever being really awake. The rarely achieved state of being truly awake is referred to in Buddhist teaching as *Satipatthana* – mindfulness. For Erich Fromm the cultivation of this state is an important extension of PSYCHOANALYSIS which he refers to as TRANSTHERAPEUTIC ANALYSIS. 'Mindfulness is practised not only in daily meditation exercises in which awareness of breathing is the central issue, but it is equally to be applied to every moment of daily living. It means not to do anything in a distracted manner, but in full concentration on what is at hand, whether this is walking, eating, thinking, seeing, so that living becomes fully transparent by full awareness.'[57] Buddhists also stress the simplicity of this state of mind: 'In its spirit of self-reliance *Satipatthana* does not require any elaborate *technique* or external devices. The daily life is its working material. It has nothing to do with exotic cults or rites nor does it confer "initiations" or "esoteric knowledge" in any way other than by self-enlightenment.'[134]

MISONEISM/MISONEIST Psychologists and anthropologists refer to a deep-seated fear or hatred of anything new or unknown as misoneism. Jung attacks those who deny the existence of the UNCONSCIOUS as misoneistic: 'Quite apart from the evidence that medical research has accumulated, there are strong grounds of logic for rejecting statements like "There is no unconscious." Those who say such things merely express an age-old "misoneism" – a fear of the new and the unknown.'[99]

MONOIDEISM James Braid (1795–1860) first coined the word HYPNOSIS from the Greek root for 'sleep'. With his further investigations into the phenomenon, he realized that the supposed connection with sleep (even the 'sleep of the nerves' implied by his first coinage, 'neur-hypnotism') was erroneous. His revised theory included the notion that focusing the mind on a single idea could lead in about 10 per cent of the people he investigated to hypnosis and increased suggestibility. He coined the word 'monoideism' to refer to this mental focusing on one idea.

MORAL INSANITY 'Moral insanity' was a term coined by James Cowles Prichard in his *Treatise on Insanity* in 1835. The French equivalent was *folie lucide* – 'lucid insanity', 'lucid' presumably to avoid the possible implication that the condition involved a loss of reasoning power. Although so-called moral insanity was accepted as justifiable grounds for committing someone (most frequently women) to a mental asylum, it actually signified little more than that such individuals did not live in the way society (or often, in the case of women, their husbands) wished them to live. Cure was conditional on the 'patient' achieving INSIGHT: accepting that they were ill and recognizing the need to conform to current standards of behaviour as decreed by society. Psychiatrists such as R. D. Laing, leading light in the ANTIPSYCHIATRY movement, have seen much the same phenomenon occurring today (schizophrenia being the equivalent modern diagnosis) and describe it in terms of the social reaction theory or LABELLING THEORY.

MOTHER TINCTURE In HOMOEOPATHY remedies are prepared by a process of progressive dilution (or 'attenuation') known as POTENTIZATION. The mother tincture is the solution from which successive degrees of attenuation are prepared.

MOTHER-SON RELATIONSHIP In ACUPUNCTURE the five elements and the yin organs associated with them are said to be in a nourishing cycle. Treating the lungs (metal), for example, will also provide more energy for the kidneys (water), since these are in a 'mother-son' relationship (metal holds water).

MOXA/MOXIBUSTION Moxa is the name given to dried mugwort (*Artemesia vulgaris latiflora*) as it is used in moxibustion. The word is derived from the Japanese *moe kusa*, meaning 'burning herb'. (The Chinese word for moxbustion is *jiu*, which means fire and is also the second element of the Chinese for 'acupuncture'.) In moxibustion ACUPUNCTURE points are treated with this smouldering herb instead of being needled. This warms the patient's CH'I, as is often required when the patient is deficient in yang energy. It is used particularly in winter with people who feel the cold unduly (a sign of possible yang deficiency).

In one method a small cone of dried or powdered leaves of the herb is placed on an acupuncture point, lit, and allowed to smoulder until it gets too warm for the patient, when it is briefly removed and then replaced several times. A cigar-shaped stick of moxa is used in a similar way – held over the appropriate point as it smoulders (this has the added advantage that it can be self-administered). Moxa may also be wrapped around the end of a needle, which is applied in the normal way, conducting the heat (and energy) of the smouldering leaves to the meridian.

MU POINTS In ACUPUNCTURE *mu* points are particular points on the front of the body which become more sensitive when the associated organs are affected. Since they indicate certain conditions which need treatment they are known as ALARM POINTS.

MUSCLE TESTING See KINESIOLOGY and BIOKINESTHESIOLOGY.

MUSIC/MUSIC THERAPY It has long been recognized that music can affect the emotions. It is also clear that music can help people in physical tasks inasmuch as martial music keeps soldiers marching in step and rhythmic songs have supported various types of manual labour throughout history, an effect that has more recently been exploited in the treatment of patients with neurological diseases that cause movement disorders. It has now been shown that music can have a direct physiological effect on the body too, and there is growing evidence that it can also affect the mind. So our response to music is emotional, physiological and mental, and, some would add, spiritual.

Listening to music with some degree of concentration causes increased arousal – heightened alertness, awareness and excitement – which manifests itself in various physiological changes characteristic of the FIGHT-OR-FLIGHT RESPONSE: changes in brain wave pattern, reduced electrical skin resistance, pupil dilation, changes in the respiratory rate, increase in muscular tone and sometimes physical restlessness (to the annoyance of concertgoers in neighbouring seats). When Herbert von Karajan was conducting, his pulse rate increased not when more physical effort was required but when he was most moved emotionally by the music. As psychiatrist Anthony Storr says, 'Music is said to soothe the savage breast, but it may also powerfully excite.'[167]

In treating people with neurological disorders, Oliver Sacks finds that 'The therapeutic power of music is very remarkable, and may allow an ease of movement otherwise impossible.'[154] Patients can make movements to the sound of music which without music they find impossible. On the other hand someone with 'musicogenic' epilepsy may suffer an epileptic seizure on hearing a specific piece of music: as well as affecting the listener physiologically, music can have a direct effect on the brain.

Analysing human responses to music sheds interesting light on the BICAMERAL NATURE OF THE BRAIN. Stammerers find that they can sometimes sing sentences they cannot speak; stammering, as part of speech, is usually controlled by the left hemisphere, whilst singing is predominantly the concern of the right. When people are monitored while listening to music, more activity is recorded in the right hemisphere so long as they are absorbed in responding to the music emotionally, but if asked to make a critical analysis of the music, they show more activity in the left hemisphere.

Recent research at the University of California at Irvine has shown that people perform better in spatial reasoning tasks immediately after listening to a Mozart piano sonata. Young children have also developed abstract reasoning skills more quickly if they have had some teaching in music. The theory proposed by Dr Gordon Shaw is that the firing patterns of neurones switching on and off in the brain during abstract reasoning (he monitored people playing chess) are reflected in the structure and harmony of music. It is generally accepted that the way the brain develops is partly determined by the external stimuli to which it is exposed, so it is suggested that exposure to music with a certain degree of structural and harmonic complexity could facilitate the establishment of neural networks which improve abstract reasoning. As Anthony Storr says, 'I find it unsurprising that musical education has a good effect upon studying other subjects; but this is not generally appreciated by educational planners and politicians. My guess is that future research will disclose that those who have been lucky enough to receive an adequate musical education in early life are better integrated in every way when they reach maturity; and are therefore likely to be both happier and more effective. I agree with Plato that music is "a heaven-sent ally in reducing to order and harmony any disharmony in the revolutions within us".'[167]

Throughout history, music has been associated with healing. Apollo was the Greek god of both healing and music; and the German romantic poet Novalis (1772–1801) wrote, 'Every disease is a musical problem; every cure a musical solution.' Today music therapy can be either active or receptive (or both). As a participatory therapy it has been used extensively in the treatment of handicapped children. People who cannot coordinate their movements adequately to tie their shoelaces have learned to perform such tasks successfully while singing the instructions to themselves. Active music therapy also works as an aid to self-expression and social rehabilitation and as a way of losing inhibitions (comparable to DANCE THERAPY and to some extent ART THERAPY), and this use is not, of course, restricted to those who are emotionally or mentally disturbed. Anthony Storr sees music as particularly important for people who are 'somewhat alienated from the body', because it can put them in touch with their physical being. He notes that 'Music began as a way of enhancing and coordinating group feelings. Today, it is often a means of recovering personal feelings from which we have become alienated.'[167]

The use of music as a means of reconnecting with our feelings takes many different forms and often becomes a means of reconnecting at a deeper level. The spiritual dimension is sometimes approached through CHANTING and 'toning' (singing single tones). Many spiritual disciplines teach that each individual soul has its own note. According to the Hekalot scriptures, esoteric Jewish writings on the heavenly spheres, when a new soul is incarnated it sends forth a vibration that resounds through the entire cosmos, continuing to sound throughout the incarnated life of that soul. Other spiritual disciplines have similar teachings about a person's 'own note' and about universal qualities of specific tones (just as some qualities are associated with specific colours). Mary Masselos, an Australian musician and psychotherapist, has drawn on some of these ancient ideas and her Jungian training to develop her own technique of exploiting a person's reactions to single tones. Finding the note which evokes negative feelings in the client, as well as the favourite tone, enables her to ease the pain associated with the memories that arise out of the unconscious by weaving a healing improvisation around the actual tones concerned. Perhaps we are now rediscovering the ancient healing art which was practised when King Saul's 'madness' was cured by David's harp music. (See also SOUND THERAPY and CYMATICS.)

MYOTHERAPY As a generic term 'myotherapy' (from the Greek *myo*, 'muscle') simply means treating muscles and may feature in the description of many forms of massage, but as a specific technique it refers to Bonnie Prudden's method of relieving pain by applying pressure to trigger points. Bonnie Prudden was an American physical fitness expert who achieved fame by treating Senator, later President, J. F. Kennedy for chronic back pain. At that time she injected a solution of saline and procaine into the painful muscle at trigger points – *trigger point injection therapy* or TPIT. Only in 1976 did she discover that acute (and incidentally very painful) pressure on the same trigger points could also solve many such problems. She has identified two categories of trigger point: matrix and satellite. Matrix points are the primary source of both local and referred pain; satellite points may arise near the original problem, but also require treatment, otherwise they are liable to trigger pain again even if the matrix has been adequately treated.

NADIS In YOGA and AYURVEDIC MEDICINE the nadis are the channels in the subtle anatomy along which LIFE-FORCE (*prana*) flows (comparable but not identical to the MERIDIANS in Chinese medicine). There are approximately 72,000 nadis in the human body, although the important ones are said to number 200; there are fourteen principal nadis, of which the three most important are the central *sushumna* nadi and the *ida* and *pingala* to the left and right of it. The main CHAKRAS lie along the central sushumna nadi. The ida and pingala nadis pass from the *muladhara* chakra at the base of the spine to the *ajna* or brow chakra, moving around each of the main chakras in turn. It is said that the symbol of the medical profession, the caduceus, is a representation of these three nadis, the wings at the top representing the crown chakra (*sahasrara*). These are the three nadis referred to in laya yoga and kundalini MEDITATION.

NAPRAPATHY Naprapathy is a manipulative technique, comparable to ROLFING (but not so widely practised), developed by American naturopath, Oakley Smith (1880–1970). Shrunken ligament tissue, mainly in the spine and supporting muscles, is stretched to bring blood flow back to its normal state.

NATAL THERAPY Natal therapy is a form of REBIRTHING developed by a psychotherapist, Elizabeth Fehr. When undergoing the rebirthing experience the rebirthers push themselves along a thirty-foot carpet.

NATURAL CHILDBIRTH/NATURAL BIRTH TECHNIQUES
There is no single method implied by the term 'natural childbirth', but it suggests less reliance on technology and drugs than is general in most western maternity units. The proportion of births at home in Britain declined from 33 per cent in 1961 to 3 per cent in 1976, and it was in this period that the attraction of so-called natural

birth techniques started to grow: mothers had an increasing sense of being on a production line, and little if any attention was paid to the feelings of the mother or of the child. In his book *Birth Without Violence* (1975) the French obstetrician Frederick Leboyer recommended that birth should take place in a quiet room with dim lighting, a far cry from most hospital delivery rooms. Among his other recommendations was that the newborn baby, before the cord was severed, should be placed immediately on the mother's warm stomach; gentle massage and immersion in tepid water would also lessen the trauma of birth. Leboyer noted that babies delivered in this way actually smile rather than cry.

Under Dr Michel Odent, the maternity unit in the hospital at Pithiviers, near Paris, became the pioneer and foremost exponent of natural childbirth in Europe. Women there choose how they wish to give birth: most opt for a squatting position, some relax in warm water until delivery, and some give birth underwater. Fear and anxiety during labour are known to exacerbate pain, so pain is minimized by the use of relaxation techniques in a generally supportive atmosphere. Anaesthetics and pain-killing drugs are not used, avoiding many unwanted side effects and reducing the risk of post-natal depression.

NATURAL HEALING A belief in the body's own SELF-HEALING power is fundamental to all NATURAL THERAPIES. In the words of Paracelsus, 'Man is his own doctor and finds healing herbs in his own garden. The physician is in ourselves, and in our own nature are all the things we need.' Even CONVENTIONAL MEDICINE has to admit that after an operation the surgeon can only sew the sides of the wound together and wait for the patient's self-healing abilities to seal it.

NATURAL THERAPIES See NATUROPATHY.

NATURAL VISION/NATURAL VISION IMPROVEMENT Natural vision improvement is a development of the BATES EYE METHOD, combined with modern theories of character and brain function, particularly the so-called integration of left and right hemispheres. It is a 'lifestyle' method of improving and maintaining eyesight without the use of optical devices, although 'transition glasses' with undercorrected lenses may be used for work and leisure until they can be dispensed with altogether.

NATUROPATHY The fundamental principle underlying all natural therapies is *vis medicatrix naturae* – the healing power of nature, i.e. the body's innate capacity for self-healing. Symptoms are regarded as evidence that the body is already healing itself, and suppression of these symptoms will probably obstruct the natural healing process. Naturopathic medicine covers a variety of therapies, the one common factor being that they use only natural forces (such as sunlight and water) and diet; if medicines are required they are compounded from natural substances (mainly plants). The basic techniques of naturopathic medicine are therefore HYDROTHERAPY, HELIOTHERAPY, nature cures such as the KNEIPP CURE, DIETARY THERAPIES, HERBALISM and HOMOEOPATHY. MASSAGE, OSTEOPATHY and CHIROPRACTIC are also regarded as naturopathic disciplines.

NAULI Nauli is an exercise in yoga for cleansing the bowel. See HYDROTHERAPY.

NEEDS Classical Freudian psychology regarded the human being as driven by certain needs which could be isolated and studied individually. It was Abraham Maslow's view that these basic needs in fact form a hierarchy and that new needs are felt with the satisfaction of lower needs on each successive level of that hierarchy. The hierarchy ranges from physiological needs, through safety needs, love needs and esteem needs, to self-actualization needs. The basic needs are deficiency needs, but beyond them Maslow saw a higher category which he called metaneeds, GROWTH needs or BEING-VALUES (or B-values) such as truth, beauty, individuality, justice, meaningfulness. These are different aspects of self-actualization needs and it is not possible to place them in any hierarchy. It is these higher needs which form the basis of HUMANISTIC PSYCHOLOGY and distinguish it from behaviourism and Freudian psychology.

Maslow defined a basic need as one which satisfies the following five conditions:

1. Its absence breeds illness.
2. Its presence prevents illness.
3. Its restoration cures illness.
4. Under certain, very complex, free-choice situations, it is preferred by the deprived person over other satisfactions.
5. It is found to be inactive, at a low ebb, or functionally absent in healthy persons.[125]

The most basic needs are physiological: the need for oxygen, food, drink, shelter, sleep and sex. These needs will take precedence over whatever other needs are felt: someone who lacks food, self-esteem and love will demand food first, and only when this need is satisfied will the other needs receive full attention. When the physiological needs are satisfied, 'other (and higher) needs emerge, and these, rather than physiological hungers, dominate the organism. And when these in turn are satisfied, again new (and still higher) needs emerge, and so on. This is what we mean when we say that the basic human needs are organized into a hierarchy of relative prepotency.'[126]

After the physiological needs are satisfied the individual is driven by safety needs – the need for security, order and stability. When the safety needs are met, the next to emerge are needs for love, affection and a sense of belonging. 'Love hunger is a deficiency disease,' says Maslow,[125] and he notes also that 'The love need involves both giving and receiving love.'[126]

After the love and 'belongingness' needs we feel esteem needs, both self-esteem and respect from others. The significance of the combination of these two implies that undeserved respect is never enough, hence the emptiness felt by some who may enjoy celebrity and adulation but do not feel that they themselves have achieved anything. Maslow thought that certain individuals also have strong aesthetic needs, for example for beauty, and that these were generally related to a person's self-image, inasmuch as those with low self-esteem feel that they do not deserve beauty and seem unable to enjoy it.

Finally in the hierarchy come what Maslow called the SELF-ACTUALIZATION needs, 'the desire to become more and more what one is, to become everything that one is capable of becoming.'[126] 'Related to the need for self-actualization is the desire to know and to understand, to systematize, to organize, to analyse, to look for relations and meanings, to construct a system of values',[126] a process which others have called the search for MEANING. At this level a range of BEING NEEDS, 'B-needs', come into play, such as the need for personal GROWTH, for creative expression, for transcendence of the self and for peak experiences.

The basic deficiency needs ('D-needs') are usually discovered, desired and where possible satisfied in order according to their position in the hierarchy, although there are exceptions to the rule, such as when idealistic individuals disregard their own needs for the sake of some greater purpose. There is also a certain flexibility between adjacent levels: for example, the need for security may well start to emerge before the need for food has been fully satisfied. People may also not advance beyond the level of esteem needs, and even if all these are fulfilled the need for self-actualization does not necessarily develop, perhaps because of inertia.

It has often been noted that this hierarchy represents a synthesis of many theories, each of which in isolation paints only a partial picture. If we base our understanding of human nature solely on the first two levels of needs, physiological and security, we arrive at a Marxist view of mankind. Freud's view too was rooted in the physiological and security needs experienced in childhood, plus the physiological need for sex, perhaps with the added consideration of the next level, the hunger for love. Reich too stressed love and attachment, but Adler was the first to recognize the importance of self-respect and the esteem of others and based his psychology on this level of esteem needs. Then Goldstein came up with the notion of self-actualization, the urge to become whatever we have it in ourselves to be, and Jung too developed his concept of INDIVIDU-ATION, the search for self-fulfilment. Maslow synthesized all these viewpoints in one structure, the hierarchy of needs, as an integral part of HUMANISTIC PSYCHOLOGY.

NEGATIVE ASSERTION One of the techniques for responding to criticism in ASSERTIVENESS TRAINING.

NEGATIVE ENQUIRY One of the techniques for responding to criticism in ASSERTIVENESS TRAINING.

NEGATIVE ION THERAPY See IONIZATION THERAPY.

NEIGUAN The neiguan is an acupuncture point inside the forearm which is pressed by a band worn to prevent or reduce travel-sickness.

NEOPSYCHE/NEOPSYCHIC In TRANSACTIONAL ANALYSIS the neopsychic ego state is more commonly referred to as the Adult.

NEURO-EPIDEMIC Neuro-epidemics are outbreaks of diseases of the nervous system that cannot be accounted for by standard transmission of airborne viruses from person to person or by other forms of contact and seem therefore to have a mental cause. The best documented cases are of PARA-POLIO, which usually affects hospital staff. Lewis Thomas has suggested that 'something like the panic-producing pheromones that slave-taking ants release to disorganize the colonies of their prey' may be responsible, implying that MASS HYSTERIA may also be the result of such scent molecules.[169]

NEURO-LINGUISTIC PROGRAMMING Neuro-linguistic programming (NLP) was developed in the early 1970s by Richard Bandler and John Grinder, who based their ideas on the work of the hypnotherapist Milton Erickson, the family therapist Virginia Satir and the GESTALT pioneer Fritz Perls, and set out to identify the key factors which underlay their therapy. Rather than studying what these therapists thought about the changes taking place in their clients, they looked for patterns of communication in the therapist/patient relationship. As with HUMANISTIC PSYCHOLOGY, Grinder and Bandler were interested in psychologically healthy individuals, in excellence rather than mediocrity, and they looked for the patterns of communication used by such people, the three therapists being ideal examples. The success of these therapists lay not so much in their theories or techniques as in the care and attention they gave each individual client, adapting their behaviour to the client's specific mechanisms of perception. For example, by noting changes in pupil size, direction of gaze, breathing and head movements, the therapist can determine whether the client is using visual and auditory recall and adopt the appropriate mode in which to respond. The skills which NLP develops are used not only in therapy but also in education, the performing arts, and not least management training.

Beyond its use in developing better communication skills, NLP is a method of using mental exercises to alter ingrained behaviour patterns – overcoming phobias, eliminating recurrent and destructive emotional and intellectual reactions – so that new patterns can emerge. One learns how to create and shape inner experience, how to resolve the painful feelings around past experiences, superimposing good feelings on unpleasant past events, and how to contact one's innate wisdom and develop neglected strengths and abilities.

NEUROLOGIC Timothy Leary, guru of the 1960s drugs culture and one of the key figures in arousing popular interest in consciousness expansion, coined the word 'neurologic' to refer to the innate intelligence of the human nervous system which is encoded in DNA and which, he thought, seems to govern everything from evolution to consciousness.

NEURO-MUSCULAR TECHNIQUE Neuro-muscular technique is a form of massage in which both diagnosis and treatment work directly on the connective tissue known as the fascia, which is rich in nerve endings. It was developed in the 1940s by Stanley Lief, a chiropractor and osteopath, and Boris Chaitow, his cousin, as a simplified system covering the main reflex points through which the sensitive practitioner can detect and prevent potential problems.

NEURO-PHYSIOLOGICAL PSYCHOLOGY An alternative term for PSYCHOPHYSIOLOGY.

NEUROTIC LAYER In GESTALT psychology the neurotic layer is the second layer of the personality. It is also known as the phobic layer.

NOCEBO Not all the results of the PLACEBO effect are positive and therapeutic: placebos can produce a wide range of symptoms including palpitations, drowsiness, headaches, diarrhoea and nausea. Such placebo-induced 'side effects' are sometimes referred to as 'nocebo effects'.[60]

NON-DIRECTIVE COUNSELLING See CLIENT-CENTRED THERAPY.

NONDISEASE A nondisease is a form of IATROGENIC ILLNESS. For example, cardiac nondisease is a 'disorder' created by misdiagnosis, a condition which arises when a patient is identified incorrectly as suffering from a weak heart. When people are told that they have something wrong with their heart they are instructed to follow a regime of restricted physical activity. This can obviously have serious consequences if the patient is actually perfectly healthy, particularly if the patient is a child: restricted physical activity in children can impair intellectual development.[194] In some cases it has been shown that as many as 80 per cent of children diagnosed as suffering from heart disease have been misdiagnosed in this way.[219] (Nondiseases are not to be confused with pseudo-diseases such as PARA-POLIO, or FUNCTIONAL ILLNESSES in which the symptoms have no identifiable cause.)

NOÖGENIC NEUROSIS According to Viktor Frankl, classical PSYCHOANALYSIS ignores an important area of our psychic life which is specifically addressed in his LOGOTHERAPY, namely our

WILL-TO-MEANING. Neurosis can be caused by a sense of meaning-lessness, resulting when the will-to-meaning is frustrated, and such neurosis is described as noögenic. Frankl claims that far from wanting a totally stress-free existence, we actually need a certain kind of tension in life, 'the kind of tension that is established between a human being, on the one hand, and, on the other hand, a meaning he has to fulfil. In fact, if an individual is not challenged by any tasks to complete, and thus is *spared* the specific tension aroused by such tasks, a certain type of neurosis – noögenic neurosis – may ensue.'[46]

NOSODES In HOMOEOPATHY nosodes are taken to stimulate the body's immune system in the way that IMMUNIZATION is used in conventional medicine. They are prepared from minute quantities of diseased substance according to the principles of POTENTIZATION.

NUCIFORM SAC In his play *The Doctor's Dilemma*, George Bernard Shaw ridiculed the pretensions of the medical profession. One char-acter in the play, Cutler Walpole, developed a theory attributing all illness to pockets of infection which he called 'nuciform sacs' – nut-shaped pouches of membrane surrounding the toxic matter. In medical circles in the 1920s there was in fact a similar theory that any disease could be cured if one could simply find the 'focal sepsis' which was at its root and cut it out. Inflamed tonsils were thought to be just such a focus of infection and children's tonsils continued to be excised unnecessarily for several decades, to the extent that tonsillectomy could almost qualify as an example of PLACEBO surgery.

NUTRITION 'Food or drink which is in itself slightly inferior but more pleasant should be preferred to that which is better in itself but less pleasant.' So wrote Hippocrates. In recommending that we judge the worth of food by its pleasant taste he was showing his inclination towards natural healing and the view that the body knows best what is good for it. Many people still feel that, when sick, whatever they have a craving for will do them good, but in general our taste buds have been distracted through the artificial sweetening of food to the extent that our instincts can no longer be relied on as a guide to general nutrition.

Nutrition forms an integral part of all ancient healing systems such as AYURVEDA and Chinese medicine. The distinction the Chinese made between *yin* foods and *yang* foods has been revived and extend-ed in MACROBIOTICS. A similar balancing of foods is recommended in the Hay Diet, which became popular in Britain and the USA in the 1930s, although in this case it is the acid–alkali balance which is paramount. As well as DIETARY THERAPIES which dictate or recommend what should be eaten, there are various therapies which make use of supplements – of vitamins in MEGAVITAMIN THERAPY and of minerals or 'tissue salts' in BIOCHEMICS.

OCEANIC FEELING The oceanic feeling is usually likened to the state of mind experienced by mystics when they feel at one with themselves and with the universe – 'cosmic consciousness'. Freud defined the oceanic feeling as 'a feeling of an indissoluble bond, of being one with the external world as a whole'.[48] He adopted the term coined in a letter to him by Romain Rolland, who complained that Freud did not understand the true origin of religious feelings (as expressed in *The Future of an Illusion*). The religious impulse came, said Rolland, from 'a sensation of "eternity", a feeling as of something limitless, unbounded – as it were, "oceanic".'[48] Freud regarded the oceanic feeling as originating in the actual sensation of the foetus in the womb and representing (in the adult) a longing to merge again with the mother.

OCULAR SEGMENT In REICHIAN THERAPY the first of the seven body areas is the ocular segment, covering the eyes, forehead and scalp.

OD/ODIC FORCE The German chemist Baron Karl von Reichen-bach (1788–1869) found that some people were able to identify the north pole of a magnet by the presence of a cold current or a bluish haze around it. Different colours were said to emanate from different CRYSTALS. Reichenbach postulated the existence of these radiations in the whole of nature, including the human body around which they formed a kind of AURA. He named this energy od (after the Norse god Odin) to distinguish it from electromagnetic radiation.

O-FIELD An American journalist, Edward J. Russell, suggested that everything in nature has an O-field or organizing field (comparable to Burr's L-field), which acts as a master blueprint for its material form. Like T-FIELDS, O-fields could link across space, and this was Russell's explanation of how DOWSING, RADIESTHESIA and RADIONICS work. In radionics the DIAGNOSTIC WITNESS enables the practitioner to establish direct contact between his O-field and that of the patient.

OK According to Thomas Harris, author of *I'm OK – You're OK*, which did much to popularize TRANSACTIONAL ANALYSIS, there are four 'life positions' which we adopt with respect to ourselves and others. These are:

1. I'm OK – You're OK.
2. I'm OK – You're not OK.
3. I'm not OK – You're OK.
4. I'm not OK – You're not OK.

The first position is adopted by people who feel good about themselves, are aware of their strengths, accept their limitations, and are able to compromise. People who adopt the second life position operate like the critical Parent – authoritarian, arrogant, smug – whilst those in position three operate like the needy child – a victim, dependent, seeking approval. Those in life position four behave as victim through and through, with no prospect of help from the outside world. One of the positive aspects of Harris's approach (reflected in the original title of his book, *The Book of Choice*) is that he emphasizes our ability to change. 'The goal of Transactional Analysis is to enable a person to have freedom of choice, the freedom to change at will, to change the responses to recurring and new stimuli.'[80] This involves adopting the first, 'Adult' position, which is capable of evaluating.

OMT OMT is a common abbreviation for 'osteopathic manipulative therapy'. (See OSTEOPATHY.)

OPHTHALMIC SOMATOLOGY An alternative term for IRID-OLOGY.

OPTIONAL ALLERGY The neurologist Oliver Sacks has argued that there is often an unconscious psychological element in migraine. He cites one example of a patient whose migraine he had successfully treated with drugs only to have him return asking for the condition to be given back to him, since without the migraines a previous condition of severe asthma had returned more virulently than ever.[153]

ORAL SEGMENT In REICHIAN THERAPY the oral segment is one of the seven areas of the body, covering most of the muscles of the face below the eyes.

ORGONE/ORGONE THERAPY/ORGONOMY Wilhelm Reich (1897–1957) believed that we are surrounded by a continuum of life-energy, a fundamental energy which he called Primordial or Cosmic Orgone Energy. (Antecedents of this idea can be seen in the eastern belief in a LIFE-force – *prana* and *ch'i* – and in Mesmer's notion of 'animal magnetism', which he exploited in MESMERISM.) This energy, Reich said, is distinct from electromagnetic energy; it is in constant motion, usually pulsating from east to west. Living organisms absorb orgone and discharge what is surplus to their requirements. Since orgone is attracted to vegetable matter and reflected by metal, Reich constructed an orgone accumulator consisting of layers of wood and metal. The orgone trapped inside this device could be channelled through a tube and used for healing purposes, and patients could actually be seated inside larger accumulators. Rapid healing of wounds and burns without scarring was reported with orgone accumulators or 'shooter' devices, and Reich proved at least to his own satisfaction that cancers arose in areas of the body where orgone was not flowing properly.

During an experiment in 1950 in which Reich was investigating the use of orgone to counteract the dangers of radiation, many workers in the Orgone Institute in New York suffered radiation sickness and background radiation was reported to be raised for 600 miles around the Institute. Reich believed that a reaction between orgone and nuclear fission in the radium he was using had created a new radiation, which he called Deadly Orgone or DOR. He claimed that DOR was also produced by nature over deserts, and further that this process was increased by nuclear tests in those areas, creating high concentrations of DOR in the clouds which led to the deserts' rapid encroachment on the surrounding arable land. Reich's continued research into orgone and radiation was in defiance of a court order and it was while working on ways of dispersing clouds supposedly containing DOR in the Arizona desert that Reich was arrested for contempt of court, but the campaign against him proved unsuccessful in 1950. By 1954, however, the

US Food and Drugs Administration had mounted another attack on Reich's work and were successful in demanding the destruction in a Long Island incinerator of all his research records as well as all orgone accumulators 'on the grounds that orgone energy does not exist'. Sentenced to two years imprisonment, Reich died from a heart attack while still in prison.

Reich distinguished between two forms of orgone therapy – physical and psychiatric – the accumulators being used only in physical orgone therapy. Today he is better known (and respected) for his psychological theories and his input into BODY-ORIENTED PSYCHOLOGY through REICHIAN THERAPY (which includes, for example, breathing exercises which Reich maintained increased the flow of orgone energy in the body). One of his most influential disciples, Alexander Lowen, continued to develop his methods and ideas of somatic psychology in BIOENERGETICS but totally rejected Reich's theory of orgone. However, traces of some of the principles behind (physical) orgone therapy may still be seen in practices such as RADIONICS and PSIONICS, and some have considered it has similarities with IONIZATION THERAPY.

ORTHODOX MEDICINE See CONVENTIONAL MEDICINE.

ORTHOMOLECULAR PSYCHIATRY This was the original name for what became more generally known as MEGAVITAMIN THERAPY. Initially it was used to treat psychiatric conditions, in particular schizophrenia, but it was later applied to other illnesses.

ORTHOPTICS Orthoptics is a method of exercising eye muscles to correct crossed eyes.

OSCILLOCLAST In the early days of RADIONICS, an oscilloclast was an instrument used to treat patients with pulsed weak electromagnetic energy with the intention of restoring the balance of their own electromagnetic field.

OSTEOPATHY Osteopathy was founded and named (from the Greek *osteon*, meaning 'bone', and *pathos*, disease) by Andrew Taylor Still (1828–1912). He was born in Jonesborough, Virginia, the son of a farmer and physician who was also a Methodist minister, and taking up medicine himself he practised as an army doctor in the civil war (on the Union side). In 1874 he lost three of his children in an epidemic of viral meningitis in Missouri. It was Still's belief that all diseases were effects, the cause being the failure of the blood adequately to nourish the nervous system: as he said, 'Interfere with the current of the blood, and you steam down the river of life and land on the ocean of death.'[93] He thought that the harmonious flow of arterial blood could also be adversely affected by the position of the body, and he started to develop a theory based on the premise that dysfunction is caused by alteration in the structure of the body. According to this view, any alteration in the structure of the skeletal system and the muscles will affect the function of the associated organs; so the remedy for disease lies within the patient. If the spine was adjusted by manipulation, the blood flow would be restored to normal, and the symptoms would disappear. 'All the remedies to human health exist in the human body. They can be administered by adjusting the human body in such a manner that the remedies may naturally associate themselves together, hear the cries and relieve the afflicted.'[93]

Still formulated the 'rule of the artery', which states that wherever the circulation of the blood is normal, disease cannot develop because our blood is capable of manufacturing all the necessary substances to maintain natural immunity against disease. Disease prevention is therefore possible by maintaining healthy circulation. At the root of all diseases lie 'lesions'. Osteopathic lesions may be described as 'chronic' if they are long-standing, or 'acute' if they are of recent origin, and the osteopath works on these structural abnormalities directly. There are three main types of technique in osteopathy: rhythmic (e.g. kneading, springing, EFFLEURAGE), THRUST (e.g. high velocity thrust) and stress (also called low velocity stress). (See also PALPATION, CRANIAL OSTEOPATHY and CHIROPRACTIC.)

OTTO Used for example in the expression 'rose otto', otto is an alternative form of the word ATTAR, meaning essential oil.

PADMASANA In HATHA YOGA the lotus position is known as *padmasana*.

PAIN Mental attitude and bodily sensation are inextricably linked in the experience of pain. If we are injured in an emergency and have to escape as quickly as possible, then we are less likely to notice any pain until the emergency has passed and we are out of danger; the fact that we are preoccupied with a situation that is more urgent distracts our attention from pain. If on the other hand we anticipate pain, as we might at the dentist's, or prior to being given an injection, then the pain we feel is more severe. There is also the question of where PHANTOM LIMB PAIN originates in amputees. Only in recent decades has it been recognized that the intensity of a pain cannot be equated with the severity of an injury, and that in some cases pain might not even be related to any specific physical cause at all.

In a study of soldiers wounded on a beach-head in the Pacific during the Second World War, Henry Beecher (who was to become famous for his research into the PLACEBO EFFECT) noticed that only a quarter of the wounded needed medication for their pain. He recognized that pain for a soldier was significantly different from pain experienced by other people in other circumstances. Furthermore there were interesting variations in the soldiers' reactions: those who were less badly hurt apparently experienced more pain and required more pain medication. These soldiers knew that their less severe wounds meant they would be patched up and sent back to fight, so they felt the pain more. For the more severely wounded, on the other hand, their injuries were their passport home, and their overriding joy at this prospect must have been a significant factor in reducing the level of pain felt.

This shows to what extent pain is a totally subjective experience, and underlines the importance not only of the mental attitudes and emotions surrounding the pain but also of the intrinsic meaning which the pain has for the individual. With the mental component so significant in the experience of pain it is perhaps not surprising that pain can be reduced by placebos, but the extent to which placebos are effective will still depend partly on the meaning of the disorder or illness to the person. Whatever the sufferer may consciously wish for, there may be SECONDARY GAINS in continuing to suffer.

Symptomatic treatment of pain, although the least effective method in the long term, has been by far the most common way to deal with it. This is true both of CONVENTIONAL MEDICINE, from the use of cold compresses to taking aspirin, and of many ALTERNATIVE remedies, from ACUPUNCTURE to feverfew in HERBALISM and even arnica in HOMOEOPATHY. In general, conventional medicine has been rather unsuccessful in countering pain, and this is probably because it has concentrated on symptomatic treatment. Practitioners of alternative therapies are more likely to concentrate on finding the root cause of the lower-back pain or the headache, and this may be environmental as well as internal. Headaches among office workers, for example, have been reduced by IONIZATION of the office atmosphere.

Apart from the therapies based on MANIPULATION (OSTEOPATHY, CHIROPRACTIC, etc.) and acupuncture (with or without TRANSCUTANEOUS ELECTRONIC NERVE STIMULATION), the most effective alternative measures against pain have been therapies which involve the mind directly: BIOFEEDBACK (including AUTOGENIC TRAINING), RELAXATION and MEDITATION, COUNSELLING and PSYCHOTHERAPY, and – most effective of all – HYPNOTHERAPY. In one pain control experiment the effectiveness of various drugs (morphine, aspirin and benzodiazepine), placebos, acupuncture (both at true ACUPOINTS and at random positions) and hypnosis were compared. Hypnosis proved to be the most effective treatment by far, with acupuncture (using true acupoints only) and morphine in second place.[227]

Ivan Illich has drawn attention to the cultural factors in the perception of pain. For example, it is culture that determines whether the mother or father or both are expected to groan when their child is born. In traditional cultures pain is perceived as a necessity and is therefore to some extent more tolerable than in the 'civilized' West, which Illich describes as 'the twentieth-century dystopia', where we have been conditioned to regard pain as controllable: 'pain is treated as an emergent contingency which must be dealt with by extraordinary interventions.'[91] Medical civilization has objectified pain, regarding it as something which can be verified, measured and regulated, and referring to it as 'pain behaviour' or even 'learned pain behaviour' rather than as a subjective response. The worst aspect of the MEDICALIZATION of pain, as Illich sees it, is that the individual's experience is somehow invalidated and misappropriated: 'The medical profession judges which pains are authentic, which have a physical and which a psychic base, which are imagined, and which are simulated . . . The person in pain is left with less and less social context to give meaning to the experience that often overwhelms him.'[91]

It is partly as a reaction against this phenomenon of 'medicalization' that people have been turning to alternative medicine in greater numbers in recent years. Many alternative therapies emphasize the importance of assuming responsibility for one's own state of health, and recognizing the meaning of one's own pain is the first step towards owning it and controlling it, if it is controllable.

PAINMANSHIP In the 1960s Thomas Szasz coined the word 'pain-manship' to refer to the use of pain as an instrument of interpersonal control, whether by the one suffering the pain (SECONDARY GAINS) or by those relating to the sufferer (TERTIARY GAIN).

PALMING Dr William Bates, author of the BATES METHOD of eyesight training, believed that most people could benefit from closing the eyes and relaxing the eye muscles. To prevent light from passing through the closed eyelids, the eyes are further shielded with the hands: in 'palming' the cupped palms are gently placed over the closed eyes, avoiding contact with the eyes themselves, with the fingers overlapping on the forehead. The near total exclusion of light is said to encourage more complete relaxation. Whilst in this relaxed state the patient is sometimes asked to remember or imagine a particular colour or image.

It was partly Bates's accidental discovery of palming which led him to develop his method. After a busy series of consultations with patients one day, when he was still working as a conventional ophthalmologist, he took of his glasses and, leaning his head in his hands, covered his eyes. After relaxing in this position for about ten minutes, he took his hands away from his eyes and noticed that everything seemed brighter and clearer than before.

PALMISTRY The study and analysis of hands, *chirology*, can be divided into three areas. Palmistry is usually equated with *chiromancy* (from the Greek for 'hand' and 'prophecy'), which nowadays is taken to mean the analysis of the lines on the palm; in *chirognomy* (the study of hand types) the shape, texture and general appearance of the whole hand is considered; and *dermatoglyphics* is concerned with skin patterns, particularly those used in fingerprinting.

The last of these acquired the status of a science when the scientist and explorer Sir Francis Galton (1822–1911) established the uniqueness of each individual's fingerprints and developed a system of describing and categorizing the loops, arches and whorls, enabling it to be used as a method of detecting criminals. In spite of this, the scientific community has been reluctant to accept the notion that there could be a link between the unique patterns on a person's hand and any other aspect of that individual's condition.

Palmistry has always dealt as much with personality traits as with prophecy. Foretelling the future is more often understood nowadays as showing certain predispositions in the individual which make certain events more likely. In the same way modern palmistry may draw attention to the risk factors involved in being a particular 'type' and reveal predispositions to certain illnesses. This can apply to both physical and mental conditions. Doctors working at Osaka Hospital in Japan in the 1960s claimed that they were able to predict patients' susceptibility to specific diseases by studying their palm prints. In the 1950s researchers at the Galton Laboratory noticed that in three out of four cases of Down's syndrome the two lines across the palm associated with the head and the heart were replaced by a single 'simian crease', a line that had also been associated with criminality and so called because it is common in apes. Another group of abnormal handprints was recorded among babies in New York in 1966, and it was discovered that they had all been born during an epidemic of German measles. Modern practitioners of *psycho-chirology* or psychological palmistry can also ascertain from a client's hand whether problems that have led to psychotherapy have been adequately resolved or not – certain configurations of lines actually change according to one's psychological condition.

PALPATION Dr Andrew Still, founder of OSTEOPATHY, used the term 'palpation' to refer to the diagnosis by touch of the speed, heat and quality of blood flow to a particular area of the body. After examining a patient's posture visually the osteopath uses a highly refined sense of touch to assess tissue states, particularly in the joints and muscles of the back, pelvis, neck and shoulders. Although conventional orthopaedists also use palpation, their technique is essentially quantitative, measuring four types of symptom: areas of unusual warmth or coldness, deviations from the normal shape and outline of bones, changes in the muscle and tissues, and areas of abnormal tenderness. Osteopaths, on the other hand, adopt a much more qualitative approach, as can be seen from a list of some of the terms they use to describe what they identify by palpation: compression, decompression, tensity, flaccidity, stress, drag, sag, strain, sprain, shock, contraction, expansion, torque, rotation, agitation, restriction, fullness, flatness, force, vitality, tone, power, balance, fluctuation, and many more.

PANACEA From the Greek *pan*, 'all', and *akos*, 'cure', a panacea is literally a remedy for all ills, a cure for all diseases. The root GINSENG (the genus is called *Panax*), with its reputation as an ELIXIR, is widely regarded as a general panacea and does seem to stimulate the immune system. But in common usage the word 'panacea' has lost much of the strength of its original meaning, bringing it closer to the notion of a palliative, or, more derogatorily, a nostrum (or quack remedy). The need for a panacea seems to be part of human nature (rather like our tendency to believe in the MAGIC BULLET approach), to such an extent that we are relatively easily persuaded to take a daily dose of the latest cure-all. This tendency is just as rife, if not more so, among those who subscribe to ALTERNATIVE MEDICINE, whether they swear by ginseng or evening primrose. For those in the mainstream of CONVENTIONAL MEDICINE the most common panaceas are supplements of vitamins and minerals, perhaps influenced by the ideas around MEGAVITAMIN THERAPY. The notion of a genuinely universal panacea is alien to conventional medicine, with its attachment to the principle of SINGLE CAUSE, SINGLE CURE. If as a self-help measure someone does take an alternative remedy such as ginseng for a period of time, rather than consult a physician and have a specific drug prescribed, sceptics may still ascribe any improvement in the condition to the PLACEBO EFFECT.

PARADOXICAL SLEEP So-called paradoxical sleep, also known as rapid-eye-movement (REM) sleep, was discovered in 1952 by Eugene Aserinsky and William Dement, two students of Nathaniel Kleitman, who was a pioneer of SLEEP research at the University of Chicago. It occurs during sleep periods for about thirty minutes at roughly ninety-minute intervals and is accompanied by sudden relaxation of body muscles. When woken during REM sleep people report that they were dreaming, and the simultaneous relaxation of body muscles may explain why in many DREAMS we have the sensation of 'walking through treacle' or trying unsuccessfully to move. The brain activity in this state is the same as in wakefulness, whereas in deep sleep (also called 'slow wave sleep') the BRAIN WAVES are the slower delta type (0.5–8.5 cycles per second). Sleep is restorative, particularly REM sleep, and in experiments people deprived of REM sleep have become increasingly disoriented.

PARA-POLIO Para-polio is a mysterious disease (or pseudo-disease) which mimics the symptoms of polio such as muscle weakness and tenderness of the limbs, but without the presence of the polio virus. It cannot be attributed to any physical cause but affects many people at the same time and is the most common example of a NEURO-EPIDEMIC: the combination of an apparently mental cause among people in groups suggests a similarity with cases of MASS

HYSTERIA. An outbreak of para-polio in 1934 at the Los Angeles County General Hospital affected medical staff at a time when the general population of the city was going through a polio epidemic. Some of the victims suffered permanent effects. Other cases were reported in Iceland (1948), and in London at the Royal Free Hospital (1955), where again the majority of the sufferers were nurses. It may be significant that as polio itself has diminished in public consciousness with the routine vaccination of children and the virtual eradication of the disease (at least in the West), so the occurrence of para-polio has also declined, emphasizing the presumed mental origin of the condition.

PARASYMPATHETIC NERVOUS SYSTEM The parasympathetic system is that part of the autonomic nervous system which induces a general state of relaxation in the body, countering the effects of the SYMPATHETIC NERVOUS SYSTEM. For example, whilst the sympathetic system tenses muscles in preparation for FIGHT-OR-FLIGHT, the parasympathetic system initiates dilation of muscles as part of the so-called 'relaxation response'. This aspect of the nervous system acts as an energy conserver by inducing rest.

PARENT See TRANSACTIONAL ANALYSIS.

PARTICULANTS Positive ions in the air we breathe have been described as pollutants by those who recommend IONIZATION THERAPY. One such individual is Roger Wasmer of Alpha-Omega, a US firm that had sold over three million ionizers by 1981. When marketing his firm's product he coined the word *particulant* to refer to the positive ions in the atmosphere – a portmanteau word from 'particle' and 'pollutant'.

PAST LIFE THERAPY In past life therapy a person is encouraged, usually under light hypnosis, to bring to mind the experiences of other personalities which appear to be part of their own memory to the extent that they condition, usually in a very restrictive sense, their present life. This technique is often called hypnotic regression, because the subject is 'taken back' to relate and re-experience traumatic events from 'previous lifetimes'. Without hypnosis the techniques used to gain access to such memories are similar to those used in PRIMAL THERAPY and PSYCHODRAMA.

It would seem that the therapy presupposes a belief in reincarnation, but Roger Woolger, a psychotherapist who specializes in past life therapy (having started out as a total sceptic), tells his clients, 'It doesn't matter whether you believe in reincarnation or not; simply follow the story *as if* it were real for the duration of the session.'[185] It is then as if experiencing a possible past-life cause of a current phobia somehow releases the grip that the phobia has on the individual; bringing to consciousness one's worst fears, facing and virtually living through the worst possible scenario which that phobia represents, is a healing experience, so cathartic that the fear is totally transformed. Woolger has noted that in many successful regressions the emotional release which occurs is accompanied by physical changes reminiscent of release mechanisms experienced in BODYWORK therapies, such as STREAMING in REICHIAN THERAPY, or in REBIRTHING. (The right question at the appropriate moment during a rebirthing session can actually lead to the experience of a 'past-life' memory.)

How does this compare with standard practice in psychotherapy? 'By treating these fragments of stories *as if* they were real, the emphasis in therapy has moved away from the endless psychoanalytic *interpretation* of their meanings – therapy as an intellectual exercise punctuated with bursts of emotion – to the direct experiential reliving of a traumatic event buried in the unconscious.'[185] Dr Woolger is fond of quoting Jung's principle that 'We do not become enlightened by imagining figures of light, but by making the darkness conscious.'[100] Jung was referring here primarily to work with the SHADOW, but the same applies to any negative complexes, and past life therapy is one way not only of acknowledging such complexes but of releasing oneself from them by experiencing them emotionally. Jung states that 'A complex arises where we have experienced a defeat in life' (leading to what Freud referred to as 'repetition compulsion' and Perls's notion of 'unfinished business'). Woolger sees a need to extend this 'across lives': 'It is as though each of us is born with a portion of the unfinished business of humanity at large which it is our personal and karmic responsibility to complete in one way or another.'[185] He reminds us of Jung's comment that in the collective unconscious 'nothing has finally disappeared and nothing has been made good' and 'none of us stands outside humanity's blackest shadow.'[105]

PASTIMES In TRANSACTIONAL ANALYSIS pastimes are patterns of behaviour which occur typically in social gatherings when people adopt particular roles or attitudes for the purpose of relating to each other for a limited time period. They are conditioned by social programming rather than individual programming. Berne writes, 'Besides structuring time and providing mutually acceptable STROKING for the parties concerned, pastimes serve the additional function of being social-selection processes.'[12] This can be a means of deciding whether a more complex relationship might be worth pursuing.

PATIENCE/PATIENTS It is generally accepted that a passive attitude is not always conducive to recovery from illness. Cancer patients who accept their condition and behave most 'patiently' (see CANCER PERSONALITY) have a very poor rate of recovery when compared with 'difficult' patients. The same phenomenon has been noted with people with HIV and AIDS, a fact that is reflected in the drive (particularly in the USA) to refer to people with AIDS as just that – *people* with AIDS, rather than 'patients' or, worse, 'victims'. It is a matter for speculation whether subliminal acceptance of the passivity inherent in the word 'patient' has abetted the process of MEDICALIZATION in western society, which encourages people to surrender power to the medical authority and about which Ivan Illich complains in *Limits to Medicine: Medical Nemesis*.

PATTERN THERAPY The theory behind pattern therapy is that certain shapes can focus the earth's electromagnetic waves or more SUBTLE ENERGIES to produce particular effects. If beer is stored in rectangular rather than round containers, the taste is different; the shape of certain yogurt containers increases the bacterial action. The supreme example is the PYRAMID, which seems to have pre-serving and healing powers, but other shapes have been shown to be therapeutic. Mice have been shown to heal faster in spherical cages; schizophrenic patients improve in wards shaped like a trap-ezoid. According to the beliefs and practices of many people, from classical architects using the golden mean ratio (1:1.618) to Chinese practitioners of FENG SHUI, we are all affected by the shape of the buildings we are in. When viewing a potential new home we may even mention 'getting good vibes' from it, indicating the possibility that when we open ourselves to such influences we are perhaps able to register the *vibrations* of a building in the manner of people referred to as sensitives. Pattern therapy can therefore be regarded as one of the VIBRATIONAL THERAPIES.

PEAK EXPERIENCE The term 'peak experience' was coined by Abraham Maslow to refer to those almost inexplicable ecstatic moments when people feel fulfilled, aware, both truly themselves and at one with the world. They range from experiences of spiritual ecstasy among the religious or the mystically inclined to feelings of high creativity among artists and moments of supreme physical prowess among athletes. Although Maslow identified the phenomenon initially by studying the characters and lives of great people (to ascertain what it means to be 'fully human'), he recognized that everyone is capable of such experiences, and most people do seem able to report such events in their lives, even in relatively mundane circumstances, such as the mother who experiences a flood of happiness, love for her family and the feeling that all is right with the world, while washing the dishes.

All peak experiences are rare events, often once-in-a-lifetime experiences. Indeed, the feeling that one has never felt like this before is usually an essential part of the experience, together with an element of surprise and disbelief. Maslow has described peak experiences as 'life-validating, i.e. they make life worthwhile'. Peak experiences are always accompanied by a strong sense of oneness: they are 'integrative of the splits within the person, between persons, within the world, and between the person and the world'. Dichotomies are fused, conflicts are resolved, polarities are transcended. In peak experiences time seems to stand still, and the peaker has the feeling of being outside space and time. There is often a feeling of awe, reverence, surrender; any fear, anxiety or inhibition disappears. As well as feeling more integrated, the person enjoying the peak experience feels more active and more responsible, the 'creating centre' of their actions and perceptions, more self-determined and 'more like a prime mover'.[125] Some of these feelings may be carried over into the individual's life following the peak experience, making it in a sense a rebirth (one of the characteristics which distinguish it from the PLATEAU EXPERIENCE). The possibility of such a personal transformation is one of the key principles of HUMANISTIC PSYCHOLOGY.

PELVIC SEGMENT The pelvic segment is one of the seven body segments in REICHIAN THERAPY, covering the legs, pelvis and genitals. It is regarded as particularly sensitive and is usually the last to be treated.

PENDULUM A pendulum is used as a diagnostic dowsing tool in RADIESTHESIA and RADIONICS. People may also dowse to see which of a batch of remedies would be most beneficial to them at a particular time, holding a pendulum over different remedies in turn until the 'Yes' swing is obtained. Some find this particularly useful when using AROMATHERAPY oils on a self-help basis, or when trying to decide which of the BACH FLOWER REMEDIES would be most helpful. Others might use a pendulum when trying to assess the freshness of the fruit and vegetables they are buying.

There is no universal rule as to which swing or rotation means 'yes' and which means 'no'. If you want to use a pendulum for this purpose you should start by asking an obvious question to ensure the answer 'No', followed by an equally obvious question to elicit 'Yes'. You can then ask to be shown the movement for 'Maybe' if that seems to be useful. There is no guarantee that you will use the same motions with a different pendulum, nor that they will be the same for other people using it. In fact if others have used your pendulum, it is advisable to check that your answering system has not been affected. But if you use the same personal and private pendulum all the time, the motions should remain consistent.

There are two main theories to explain how the pendulum works. Some people regard its movements as controlled unconsciously by the person holding it. In this case the information is picked up (again unconsciously) by some form of extrasensory perception. According to the second theory the movements are influenced by the SUBTLE ENERGIES which pervade the whole universe, although they may also depend on the person holding the pendulum being a kind of receiving station. When holding the pendulum over a potentially useful remedy, particularly one which works in a VIBRATIONAL way, it may be thought that some sort of RESONANCE is set up between the remedy and the subtle body of the person consulting the pendulum. This seems quite a neat theory until one realizes that people can diagnose remedies for each other (some even say more effectively than for themselves) when the patient's body is nowhere near the pendulum.

PERSONA The process of socialization results in a compromise between the individual and society: to a certain extent each one of us has to play the part that society has laid down for us, appearing to be what society thinks we should be, and this leads to the formation of the persona, Jung's term for that part of our personality which we show to the world. *Persona* is the Latin word for the mask worn by actors in ancient Greek drama, and the persona is the face we put on when we have to relate to others. To a certain extent we choose the roles we think we are suited for, but the persona can never be the whole man or woman and is clearly only a fragment of our personality, albeit a very useful one. Jung described it as 'a functional complex that comes into existence for reasons of adaptation or personal convenience, but is by no means identical with the individuality.' It has been described as 'the packaging of the EGO' or 'the ego's PR man or woman, responsible for advertising to people how one wants to be seen and reacted to'.[162] As such it simplifies our contacts and dealings with others, and people who do not develop an adequate persona tend to be gauche, easily offending others. Trouble also arises if one tries to wear a persona which is unsuitable, perhaps pretending to fulfil a role which one cannot maintain (so one ends up by 'losing face'). Other problems emerge if someone identifies too strongly with their persona, merely playing a part and denying the rest of the personality. The formation of the persona out of the approved, socially acceptable qualities in one's personality is accompanied and balanced by the formation of the SHADOW out of one's unacceptable characteristics.

PERSONAL CONSTRUCT THERAPY Personal construct theory was proposed by George Kelly in 1955. The theory is that we construe our perception of people, events and situations in a distinctly personal way. Therapy involves coming to understand one's own construct system and that of others, seeing how others see us and how people relate to each other. Therapy can be in groups as well as one-to-one. Various techniques are used, such as repertory grid analysis, self-characterization, enactment and fixed role therapy. The repertory grid technique is a way of analysing the way the client views the world with the help of a questionnaire. Self-characterization refers to a method of evaluating the client's self-image from a biography written from the (imagined) point of view of a good friend. In enactment, the client and the therapist act out a familiar situation to help the client achieve a fresh and detached view of it. The fixed role technique involves the creation (by the therapist) of a fictional character who views the world differently from the client (although the new position must not be diametrically opposed to the client's habitual one); the client is then asked to pretend to 'be' that fictional person for a week to experience the reactions of others to this new character.

PERSONALITY TYPES AND DISEASE In recent decades there has been increasing interest in the possible relationship between personality traits and susceptibility to specific diseases. Research has focused particularly on the CANCER PERSONALITY and the so-called TYPE A personality in connection with heart disease. There has also been research with sufferers from diseases which seem to have a strong PSYCHOSOMATIC component, such as PSORIASIS, and there is evidence that certain types of people seem to be more susceptible to rheumatoid arthritis, others to MIGRAINE.

People with rheumatoid arthritis tend to be shy, inhibited, self-conscious, conforming, perfectionist, interested in sports, and self-sacrificing, even masochistic. Female rheumatoid patients are nervous, tense, worried, moody, depressed, and typically had mothers who they felt rejected them and fathers who were unduly strict; they also have difficulty in expressing anger. There are some similarities with the CANCER PERSONALITY here. (See also RELATIONSHIPS.)

Migraine sufferers too are typically perfectionist, but also ambitious, excessively competitive, unable to delegate responsibility, and afraid of failure. They can be fanatical, self-righteous and also self-sacrificing; they may try too hard and defeat themselves in the process, and they tend to take on more than they can manage. Those who are aggressive and egotistical are also more likely to be prone to heart disease (the Type A personality).

PETRISSAGE Pétrissage is a kneading action used on fleshy areas of the body in SWEDISH MASSAGE. The action involves kneading, rolling and squeezing in a manner similar to kneading dough. Its effect is to relax, soften and stretch muscles that are too contracted, hard and shortened. It also draws blood to the area being worked on and improves the tone of the skin.

PHANTOM LIMB PAIN After the loss of a limb it is quite common to feel PAIN in that part of the body which is no longer there. Paraplegics also experience pain from parts of their body in which it is known that through paralysis there can be no normal sensory activity. The theory is that when the central nervous system finds itself incomplete it manufactures pain in the area where there is an absence of sensory input.

PHOBIC LAYER In GESTALT therapy the phobic layer is the second level of the personality, also known as the neurotic layer.

PHONEY LAYER In GESTALT therapy the phoney layer is the first level of the personality, also known as the game-playing layer.

PHRENOLOGY Phrenology (from the Greek *phren*, meaning 'upper-middle of the chest', i.e. the area of the heart and thymus, 'diaphragm', or 'mind') is the art of determining a person's mental characteristics and personality by studying the shape and contours of the skull – 'reading the bumps'. Franz Joseph Gall (1758–1828) identified twenty-seven 'organs' on the surface of the skull. Despite accusations of superstition, the practice survived (the British Phrenological Society lasted until 1967), because its defenders claimed that certain regions of the brain governing specific skills and characteristics could be developed in much the same way that athletes develop muscles. A form of micro-phrenology was extended to facial characteristics, such that character could also be read by FACIAL DIAGNOSIS, a practice with a long tradition in China.

PHRENOMETER The Lavery Electric Phrenometer (1907) was a complicated contraption designed to measure the contours of the skull accurately for the purposes of analysis according to the rules of PHRENOLOGY.

PHYSIOLOGICAL PSYCHOLOGY See PSYCHOPHYSIOLOGY.

PHYSIOMEDICALISM See HERBALISM.

PHYTOTHERAPY (from the Greek *phyton*, meaning 'plant') An alternative term for HERBAL MEDICINE.

PILATES METHOD Pilates is a non-aerobic method of exercise designed to stretch and lengthen all major muscle groups in a balanced way. It was developed by Joseph Pilates, who conquered his own frailty as a child by working at standard body-building techniques, to such an extent that he later worked as a boxer, circus performer, self-defence teacher and model for anatomical drawings. As a German national resident in Britain he was interned during the First World War on the Isle of Man, where he started to devise his technique of physical education and posture correction. Between the wars he returned to Germany, where he worked with Rudolph Laban, the pioneer of DANCE THERAPY, and then moved to New York, where he set up his first exercise studio.

A Pilates exercise studio looks at first sight like a gym, but the apparatus used is not the same as for a conventional work-out. People pursue their individually tailored routines not to overdevelop already strong muscles but to strengthen weaker ones. There is great

emphasis on correct posture and balance, and deep rhythmic breathing is incorporated into the exercises. The atmosphere in a Pilates
studio is one of calm concentration, perhaps with a background of
classical music, with no sweating and straining – more like a yoga
class than a work-out session. The aims of optimal natural body use
without strain and tension are similar to those of the ALEXANDER
TECHNIQUE, although the method involves more activity.

PITTA One of the three HUMOURS (*doshas*) in AYURVEDIC MEDICINE,
translated as bile or fire.

PITUITARY BODY/PITUITARY GLAND The pituitary body,
situated at the base of the brain in the middle of the skull, is the size
of a small cherry. It is the main centre for the regulation of hormone
production and influences the activity of the entire endocrine system.
Pituitary hormones are discharged into the bloodstream and carry
specific messages to the other endocrine glands.

PLACEBO/PLACEBO EFFECT The term 'placebo' appeared in
medical dictionaries as early as 1811. It is Latin for 'I will please' and
originally referred to a dummy remedy administered as a palliative.
Later it was realized that for reasons which are not fully understood
such 'treatment' can have a beneficial effect. Placebos seem to bring
into action the body's self-healing powers, or in today's medical
jargon they are 'catalysts of the bio-regulatory mechanism'.[230]
Serious research into the placebo effect began in the 1950s. In
1955, Henry Beecher of the Harvard Medical School reviewed a
large number of studies and found that, on average, a third of the
people who were given placebos reported satisfactory relief of their
symptoms.[204] This figure of one third has been confirmed by many
other studies and has to be taken into account when analysing the
results of CLINICAL TRIALS.

Modern medical commentators are fond of pointing out that most
of the history of medicine until recent times can be regarded as the
history of the placebo effect. The reason for this is that in spite of
what we now regard as patently useless and quite often dangerous
treatments (such as bloodletting), people presumably often did get
better. But there is a certain arrogance in this attitude, which
assumes both the efficacy of the modern scientific methods of
CONVENTIONAL MEDICINE (which still does not understand the
placebo effect) and the uselessness of traditional methods. After
all, leeches, which were used to bleed patients, have been shown by

modern chemical analysis to contain at least four active biochemical substances that counter different diseases.[135]

In medieval times, no less than today, people were encouraged to attribute 'cures' to the authority figure in charge of their treatment, rather than to any inner healing power of their own, and part of the placebo effect is indeed the knowledge that one is being attended by a doctor. John Donne recognized this when he wrote, 'I cannot rise out of my bed till the physician enable me, nay I cannot tell that I am able to rise till he tell me so. I do nothing, I know nothing of myself: how impotent a piece of the world is any man alone! And how much less a piece of himself is that man!'[33] Donne also recognized that the patient detects and reflects the doctor's expectations: 'I observe the Physician with the same diligence as he the disease; I see he fears, and I fear with him.' This negative expectation and its fulfilment is the downside of the placebo effect and has been called the NOCEBO response.

One's EXPECTATION of recovery when ill is to some extent conditional on the faith one has in the physician, although some people of a stubbornly independent character may show a surprising lack of faith, preferring to prove everyone else wrong by resorting to a form of SELF-HEALING. Faith in the medical profession and the esteem in which it is held is inevitably affected by one's experience of the doctor-patient relationship, and the apparent authority of the prescriber (conveyed typically by the wearing of a white coat and stethoscope) generally helps the placebo effect, as do certain personality factors in the patient – over-anxiety, emotional dependence and immaturity (the reciprocal patient traits balancing the authority of the doctor).

A patient's response to a placebo can also be affected by the belief (and expectation) of the doctor prescribing it. In drug trials, when doctors knowingly prescribe the new drug their patients' condition is more likely to improve than when they think (mistakenly) they are giving them a placebo. In such situations, it is thought, the doctors somehow communicate their expectations by unintentional cues picked up subliminally by their patients, who respond accordingly (which explains the importance of the DOUBLE-BLIND condition in clinical trials). This sort of communication between doctor and patient must be extremely subtle. PAIN can be reduced by placebos, and placebos administered surreptitiously, without the knowledge of the patient, have been shown to have an analgesic effect similar to that resulting from openly administered placebos.[218]

The response to placebos varies according to the form the placebo takes. The more bitter-tasting the medicine or difficult and unpleasant the treatment, the more likely it is to succeed. Placebo injections are more potent than placebo capsules, which in turn are more potent than placebo pills. COLOUR is also significant: anxiety is best treated with green pills, depressive symptoms with yellow, and pain with red. Size is a factor too: small yellow pills work well for depression; large blue pills have a better effect as sedatives; but best of all are very large brown or purple pills or very small bright red or yellow pills.[222] Even brand names affect the placebo response.[197]

The placebo effect is not restricted to treatment with drugs: placebo surgery has also been shown to be effective. In the mid-1950s a new surgical procedure was introduced to provide relief from the symptoms of chest pain due to coronary heart disease. The procedure involved tying off an artery in the chest and was called 'internal mammary ligation'. But some surgeons doubted the validity of the treatment, so to test their theory they assigned some patients at random to receive a sham operation: their chests were cut open and closed up without the artery-tying. (Such practices in the interests of research would be considered unethical today.) The benefits from this placebo surgery were found to be as great as from the artery-tying operation itself.[193]

There has been ample research to demonstrate the existence of the placebo effect. What is perhaps still lacking is the link between different personality traits and the most effective method of administering the placebo. In some cases it might be found that direct SELF-HEALING techniques may be more appropriate for certain people. It is possible that we could one day begin a course of medical treatment with a personality assessment to determine whether the doctor's prescription should be supplemented by a particular type of placebo, or guided VISUALIZATION, or self-directed imagery.

PLATEAU EXPERIENCE Abraham Maslow describes a plateau experience as a 'serene and calm . . . response to the miraculous, the awesome, the sacralized, the Unitive, the B-VALUES'. It differs from a PEAK EXPERIENCE in that there is always a strong cognitive element (peak experiences may be purely emotional), it is less intense, and it is more voluntary. One may be marvelling, wondering, philosophizing, in a state of pure enjoyment or blissfulness, but the plateau experience lacks the 'climactic explosion' which Maslow says is a characteristic of peak experiences.[123]

PO (or *p'o*) In the traditional Chinese belief system the force which energizes the physical body is called CH'I, but the vehicle for this life-force is referred to as *po*, a kind of physical soul or etheric body, the vessel which contains the ch'i.

POLARITY THERAPY/POLARITY BALANCING Randolph Stone (1890–1981), who first produced the concept of polarity therapy, was a naturalized American, born in Austria. He was an osteopath, chiropractor and naturopath, trained in herbalism, ACUPRESSURE and REFLEXOLOGY, and studied both western and eastern medicine, incorporating some of the principles of AYURVEDA in his work. Polarity therapy is based on the fundamental principle, common to the major oriental systems of medicine, that there is a vital energy, a universal life-force flowing through the body (the Chinese CH'I, Indian PRANA, or Reich's ORGONE) and that this energy becomes *polarized* as positive, negative (like yang and yin) or neutral in specific parts of the body. The feet, for example, are regarded as negative poles, whilst the head is a positive pole; left and right are also regarded as negative and positive respectively. Illness manifests when there is an imbalance in these polarized energies. As Stone wrote in his *Health Building*, 'An excess of the positive current produces irritation, pain, swelling and heat . . . The left hand is the conductor of the negative or moon current, which is cooling, soothing, refreshing and toning. Place it over the seat of pain, where the positive currents are in excess.'[165] The interaction of the three types of energy (positive, negative and neutral) create the five ELEMENTS – earth, water, fire, air and ether (as in ayurveda), and these correspond respectively to the five centres (or CHAKRAS) from the base or coccyx (earth) to the throat or nape of the neck (ether). There are five vertical energy currents in the body (like MERIDIANS), each corresponding to a specific element, and each finger and toe carries the energy of a specific element.

Treatment involves rebalancing the energy levels and freeing any blocks in the flow. The practitioner may, for example, place the left hand, which is negatively charged, at a positive pole on the patient's body to facilitate the harmonious flow of energy. Gentle massage (usually circular, the direction depending on the polarity required) and slight pressure may also be used in the manner of SHIATSU and acupressure. As well as this special kind of manipulation the polarity therapist will recommend particular posture and stretching exercises (derived primarily from YOGA), and specific diets which are intended first to cleanse the organism and then to maintain harmonious balance. A fourth area of work is the attitude of the patient, since it is recognized that thoughts and emotions also affect the flow of vital energy through the body: POSITIVE THINKING is a crucial factor in maintaining good health.

POLYPHARMACY Polypharmacy refers to the habit of prescribing remedies which contained a witches' brew of ingredients, a practice which Paracelsus (1493–1541) was one of the first to reject but which remained common for many generations after him. Samuel Hahnemann (1755–1843), founder of HOMOEOPATHY, renewed the attack on this habit, referring to it as 'blunderbuss' treatment. He favoured the use of SIMPLES in the preparation of remedies.

POLYPHASIC Polyphasic behaviour – doing several things at once – is characteristic of the TYPE A PERSONALITY and seems to be a contributory factor in the incidence of STRESS-related diseases.

POMANDER A pomander was an early form of AROMATHERAPY, a sachet of herbs used as a method of emitting healing and protective vapours. Sometimes the herbs were carried in an orange peel. In Elizabethan times bouquets of herbs were used to ward off infection – for example, judges carried them when appearing in the crowded court, and they were believed to protect people from the plague (giving a possible origin for the nursery rhyme 'Ring-a-ring o' Roses').

POSITIVE REGARD According to Carl Rogers, one of the three essential conditions in the relationship between therapist and client in CLIENT-CENTRED THERAPY is positive regard – accepting clients as they are.

POSITIVE THINKING In the 1900s Orison Swett Marden, a graduate of Harvard Medical School and editor of *Success* magazine, developed 'mind power', a mixture of yoga and auto-hypnotic suggestion. According to Emile Coué's theory of AUTOSUGGESTION the imagination could be used more effectively than will-power to achieve one's aims; in 1922 he wrote, 'Every one of our thoughts, good or bad, becomes concrete, materializes, and becomes in short a reality.' In the 1930s Napoleon Hill wrote two books, *The Law of Success* and *How to Sell Your Way Through Life*, in which he maintained that we could send 'AFFIRMATIONS or orders to the subconscious mind'. These were all to some extent predecessors of Norman Vincent Peale (1898–1994).

At its simplest, Norman Vincent Peale's theory of positive thinking encourages us to feel good about ourselves and our prospects by focusing our attention on what is good, and on desirable rather than undesirable outcomes. The theory depends on the principle of a mental set. Our mental set determines what we notice: having recently heard about a particular book or film we tend to notice it whenever it is referred to; after reading about the symptoms of a particular illness we seem to recognize those same symptoms in ourselves. With a positive mental set we see things in a good light ('the glass is half-full'), but with a negative mental set we tend to notice the downside of every situation ('the glass is half-empty'). If we see obstacles everywhere we become discouraged, lose hope and are unlikely to succeed, because we will probably fail even to see chances that come our way, never mind seize them. Positive thinking is a way of inducing and maintaining a positive mental set, so that we notice the opportunities that will help us to achieve our aims and regard the obstacles (if we see them at all) as insignificant. The only danger is that some obstacles undoubtedly need to be taken seriously, and too much positive thinking might result in a foolhardy naivety. Perhaps this is why it has been described somewhat dismissively as 'a technique whereby a precarious ego represses recognition of its own precariousness'.[130] But thinking positively is an essential factor in, and even a prerequisite for, SELF-HEALING and therapies such as VISUALIZATION.

POSTURAL INTEGRATION/POSTURAL RELEASE See ROLF-ING.

POSTURE/POSTURAL THERAPIES
Posture is naturally one of the concerns of OSTEOPATHY and CHIROPRACTIC, but several BODYWORK therapies are aimed primarily at helping the individual to develop and maintain a better posture. Practitioners often make the comparison between the harmoniously balanced stance adopted naturally by an infant and the tense, rigid or distorted posture of an adult. Whether because of the unnatural positions we hold ourselves in at work or because of psychological ARMOURING, we tend to get into the habit of using our bodies in ways which create muscular tension and skeletal distortion. Therapies such as the ALEXANDER TECHNIQUE and the FELDENKRAIS METHOD seek to help the individual to break out of these inefficient and ultimately harmful patterns

of behaviour by relearning natural posture and movement. With ROLFING the patient adopts a more passive role while the therapist uses deep tissue massage to realign any asymmetry in the body. There is usually a further consequence of developing better posture: the individual feels better psychologically, with a greater sense of emotional and mental well-being. In some cases this may be consciously worked towards and verbalized while undergoing the physical therapy, as with HELLERWORK and BIOENERGETICS.

POTENCIES/POTENTIATION/POTENTIZATION In HOMOEO-PATHY remedies are prepared by a process of repeated dilution known as potentization/potentiation (or DYNAMIZATION), each step producing a more active, more effective, more potent dose (the so-called Law of Potentiation). One part of the MOTHER TINCTURE is mixed with 99 parts of alcohol and water and succussed (see SUCCUSSION) to produce the 'first centesimal dilution' (1c). The procedure is repeated using the new solution, often up to 30c, the most commonly prescribed potencies being 6c, 12c and 30c. If the original substance is dry it is mixed with milk sugar by a process known as TRITURATION. Hahnemann also discovered that certain substances which are usually regarded as inert (such as gold, silver and silicon) could reveal medicinal powers when triturated; and many poisons (such as belladonna, strychnine, aconite and various types of snake venom) were transformed into useful remedies through the process of potentization. However, the most controversial aspect of potentization from the viewpoint of CONVENTIONAL MEDICINE is that beyond a dilution (or ATTENUATION) of 12c it is unlikely that a remedy will contain a single molecule of the original substance. This degree of potentization is known as the AVOGADRO LIMIT. Hahnemann referred to this effect as a 'remarkable transformation of the properties of natural bodies through the mechanical action of trituration and succussion on their tiniest particles', which 'developed the latent *dynamic* powers previously imperceptible and as it were lying hidden asleep in them' – hence 'dynamization'.[68] This is a reference to the SUBTLE ENERGIES to which curative power is attributed in the BACH FLOWER REMEDIES, ANTHROPOSOPHICAL MEDICINE and various types of VIBRATIONAL HEALING. In RADIONICS distilled water or inert tablets can also be 'potentized' with the vibrational energy which the patient requires.

POTENCY SIMULATOR Potency simulators are used in RADIONICS to treat a patient either by placing a DIAGNOSTIC WITNESS in the instrument or by treating distilled water or inert tablets which will then be used as a remedy. The most widely used today is probably the Rae potency simulator, named after its inventor, Malcolm Rae, and also called the 'magnetogeometric potency simulator'. It is the latest device in a direct line of succession from the ABRAMS BOX (the infamous 'black box'). Like most other radionic instruments, the simulator contains a magnet which is said to send out the energy pattern required. This is determined in the Rae simulator by the insertion of a card on which is printed a geometric drawing of seven concentric circles with a variable number of lines pointing to the centre in critical positions depending on the condition being treated.

POWER NAP The power nap is a method of achieving total relaxation when under pressure, resting for a few minutes and reversing the various stress responses in the body. People learn to slow their pulse and breathing rate. They do this in a way resembling VISUALIZATION and AUTOSUGGESTION: closing their eyes for a short time and imagining a dial with the needle pointing to a high setting, they visualize the dial being turned down and gain control over themselves, commanding their pulse and blood pressure rates to decrease.[76]

PRANA In Sanskrit *prana* means 'LIFE-FORCE', or the 'breath of life'. As the energy which maintains life it is essentially the same as the Chinese CH'I, (Japanese *ki*).

PRANAYAMA In yoga, *pranayama* is the science of breath control. It involves breathing rhythmically, according to specific cycles – breathing in, holding, breathing out and holding according to various ratios. This may lead to an experience known as *kundalini* – when something like an electric charge is felt to rise from the base of the spine (through the CHAKRAS) to the brain, giving a sense of heightened perception and greater awareness – or it may simply induce a feeling of well-being by balancing the flow of PRANA, the life-force, around the body. Some of the methods of *pranayama* are used to assist in MEDITATION, and others have been adopted by modern therapies such as REBIRTHING.

PREBIRTHING Prebirthing, as a modification of the technique of REBIRTHING, is the name given to a method of deep breathing intended to access PRE-BIRTH MEMORIES.

PRE-BIRTH MEMORIES Researchers such as Stanislav Grof, Frank Lake, William Emerson and Thomas Verny believe that the experience of the foetus affects the way later experience is organized. A relatively constant experience of feeling good as a foetus predisposes the newborn to expect this of life. A mixture of good and bad feelings may tend to undermine later hope and trust, while a predominantly bad experience of life in the womb predisposes the newborn to expect this to continue. The everyday life of the growing foetus has a strong formative effect on our predispositions, expectations and attitudes in later life. Bad feelings are associated with terror coming in from the placenta or the umbilical cord, which it is postulated manifests in the adult as a fear of snakes or spiders. These memories may not be conscious, but METAMORPHIC TECHNIQUE is based on the idea that our future health can be affected by the mental state of the mother during the gestation period.

PRECONSCIOUS In PSYCHOSYNTHESIS the preconscious is an alternative term for the middle unconscious.

PRENATAL THERAPY See METAMORPHIC TECHNIQUE.

PRE-PATHOLOGY A certain PERSONALITY TYPE is regarded as a risk factor in heart disease. This is an example of pre-pathology, the circumstances which may give rise to illness without themselves demonstrating any sign of illness.

PRESSURE THERAPY See ACUPRESSURE, SHIATSU, REFLEXOLOGY, METAMORPHIC TECHNIQUE.

PREVENTIVE MEDICINE CONVENTIONAL MEDICINE lays greater emphasis on treatment than on prevention, whereas in all systems of ALTERNATIVE MEDICINE the maintenance of health involves avoiding rather than simply curing disease. This was exemplified in the Chinese tradition by the custom of paying the physician so long as one was well; as soon as one fell ill, payment ceased until one was well again, since the astute physician should have been able to recognize the patient's condition and take counter-measures before the disease manifested physically. It was also recognized in classical Greece that treatment was only one part of the physician's task. In Greek mythology Asclepius, the god of healing, had two daughters – Panacea (literally 'cure-all'), who had knowledge of medication and knew how to treat diseases, and Hygeia (from which we derive the word 'hygiene'), who taught how to live in harmony with nature in order to avoid disease.

PRIMAL INTEGRATION Primal integration as developed by Bill Swarbley is a technique similar to PRIMAL THERAPY but concentrating as much on the problems of adult life as on the pains of childhood. It looks at the individual's entire life, from conception and into the future, and uses all four of the Jungian FUNCTIONS – sensing, feeling, thinking and intuition.

PRIMAL PAIN/PRIMAL SCREAM/PRIMAL THERAPY/PRIMAL ZONE Arthur Janov, a navy veteran, interviewed in *Vogue* magazine in 1971, said, 'I believe the only way to eliminate neurosis is with overthrow by force and violence.' Janov's theory is that we all have a certain amount of Primal Pain inside us and that releasing it, rather like opening a pressure valve to let off steam, will help to overcome all psychological problems. The result of encountering this repressed pain and releasing the pressure is the *primal scream*. Confronting the pain enables one to disempower it and empower oneself. But this confrontation is not on a cognitive intellectual level; the insight which psychoanalysis aims for plays little or no part in Primal Therapy. 'The beginning of feeling is the end of philosophy,' Janov wrote; and 'Until we feel the pain, we suffer.'

Repression of pain leads to the formation of an 'unreal self' which develops from about the age of six until the teens. This unreal self refuses to acknowledge deep pain and builds up neurotic defence patterns to shield the individual from experiencing it. Janov identifies three levels of pain: first the pain of birth itself; second the pains of childhood when all the dependent child's unmet needs and the anger of others are seen as signs of rejection; and third the pains of adult life such as rejection by a lover or fear of failure. In primal therapy these three levels of pain are tackled in reverse order (the most recent first). When 'primalling', people are encouraged to wail just like babies.

Learning of some of the reports of the questioning techniques of Primal therapists one is perhaps not surprised that the reaction of some of the patients is sooner or later simply to scream. When expressing anger at someone the patient will be asked, 'Who is it really?', the implication being that the feelings of frustration should be directed against the patient's mother. Criticism of another person's behaviour will usually attract the question, 'Who else did that?', again inviting connections to be made with parental behaviour. At the same time the therapist constantly reminds the patient not to intellectualize and to stay with any negative feeling that arises. If they dare to criticize or disagree with the therapist, the patient is told 'That's a feeling', and there is no possibility of discussion.

PROCESSING The verbal self-expression and dealing with 'unfinished business' which is characteristic of EST training is sometimes called 'processing'.

PROGRESSIVE RELAXATION A simple method of inducing RELAXATION is to relax groups of muscles in sequence starting at the feet and progressing up to the head, usually while lying down and contracting each muscle or muscle group before relaxing it fully. This is known as progressive relaxation.

PROJECTION Projection is the process by which we externalize subconscious feelings, usually feelings about ourselves onto others. When we find in another person, an institution or an object some echo of a part of ourselves that we lack, hate, or refuse to accept, we escape the inner discomfort by attaching our disowned qualities to them. We can then convince ourselves that they don't belong to us. Positive as well as negative characteristics may be projected in this way. The mechanism operates in hero-worship as well as in witch hunts, scapegoating and racism. The phenomenon was recognized long before modern psychology gave it a name: Thomas à Kempis (1379–1471) said, 'What a man is inwardly, that he will see outwardly.'

It has been noticed that projection plays a significant part in the healing profession. Anxiety can lead to a desire to help because one's own helplessness is projected onto others, and the greater the subconscious anxiety the greater the desire to externalize. It has been suggested that most members of the healing profession are driven and motivated by just this unconscious process, projecting their own anxiety. The fact that their level of anxiety is higher than average (i.e. before they join their particular profession) may partly account for the high rates of suicide, divorce and alcoholism amongst doctors and psychiatrists.

PROPRIOCEPTION Proprioception, or self-observation, forms the basis of much of the ALEXANDER TECHNIQUE, since it was through self-observation that F. M. Alexander first realized that he was misusing his body and was led to the belief that such misuse played an important part in disease. Becoming an observer of at least an aspect of oneself is an essential part of certain psychological therapies (for example when acting out the dialogue between various SUB-PERSONALITIES), although in others (such as PSYCHODRAMA or PRIMAL THERAPY) one is encouraged never to step outside the experience and observe.

PROVINGS In developing HOMOEOPATHY, Hahnemann went to great lengths to test his remedies on himself, judging the varying effect of different doses. These tests he referred to as 'provings'.

PROXEMICS Proxemics is the study of a particular area of BODY LANGUAGE – territorial personal space, i.e. the distance people stand apart when dealing with each other or when obliged to be in 'proximity' with each other for other reasons. According to Edward T. Hall, professor of anthropology at Northwestern University, who coined the term, there are four main zones depending on the degree of intimacy between the people concerned: intimate distance, personal distance, social distance and public distance. The actual measurements of these distances vary greatly from one culture to another.[71,72]

PSIONICS/PSIONIC MEDICINE Psionic medicine was developed by Dr George Lawrence, who founded the Psionic Medical Society in 1968. It combines elements of certain VIBRATIONAL THERAPIES, using RADIESTHESIA as a diagnostic method with the rationale and remedies of ANTHROPOSOPHICAL MEDICINE and HOMOEOPATHY. Basic to all types of vibrational medicine is the notion that everything in nature vibrates and emits radiations which enable both diagnosis and treatment. Treatment with homoeopathic remedies provides corrective radiations to bring the flow of LIFE-FORCE or bioenergy back into balance. These remedies do not attack the symptoms of disease but are directed at the underlying MIASM which gives rise to the disease. Miasms are irregularities in the body's capacity for self-healing and its flow of life-energy. They may be inherited (e.g. the tuberculosis miasm) or acquired (e.g. measles and chickenpox).

PSORIASIS Psoriasis is a disorder of cell growth, like cancer.

In psoriasis there is an overproduction of skin cells, but unlike cancer the excess growth is restricted to skin cells and does not invade other organs, and the cells thus produced are normal (not abnormal as in cancer). One long-established treatment of psoriasis is to plaster coal tar on the affected skin. Coal tar is carcinogenic, but this treatment has never been known to result in skin cancer in psoriasis patients. In those patients who do develop cancer the psoriasis immediately clears up.

It has been suggested that the disfigurement which psoriasis causes may be a reflection of a pre-existing lack of self-esteem, rather than simply a cause of the loss of self-esteem. According to this theory, the mind/body creates a justification for the mind/personality to feel it is lacking in worth. There is certainly evidence for a strong psychosomatic component in certain cases of psoriasis: for example, when manic-depressives are depressed, their psoriasis breaks out, but in their manic phases it recedes – in other words, when they behave in an uncontrolled way, their skin cells do not.

Dermatologist R. H. Seville believes that 'severely felt, but suppressed emotional stress can lead to an outbreak of psoriasis within a month, and clearance of the disorder can be related to the insight gained by the patient into the nature of the emotional trauma.' This insight means a particular kind of self-knowledge: 'observation and appreciation by the patient of the significance of what has happened that upset them, resulting in understanding in depth, with acceptance of reality – the veneer of superficial recognition only evades real awareness.' Furthermore, when Seville assessed the degree of insight gained by his patients, those with greater awareness and understanding were less likely to suffer a later relapse of symptoms.[225]

PSYCHIC SURGERY (not to be confused with PSYCHOSURGERY, the treatment of severe mental disorders by operating directly on the brain). Psychic surgery is the paranormal practice of surgery, allied to magic and shamanism, whereby a patient appears to undergo an operation to remove a pathogenic object from the body. Psychic surgeons may use a knife to open up the patient's body, as does the most famous Brazilian psychic surgeon, Arigo (José de Freitas), or they may draw out the poison simply by manual contact, the preferred method in the Philippines. In a European variant of psychic surgery the healer, usually in trance, appears to go through the motions of performing an operation *above* the patient's body, supposedly on the ETHERIC BODY. In all such operations the tumour or toxic substance simply dematerializes, the patient feels no pain, and the wound heals extremely rapidly, leaving only a very faint scar.

PSYCHOANALYSIS Psychoanalysis is based on the theories of Freud (most of which are unproven) and such concepts as REPRESSION, RESISTANCE, TRANSFERENCE and COUNTER-TRANSFERENCE. Although usually considered as part of mainstream health care, the process is increasingly regarded as scientifically suspect. Its main aim is to plumb the depths of the UNCONSCIOUS, to bring the patient's unconscious to conscious awareness, with everything the patient says seen as relevant to revealing the unconscious. It requires a fair degree of articulacy on the part of the patient, since the method is wholly verbal – a 'talking cure'. It is a very long process, potentially unending, and in its true 'classical' form is the least commonly practised form of PSYCHOTHERAPY, which comes in many guises. Psychoanalysis is much more specifically Freudian than other forms of psychotherapy; the basis of Jungian analysis is referred to as 'analytical psychology' to distinguish it from the Freudian version.

Freudian psychoanalysis is sometimes referred to as *classical* psychoanalysis. The analyst, often described as 'cold' as well as analytical, remains detached and aloof, offering interpretations of what the patient says but never encouraging or directing or even showing sympathy. (As Charles Brenner explains, 'For the analyst to express sympathy for a patient who has just lost a close relative may make it more difficult than it would otherwise be for the patient to express pleasure or spite or exhibitionistic satisfaction over the loss.'[121] Sessions are frequent and the patient usually lies on a couch, thus avoiding the gaze of the analyst, a system which, it is claimed, not only allows more spontaneous, less inhibited talking, but also reduces the influence of TRANSFERENCE.

Talking openly about one's preoccupations and one's past is supposedly also encouraged by the patient's total ignorance about the life of the analyst. In this respect Freud said, 'The doctor should be opaque to his patients and, like a mirror, should show them nothing but what is shown to him.'[51] There is no pressure for the two people to relate to each other in a normal sense, for this would inhibit the patient. This is why long silences are permitted – the patient is the motivator, it is claimed, not the analyst. (But this argument avoids the issue of how the patient perceives the silences: the analyst's silence can easily be interpreted as a mean-spirited, aggressive act of indifference, increasing the patient's apprehension and sense of insecurity.) Analysts maintain that they restrict themselves to saying what they believe is true of their patients without attempting to manipulate or act on them in any way, but this again disregards (or accepts as part of the treatment) the way in which patients might *perceive* what is said of them as judgmental and manipulative.

Freud himself placed psychoanalysis on a par with the revolutionary work of Copernicus and Darwin. Copernicus had shown that the earth was not the centre of the universe, Darwin had shown that man was not a unique creation, and psychoanalysis showed that man was not even master in his own house. There was always a streak of pessimism in Freud's thinking: he never saw psychoanalysis as a means of 'self-improvement' or fulfilment; his concern was, for example, to find a means of 'transforming your hysterical misery into common unhappiness'.[50] Freud regarded psychoanalysis as suitable in the treatment of 'transference-neuroses, phobias, hysterias, obsessional neuroses, and besides these, such abnormalities of character as have been developed instead of these diseases'; he did not deem it suitable for psychotic conditions.[174]

Sandor Ferenczi (1873–1933), a Hungarian-born medical doctor who became a colleague of Freud's, kept a private diary from 7 January to 2 October 1932, which was not published for fifty-three years, appearing for the first time in 1985 in French. In it he reveals that Freud referred to his patients as riffraff (German: *ein Gesindel*), saying that the only thing patients were good for was to help the analyst make a living and to provide material for theory, and that there was no hope of actually helping them. 'This is therapeutic nihilism,' wrote Ferenczi. 'Nevertheless we entice patients by concealing these doubts and by arousing their hopes of being cured.' Ferenczi had become thoroughly disillusioned with Freud and his methods. 'He looms like a god above his poor patient, who has been degraded to the status of a child. We claim that transference comes from the patient, unaware of the fact that the greater part of what one calls the transference is artificially provoked by this very behaviour.' Ferenczi claimed that the analyst infantilizes patients: 'Far from helping them to overcome infantile problems, the analyst resubmerges them in an infantile relationship in which it is the analyst who emerges as all-powerful' (reported by Jeffrey Masson in *Against Therapy*[128]). Psychoanalysis has often been condemned, not only for appearing to interpret everything in sexual terms, but for 'its unquestioned dogma that everything *must* originate in early childhood'.[185]

Analysts have changed over the years. Just as 'there are very few analysts who would now subscribe wholesale to the Freudian system, with its eccentric baggage of drives, and its concept of oral, anal, and phallic stages',[136] so there are now many who put much greater emphasis on qualities such as patience, tolerance, reliability and empathy, which would not have been high on the list of an analyst's priorities fifty years ago. Freud and the early Freudians maintained that the personality congeals in early childhood, that all attitudes, feelings and impulses become frozen and dictate behaviour for the rest of one's life. According to this view, as a patient in psychoanalysis the individual is also totally passive, incapable of real change. Some of Freud's successors moved away from this position and accepted that a person's actions continue to have a formative influence on personality, through the reactions they evoke in others; thus was formed what has been called the *interpersonal* school. Then a third generation of analysts rejected Freud's view that the individual has no power to change, embracing the aim of analysis as a means whereby patients cure themselves. 'Every choice, small or large, reinforces the underlying feelings, attitudes and beliefs, the view of life that motivated the choice.'[179] Making different choices helps the individual to change inside – the so-called *action approach*.

Erich Fromm believes that the classical concept of psychoanalysis 'does not do justice to the real depth and scope of Freud's discoveries.' He maintains that Freud's original presentation of his ideas was limited and even distorted by the 'thought patterns and categories of his culture', which determined what was 'thinkable', to the extent that 'The original idea must be expressed at first in erroneous forms.' 'Freud's theory of the conflict between libido and ego as the central conflict in man was therefore a necessary assumption, which enabled him to express his fundamental discovery in "thinkable" terms. Freed from the shackles of the libido theory, the essence of psychoanalysis can be defined as the discovery of the significance of conflicting *tendencies in man*, the power of the "resistance" to fight against the awareness of these conflicts, of the rationalizations that make it appear that there is no conflict, and of the liberating effect of becoming aware of the conflict, and of the pathogenic role of unsolved conflicts.'[57] Fromm admires Freud's contribution because he 'smashed the conventional view that man's thinking and his being are identical . . . he unmasked hypocrisy . . . he questioned all conscious thought, intentions, and virtues and demonstrated how often they are nothing but forms of resistance to hide the inner reality.' Fromm still sees great value in psychoanalysis, but not simply as therapy for neuroses:

the new function of analysis is what he calls TRANSTHERAPEUTIC ANALYSIS, through which one may hope to achieve self-awareness and self-liberation.

Bruno Bettelheim decided that psychoanalysis was 'by no means the most effective way to *change* personality', adding that while it 'told much about the "hidden" in man, it told much less about the "true" man.' He regarded psychoanalysis as a useful method of observation rather than a body of theory or a therapy: it helped him to understand what might be going on in the unconscious minds of prisoners and guards in Dachau and Buchenwald – 'an understanding that on occasion may have saved my life, and on other occasions let me be of help to some of my fellow-prisoners, where it counted.' He concluded that the trouble with psychoanalysis lies in its concentration on what has gone wrong. In particular it has little to say about 'what makes for "goodness" or "greatness" in a life'.[14] It was for this reason that Abraham Maslow created his 'third force' or HUMANISTIC PSYCHOLOGY.

PSYCHOBABBLE 'Psychobabble' is a word invented by the American writer R. D. Rosen in 1975 to denote the meaningless clichés characteristic of the talk about therapies in the 'manic, self-regarding, relentlessly psychological atmosphere' of American society in the 1970s: 'This therapeutic age has culminated in one profuse, steady stream of self-revelation, confessed profligacy, and publicized domestic and intrapsychic trauma.' 'Psychological Man has regressed in the seventies to an adolescent – not just the victim of his own interminable introspection but also the victim of his own inability to describe behaviour in anything but platitudes.' The jargon that was invented supposedly to communicate emotion actually blocks rather than facilitates insight into oneself. Considering Tom Wolfe's description of the 70s as the 'me decade', Rosen remarked, 'These people seem barely to be talking about themselves at all. Their words don't belong to them so much as to the current guru of choice or best-selling self-help book.'[151] (See also SANSUKI.)

PSYCHOBIOLOGY An alternative term for PSYCHOPHYSIOLOGY, or *physiological psychology*.

PSYCHOCYBERNETICS Cybernetics is the study of control systems, the branch of science which compares automatic communication and control functions in living organisms with man-made mechanical and electronic devices such as computers. Psychocybernetics, a concept developed by Maxwell Maltz, focuses on the interaction and interdependence of mind and brain. One of its basic tenets is that disease can be eliminated only if the brain communicates the concept of health to the cells of the body. The patient must therefore be convinced of the feasibility of a cure. There are echoes of POSITIVE THINKING and SELF-HEALING here, and to some extent psychocybernetics represents a re-emergence of these in more scientific language. The programme of exercises Maltz designed enables people to create a positive and realistic self-image by means of auto-suggestion, goal-seeking and behaviour modification.

PSYCHODRAMA Psychodrama was developed by Jacob Moreno (1892–1974), a Viennese psychiatrist and contemporary of Freud who settled in America. It was originally conceived as an alternative to the very verbal, one-to-one approach of PSYCHOANALYSIS. Individuals act out their feelings, beliefs and attitudes in improvised situations related to their past, present or future. The therapist is referred to as the director, the client as the protagonist; other participating members of the group are the cast and those with no parts to play are the audience. Psychodrama is a way of exploring the origins of past emotions, expressing feelings openly in a safe and supportive environment, and trying out new roles by enacting a future event. The possible benefits are reduced inhibition, release of suppressed emotions in CATHARSIS, greater empathy with others in a given situation, and greater ease when adopting a new way of behaviour or 'role-switching'.

PSYCHOGENESIS Groddeck proposed that when we fall ill it is because at some level we choose to fall ill – our IT decides to follow that course. This mental or emotional point of origin for disease is now referred to as 'psychogenesis'. 'The psychogenesis of a disorder can be described as follows: An individual is confronted with a stressful situation which is extremely difficult for him or her to resolve. This situation becomes overwhelming, and he sees no respite from it. As a result, he makes an unconscious choice which allows him a means of coping with this irresolvable situation. One means of resolution is to develop a PSYCHOSOMATIC disorder, such as a MIGRAINE headache, which affects him so severely that he is incapacitated and released from the responsibilities which weigh so heavily upon him. These symptoms allow an individual to remove himself from an untenable situation when he cannot extricate himself by any other means.'[139]

PSYCHOGENIC 'Psychogenic' means 'having its origin (genesis) in the mind (psyche)'. Just as a PSYCHOSOMATIC illness results from a psychological condition, psychogenic pain is pain which has a psychological rather than a physical cause. A blush can also be described as psychogenic, if its origin is mental as in the case of embarrassment.

PSYCHOIMMUNITY When increased physical immunity from disease is attributed to mental techniques (i.e. those involving the psyche) such as VISUALIZATION, SELF-HYPNOSIS and BIOFEEDBACK, it is referred to as 'psychoimmunity'. It is the balancing factor when considering PSYCHOSOMATIC disorders. The area of research which deals with this type of immunity is known as PSYCHONEUROIMMUNOLOGY.

PSYCHOLOGICAL TYPES (See also PERSONALITY TYPES and TEMPERAMENTS.) Having established that people can be divided into two groups according to their general attitude to life – EXTRAVERT/INTROVERT – Jung decided on four more categories, which he called EGO FUNCTIONS, representing ways in which we orient ourselves in the world: thinking, feeling, sensation and intuition. Each of us relates to the world predominantly through one of these four functions, our 'most developed function', although this is not all that we are capable of. 'Just as the lion strikes down his enemy or his prey with his forepaw, in which his strength resides, and not with his tail like the crocodile, so our habitual reactions are normally characterized by the application of our most trustworthy and efficient function; it is an expression of our strength.'[101] The four basic types categorized by function can then be further subdivided by bringing in the two attitudes (extravert and introvert), thus producing eight types in all.

First Jung recognized the *thinking* type and its polar opposite, the *feeling* type. 'I was struck by the fact that many persons habitually do more thinking than others, and accordingly give more weight to thought when making important decisions ... and whatever happens to them is subjected to consideration and reflection, or at least reconciled with some principle sanctioned by thought. Other people conspicuously neglect thinking in favour of emotional factors, that is to say, feeling. They inveterately follow a "policy" dictated by feeling, and it takes an extraordinary situation to make them reflect.'[101] In some respects feeling is not the same as emotion, since all functions can lead to emotional responses; it is rather a non-thinking way of knowing. These two functions combine with the two attitudes (extravert and introvert) to produce four of the eight basic types.

The *extravert thinking* type likes logic and order, habitually 'thinks things through' and comes to conclusions based on data regarded as facts; the explanations which this type might offer for any particular course of action are given the status of absolute truth, which can lead to fanaticism, despite an intense dislike and fear of irrationality. Emotion and feeling tend to be repressed in the thinking type and in the extravert this can result in an individual who comes across as cold, intolerant and lacking in understanding of human frailty.

The *introvert thinking* type is less interested in facts than in ideas, directing the thinking inwardly without any desire to impress or influence others. This is often an eccentric character, the stereotypical absent-minded professor, shy, quiet, paying little attention to relationships and what is going on in the world and not really understanding what makes people tick.

The *extravert feeling* type is usually regarded by others as well-adjusted, enjoying social activities ('the life and soul of the party'), a person with tact and charm, able to smooth ruffled feathers, and generally help other people to get on with each other. Although sympathetic this type risks coming across to others as superficial and insincere.

The *introvert feeling* type, being ruled by subjective factors, appears to the world at large much more reserved than the warm, friendly extravert, but will be valued much more by close friends as someone who is genuinely sympathetic and understanding. This individual cannot dissemble or adapt, and having to play a role may result in self-destructive behaviour. Religion, poetry and music are typically associated with the introverted feeling type.

Both thinking and feeling are regarded by Jung as rational, compared with the sensation/intuition polarity, because they are discriminating and operate with a particular end in view: 'When we think, it is in order to judge or to reach a conclusion, and when we feel it is in order to attach a proper value to something; sensation and intuition, on the other hand, are perceptive – they make us aware of what is happening but do not interpret or evaluate it . . . Lack of rationality is a vice where thinking and feeling are called for – rationality is a vice where sensation and intuition should be trusted.'[101] It is rather confusing that both sensation and intuition may be referred to in everyday speech by the word 'feeling': the feeling function is not involved in the 'feeling' 'that the weather will change or that the price of our aluminium shares will go up', which Jung calls respectively sensation, 'perception through conscious sensory processes', and intuition, 'perception by way of unconscious contents and connections'.[101]

The *sensation* type takes experience as it comes, unaffected by thought or imagination; there is neither logic nor consistency in the experiences of the senses, and different sensations may be evoked by the same situation at different times. The sensation type is often an easy-going person, with a great capacity for enjoyment, the danger being that the world of the senses might become overvalued, leading to a restless life of pleasure-seeking, especially in the case of the *extraverted sensation* type, for whom the object which arouses the sensation is of prime importance. For the *introverted sensation* type the sensation itself is most important; such individuals, immersed in their own sensation, often have difficulty expressing themselves to others, although their need for self-expression manifests in their becoming artists or musicians.

Both sensation and intuition are irrational functions, but for the *intuitive* type much of what could be perceived via the senses never reaches consciousness. 'Intuition is a perception of realities which are not known to consciousness, and which goes via the unconscious.'[234] Intuition can come into play when there is no scope for thinking or feeling: 'Wherever you have to deal with strange conditions, where you have no established values or established concepts, there you will depend on the faculty of intuition.' (*Fundamental Psychological Conceptions*.) The *extraverted intuitive* has no time for either established values or established concepts: whatever is familiar, conventional or safe is seen as limiting, and what really matters to this type is the fact that 'anything is possible'. This makes the extraverted intuitive a supremely adventurous personality, who could sacrifice everything on a hunch for a future which will probably never materialize because other 'possibilities' almost invariably beckon before any becomes permanently established.

With the *introverted intuitive* the faculty is directed not to the outer world but to the inner life of fantasy, imagination and the collective unconscious. This is the type that sees visions and has prophetic dreams. 'The peculiar nature of the introverted intuition, when

307

given the priority . . . produces a peculiar type of man, viz. the mystical dreamer and seer on the one hand, or the fantastical crank and artist on the other.'[234] Shamans and prophets, cult leaders and religious fanatics belong to this type. William Blake has been cited as a good example of an introverted intuitive artist and poet.

It is possible to categorize people by ego function, because most people use one function much more than the other three, the diametrically opposed function being a strong force in the SHADOW. Neurosis often means that one function is developed to the virtual exclusion of all others, but for many people a second function may also be significant: if their predominant function is rational, the secondary function will be non-rational, and vice versa. The process of INDIVIDUATION involves bringing all the functions into one's repertoire, particularly the 'repressed' faculties (third and fourth functions) which have been relegated to the shadow.

PSYCHONEUROIMMUNOLOGY As the area of research which investigates the effect of mental and emotional states on the immune system, psychoneuroimmunology is one of the most important disciplines in studying the interaction or even inseparability of mind and body. It considers PSYCHOSOMATIC conditions, and the ways in which the immune system can be weakened by such experiences as bereavement and grief, [213] or strengthened as PSYCHO-IMMUNITY.

PSYCHOPERISTALSIS The contractions of the intestines induced by digestive juices is called peristalsis. Psychoperistalsis is a form of peristalsis which is induced, according to Gerda Boyesen, the Norwegian psychotherapist who developed the idea, 'to dissolve and discharge residual metabolic waste products of psychosomatic origin'.[88] In other words, the aim is to release visceral tension along with the nervous tension and repressed emotions which gave rise to it (hence *psycho*peristalsis, linking the mind and the digestive process). This tension is an example of body ARMOUR, a central concept in all types of BODY-ORIENTED PSYCHOTHERAPY, and the end result in successful psychoperistalsis is ABREACTION, the release of repressed emotion. In therapy the hypertonic flexor muscles are massaged and manipulated, sometimes inducing a 'startle reflex' which may signal a chain reaction of internal movements and rumblings indicative of peristalsis. The therapist monitors such internal changes by placing a stethoscope on the patient's abdomen.

PSYCHOPHARMACOLOGY Psychopharmacology is the study of mood-altering (psychotropic) drugs, including the effect of natural chemicals such as ENDORPHINS in the brain.

PSYCHOPHOBIC R. D. Laing, who conceived the idea of ANTI-PSYCHIATRY, believed that we in the West have become 'psychophobic' – terrified of the psyche and of inner experience. He held that the use of psychiatric labels for mental disturbance was just as alienating as the repressive use of chemicals. Denial of the rich life of the psyche is so common in western society that certain inner experiences are only made acceptable by being regarded as so-called channelling – i.e. the influence of entities *outside* the individual. If we were not so 'psychophobic' we would recognize that such events may well be a natural part of our own psychic life.

PSYCHOPHYSICS Psychophysics was a term coined by Gustav Theodor Fechner (1801–87) to refer to a particular type of science of the mind, which suggested that mental events could be defined in the same way as events in the natural world are accounted for by the laws of physics, and that sensations could therefore be measured. One consequence of this notion is the practice of defining sound level on a logarithmic scale in decibels, but all research has shown that people cannot agree on quantitative judgments such as 'half as loud'. All mental events, from PAIN to the perception of sound and COLOUR, are both subjective and unquantifiable.

PSYCHOPHYSIOLOGY Psychophysiology, also known as *psychobiology* or *physiological psychology*, is the study of the physiology of different psychological experiences – brain wave changes, heart rate changes, sweating, etc. (The lie-detector is one of the instruments which measure psychophysiological effects.) Physiological psychologists specialize in researching the effects of biochemicals on the brain and behaviour. In *transactional psychophysiology* the study focuses on the physiological changes that take place when people are affected by their interaction with each other. For example, social pressure (such as being interviewed by someone with higher status) increases blood pressure, and may result in BLUSHING. Some specialists in transactional psychophysiology use BIOFEEDBACK techniques: patients are shown the changes in their blood pressure while they are talking to their doctor, so that they can learn to change the way they respond to people, and keep their blood pressure down.

It may seem strange to some that specialists in physiological psychology are called psychologists at all since they reduce all mind and body functions and behaviour to a matter of genetics and chemistry.

PSYCHOSOMATIC EFFECTS In conventional medicine the term 'psychosomatic' is used to refer to symptoms which persist in the absence of organic pathology; the patient continues to complain of painful or otherwise distressing physical conditions which have no apparent physical or physiological cause. In such a situation it is quite common for a physician to conclude that the disorder is nonexistent, imaginary or hypochondriacal; in short, it has no real basis. In this way, for some people the term 'psychosomatic' has become virtually synonymous with 'imaginary'. But psychosomatic conditions are not imaginary, and their symptoms are not unreal. Such conditions are better termed 'hysterical'. Nor does 'psychosomatic' mean simply 'induced by the mind', as with a blush of embarrassment. For that we have the description 'psychogenic'. The term 'psychosomatic' can be used more accurately to convey the notion of a fundamental *interaction of mind and body* which is involved in all matters of health and disease.

The fact that there is a mental or emotional element among the factors which produce disease was known as early as 500 BC if not before. Socrates said, 'There is no illness of the body apart from the mind.' But given that people have always seen illness as an affliction, there has been an understandable reluctance to accept the personal responsibility for a condition that the psychosomatic principle seems to require. Nevertheless there have been intermittent reminders that this principle has validity. Two centuries ago (on 31 August 1772) Dr Samuel Johnson wrote his commiserations to a sick friend, John Taylor, including the comment, 'There is no distemper, not in the highest degree acute, on which the mind has not some influence, and which is not better resisted by a cheerful than a gloomy disposition.' Or in modern terminology, the mind influences all diseases and being cheerful bolsters our immune system (a foreshadowing of Norman Cousins's LAUGHTER cure).

Before the word psychosomatic was current, it was quite common to attribute symptoms which could not be satisfactorily explained to hysteria: backache was referred to as 'spinal hysteria'. But when hysteria fell into disrepute as a reliable diagnosis, few medical authorities saw fit to pursue their investigations into a possible psychogenic element in physical health. One exception was a

London surgeon, Daniel Hack Tuke, who in 1872 published his *Illustrations of the Influence of the Mind upon the Body in Health and in Disease*. But he was running against the tide of the times: mechanistic medicine had just had the impetus of Pasteur's GERM THEORY and it was generally believed that all disease must have a physical cause.

Just before the Second World War a Scottish doctor, J. L. Halliday, argued that lumbago and sciatica should be renamed 'psycho-neurotic rheumatism', because he believed he had identified a common pattern in which certain PERSONALITY TYPES suffered those physical symptoms when failing to express emotional tensions in any other way. He believed that psychological factors could affect the chemistry and even the structure of the body.[202] His ideas were later published in book form as *Psychosocial Medicine*.[73] At about the same time, Flanders Dunbar started using the word 'psychosomatic'.[34]

The impetus for this new interest in psychosomatic elements had perhaps come from psychology. Groddeck had put forward his theory of the IT, Freud had to a certain extent redefined hysteria through his exploration of the UNCONSCIOUS mind, and Reich had shown how emotional conditions could become locked in the body in the form of ARMOURING, giving rise to a range of BODY-ORIENTED PSYCHOTHERAPIES. In more recent years the impetus has come from research into the causes of killer diseases such as cancer and heart disease, and it is increasingly clear that genetic and environmental considerations are not the full answer. TYPE A/TYPE B behaviour is primarily an attitude of mind, as is the CANCER PERSONALITY. It has even been suggested that some diseases could better be described as 'degenerative processes', and that they can be reversible if something in the patient's mental attitude changes. For many people the mind has been shown to be an effective agent for SELF-HEALING, whether by taking a PLACEBO, or by using techniques such as VISUALIZATION and RELAXATION, or by simply being a stubborn, 'difficult' PATIENT. A HOLISTIC approach should recognize the interaction of mind and body implied by the nostrum 'We believe in treating the whole person', but all too often ALTERNATIVE practitioners still find themselves treating people who want a quick fix without taking any personal responsibility for their present or future condition.

PSYCHOSURGERY In 1935, at a conference of neurologists in London, Jacobsen and Fulton described how tantrums in a rather temperamental chimpanzee (understandably frustrated by the neu-rologists' attempts to train it to remember where they had hidden

311

its food) were successfully reduced by the surgical removal of part of the frontal lobes of the cerebral hemispheres. This operation severed the links between the emotional centres of the limbic system and the areas of the cortex that control behaviour. Frontal lobotomy was immediately seized on as a possible 'cure' for deranged behaviour in humans, and by 1950, 20,000 people around the world had been lobotomized. The first to prescribe such surgery was a Portuguese neuropsychiatrist, Egas Moniz (1874–1955), who was awarded the Nobel prize for Medicine in 1949 and was eventually shot by one of his lobotomized patients.

The drastic practice of lobotomy declined in the 1950s but other examples of psychosurgery persist. Extreme aggression is sometimes treated by removal of the amygdala, part of the limbic system, or by lesions in part of the hypothalamus. The justification for such operations is regarded by many as specious to say the least; it often uses comparisons with animal brains, which do not even have the same definition of brain areas. The whole subject of psychosurgery is disquietingly reminiscent of the medieval practice of TREPANNING.

PSYCHOSYNTHESIS Psychosynthesis, as its name implies, differs from PSYCHOANALYSIS in the emphasis laid not just on uncovering what is repressed in the unconscious, but also on putting all the pieces back together again. It is also more interested in the TRANSPERSONAL and has been called a 'psychology of the soul'. It was developed by Roberto Assagioli (1888–1974), an Italian psychiatrist who was involved in the early development of psycho-analytic theory but who also drew on the insights of spiritual traditions and mysticism. He presented the essentials of psychosynthesis in two books published towards the end of his life: *Psychosynthesis*[4] and *The Act of Will*.[5]

In Assagioli's view, an individual is a soul who has a personality, and through psychosynthesis one becomes not only more aware of one's own soul – who one really is – but also more aware of the soul in others. The soul, Higher SELF or transpersonal Self, is in a region of the unconscious which is referred to as the superconscious. There are two other aspects of the personal unconscious: the lower unconscious and the middle unconscious. The lower unconscious contains primitive urges, basic psychological drives, emotional complexes (often originating in childhood), and various compulsions, phobias, obsessions and delusions. The middle unconscious is the most accessible part of the unconscious: 'In this inner region,' says Assagioli, 'our various experiences are assimilated, our ordinary mental and imaginative activities are elaborated and developed in a sort of psychological gestation before their birth into the light of consciousness.'

It is in the middle unconscious that our various subpersonalities develop. These influence our behaviour and their absorption into the conscious self is an essential part of the process of synthesis. 'The concept of subpersonalities is essentially a dynamic one, assuming that new attributes emerge in us all our lives, if we allow them to, and that people can change and go on changing until the moment they die.'⁷⁷ These subpersonalities cover a much wider variety of roles than those used in other therapies such as TRANSACTIONAL ANALYSIS, and may include the rebel, the intellectual, the critic, the seducer, the saboteur, the organizer, the gourmet. As Piero Ferrucci says, 'Each of us is a crowd.'⁴² Subpersonalities are discovered and worked with in psychosynthesis through techniques such as guided imagery and visualization. Once we have identified a subpersonality we learn to step outside it and observe it – a process called *disidentification*.

Another crucial aspect of psychosynthesis is the use of the will. Although we are often driven by instinctive mechanisms, act on automatic pilot or behave according to the limited agenda of a subpersonality, we can also act with autonomy. 'We can truly and freely choose, bearing the full responsibility of self-determination. It is this evolutionary acquisition, still very much in development, that we give here the name of will.'⁴² It is through the will that we have the power to effect changes in our lives, a belief which makes psychosynthesis one of the most optimistic of psychological therapies.

PSYCHOTHERAPY In 1959 a book appeared in the USA with the title *Psychoanalysis and psychotherapy: Thirty-Six Systems.*⁷⁹ By 1980 the thirty-six therapies identified in that book had grown to well over 250 in two new books, *Handbook of Innovative Psychotherapies,*²⁷ and *The Psychotherapy Handbook.*⁸²

The history of psychotherapy starts with Freud's invention of PSYCHOANALYSIS. Many of the rules of psychoanalytic practice have been carried over to a greater or lesser extent into psychotherapy. For example, although there are degrees of strictness, the therapist generally discloses nothing about his or her own life. As the American psychotherapist George Weinberg writes, 'A good principle is that it's never wrong not to talk about ourselves, and it is often wrong to do so.' But a few paragraphs later he adds, 'However, if there is any reason for us to talk about ourselves, I think revealing a weakness is the best one. Often we can gain a person's confidence in this way, and can help him see that, even if he doesn't share our failing, he can do well in spite of some other failing of his.' Yet in this concession, what stands out is the inequality in the therapist-patient relationship. This too Weinberg recognizes: 'The nature of the relationship is that of a success talking to a failure . . . Humaneness requires taking steps not to let this inherent imbalance undermine the patient.' Weinberg also emphasizes the need for the therapist to react, which contrasts starkly with the cold, detached, impassive attitude adopted by 'classical' Freudians. 'The ability to react is a first-order requisite,' according to Weinberg, 'and those who possess it become the more successful therapists.'[179] In the words of a less conventional therapist, R. D. Laing, 'Psychotherapy must remain an obstinate attempt of two people to recover the wholeness of being human through the relationship between them.'[114]

Whilst many have adopted the psychotherapeutic method, some have condemned it as irremediably flawed. In *Against Therapy*, Jeffrey Masson attacks the whole structure of psychotherapy and talks of the 'covert sadism in psychotherapy'.[128] The subtitles of his book show his basic attitude to the practice: *Emotional Tyranny and the Myth of Psychological Healing* (in the American edition) and *Warning: Psychotherapy May Be Hazardous to Your Health* (in the British edition). He believes that 'The structure of psychotherapy is such that no matter how kindly a person is, when that person becomes a therapist, he or she is engaged in acts that are bound to diminish the dignity, autonomy and freedom of the person who comes for help.' He argues that all types of psychotherapy put excessive power in the hands of the therapist: 'The therapeutic relationship *always* involves an imbalance of power. One person pays, the other receives. Vacations, time, duration of the sessions are all in the hands of one party. Only one person is thought to be an "expert" in human relations and in feelings. Only one person is thought to be in trouble. This cannot but affect the judgment and perception of the party less powerful.'

Dorothy Rowe, the renowned psychotherapist who wrote a preface to Masson's book, supports him in his basic premise. She agrees that psychotherapy can be used 'to manipulate, control and humiliate people', and when it is employed by psychiatrists this is often what happens. 'Psychiatrists talk not of curing patients, but of "managing" them. Psychiatry is concerned with power, the power of individual psychiatrists and the power of the State.' This

hierarchical power structure, Rowe says, is reflected in psychotherapy: 'The psychotherapist is superior, the patient inferior. The
psychotherapist, by virtue of his knowledge, training and special
insight has access to truths above and beyond the capacity of the
patients. The psychotherapist's truths have a higher true value than
the patient's truths. The psychotherapist interprets the patient's
truths and tells him what they *really* mean.' This means that the
patient's version of reality is invalidated. 'Everything the patient
says,' writes Rowe, 'is taken, not as a statement of the patient's
truth, but as a projection of the patient's fantasy.'

Masson claims, 'It is in the nature of therapy to distort another
person's reality.' He traces the roots of analysis and therapy back
to the nineteenth-century diagnosis of MORAL INSANITY, claiming
that 'The tyranny of judging another person's life to be inadequate
was and is the very wellspring of psychotherapy', and 'Blaming the
victim . . . is the hallmark of psychotherapy.' Statements such as
these are reminiscent of ANTIPSYCHIATRY. As Dorothy Rowe says,
'The most dangerous people in the world are those who believe that
they know what is best for others.' But she does not have quite such
a jaundiced view of psychotherapy's past, pointing out that it was
originally concerned with 'the gentle building-up of the patient's
self-confidence by creating a trusting relationship between patient
and therapist (a model still used by many of those people who call
themselves counsellors).' COUNSELLING, with its CLIENT-CENTRED
approach, probably owes its very existence to the unfortunate fact
that for the 'healthy neurotic' or the 'worried well', psychotherapy
has not lived up to expectations.

There was awareness of the poor results of psychotherapy as early
as 1952, when H. J. Eysenck wrote an article entitled 'The effects
of psychotherapy: an evaluation'.[199] Eysenck concluded that 'There
appears to be an inverse correlation between recovery and psychotherapy; the more psychotherapy, the smaller the recovery rate . . .
roughly two-thirds of a group of neurotic patients will recover or
improve to a marked extent within two years of the onset of their
illness, whether they are treated by means of psychotherapy or not.'
By 1960 he could state even more categorically that psychotherapy
was a failure: 'Psychologists and psychiatrists will have to acknowledge the fact that current psychotherapeutic procedures have not
lived up to the hope which greeted their emergence 50 years ago.
All methods of psychotherapy fail to improve on the recovery rate
obtained through ordinary life experiences.'[39]

Dorothy Rowe points out that the basic questions which lead some people into therapy are often totally ignored or misunderstood by the psychotherapist. 'Surveys show that between 60 and 90% of the population in the UK and the USA believe in God and in the relationship between God and human goodness and wickedness. Thus, most of the people who come to psychiatrists and psychologists for help are not asking, "How can I be happy?", but "How can I be good?" Lacking a belief in God and the life hereafter, psychologists and psychiatrists consider that the only sensible question to ask is, "How can I make the most of my life (my only life)?" When the therapist and the patient have different and unspoken aims, the course of the therapy is doomed to failure.' (There are, of course, many other therapies to which this contradiction does not apply, such as PSYCHOSYNTHESIS.)

Other critics have drawn attention to the fact that for a century psychotherapy has supposedly been making people more sensitive – and influential people at that – and yet the world they inhabit seems to get worse rather than better. In *We've Had a Hundred Years of Psychotherapy – And the World's Getting Worse*, James Hillman says, 'Therapy goes on blindly believing that it's curing the outer world by making better people', despite the fact that this is ostensibly not so. The one does not translate into the other, he suggests, because therapy deals only with 'going inside'. His co-author Michael Ventura comments, 'A therapist told me that my grief at seeing a homeless man my age was really a feeling of sorrow for myself.'[84] Hillman also blames the current preoccupation with what therapy calls the inner child, which he sees as disempowering. He suggests that psychology in its present state is actually part of the disease rather than a possible cure. The present is converted into the past, and outrage about the external world is converted into inner emotions, so not surprisingly the patient feels cut off from the outside world, which appears to be nothing but dead matter. On top of this, therapy encourages unrealistic expectations from close personal relationships (but not from working and community relationships) and a belief in 'the fantasy of GROWTH, the fantasy of the ever-expanding, ever-developing person', without recognizing that there is also something changeless inside people and that growth almost always involves loss. As another critic of psychotherapy has said, 'The way to alleviate and mitigate distress is for us *to take care of* the world and the other people in it, not to *treat* them.'[160]

PSYCHOVISUAL THERAPY The term 'psychovisual' usually refers to creative VISUALIZATION.

PULSED HIGH FREQUENCY THERAPY One of the main effects of ELECTROTHERAPY, particularly those forms which use high frequency waves (DIATHERMY and ULTRASONICS) is that heat is thereby generated within the body tissue, and it has often been suggested that this heat accelerates the body's natural healing process. But Dr Abraham Ginsberg of New York believed that the radio waves themselves were more significant than the heat they generated. So in 1934 he cut out the thermal effect by devising a machine which emitted short bursts of high frequency radio waves. In modern PHF generators these are typically of 65 microseconds duration with an interval of 1,600 microseconds before the next burst of energy, allowing any heat generated in the body to be dissipated. The healing of both bone and tissue is accelerated by pulsed high frequency therapy. The natural healing process at the cellular level involves the flow of current from healthy cells to those which have lost their electrical potential through damage or disease. When bombarded briefly with radio waves these damaged cells align themselves temporarily with the electromagnetic field, and the stress caused by this repeated realignment is thought to make the cells more receptive to the body's own natural flow of healing current.

PULSES/PULSE DIAGNOSIS The way conventional doctors and nurses feel a patient's pulse is an extremely basic, some would say debased, version of what to physicians in other traditions is a very subtle method of diagnosis. Galen of Pergamum (c.130–201) wrote eighteen works on subtle pulse diagnosis, describing over a hundred different pulse qualities. Today this form of diagnosis is still used in traditional ACUPUNCTURE and SHIATSU. The therapist feels the pulse of the radial artery in six different positions (three on each wrist) and at two different pressures – superficial and deep – so as to feel the pulse of each of the twelve so-called Officials corresponding to the twelve meridians. Each of these twelve pulses is evaluated in terms of twenty-eight different qualities, described for example as full, empty, floating, rapid, slow, intermittent, wiry, slippery, hollow, knotted, deep or tight. At the end of the shiatsu or acupuncture session the therapist again feels all twelve pulses to register the changes that the treatment has effected.

PUT-DOWN A form of manipulative criticism which one learns how to counteract in ASSERTIVENESS TRAINING.

PYRAMIDOLOGY/PYRAMID ENERGY/PYRAMID THERAPY

A pyramid is a geometrical solid with a square base and four equal triangular faces with a slope angle of 51°52′ (approximately one seventh of 360°). Pyramidology is primarily the study of the geometry and mathematical design of pyramids, particularly those in Egypt, with a view to speculating on their astronomical and/or religious significance and decoding any information which their design might contain. This study was then extended to investigations into the effect of placing objects inside hollow pyramids or wire-frame pyramid constructions in the position corresponding to that of the King's Chamber in the Great Pyramid, i.e. below the apex at a distance from the base of about one-third of the height. In the 1930s Antoine Bovis, a French explorer, found the dehydrated bodies of dead animals in the King's Chamber and noted with surprise that they had not decayed. It is claimed that meat and milk remain fresh for long periods (and razor blades are sharpened) if left in this position with the pyramid correctly aligned with the points of the compass. Small pyramid frames are used over food to keep it fresh, or to dehydrate fruit and vegetables without losing flavour, to enhance the taste of tap water and of cheap wine, and to stimulate plant growth. People sometimes sit inside larger pyramid frames during MEDITATION, thereby, it is suggested, improving their connection with the universal LIFE-FORCE. Pyramid therapy is just one aspect of PATTERN THERAPY.

QALY QALY stands for Quality Adjusted Life Year, a term invented by economists at the Centre for Health Economics at the University of York. It is a way of assigning a numerical value to the quality of any extra years of life which a particular person's treatment, if successful, is likely to yield. It represents an attempt to reduce all dilemmas about priorities in (conventional) treatment to a mathematical calculation. The procedure enables administrators to decide who to treat by dividing the expected cost of the treatment by the number of QALYs, giving a prediction of the return society can expect from its investment. Although not yet used officially as a yardstick of economic efficiency in the National Health Service, it was taken seriously enough for a BMA seminar to be held on the idea in 1986.

QI 'Qi' is the modern spelling of CH'I (both pronounced 'chee', as in 'cheese'). 'Ch'i' was so well established before the modern spelling was introduced that it is still the more common spelling in Europe, except in the combination QI GONG.

QI GONG Qi Gong is literally 'manipulation of Qi'. But Qi (or ch'i) can mean 'breath' as well as 'life force', so Qi Gong can be interpreted as both 'breathing skill' and 'control of vital energy'. It is a form of meditative breathing, sometimes referred to in the West as 'Standing Zen'. Taoist and Buddhist monks are said to be able to influence the Qi in their bodies with special breathing exercises, arm and hand movements, physical training and intense concentration, directing their 'vital energy' to any part of the body in order to perform extraordinary feats. This may also be what people in extreme emergencies do, as for example when a woman is able to lift a great weight, such as a car, which would otherwise crush her child to death. Qi Gong predates and underlies all other MARTIAL ARTS.

Some 'Qi Gong Masters' have also claimed to be able to direct their Qi outside their body, in the way that psychokinesis is hypothesized in the West, and Qi Gong has been associated with telepathy.[37] Chinese medical practitioners who are also masters in Qi Gong direct Qi to their patients in the manner associated in the West with the laying on of hands, but usually without physical contact (comparable to the techniques of REIKI).

When patients attending a hypertension unit in a Shanghai hospital were given regular Qi Gong exercises it was found to be very beneficial: the effects were reductions in blood pressure, pulse rate, metabolic rate and oxygen demand. These physiological effects are comparable to those of MEDITATION.[37]

Millions of people in China, including the terminally ill, practise Qi Gong exercises at dawn every day, combining the movements of TAI JI QUAN with meditation, relaxation and breath control. They then focus their Qi on a particular point deep in the centre of the body, a little lower than the navel, known as the *dan tian*, or 'vital centre', from which Qi is believed to be distributed to all other parts of the body. Other traditions would refer to this point as the solar plexus centre, the CHAKRA known as *manipura* in the Indian tradition, or HARA in Japanese. It is also one of the most favoured parts of the body to which healers direct their attention, second only perhaps to the head region in the practice of laying on of hands.

QUACKBUSTERS See HEALTH WATCH.

RADIANCE TECHNIQUE An alternative term for REIKI.

RADIATIONS See RADIESTHESIA, RADIONICS and VIBRATIONAL THERAPIES.

RADIESTHESIA Radiesthesia (literally 'sensitivity to radiations') is a form of medical dowsing using a PENDULUM. The term was coined in the 1920s by a French priest, the Abbé Mermet, who first had the idea of using the principles of water divining on the human body. If with a pendulum one could diagnose the condition of an underground stream, he speculated, one could also use a pendulum to diagnose the condition of a patient's blood stream, and he proceeded to do just that, diagnosing all manner of diseases. A pendulum is used in this way by certain practitioners of HOMOEOPATHY, HERBALISM and AROMATHERAPY, and radiesthesia is an integral part of PSIONIC MEDICINE and RADIONICS. (A traditional form of radiesthesia is the practice – some would say superstition – of trying to ascertain the sex of an unborn child by holding the mother's wedding ring suspended over her abdomen. It is said that if the swing is circular the baby is a girl, and if to and fro it is a boy.)

RADIO WAVES See MICROWAVE DIATHERMY and PULSED HIGH FREQUENCY THERAPY.

RADIONICS Radionics belongs to a group of therapies that can be classified as VIBRATIONAL and involves diagnosis and treatment at a distance. In addition to using special radionics equipment, practitioners may also confirm diagnosis and treatment through RADIESTHESIA with a PENDULUM, a technique which is also thought to work on 'vibrations'.

Radionics was developed by Albert Abrams (1863–1924), a distinguished American neurologist, who developed his theory of *biocurrents* as a result of his investigations into 'percussion' – tapping a patient's body and noting the sound this produced. While percussing the abdomen of a cancer patient, he noticed that the resonance of the note given off by a particular area above the navel changed when the man faced west. He found that the same occurred with other conditions but in different areas; for example, for patients with tuberculosis the critical area was below the navel. Abrams believed this phenomenon to be electromagnetic, so he devised a box containing resistors and measured the disease reactions in ohms. Cancer was found to react at 50 ohms, syphilis at 20 ohms, tuberculosis at 15 ohms.

Next he discovered that he could also diagnose a patient's complaint without the patient needing to be present. By placing in the box a tissue sample or drop of blood (the diagnostic *witness*) from the patient, and attaching the electrode to the forehead of a healthy person standing on earthed metal plates, Abrams was able to make an accurate diagnosis by tapping the abdomen of this third party and going through the known rates of resistance. Abrams concluded that the diseased tissue or any organic material from the patient, even dried blood, emitted detectable radiations. In finding the particular resistance which would cancel out the effect of these radiations, he could not only make a far more discriminating diagnosis than with the basic percussion method but also provide corrective therapy by transmitting the precise radiation to balance the defective biocurrent. Abram's 'black box' became the standard piece of equipment in radionic therapy.

Abram's theories were ridiculed during his lifetime. After his death his work was continued in California by Ruth Drown and in Britain by George de la Warr. It was Ruth Drown who discovered that treatment as well as diagnosis could be made at a distance. This signalled a slight shift away from Abram's anatomical and electromagnetic view of biocurrents and radionics to a more oriental or theosophical view. Present-day radionics practitioners talk less of electromagnetic radiations and more in terms of ETHERIC forces or BIOENERGY, the fourfold nature of a human being – mental body, emotional body, etheric body and physical body – and the state of the CHAKRAS. Although they usually still use the black box to help them focus on the diagnosis as well as to beam back the corrective radiation, it is seen by some commentators as less significant than Abrams believed. 'It is likely that the instruments, although useful as a focus for the mind of the practitioner, do not in themselves have any intrinsic value beyond the fact that they can be used to objectify a process going on at mental levels. Thought connects the practitioner to the patient, and thought initiates the treatment process. Radionics is a form of mental healing. When a practitioner tunes in to the patient, he literally brings that patient "to mind" and on that plane of consciousness distance does not exist. At this level the very act of making a diagnosis sets up a form of energy exchange which has therapeutic impact upon the patient.'59

RADIX THERAPY Radix therapy is a neo-REICHIAN THERAPY developed by Chuck Kelley, using BIOENERGETIC techniques to overcome pain, anger and fear.

RAE POTENCY SIMULATOR See POTENCY SIMULATOR.

RAINBOW EFFECT When Jean-Martin Charcot was investigating hysterical patients at the Salpêtrière Hospital in Paris, he noticed that whilst lying down they would often arch their bodies, resting simply on the head and heels. This was referred to as the 'rainbow effect'.

RAINBOW HEALING As a form of COLOUR THERAPY, rainbow healing is one of the simplest ways to get colour into the body. Drinking water is poured into coloured glasses and placed in sunlight, so that it takes on the energies of the colour of the container. Those energies are then absorbed by the person drinking the water.

RASA *Rasa* is a Sanskrit word meaning 'essence' or 'taste'. In AYUR-VEDIC MEDICINE the taste of a herb is believed to give a clear indication of its essence and hence its medicinal properties.

RATIONAL EMOTIVE THERAPY Rational emotive therapy is a method of achieving greater inner harmony, developed by Albert Ellis. As the name suggests, the technique involves rational management of the emotions, which is regarded as essential for greater self-awareness, and a step towards SELF-ACTUALIZATION. The rational-emotive therapist encourages the client to bring to awareness beliefs that have been unconsciously internalized and which give rise to a false self-image, false expectations, and ultimately neurosis when the expectations are not realized.

REACTION-FORMATION Reaction formation was identified by Freud as one of the DEFENCE MECHANISMS which people employ to avoid facing the truth about their feelings or anxieties. It is a case of 'The lady doth protest too much, methinks' (*Hamlet*), and refers to the way in which we can mask undesirable feelings by behaving in a way that is contrary to our natural inclination, as when someone who hates children conceals the fact by going out of their way to appear affectionate towards them.

REAL PERSON In his 1943 *On Being a Real Person*, Harry Emerson Fosdick said, 'Integration is an affair of psychological government, with all the recurrent dissents, tensions and revolts to which government, however united and strong, is subject.'[44] His use of the term 'a real person' was not as glib as that of some therapists and counsellors in the following generation. He maintained that 'Therapy directed merely toward a happy adjustment to life is by itself alone superficial.'

REALITY THERAPY Reality Therapy was devised by the American psychiatrist Dr William Glasser in the 1960s. When he asked himself why people needed psychiatric treatment he decided that it was because they were not satisfying two basic human needs – relatedness and respect. Such people have no sense of belonging and lack both self-respect and the respect of others. Their condition is one of *under*-socialization. This is not the view of standard psychoanalytic theory, which regards neurotic behaviour as arising out of *too much* training during childhood from parents and other authority figures. To satisfy the needs of relatedness and respect these psychiatric patients need to become more realistic and act more responsibly. Instead of speculating *why* they behave the way they do by delving into the past, which cannot be changed, they need to accept responsibility for their present behaviour. 'Responsibility, a concept basic to Reality Therapy, is here defined as the ability to fulfil one's needs, and to do so in a way that does not deprive others of the ability to fulfil their needs.'[64] This means discussing their behaviour – what they want out of life and how they can best go about achieving it – in as practical a way as possible. In conventional PSYCHOTHERAPY the therapist is expected to remain as impersonal and objective as possible, not getting involved with patients or forming real relationships with them. In reality therapy the therapist becomes involved in a very real way. The relationship has to be deep enough for the patient to realize that the therapist

323

'cares enough about the patient to make him face the truth that he has spent his life trying to avoid: *he is responsible for his behaviour.* Now, continually confronted with reality by the therapist, he is not allowed to excuse or condone any of his behaviour.'[64] The therapist challenges the patient to decide whether or not a proposed course of action is that of a responsible person. Questions of right and wrong, ignored by conventional psychotherapy, are crucial in reality therapy. As Glasser says, 'We emphasize the morality of behaviour . . . People come to therapy suffering because they behave in ways that do not fulfil their needs, and they ask if their behaviour is wrong. Our job is to face this question, confront them with their total behaviour, and get them to judge the quality of what they are doing. We have found that unless they judge their own behaviour, they will not change . . . Treatment, therefore, is not to give him understanding of past misfortunes which cause this "illness", but to help him function in a better way right now . . . People do not act irresponsibly because they are "ill"; they are "ill" because they act irresponsibly.'[64] Such people can break old patterns of behaviour only by learning new ways of behaving; reality therapy means facing up to the reality of living and participating responsibly in society as it is.

REBALANCING An alternative term for DEEP TISSUE MASSAGE.

REBIRTHING Modern psychoanalytic theory regards the birth trauma as just one of many possible factors contributing to neurotic behaviour and not the ultimate cause of all anxiety. Freud was the first to suggest that the anxiety of the birth experience was the prototype for later anxieties. His pupil, the Viennese psychoanalyst Otto Rank, developed this theory further in *The Trauma of Birth* (1923), suggesting that since all anxieties originated in the traumatic experience of separation from the mother at birth, overcoming that original anxiety would enable all others to be overcome. He regarded successful psychoanalysis as 'belated accomplishment of the uncompleted mastery of the birth trauma'.[148] Although Rank eventually abandoned this view, it gained a considerable following in America, where Rank settled. L. Ron Hubbard picked up the idea and developed it further in his *Dianetics* of 1950, claiming that the foetus picked up impressions which formed memory traces (ENGRAMS) in the unconscious ('reactive') brain.[87]

Rebirthing as a therapeutic physical and psychological experience was first developed by Leonard Orr, an ex-consultant to EST who founded the organization Theta, and Stanislav Grof. The technique, derived in part from the yogic science of breathing (PRANAYAMA), uses breathing and hyperventilation to achieve an emotional climax and catharsis, specifically the release of emotions, memories and physical holding patterns which seem to originate in the trauma of birth. In the authentic rebirthing experience (now known as 'wet rebirthing') the client is led naked apart from nose-clip and snorkel into a small pool of warm water (37°C) and held face down. The assistant or 'rebirther' instructs the 'rebirthee' in 'connected breathing' (without pausing between breathing in and breathing out) and delivers comforting 'affirmations' to reassure and ease passage into the outside world. This eventually evokes memories and sensations from the actual birth experience, the primal panic of the original birth trauma, which Leonard Orr called 'the creeping crud'. Later practitioners dispensed with the water and rebirthed their clients on a bed ('dry rebirthing'). Stanislav Grof (who also worked on PREBIRTHING) uses music to assist the process ('Grof breathing'). In NATAL THERAPY a carpeted floor is sufficient. PRIMAL THERAPY is another descendant of the rebirthing tradition, although its founder, Arthur Janov, in his desire to appear revolutionary, is loath to acknowledge antecedents.

RECESSED HEEL FOOTWEAR Wearing shoes with a recessed heel is a way of adopting a more natural posture when standing and walking. A Danish yoga teacher marketed the first successful shoes of this kind. She had noticed that standing barefoot on soft ground the heels sink into the ground more deeply than the rest of the foot, which makes the pelvis tilt slightly and the spine straighten. High heels have the reverse effect and are responsible for a great deal of bad posture and back pain. Whilst the lower heel may not seem 'natural' per se, it is the best counter-measure against the unnatural practice of having to walk on hard concrete surfaces. As well as a lower heel, recessed heel footwear should have varying degrees of flexible arch support, a broad toe area which gives the toes ample space to flex, a snugly fitting heel which does not allow slipping or rocking, and a curved sole that facilitates transfer of weight from heel to toe and forward propulsion.

RECOVERED MEMORY THERAPY An alternative term for RE-PRESSED MEMORY THERAPY.

REDUCTIONISM Many of the criticisms levelled by alternative therapists against CONVENTIONAL MEDICINE are attacks on the principle of reductionism which has dominated science over the last three centuries. Knowing how an organism works is seen as no more than knowing how all its component parts operate; organs are broken down into ever smaller units, and life is a matter of chemical reactions, each DISEASE having a SINGLE CAUSE and a single cure. This process started with Descartes's separation of mind and body. 'I consider the human body as a machine,' he wrote. 'My thought compares a sick man and an ill-made clock with my ideas of a healthy man and a well-made clock. I say that you consider these functions occur naturally in this machine solely by the dispositions of its organs not less than the movement of a clock.'

Viktor Frankl describes being told as a schoolboy that in the final analysis life was 'nothing but a combustion process, an oxidation process',[45] and he often refers to this 'nothing-but-ness' which reductionism encourages. He defines reductionism as 'a pseudo-scientific procedure that either reduces human phenomena to or deduces them from subhuman phenomena'.[45] So 'conscience is reductionistically interpreted as nothing but the result of conditioning processes', and love is interpreted 'as the sublimation of sexual drives and instincts which man shares with the other animals'.[45,46] Frankl shows how psychotherapy has also suffered from a reductionist approach: according to reductionism 'values are nothing but reaction formations and defence mechanisms. As for myself, I am not prepared to live for the sake of my reaction formations, even less to die for the sake of my defence mechanisms.'[45]

Reductionism has had its successes in developing such treatments as polio vaccine, the synthesis of hormones, antibiotics, tissue-grafting for burns and the use of artificial limbs and joints. Large-scale killers such as leprosy, rickets, syphilis, smallpox, scurvy, yellow fever and typhus have been conquered by eliminating, avoiding or being able to 'knock out' what has been identified as the causative factor. But focusing so exclusively on single causes and single cures has meant that the conditions or circumstances in which a particular disease arises have been ignored until relatively recently, and the 'connectedness' of contributory factors is little understood. A prime example is diabetes: although medicine is successful in treating diabetics with insulin it has not satisfactorily confronted the cause of the illness. Dr Patrick Pietroni has described this as 'a pharmacological equivalent of spare-part surgery', and admits, 'There is a growing crisis of faith not only in medicine's power to cure, but in its power to explain.' He sees what he calls the 'greening of medicine' as involving primarily a 'shift from causality to connectedness'.[143] The view that phenomena are explicable only in terms of a complex interaction of a plurality of causes is the view of HOLISM, which is diametrically opposed to reductionism. In matters of health this plurality of factors may involve PSYCHOSOMATIC elements – emotional, mental and even spiritual considerations. (Incidentally, if the term 'psychosomatic' sounds derogatory when used diagnostically it is because it is being understood in a reductionist way as the single cause.) The reductionist view also finds it difficult to appreciate HEALTH as anything other than the absence of DISEASE, whilst holism has a much more rounded view of what constitutes good health and WELLNESS.

RE-EVALUATION COUNSELLING Re-evaluation counselling is an alternative term for CO-COUNSELLING.

REFERRAL ZONE The zones used in REFLEXOLOGY are sometimes called referral zones since the treatment (and possibly pain) in one area may refer to another part of the body in the same zone.

REFLEXOLOGY Reflexology is an ancient form of healing which uses pressure in the manner of SHIATSU or ACUPRESSURE, particularly on the feet. It was practised in ancient China alongside ACUPUNCTURE, and an illustration on the walls of the so-called Physician's Tomb at Saqqara shows that it was also practised in Egypt around 2330 BC.

Western interest in reflexology began in the 1920s with the work of Dr William H. Fitzgerald, an American ear, nose and throat specialist. He was led to rediscover the practice of reflexology by noticing that it was possible to anaesthetize the ear by applying pressure to a certain area of the foot. He divided the body into ten vertical zones (hence the term ZONE THERAPY), five on each side of the body, and found that by pressing points in one zone he could relieve pain in other areas within the same zone. He then discovered that pressure at the end of a finger or toe could affect all areas within the relevant zone; similarly the tongue and ears (as in AURICULOTHERAPY) could be divided into ten zones for the purposes of treating the whole body.

For the most part, reflexologists use the zones of the feet. By feeling the patient's feet the reflexologist can detect in which zone there is a blockage in the flow of energy. (KIRLIAN PHOTOGRAPHY of the hands or feet may also be used to help in this diagnosis.)

These blockages, described as crystalline deposits under the skin, are felt as tiny lumps or gritty granules, and they are dispersed by applying pressure and massage. They often feel very tender to the patient and pressure on them can be quite painful, or there may be pain in another part of the body corresponding to that zone. Pressure on these areas may also produce emotional reactions in the patient (reminiscent of ABREACTION in various types of BODY-ORIENTED PSYCHOTHERAPY).

Although the principle behind the zones is similar to the system of MERIDIANS in acupuncture, the two sets of pathways along which energy (or CH'I) is said to flow do not exactly coincide. With the whole body mapped out on a drawing of the feet one can to a certain extent practise reflexology on oneself. According to traditional Chinese medicine certain areas of the feet relate to prenatal development and these are treated specifically in METAMORPHIC TECHNIQUE.

REGRESSION The evocation of past experiences is generally referred to as regression. This may mean regression to early childhood as in standard psychoanalysis, or to the events experienced by another personality as in PAST LIFE THERAPY, both of which usually involve HYPNOSIS. Other therapies, such as REBIRTHING and REICHIAN THERAPY, achieve regression to birth or other traumatic events in one's life through bodywork techniques.

REICHIAN THERAPY Wilhelm Reich (1897–1957) was a student and later a colleague of Freud. He broke away from Freud, believing that verbal PSYCHOANALYSIS ignored the physical effects of repressed sexuality, and in his ideas about the relationship between psychology and posture he laid the foundations of all later forms of SOMATIC PSYCHOLOGY. He provides a link between Freud and many later therapies, counting among his own patients and students, for example, Alexander Lowen, who founded BIOENERGETIC ANALYSIS, Gerda Boyesen, who created BIODYNAMIC PSYCHOLOGY, and Fritz Perls, who developed GESTALT THERAPY. The bioenergetic principles of Reichian therapy have been continued and extended in the work of Stanley Keleman and in the BIOSYNTHESIS of David Boadella.

It was the publication of Reich's *The Function of the Orgasm* which brought the final rupture between Reich and Freud. Reich believed that sexual repression leads not only to psychological neurosis but also to rigidity in the body (and incidentally to a similar rigidity in authoritarian systems in society): energy which fails to be released in orgasm becomes dammed up in muscular tensions (part of ARMOURING), which leads to bad posture, poor circulation and shallow breathing. The aim of Reich's therapy, which he initially called *vegetotherapy*, was to unblock body tensions and free breathing patterns, thus increasing the flow of biological energy (which Reich called ORGONE) through the body.

In *Character Analysis* (1933) Reich describes seven rings of tension caused by muscular armouring. These lie at right angles to the main axis of the body and divide the body into horizontal segments. (The limbs can also be divided into segments, and parallels are drawn between the hands and feet and the head, between the wrists and ankles and the neck, between the forearm and lower leg and the heart, etc.) There are two segments on the head – the *ocular* segment, which includes the forehead and scalp muscles, and the *oral* segment, which includes the muscles of the lips, chin, jaw and cheeks, but not the tongue. Armouring can build up in the ocular segment at birth as a result of intense bright light in the delivery room, and this can lead to symptoms ranging from dizziness to schizophrenia. In the oral segment armouring may result from deprivation at the mother's breast, and may manifest as tight or constricted facial expressions and voice tone. The third segment, the *cervical*, covers the neck muscles, including those of the tongue, throat and larynx. Armouring here is associated with sadness and fear, sometimes the result of trying to 'keep one's head above water', and therapy in this segment may involve shouting. The fourth segment, the *thoracic*, contains the heart, rib-cage, lungs and arms. Emotions including anger, pain, fear and love may be blocked in the armouring of this segment. The fifth is the *diaphragmatic*, covering the stomach, pancreas, liver, kidneys and solar plexus, where armouring often associated with fear may lead to stomach ulcers, liver conditions and diabetes. The sixth segment, the *abdominal*, covers the intestines and lower back, and armouring here is usually a result of sexual repression (which inhibits the normal motion of the abdomen during orgasm). Armouring in the seventh segment, the *pelvic*, covering the pelvis, genitals and legs, also results from repression and fear and is usually the last to be treated. These seven segments are closely related to the eastern system of CHAKRAS.

Reichian therapy involves fairly violent massage as well as deep breathing exercises and sometimes shouting. Working through the seven different zones of the body, the layers of pent-up emotions are dismantled one by one. Emotional ABREACTION is often preceded by a physical sensation known as STREAMING, a feeling of melting while streams of newly released energy flow through the body.

REIKI Reiki (Japanese *rei*, 'boundless and universal', and *ki*, 'life-force') is a cross between the laying on of hands and QI GONG involving the transfer of *ki* to the patient. It was developed in the nineteenth century by Mikao Usui, a Japanese Christian theologian who rediscovered ancient Tibetan healing practices and reinterpreted them in the light of his understanding of the healing methods of Jesus. Reiki treatment can be a relaxing, meditative and/or invigorating experience for the patient. There are twelve basic hand positions which the therapist usually holds for about five minutes each, although intuition may guide the practitioner to spend more time on problem areas and adopt other positions as necessary. The overall effect is seen as opening the CHAKRAS and attuning the patient to the 'universal life energy' (reiki) so that it can be received in a spirit of unconditional love. Although the hands are always used when the patient is present, reiki can also be used for people who are not present.

RELATIONSHIPS It is becoming increasingly apparent that just as certain PERSONALITY TYPES seem more susceptible to some diseases, relationships are an important factor in resistance to disease. One very simple conclusion to be drawn from the existing research is: 'The more social connectedness, the lower the death rate.'[135]

Statistics show that people who are single, widowed or divorced, with few close friends or relatives, and who tend not to join or participate in community organizations, are two to five times more likely to die prematurely than those with more extensive social ties. This is a general tendency, not associated with any particular disease. Death rates for people who are not in stable relationships and not well integrated socially are higher for all types of disease, including heart disease, cancer, infections and even accidents. The effect of divorce on health has been equated with that of smoking more than twenty cigarettes a day. Men's health benefits more from marriage than does women's, and suffers more from bereavement: men react more strongly to the death of a spouse than do women, perhaps because women have a broader social network and are more likely to confide in friends and relatives. 'This suggests that social isolation and disconnectedness somehow increase susceptibility to disease in general', and that 'social support increases all resistance to disease.'[135]

Further support for this conclusion can be drawn from research into heart disease. Japan has the highest life expectancy in the world and one of the lowest rates of heart disease, only one fifth of the rate in the USA. But this holds only for those Japanese who live in Japan; it is as if the farther the migrants get from Japan (or the closer to California), the higher the disease rates. This might at first suggest environmental or dietary considerations, but one subgroup of Japanese migrants to California was found with low rates of heart disease despite the fact that their diet, consisting of western foods, was high in fat, and they smoked cigarettes and had high blood pressure. The crucial factor was that they had close ties to the traditional Japanese community.[190] 'But what does having "close ties to the Japanese community" mean for health? . . . They maintained a stable view of the world and were able to rely on friends for help and support, thus avoiding the panic, indecision, instability and illness which often accompany major changes in geographic and cultural circumstances.'[135]

One of the most fundamental human NEEDS is that we should have a stable place in the world, and Japanese society perhaps addresses this need more than other societies do. This protects the heart. The same applies to Irish communities in the USA. Social interaction has been shown to prompt measurable changes in endocrine production, boosting the immune system and therefore improving the chances of maintaining good health. Other studies have suggested that owning a pet reduces the chances of death occurring within a year of having a heart attack. (Merely stroking a pet reduces tension.) 'The sense of connectedness and RESPONSIBILITY, whether it be to people, pets, or plants, seems to draw us out of ourselves and link us to the larger world. The predisposition to communicate with others, to bond, appears to be vital to our health.'[135]

These findings have led to some controversial comment on social trends and attitudes. 'If the cardiovascular system is a mirror of the mind, people who are excessively self-centred are doing themselves harm. The "me decade" of the 1970s may have backfired. Self-centred, hostile people set themselves apart from the world rather than seeing themselves as part of it. They are cut off from the normal give-and-take of social intercourse, and the result may well break their hearts.'[135]

RELAXATION With the high degree of STRESS experienced in western life, caused primarily by our inability either to control or to allow full release of the FIGHT-OR-FLIGHT RESPONSE (what

Herbert Benson has called an 'arousal disorder'), the value of relaxation is increasingly evident. Just as it is impossible to separate mental stress from physical effects, so the effects of relaxation are both psychological and physiological, although the entry point one chooses may focus primarily on either the mind or the body.

Just as the fight-or-flight response brings an increase in breathing rate, heart rate, blood pressure, metabolism and activity in the sympathetic nervous system, so relaxation induces a decrease in all these areas. BREATHING is one of the most direct ways of inducing the RELAXATION RESPONSE. When tense we tend to take short, shallow breaths – thoracic breathing, as it is called – which curtails the oxygen–carbon dioxide exchange taking place in the tissues and causes waste products to accumulate. Breathing is important in HATHA YOGA and many MARTIAL ARTS, other approaches to relaxation which are both physical and mental. Other ways of inducing relaxation range from MASSAGE at one end of the physical spectrum to SENSORY DEPRIVATION at the other. It is impossible to exclude consideration of the mind from any of these relatively physical relaxation methods, but much more attention is paid to mental activity (or passivity) in methods such as BIOFEEDBACK, AUTOGENIC TRAINING and MEDITATION.

RELAXATION RESPONSE The 'relaxation response' (so called by Herbert Benson) is the direct opposite of the FIGHT-OR-FLIGHT RESPONSE. It is controlled by the PARASYMPATHETIC NERVOUS SYSTEM. The sensations associated with the functioning of this aspect of the autonomic nervous system are feelings of being 'warm-hearted', 'swollen with pride' and 'flushed with excitement' (though not the tense excitement of the fight-or-flight response).

RELAXOMETER The Relaxometer is a device used in BIOFEEDBACK to measure electrical skin resistance. Electrical resistance in the skin is affected by blood flow, and by monitoring this with an ESR meter one can learn to control the relaxing influence of the PARASYMPATHETIC NERVOUS SYSTEM and thus reduce one's state of arousal.

REM Rapid-eye-movement sleep (REM) is also known as PARADOXICAL SLEEP.

REPARENTING The term 'reparenting' is used in two senses: as an aspect of the process many people go through in general

COUNSELLING, and as a specific regressive technique in psychotherapy. Both are ways of overcoming the effects of what is seen as an unsatisfactory childhood.

In its weaker sense, reparenting means little more than thinking deeply about one's childhood (dealing with the INNER CHILD) in order to understand oneself better and to do for oneself what one's parents failed to do – nurture oneself, develop a sense of self-respect, learn how to develop a healthy relationship with the outside world, and find the right balance between self-reliance and dependency.

The regressive technique of reparenting is aimed at those with more pronounced inadequacies in these areas. It is one of the more controversial unorthodox therapies and is not practised by psychiatrists but by a few clinical psychologists with lay therapists as helpers. It originated in the USA in the 1960s when a psychotherapist (Jacqui Schiff) adopted a young schizophrenic man and became his surrogate mother. She later treated many other schizophrenics in the same way, as described in her book *All My Children*. The theory behind this rather extreme approach is that by taking the patient back to a babylike condition and creating a new child-parent relationship it is possible to undo the damage done by the original parents. The re-creation of babyhood can be quite detailed, even to the extent of wearing nappies and drinking juice from a bottle, and the patient and therapist may even be connected by a cord for two or three days (a procedure known as being 'on the rope'). Although these more dramatic aspects of reparenting take up a very small proportion of the time, they show how much psychic energy is invested in the idea of reinventing a more satisfactory experience of being parented. (The reparenting method is sometimes known as *cathexis*, Schiff's preferred term, which in a more general sense means the investment of mental energy in a particular object, person or idea.)

The validity of reparenting as a therapy is disputed by orthodox psychiatrists, who see it also as too open to abuse, but its proponents believe it is the only solution for a minority of seriously disturbed people. It is not intended for the neurotic, but for those who tend to lose touch with reality, for people who are inclined to 'act out' or 're-live' their past experiences and repressed memories rather than talk about them in conventional therapies for whom ordinary psychotherapy is unsuitable.

REPRESSED MEMORY THERAPY Also known as 'recovered memory therapy', this form of psychotherapy deals with traumatic events which the patient has blotted out or blocked from conscious memory. The therapist encourages the patient to bring these memories back to conscious awareness, but critics maintain that on the one hand this can cause unnecessary pain and on the other it can often lead to unconscious invention. In the 1980s, when there was growing public awareness of child sexual abuse, the use of this form of therapy mushroomed, but many who 'remembered' abuse by their parents later recanted and became reunited with their families. Since 1992 some of these people have sought help from the False Memory Syndrome Foundation, based in Philadelphia and founded by Pamela Freyd.

REPRESSION The unconscious process by which painful memories are 'forgotten' whilst still lying hidden in the unconscious was named repression by Freud, although the phenomenon was recognized before it was given a name. Nietzsche understood that something in our emotional make-up was capable of distorting memory: ' "I did this," says my memory. "I cannot have done this," says my pride . . . and remains inexorable. In the end – memory yields.' Critics of Freud and the methods of PSYCHOANALYSIS maintain that there is no scientific evidence for the reality of repression and consider that encouraging people to remember (or fantasize about) disturbing childhood events (REPRESSED MEMORY THERAPY) can actually be harmful.

RESCUE REMEDY One of the most popular of the BACH FLOWER REMEDIES is a composite of five flower remedies: Impatiens (for nervous impatience), Star of Bethlehem (for shock), Cherry Plum (for irrational fear and despair), Rock Rose (for panic and terror) and Clematis (for listlessness and inattention). This combination, known as the Rescue Remedy, is recommended for emergency use as a first aid when one suffers shock or stress of any kind. Instead of drops of the remedy being added to water, two drops are often taken neat on the tongue. People also administer it to their pets by rubbing two drops on the animal's brow.

A form of COLOUR THERAPY known as 'AURA-SOMA', using oils of different colour combinations, also includes a 'rescue' bottle for emergencies, headaches, neuralgia, insomnia, sciatica, diarrhoea, high blood pressure and other acute conditions. It is a combination of blue and purple, both of which are generally regarded as particularly healing colours.

RESISTANCE Anyone in psychoanalysis may feel disinclined to face certain truths, even though the uncovering of these truths is one of the main aims of analysis. When a patient is expected to say whatever comes to mind, a certain amount of monitoring comes into play, as well as unconscious defence mechanisms which aim to keep what has been repressed hidden from consciousness. Freud gave the term resistance to these efforts to thwart the psychoanalytic process. Resistance is the interpersonal counterpart of REPRESSION.

RESONANCE See VIBRATIONAL HEALING.

RESPONSIBILITY CONVENTIONAL MEDICINE is often criticized for effectively relieving the patient of responsibility. Ivan Illich regards this usurping of the patient's rights as 'social and cultural IATRO-GENESIS' and a direct result of the MEDICALIZATION of life in the West. In contrast, many systems of ALTERNATIVE MEDICINE empha-size the patient's own responsibility, if not for the condition, at least to some extent for the healing process, in which lifestyle, diet and mental attitude will all play a significant part. Before SELF-HEALING can occur we must assume responsibility for our own health, rather than regard our bodies as a passive object which only the medical experts can influence. The very fact that someone seeks out treat-ment from an alternative therapist is a sign that in some way they have already assumed more responsibility than the average patient who consults their general practitioner. The growing popularity of alternative therapies is sometimes seen as an indictment of the way many general practitioners tend to treat their patients, prescribing without explaining, demanding cooperation irrespective of whether the patient understands, and expecting unquestioned faith in their expertise, all of which diminishes the patient's sense of responsibility for what is happening to them.

A sense of responsibility for things outside oneself is an important factor in one's chances of recovery, as has been shown by the research into the importance of RELATIONSHIPS and a sense of connectedness with the world. Field experiments in nursing homes have shown that patients who feel some personal responsibility and control over their lives fare better physically and mentally than those who remain in a more dependency-producing environment. One of the most amazing aspects of these experiments is that responsibility enhancement can come from such simple activities as choosing and regularly tending a plant.[214]

RESURRECTION MEDICINE/RESURRECTION MODE When

people are brought back from death's door, perhaps with emergency surgery, this is sometimes referred to as 'resurrection medicine'. It often implies high-tech medicine at high financial cost. Some people in the medical establishment are beginning to ask themselves why so much effort is put into resurrection medicine and so little into PREVENTIVE MEDICINE. One suggested reason is the esteem in which doctors in 'resurrection mode' are held when the patient can say, 'You've saved my life.' As David Smith, Commissioner of the Texas Department of Health, says, 'We don't feel as wonderful about doing prevention, even though it's cheaper. What happens in the resurrection mode is that we end up paying more later, and the patient is worse off because the condition has gotten more serious in the meantime.'[133] We find a parallel with these two modes in the contrast between HOLISTIC MEDICINE, in which the focus is on HEALTH, and CONVENTIONAL MEDICINE, which seems to be preoccupied with DISEASE and pathology.

RIGHT BRAIN/LEFT BRAIN See BICAMERAL NATURE OF THE BRAIN.

ROGERIAN THERAPY The CLIENT-CENTRED THERAPY developed by Carl Rogers in the 1940s is sometimes referred to as Rogerian therapy.

ROLFING Rolfing takes its name from the Swiss-born American biochemist, Dr Ida Rolf (1896–1979), who developed a system of bodywork techniques involving deep massage, which had as their prime purpose the rebalancing of the body and the restoration of proper vertical alignment. (Misalignment could be the result of injury, bad postural habits, or emotional trauma.) For whatever reason, most people tend to hold their bodies in unnatural positions, using energy to fight against gravity instead of relaxing into a natural posture. Rebalancing or realigning the body means that weight is distributed as evenly as possible around the vertical axis. The rolfer typically spends ten one-hour sessions enabling a client to achieve this vertical realignment, and during these sessions certain emotional and psychological insights may be achieved, sometimes involving the release of emotional pain.

This psychological bonus was not originally part of Ida Rolf's concept of structural integration. Her original ideas were influenced by YOGA, the ALEXANDER TECHNIQUE and osteopathy. But as Rolf gained more experience with her clients she realized that a further effect of deep massage and structural realignment was the freeing of the mind and emotions as well as the body from their negative conditioning: energies that are locked in 'ARMOURING', the permanent tension of large muscle groups, are freed and the so-called *postural release* is accompanied by insight into the anxieties or trauma that produced the body armouring in the first place. This release of stored trauma during a course of rolfing treatment became a common occurrence: one well-documented early example of this took place when Ida Rolf was treating Fritz Perls at ESALEN.

Many of Rolf's successors have laid greater emphasis on this psychological aspect of their own versions of bodywork. In sessions of HELLERWORK, for example, Joseph Heller encourages greater self-awareness by incorporating verbal expression of the issues which the work on muscle tissues brings to the surface.

ROSEN METHOD Marion Rosen was a refugee from Nazi Germany who settled in California, where she worked as a physical therapist treating injured workers from the San Francisco shipyards. Seeing a marked improvement in one of her patients following his participation in an early EST seminar, Rosen underwent est training herself and decided that verbal expression could be combined with her own bodywork methods. The philosophy she developed includes the idea that socialization leads to repression and the building of a persona which is both emotional and physical. The Rosen method uses both touch and verbalization to induce muscular relaxation, greater body self-awareness and release from the restrictive attitudes that have been induced by past emotional experiences. In a supportive, non-threatening atmosphere the therapist asks questions which help the client to evoke memories of events that may be locked in muscular tension, as well as using touch and movement exercises. Seeing a particular muscle quiver may prompt the therapist to ask what the client is thinking or feeling at that moment. Breathing is also an important part of the therapy, being, as Rosen says, the intersection between conscious and unconscious processes, since it can be under either voluntary or autonomic control. The Rosen method is one of the gentler therapies in the area of BODY-ORIENTED PSYCHOLOGY.

RUSSIAN BATH See HYDROTHERAPY.

S

SAD Abbreviation for SEASONAL AFFECTIVE DISORDER, which can be treated with HELIOTHERAPY or LIGHT THERAPY.

SAMADHI TANK The samadhi tank is a sensory isolation tank which was developed following John Lilly's investigations into SENSORY DEPRIVATION. The name derives from the Sanskrit term for enlightenment, chosen because of the ecstatic feelings of cosmic consciousness sometimes induced by the experience of floating in the tank with no sensory input whatsoever for the brain to monitor.

SANDPLAY Sandplay is a technique employed by some psychotherapists (often Jungian). The client forms a landscape in a sandbox, adding trees, animals, buildings, vehicles or other objects and peopling it with assorted figures, all selected from a large bank of such models. The technique has the advantage of avoiding verbalization by both client and therapist, as in ART THERAPY, whilst enabling the unconscious to be represented symbolically in tangible form. In this way the therapist may get a clearer idea of which ARCHETYPES are most active at that time, but even without retrospective interpretation the main benefit is to the client. With the client having no preconceived idea as to what might be depicted in the sand scene, the activity of the unconscious is brought to conscious awareness, albeit symbolically, as if in a waking dream, and the very act of producing the scene is enlightening and therapeutic (just as the dynamic act of working with DREAMS can be more beneficial than the more static interpreting of them).

SANSUKI In 1972 two American journalists invented an imaginary commune as a spoof of 'the various cults that had recently won the attention of the mass media'. They described it in great detail, filling their account of its principles and procedures with 'neurophysiological gibberish'. The commune was called Sansuki. Many readers took it seriously enough to write in asking for further information. One of the instigators of the spoof, R. D. Rosen, later wrote *Psychobabble* in protest at the bewildering proliferation of self-improvement manuals and popular psychotherapies.

SAUNA See HYDROTHERAPY.

SCANNING In the BATES METHOD one of the common exercises to strengthen the eye muscles involves moving the eyes rapidly from one focus of attention to another, a practice known as scanning.

SCIENTOLOGY See DIANETICS.

SCOTOPIC SENSITIVITY See IRLEN SYNDROME.

SEASONAL AFFECTIVE DISORDER Some people seem generally far less resilient during the winter months, when there is less natural light. Since the main effect of this seasonal condition is psychological, affecting mood, it is known as seasonal affective disorder, which happens to have the conveniently apt acronym SAD. The most common treatment for SAD is LIGHT THERAPY.

SECOND ADOLESCENCE Jung defined 'second adolescence' as a period of life roughly between the ages of thirty-five and fifty, when the orientation of our lives is concerned less with the opinions of others and more with the growth of the self, the closer alignment of the EGO with the SELF through a process he called INDIVIDUATION. In alchemy fifty was the symbolic age at which an individual achieved wisdom and spiritual maturity, which Jung reinterpreted as the individuated personality.

SECONDARY DOCTOR TECHNIQUES Conventional doctors sometimes attend short weekend courses on SYMPTOMATIC ACUPUNCTURE and then claim that they are acupuncturists. But the skills they have acquired are only 'secondary doctor techniques': they gain no real understanding of the patient's basic disorder according to the principles of Chinese medicine and are concerned only with relief of the symptoms.

SECONDARY GAINS The benefits from being stricken by illness are referred to as secondary gains. In the words of Carl Simonton, the cancer specialist and exponent of VISUALIZATION techniques, illness 'serves as a "permission giver" by allowing people to engage in behaviour they would not normally engage in if they were well.'[159] The benefits he cites from being ill include increased love and attention, time away from work, and reduced responsibility. (He notes also that the CANCER PERSONALITY is typically someone who always puts the needs of others first, and that suffering from cancer is one way, albeit drastic, of giving oneself permission to attend to one's own needs.) This does not imply that we deliberately fall ill with a conscious, ulterior motive, but rather that at a deeper unconscious level part of our psyche (Groddeck's notion of the IT) chooses to inflict the condition on us and that there is therefore a purpose behind our illness. For example, if we suffer from migraine we may unconsciously be using our attacks as a means of getting a few moments of privacy from a demanding family. Cure often depends on our recognizing the secondary gains that our particular disease brings us. (See also PAINMANSHIP.)

SEIZA Seiza is a Japanese term used in BODYWORK therapies to denote the position of kneeling and sitting on one's feet, keeping the back straight.

SELF In Jungian psychology the Self is distinct from the EGO, which arises from it and mediates between it and the outside world. The Self is the central nucleus of the psyche and through its relationship with the ego gives rise also to the formation of PERSONA, SHADOW and ANIMUS or ANIMA. 'The Self is not only the centre but also the whole circumference which embraces both conscious and unconscious; it is the centre of this totality, just as the ego is the centre of the conscious mind.'[103] The goal of the Self is wholeness, Self-realization, the assimilation of all these fragmentary aspects of consciousness into ego-awareness, a process Jung called INDIVIDUATION.

Whereas the ego has access only to what we are consciously aware of, the Self inhabits a much larger realm of psychic experience; and whilst it is regarded as a biological entity which has evolved with the function of controlling the development of the personality, it also possesses qualities commonly associated with the soul. In DREAMS, God and the Self share the same symbolism. The Old Testament representation of man created in God's image is seen as analogous to the birth of the ego out of the Self, and visions of God are encounters (of the ego) with the Self.

SELF-ACTUALIZATION In HUMANISTIC PSYCHOLOGY self-actualization is Maslow's term for the process of living up to one's full potential as a unique human being, with 'the full use and exploitation of talents, capacities, potentialities' which are innate in human nature. This is the final level of psychological development, which is embarked upon only when basic NEEDS are fulfilled. (For Kurt Goldstein, the theorist who originally coined the term, self-actualization was understood not as a level of development but as the motive which underlay all other motives; in his view everything a person did was motivated by the drive to realize all one's potentialities.) Self-actualization is to some extent Maslow's equivalent of Jung's concept of INDIVIDUATION. As with individuation one can never say that it has finally been achieved, since once begun it is a constant process rather than an event: living in accordance with one's true nature as if moving towards a goal, rather than attaining it and developing no further. 'Self-actualization is not a static, unreal, perfect state in which human problems are transcended, and in which people "live happily ever after" in a superhuman state of ecstasy.'[125] This misunderstanding of self-actualization is perhaps a result of confusion with the more abstract notion of SELF-REALIZATION. Maslow estimated that less than one per cent of the population were 'self-actualizers'. Viktor Frankl, creator of LOGOTHERAPY, sees something self-contradictory in aiming at self-actualization. For him, the basic motivation of the will-to-meaning involves self-transcendence. 'What is called self-actualization is, and must remain, the unintended effect of self-transcendence; it is ruinous and self-defeating to make it the target of intention.'[46]

SELF-ANALYSIS In developing his ideas on PSYCHOANALYSIS Freud set great store by his discoveries from his own self-analysis, so it is perhaps surprising that so few of his successors have suggested that self-analysis might be a real possibility. Karen Horney is one. Another is Erich Fromm, who speculates that 'The main reason for the fact that self-analysis has been so neglected as a curative possibility lies probably in the conventional bureaucratic concepts of most analysts about their role and that of the "patient". As in general medicine, the sick person is transformed into a "patient" and the belief is fostered that he needs a professional to get cured. He is not supposed to cure himself.'[57] Fromm sees self-analysis as adopting all the customary concerns and procedures of PSYCHOANALYSIS, although it can only follow on from initial work with an analyst. There may even be slight advantages in self-analysis in that verbalization is not required and one can perhaps enter more

341

fully into the feeling of emotions. Fromm criticizes what he calls 'the "cerebralization" of affective experience'[57] in much that passes for psychoanalysis. He recommends that self-analysis should be done for at least thirty minutes every morning. 'Self-analysis becomes a cleansing ritual, not because one is so concerned with one's ego but because one wants to free oneself from egoism by analysing its roots. Self-analysis becomes a daily practice that permits one to be minimally concerned with oneself the rest of the day.' In this Fromm shows his inclination towards the Buddhist view that self-awareness can lead to self-liberation, the aim of his conception of TRANSTHERAPEUTIC ANALYSIS.[57]

SELF-AWARENESS Self-awareness usually means being aware of one's existence as an individual and appreciating to some extent one's personal nature and identity. Psychological therapies such as GESTALT and many others in the 'personal growth industry' seek to increase one's self-awareness in the sense of giving one a greater understanding of one's true nature. Erich Fromm sees true self-awareness coming from PSYCHOANALYSIS and in particular from what he described as TRANSTHERAPEUTIC ANALYSIS. Insight into one's own psychological and emotional constitution can also be gained from many BODYWORK therapies in the tradition of ROLFING and REICHIAN THERAPY. In more specifically body-oriented therapies such as the ALEXANDER TECHNIQUE and the FELDENKRAIS METHOD, self-awareness denotes one's kinaesthetic sense or body-awareness, the recognition of what the body is doing and conscious control over how one is using it.

SELF-CONSCIOUSNESS Self-consciousness (apart from its secondary sense of 'embarrassment') is similar in meaning to self-awareness, although it implies an additional appreciation of the fact that other individuals also have an awareness of oneself.

SELF-DIRECTED IMAGERY The VISUALIZATION technique pioneered by Dr Carl Simonton whereby a patient uses a form of self-hypnosis to boost the body's self-healing powers (particularly in the treatment of cancer) is sometimes called self-directed imagery (as distinct from guided imagery, in which the visualization is directed by the doctor or therapist).

SELF-ESTEEM The word 'esteem' usually has a positive connotation, but 'self-esteem' can range from high to low, representing the degree to which one values oneself. Low self-esteem is typically seen to be at the root of many psychological problems in the more popular (or populist) forms of CLIENT-CENTRED THERAPY, COUNSELLING and CO-COUNSELLING that have burgeoned in recent decades. Healers such as Meir Schneider also consider low self-esteem to be a significant factor in many physically debilitating conditions, and part of their treatment involves increasing the patient's self-esteem in order to activate their own powers of SELF-HEALING.

SELF-HEALING Self-healing is the basic principle behind many traditional forms of medicine. Hippocrates referred to the healing force of nature, 'vis medicatrix naturae'; and speaking in his role as physician, Albert Schweitzer said, 'Each patient carries his own doctor inside him. They come to us not knowing that truth. We are at our best when we give the doctor who resides within each patient a chance to go to work.'

Western CONVENTIONAL MEDICINE, with its interventionist methods, has tended at best to belittle and more often to ignore and even deny the existence of this 'inner doctor', encouraging a totally passive attitude on the part of the patient (who must indeed be the epitome of patience in the hands of the medical expert). Ivan Illich has referred to this wresting from the sick of their own individual responsibility as social and cultural IATROGENESIS, which ultimately weakens the individual and increases disease. The prescription of ALLOPATHIC drugs is in principle a further denial of the body's own healing powers, and the body is seen as a battlefield where war is waged between pathogens and the weapons of modern medical science (with its MAGIC BULLET approach).

Most forms of ALTERNATIVE MEDICINE regard the diseased body as 'out of balance' in some way, or as a sign that the individual is mentally, emotionally or spiritually out of harmony. They use techniques which are intended to promote self-healing in the organism, whether by encouraging the body to improve its own defences against external attack (by introducing HERBAL or HOMOEOPATHIC remedies, for example), or by seeking to rebalance the energies at a more subtle level (with therapies such as ACUPUNCTURE, or remedies that work at a VIBRATIONAL level such as CRYSTAL THERAPY or the BACH FLOWER REMEDIES), or by trying to access and modify the emotional or psychological factors in the disease – the reasons why the IT (according to Groddeck) has decided to make the body suffer this particular illness (many BODY-ORIENTED PSYCHOTHERAPIES and BODYWORK therapies can be used in this way).

The self-healing powers of the body are also called upon even more directly by techniques such as VISUALIZATION, and many healers consider that their role is simply to help people access their own inner resources and use them to achieve good health. One such healer is Meir Schneider (born in Russia, brought up in Israel, and now living and working in California), who set up the Center for Conscious Vision in 1977 and Center for Self-Healing in 1980, both in San Francisco.

Schneider maintains that he is not a healer but that he helps others to heal themselves. (He actually calls himself 'a teacher of movement'.) Having overcome his own blindness through exercises based on the BATES METHOD, he decided to help others to take responsibility for their own healing. When treating people with physical disabilities he uses massage and encourages self-massage as well as exercises to reduce tension and improve circulation. 'Most people do not use their bodies properly and have a strong resistance to learning how. This is especially pronounced in the handicapped. They try to separate themselves from the part of the body which is crippled, so it is hard for them to work on those areas. My task was to try to help them come into touch with bodies from which they had become alienated. I was trying to help them regenerate functions which they had given up hope of ever regaining, or even to gain functions which they never had before. I was discovering something about the psychology of illness, as well as the physiology. I learned that a person must be *willing* to recover in order to overcome limitations.'[157]

Schneider also has his own theories about the causes of disease. Multiple sclerosis is a disease of the central nervous system, in which the myelin sheath, the fatty tissue which protects the nerves, begins to break down, making it difficult for messages to be transmitted from the brain to the rest of the body. Attacks often come in waves, and are often the result of some kind of shock. Current medical opinion tends to discount the theory of infection by a virus, favouring the idea that a breakdown or failure in the immune system is responsible. Schneider speculates otherwise: 'In my opinion, multiple sclerosis is related to an overload of the central nervous system due to overusing some neural pathways and underusing others. This is a result of stiff and unbalanced use of the body. A typical multiple sclerosis patient has poor posture and a rigid spine . . . extreme tension of muscles and organs leads to neurological dysfunction. The disappearance of parts of the myelin sheath is not the cause of multiple sclerosis, but is simply one of the worst symptoms, a result of misusing the body.'[157]

While encouraging better use of the body and faith in its own restorative powers, Schneider encourages his patients to use visualization (for example, visualizing suppleness in the affected part of the body while exercising the unaffected part, or in the case of people with arthritis 'sending' oxygen to affected joints, and visualizing a pleasing colour to induce relaxation). He believes low self-esteem is often a factor in debilitating illness, and consequently that belief in oneself, as well as the will to be whole, are crucial to recovery.

SELF-HELP Originally the term 'self-help' denoted the practice of working towards psychological health without direct contact with a psychoanalyst. It represented an attempt to educate the public in the principles of Freudian or post-Freudian psychology, emphasizing the health-oriented rather than the pathological aspects of such psychology. Self-help soon became associated with HUMANISTIC PSYCHOLOGY and the HUMAN POTENTIAL MOVEMENT, with the emphasis on encouraging people to grow and to assume responsibility for themselves without depending on psychotherapists.

SELF-HYPNOSIS In the late 1880s Oskar Vogt, the Berlin brain physiologist, realized that people were able to hypnotize themselves. He also noticed that by practising self-hypnosis several times a day patients could reduce their stress-induced tension and headaches. His ideas were later incorporated and developed further in AUTOGENICS. In more recent times it has been suggested that all HYPNOSIS is in fact self-hypnosis: '. . . hypnosis is achieved by the person himself as opposed to being achieved by the hypnotist. There is only auto- and never hetero-hypnosis. What the person expects to happen – does happen.'[47] The possible effects of some form of self-hypnosis may be seen in a variety of phenomena ranging from STIGMATA to SELF-HEALING.

SELF-IMPROVEMENT The notion of self-improvement probably originated with the POSITIVE THINKING movement in the early 1900s, but it became more of a movement in its own right and acquired more of a psychological bias with the birth of ENCOUNTER GROUPS in the 1950s, the subsequent proliferation of new therapies such as GESTALT, and the development of HUMANISTIC PSYCHOLOGY with its emphasis on SELF-ACTUALIZATION. Self-improvement in this sense became virtually synonymous with GROWTH. Self-improvement also covers techniques of mental training, such as the SILVA

METHOD, aimed at improving all mental powers and promoting health.

SELF-REALIZATION Although sometimes confused with SELF-ACTUALIZATION, self-realization usually refers to that sense of inner understanding or spiritual enlightenment which is the ultimate goal of the various mental disciplines taught in schools of MEDITATION and YOGA. In this sense self-realization implies not so much fulfilment of one's potential as knowledge of the inner self.

SELF-REMEMBERING Self-remembering is an important part of Gurdjieff's 'Work': it is a form of meditation in which one is constantly aware of oneself and of everything one is doing. There are similarities between this self-remembering and the relaxed attention to body movements in MARTIAL ARTS such as T'AI CHI CH'UAN, or the avoidance of END-GAINING in the ALEXANDER TECHNIQUE, in that the mind is focused on the present rather than preoccupied and distracted by imagined end-results.

SELF-TRANSCENDENCE Viktor Frankl, creator of LOGOTHERAPY, sees self-transcendence as an aspect of the will-to-meaning, the basic human motivation. 'Human existence – at least as long as it has not been neurotically distorted – is always directed to something, or someone other than itself – be it a meaning to fulfil or another human being to encounter lovingly. I have termed this constitutive characteristic of human existence "self-transcendence". What is called "self-actualization" is ultimately an effect, the unintentional by-product, of self-transcendence.'[45] It is much more significant in his view than SELF-ACTUALIZATION, which in his estimation it is 'self-defeating' and 'ruinous' to make the purpose of one's life. This aspect of the will-to-meaning is comparable to Jung's notion of the TRANSCENDENT FUNCTION. Self-transcendence is central to all forms of TRANSPERSONAL PSYCHOLOGY.

SENSATION Sensation is one of the four EGO FUNCTIONS in Jung's theory of PSYCHOLOGICAL TYPES.

SENSITIVE CRYSTALLIZATION In ANTHROPOSOPHICAL MEDICINE sensitive crystallization is a technique devised by Ehrenfried Pfeiffer whereby it is claimed one can obtain a representation of the ETHERIC forces of a plant, animal or human being. A few drops of liquid from the living organism (sap or blood) are added to a solution of copper chloride and it is allowed to crystallize. The pattern thus obtained is unique to that organism.

SENSITIVITY TRAINING An alternative (and later) name for T-GROUP training.

SENSORY DEPRIVATION/SENSORY ISOLATION In the 1950s Dr John Lilly developed isolation tanks in which a person could float naked, enclosed and completely cut off from all external stimuli. The water in the tanks is kept at body temperature (so that after a while it is not felt against the skin) and contains salts to ensure that the person floats automatically. Without stimulation the brain eventually starts to hallucinate. Initially Lilly used this method to investigate altered STATES OF CONSCIOUSNESS, some people claiming that this was a quick way to experience nirvana or SAMADHI. In *flotation/ floatation therapy* the purpose is to relax, reducing stress and tension. In MEDITATION, which can achieve the same purpose, external stimuli are excluded, rejected or ignored by conscious mental control rather than by mechanical means, but the immediate effects are similar, at least superficially. It is also claimed that with the relative inactivity of the brain, the left hemisphere in particular, the right hemisphere functions are stimulated, thus enhancing one's creative and intuitive capacities.

SENSORY THERAPIES Sensory therapies are a category of ALTERNATIVE THERAPIES which make use of the senses, e.g. the sense of smell (AROMATHERAPY) or the visual sense (COLOUR THERAPY). Vision is also used in ART THERAPY, which is usually not only sensory but also creative. In the case of MUSIC THERAPY there is also often a creative element. BODYWORK therapies might also be regarded as belonging to the sensory group in that they involve body awareness, the kinaesthetic sense, but the category is generally restricted to the senses of sight, hearing and smell. Many other types of psychotherapy also involve working with the senses (e.g. GESTALT), but these would not usually be regarded as sensory therapies.

SENTICS/SENTIC CYCLE Dr Manfred Clynes, a Viennese-born physiologist and musician, developed a system of classifying emotions known as sentics. He believed that each emotion required a particular amount of time for its characteristic expression, ranging from 4.8 seconds for anger to 9.8 seconds for reverence, and he produced recordings to guide his clients through the expression of each of the seven basic emotions in the so-called 'standard sentic cycle': anger, hate, grief, love, sex, joy and reverence.

SETSU-SHIN Setsu-shin is diagnosis through touch, mainly of the PULSES, as practised in ACUPUNCTURE.

SHADOW Through the process of education and socialization a child's disagreeable characteristics are restrained and pushed into the background. As we grow up we forget or ignore the fact that these negative traits are actually part of our psychic make-up, and as adults we tend to deny that they exist, even though they live on as repressed tendencies in the unconscious. These impulses come together in the personal unconscious to form what Jung called the shadow. (Its formation during the process of socialization mirrors the formation of the PERSONA.) 'The shadow personifies everything that the subject refuses to acknowledge about himself and yet is always thrusting itself upon him directly or indirectly.'[97] It is the shadow that wants to do all the things we do not allow ourselves to do, and if we do kick over the traces and act 'out of character' (the idealized character our EGO has constructed for itself), it is in accordance with the desires of our shadow. The shadow represents everything that we are ashamed of in ourselves. If we dislike someone intensely it is often because we project our shadow onto that person, as if condemning a trait in someone else somehow distracted attention from that quality in ourselves. This PROJECTION is a typical ego DEFENCE MECHANISM, a way of making the ego seem pure and unblemished by denying that the shadow exists. But constant repression of the shadow seems to increase its strength, so that when it breaks through the defences and affects behaviour it seems violent and uncontrollable. This accounts for much of the bigotry in life and the practice of scapegoating. (At the heart of the shadow is the ARCHETYPE of the enemy, the treacherous stranger.) Jung believed that it is essential for everyone to find some way of acknowledging their dark side; mental and physical health depend on owning the shadow and living with it, however painful that experience might be. 'One does not become enlightened by imagining figures of light, but by making the darkness conscious. The latter procedure, however, is disagreeable and therefore not popular.' This assimilation of the shadow is one of the key aspects of INDIVIDUATION.

SHAMANISM Shamans are originally tribal medicine men (seldom women) or witch-doctors. Their powers and responsibilities have meant that in most parts of the world they act as priest, prophet and doctor, healing body, mind and spirit and offering guidance on all aspects of life. Much of their work may be done in trance. In principle if not in practice, the spiritual HEALERS of the West have a certain amount in common with shamans, substituting some form of LIFE-FORCE or the will of the Holy Spirit for the *mana* of shamanistic beliefs, but when westerners adopt shamanism today they tend to include the whole spiritual system, not just the healing aspect. This usually includes reference to spirit guides, power animals (a witch's familiar in the form of a black cat is a survival of this in our western culture) and in the North American tradition the medicine wheel – a ceremonial circle in which people celebrate their connection to elements of the universe such as Sun and Moon, specific animals and certain abstract concepts such as love and trust. In 'neo-shamanism' the old rituals are combined with modern techniques of guided imagery, VISUALIZATION and counselling; establishing contact with spirit guides may be seen as a self-empowering exercise, designed to form a link with one's own inner healer, so that transformation and SELF-HEALING can take place.

SHAVASANA *Shavasana* is the Sanskrit name for the 'corpse pose' in hatha YOGA, later adopted by TRANSCENDENTAL MEDITATION. The position is taken by lying on the back on a fairly hard surface (the floor or a hard mattress) with the feet apart and relaxed; the arms should lie easily at a natural distance from the body with the palms up; the eyes are closed. While lying in this position one concentrates on one's breathing, and it is an effective way to reduce blood-pressure.

SHELL SHOCK What was called 'shell-shock' in the First World War became known as 'combat fatigue' in the Second World War and 'acute combat reaction' in the Vietnam war. Hans Selye's theory of ADAPTATION ENERGY and the general adaptation response is an attempt to explain what happens in these situations of prolonged and extreme stress.

SHEN TAO Shen tao is an old form of ACUPRESSURE, sometimes called the 'mother of acupuncture'.

SHIATSU Literally 'finger' (*shi*) 'pressure' (*atsu*), shiatsu is a modern

Japanese form of ACUPRESSURE massage which uses a rhythmic series of finger pressures along the energy MERIDIANS; ACUPOINTS (or *tsubo*) are held for only three to five seconds. This helps to stimulate or balance the flow of *ki* (energy – the Japanese equivalent of CH'I) through the body. In the words of Tokujiro Namikoshi, who first formulated the system, 'Shiatsu strives first of all to prevent illness and, by calling forth innate self-curative powers, to develop bodies capable of resisting sickness.' Namikoshi opened the first Shiatsu Institute of Therapy in 1925, and in 1940 he founded the Japan Shiatsu Institute.

As a form of first aid treatment, acupressure has traditionally been used in China and Japan by members of a family on each other, just as throughout the world when a child is hurt the mother will 'rub it better'. As this suggests, the basics of shiatsu are easily learned, and in recent decades it has become increasingly common in the West, where practitioners often combine it with AROMATHERAPY and REFLEXOLOGY. Its popularity in the West may derive in part from its effectiveness in relieving tension and fatigue and inducing relaxation.

SHINTAIDO Shintaido is a method of body movement in the Japanese martial arts tradition, developed by Hiroyuki Aoki. It combines physical exercise with poetic physical expression. Positions or 'forms' are adopted in the manner of T'AI CHI, but there are also much freer movements in which one expresses one's own inner peace.

SHRINK The choice of the word 'shrink' as a slang term for 'psychoanalyst' sheds interesting light on the extent to which people feel diminished as individuals by the process of pschoanalysis and PSYCHOTHERAPY. This has been commented on by people such as Viktor Frankl, whose so-called HEIGHT PSYCHOLOGY seeks to stretch rather than shrink the individual.

SHU POINTS In ACUPUNCTURE certain points are used in diagnosis as well as treatment. Each of these so-called ALARM POINTS relates to a particular organ in the body and is liable to become tender when that particular organ is not functioning properly. Conversely the organ may be treated via the appropriate shu point. Alarm points on the front of the body are known as *mu* points and on the back as *shu* points. The shu points are situated on the bladder MERIDIAN.

SICK BUILDING SYNDROME Certain non-specific complaints such as tiredness, stuffy nose, headaches, eye trouble and rashes have been identified as being associated with working in particular office buildings. The condition was largely unrecognized until about 1980. Several possible causative factors have been suggested, including air-conditioning facilities and the accompanying toxic effect of recycled air, the glare from VDUs, lack of natural LIGHT and the level of IONIZATION. Introducing ionizers has had beneficial effects in some cases. Open-plan offices seem more susceptible to the 'sick building' condition, which suggests that the psychological effect of the lack of privacy may also be a contributory factor. Even though sick building syndrome has no clearly identified pathology, it is recognized by the World Health Organization. A UK survey in 1987 found that 80 per cent of office workers suffered from the condition, inasmuch as symptoms often vanished when they went home.

SIDDHA MEDICINE Siddha medicine is an offshoot of AYURVEDA, the ancient healing system of the Indian subcontinent which is derived from the Vedas (Hindu scriptures). It is practised in Tamil Nadu and Sri Lanka.

SIDE EFFECTS The word 'medicine' is used to refer only to therapeutic drugs, but since the growth of public awareness of drug addiction the word 'drug' carries both positive and negative connotations, as did the Greek word for 'drug', *pharmakon*, which had the ability to kill as well as to cure. People are now recognizing that practically all drugs bring unwanted side effects. The result is IATROGENIC DISEASE: roughly 15 per cent of hospital patients are suffering from conditions induced by their medical treatment, and by far the largest number of drug 'addicts' are people who are addicted to prescribed drugs.

Mistrust of artificial drugs is not new. Over a hundred years ago, Oliver Wendell Holmes wrote, 'I firmly believe that if the whole *materia medica*, as now used, could be sunk to the bottom of the sea, it would be all the better for mankind – and all the worse for the fishes.'[85] Proponents of natural remedies such as those prescribed in HERBALISM maintain that side effects are a result of bombarding the body with an isolated chemical rather than a naturally occurring combination of chemicals. Even though HOMOEOPATHY insists on the use of single remedies – SIMPLES – such remedies are produced from the whole plant or other naturally occurring substance, which

351

inevitably includes an array of chemical compounds. CONVENTION-AL MEDICINE, in isolating the 'active ingredient', overlooks the fact that some of the other chemicals in the plant are often natural ways of preventing unwanted side effects.

SIGNALYSIS Signalysis is used both as a method of diagnosis and as a therapy. As a method of diagnosis it uses blood and urine samples. The patient's blood and urine go through a distillation process, being boiled and condensed, and crystals are allowed to form from the condensate. The form these crystals take is the basis of the diagnosis, different shapes representing different organs and their condition. As a method of diagnosis alone signalysis may be used in conjunction with other therapies such as ACUPUNCTURE. Signalysis therapy involves the preparation of a remedy, using the distillation from the patient's own body fluids but with the addition of herbs, which are chosen on the basis of the crystals produced.

SIGNATURES (DOCTRINE OF SIGNATURES) Traditional HERBALISM included the old folkloric belief that the colour and form of a plant or part of a plant were a guide to deciding which organ in the human body might benefit from its use. For example, heart-shaped seeds or leaves were used to treat the heart. ANTHROPOSOPHICAL MEDICINE, which has absorbed much of the old wisdom of traditional herbalism, also recognizes the value of this Doctrine of Signatures.

SILVA METHOD/SILVA MIND CONTROL The Silva Method (originally known as Silva Mind Control) is a method of developing and exploiting the powers of the mind, in problem-solving, raising IQ, improving memory and learning, developing creativity and helping with healing. It represents an amalgam of various techniques, including RELAXATION, MEDITATION, VISUALIZATION and AUTOGENIC TRAINING. It was developed in the 1950s and 1960s by José Silva, a Texas-born Mexican American. Investigating COUÉISM and BIOFEEDBACK, he concluded that the mind operates at optimum efficiency when in a relaxed state characterized by alpha BRAIN WAVES. The method is described as a form of 'dynamic meditation' (although the senses are shut down, the meditative state is not passive), which enables people to 'go into alpha' and use 'a deeper level of mind'. This facilitates understanding and creativity, and increases the effectiveness of AUTOSUGGESTION. If changes are desired, 'self-programming' can help in their realization and one's capacity for SELF-HEALING is enhanced. 'Going into alpha' is also thought to improve receptivity to telepathy, ESP and clairvoyance. One particular form of clairvoyance, known as 'case-working', is a technique for diagnosing the health of others.

SIMILARS See LAW OF SIMILARS and SIMILLIMUM.

SIMILLIMUM In HOMOEOPATHY the best single remedy (or SIMPLE) is the one that most exactly reproduces all the symptoms of the disease – it is the 'most similar', the simillimum. A remedy that reproduces three-quarters of a patient's symptoms is deemed of no use even if combined with another which reproduces the other symptoms.

SIMPLES One of the basic principles in HOMOEOPATHY is that any remedy should use a single naturally occurring substance, whether from plants, minerals or animals. Paracelsus, recognizing the dangers of prescribing a multitude of medicines ('polypharmacy'), was one of the first to favour such 'simples' as the best form of treatment.

This idea has also been adopted by mainstream CONVENTIONAL MEDICINE, albeit (from the ALTERNATIVE or HOLISTIC point of view) in a debased form: in orthodox ALLOPATHIC medicine the physician prescribes drugs which have been prepared by isolating what is believed to be the single active ingredient in what might originally have been a 'natural remedy', and this ingredient is usually prepared chemically. Alternative practitioners maintain that it is because the body is bombarded with drugs made up of single isolated ingredients that it suffers so many SIDE EFFECTS; the naturally occurring substance would contain many other compounds which would prevent or at least mitigate such harmful consequences.

SINGLE CAUSE, SINGLE CURE It is one of the basic tenets of CONVENTIONAL (ALLOPATHIC) MEDICINE that disease is treated by countering the symptoms and by eradicating the agent which has caused the condition. The medical establishment has been very slow to recognize that in most cases exposure to an infectious agent is not sufficient to cause disease. Although more attention is being paid nowadays to the significance of contributory factors in disease, the belief in a single cause is still relatively strong, and the practice of administering a single remedy even stronger. This attitude is demonstrated in the so-called MAGIC BULLET approach. Even where conventional medicine might have a variety of treatments at its disposal, there is still surprising reluctance to try more than one at a time. Back pain sufferers are all too familiar with being sent from one type of treatment to another – be it physiotherapy, psychotherapy, drugs or surgery. Despite the abysmal record of any one type of treatment alone, few if any patients are ever given the benefit of more than one at a time. The 'single cure' idea, which perhaps grew out of the old medical belief in SIMPLES, has also meant that patients are treated with chemicals rather than with the naturally occurring substances from which they were originally isolated – a practice which is fraught with the IATROGENIC problems of unwanted and harmful SIDE EFFECTS.

SKIN BRUSHING The skin is the largest eliminating organ in the body, weighing between six and ten pounds and covering about two square yards. It gets rid of uric acid in the form of sweat, and like the lungs it absorbs oxygen and expels carbon dioxide. If elimination is impaired, serious illness can result. Dry skin brushing is an effective way of unclogging the pores of the skin and sloughing off dead cells. The skin is massaged with a loofah or a natural bristle brush. The effect of skin brushing is invigorating, and as well as unclogging the pores, it can improve circulation and stimulate the lymphatic system.

SLEEP Our conscious EGO is in charge of our bodies only so long as we are awake, to the extent that we are not held legally responsible for actions carried out while asleep: people have been acquitted of murder on the grounds that the crime was committed in their sleep. It has been a common belief throughout most of history that the spirit leaves the body during sleep. The ancient Chinese would not wake a sleeper too quickly for fear that the spirit might not have time to re-enter the body. The ancient Egyptians slept on wooden pillows which were carved in the shape of Bes, the god of the highways, who would protect the spirit of the sleeper on its night-time journey.

In waking life the BRAIN generates predominantly beta waves. Slower alpha BRAIN WAVES predominate when we feel relaxed or drowsy and close our eyes. There are then four identifiable stages of sleep before we reach deep sleep, which is characterized by the very slow delta waves, and the cycle is repeated several times a night. In the first stage we move out of alpha, half asleep and half awake; in the second stage we are still easily woken and there are still occasional bursts of brain activity. Large, slow delta waves mark stages three and four. The waves are at their slowest and most regular in stage four, by which time blood pressure, heart rate and temperature have dropped considerably. Sleep stage four is thought to be a regenerative time for the body: it is then that growth hormones are most active, and children spend much more time in stage four sleep than adults do.

It is during stage four sleep, or just as one is emerging from it, that night terrors may occur. It is thought that the transition from deep sleep to lighter sleep may induce anxiety: after the build-up of carbon dioxide during deep sleep breathing must become faster and deeper again, and this may provoke feelings of suffocation or of being unable to breathe adequately. Nightmares, on the other hand, like ordinary dreams, occur during stage one sleep. Having passed from stage four, through stages three and two, back to stage one again, we seem to be about to wake up: brain waves, breathing and heart beat all speed up, blood flow increases, and the eyeballs move rapidly from side to side. But it is in fact difficult to rouse us from this period of PARADOXICAL SLEEP. Because the brain is so active in these periods – when, however, there is no new information being taken – it has generally been thought that this is a time for processing and sorting information that has been taken in during the previous day. Some people have thought it might be possible to learn during sleep, in these periods of higher brain activity, but SLEEP-LEARNING has had little success.

SLEEP-LEARNING Experiments in the 1950s showed that information prsented to people while they were asleep was recalled only if alpha BRAIN WAVE activity occurred during presentation, suggesting that such material was committed to memory during a state of relative wakefulness.[226] Later experiments, however, distinguished between subjects of high and low hypnotic susceptibility, all of whom were additionally motivated by the strong waking suggestion that sleep-learning was possible. It was then found that those who were more susceptible to hypnotic suggestion were able to recall more of the 'sleep-learning' material which was 'heard' *without* alpha brain-wave activity.[58] These experiments were carried out in controlled laboratory conditions and actually say little about whether what most people understand by sleep-learning (i.e. learning whilst at home, in bed, asleep, without special supervision) is a practical possibility.

SLOUGHING See SKIN BRUSHING.

SMILE THERAPY/SMILING Since Norman Cousins used LAUGH-
TER effectively to cure himself of a crippling disease in 1964,
there has been a slowly increasing amount of research into the
physiological effects of laughing and smiling. It has been shown
that deliberately smiling or frowning can create the corresponding
emotional response. Charles Darwin recognized this over a century
ago. 'The free expression by outward signs of an emotion intensifies
it. Passions can be produced by putting people into appropriate attitudes. On the other hand the repression of all outward signs softens
our emotion.'[30] In 1906 Israel Waynbaum, a French physiologist,
suggested that facial expressions affect blood flow to the brain, which
in turn create the positive or negative feelings. A psychologist at the
University of Michigan, Robert Zajonc, has more recently suggested
that the temperature of the brain as well as the supply of oxygen via
the blood might affect the production of neurotransmitters.

Paul Ekman of the University of California, the leading smile
researcher, has studied the effect of 'artificial' facial expressions.
Asked to put on expressions of fear, anger and disgust, people
manifested changes in the autonomic nervous system typical of
stress reactions, such as a rise in temperature and an increase in
heart rate, whilst assuming happy facial expressions was calming.
The effect of smiling or frowning could even apparently override a
more immediate response to external stimuli: people who were asked
to smile while watching sad or upsetting films reported feeling positive about what they had seen, whilst those asked to frown while
watching cheerful films reported feeling sad or angry despite the
images on the screen. The emotional reaction seemed to be affected
more by the physical grimace than by anything else.

At first sight this may suggest support for the 'mechanistic' view
that emotions are nothing more than our way of consciously
registering what is happening in the body, a view which can
be expressed crudely as 'I don't know what emotion I feel until
I see how my body reacts.' But if, knowing the effect of smiling, I
decide to put on a smile in order to cheer myself up, what part of
that mechanism is it that has decided 'I want to feel happy'? Other
research, involving hypnosis, suggests that the emotion itself causes
the physiological effect: blood serum from people hypnotized into
a happy state dealt more quickly with typhoid bacillus than blood
from people hypnotized into a depressed frame of mind.[29] Perhaps
it is fruitless to pursue this as a chicken-and-egg question. Rather

than showing we can dispense with the mind as a separate entity, this research provides more evidence for the interplay between mental and physical events, the unity of mind and body.

SOCIAL REACTION THEORY See LABELLING THEORY and ANTI-PSYCHIATRY.

SOCIAL READJUSTMENT RATING SCALE The social readjustment rating scale, developed by T. H. Holmes and R. H. Rahe in the 1960s, assigns numerical values to events that are typical in people's lives: divorce, marriage, death in the family, change of job, pregnancy, debt, etc. Whether positive or negative, they cause stress and take their toll on our capacity to adjust. Values range from 100 so-called life-change units (LCUs) for the death of a spouse, through 65 for marital separation and 45 for marital reconciliation, down to 13 for a holiday, 12 for Christmas, and 11 for minor violation of the law. Of 2,500 men, the 30 per cent with the highest life-change scores developed almost 90 per cent more new illnesses during the first month than the 30 per cent with the lowest scores.[203]

SOCIAL STATUS Economic recessions which result in unemployment and loss of social status are generally followed by increases in death rates from nearly every cause. Each time the unemployment rate increases by one percentage point, 4 per cent more people commit suicide, 5.7 per cent more commit murder and nearly 2 per cent more die of cirrhosis of the liver or cardiovascular disease. Some of these responses to economic decline occur rapidly with the onset of the recession while others begin to appear after one to two years. The crucial factor in this loss of social status is STRESS, and researchers have predicted the likelihood of illness occurring in particular individuals by reference to the SOCIAL READJUSTMENT SCALE first developed by Holmes and Rahe. Since stress is caused equally by positive events, which may foster the perceived need to maintain or increase social status, economic recovery and rapid growth also seem to contribute to mortality. The support an individual receives from RELATIONSHIPS when adjusting to events is another important factor in resistance to disease.

SOMATIC PSYCHOLOGY See BODY-ORIENTED PSYCHOTHERAPY.

SOMATIZATION Somatization is a result of separating the mind and the body when considering health and disease and ignoring or even denying the ways in which the body (*soma*) can be influenced by the mind. It refers to the process of interpreting psychiatric conditions as physiological, even if the root causes are clearly emotional and psychological. People often prefer to have an identifiable physical ailment rather than a mental problem. This may to some extent be a consequence of the lingering sense of social stigma attached to mental illness (in some societies more than others), but it also reflects the patient's desire to be able to identify and point to a more tangible condition for which the experts can probably provide an antidote.

An example of somatization is neurasthenia, which apparently has no physical cause although its manifestation – excessive fatigue – is clearly physical. The labelling alone, giving the malady a name, satisfies a need in the patient, although it can also seem to add permanence to the condition, fixing it as an entity which has attacked or attached itself to the patient, rather than suggesting a more transient feeling.

SOMATOGRAPHY Somatography therapy and training aims to increase self-awareness – awareness of the body and of the messages that can be received from it regarding tensions that reflect the health of the inner self as well as of the body itself. As the creation of Bryn Jones, a Welsh therapist who works on the AURA, and George C. King, a New York YOGA master, somatography has elements of both subtle and physical body work. The therapist finds blockages in the energy flow in the aura to work on and guides the patient to a recognition of similar stress signals from the muscles. Patients are taught to pay attention to their bodies and to develop awareness to the point that the constant attendance of the therapist is no longer needed.

SOMATOTHERAPY An alternative term for MASSAGE therapy.

SOUND THERAPY Sound therapy is a blanket term that can cover several different practices. In its loosest sense it can include MUSIC THERAPY and CHANTING, but the kind of sound therapy for which there is no alternative name uses artificially generated sound waves to affect specific areas of the body. The vibrations of low frequency sounds are directed at bones, muscles and joints to relieve pain in much the same way that electromagnetic waves are used in ELECTROTHERAPY. (Sound waves of a very high frequency are used in ULTRASONICS, which is sometimes considered to be a type of electrotherapy, and the ultrasonic scanner is used diagnostically in conventional medicine – to check the condition of a foetus, for example.)

Sound therapy has only been applied to a few conditions as yet, primarily arthritis, fibrositis, muscular conditions, bone fractures and sprains. Pre-operative sound treatment is sometimes used before hip replacement operations and healing after the operation is said to be quicker as a result. There has been little research into how the therapy works, but it is thought that sound waves can affect the natural vibrations of organs and indeed cells. Each organ, the theory goes, has its own vibration profile. At its most obvious this can be seen in the electromagnetic waves registered by the brain on the EEG and by the heart on the ECG, but sound therapists hold that all organs and cells behave in this way and that all disease involves a change in the fundamental frequency of the energy vibration, whether of a group of cells, a whole organ or the whole body. Sound therapy is aimed at bringing the vibrations back to normal, by cancelling out the frequencies that are generated by the disease process. (Some say there are links with COLOUR THERAPY here, in which it is light frequencies that are crucial.) A patient being treated with sound therapy does not necessarily hear or even feel the vibrations applied to a particular part of the body.

SPAGYRIC MEDICINE In the sixteenth century so-called Spagyric physicians favoured the use of chemical preparations in the treatment of disease. Their methods are echoed in the interventionist techniques of CONVENTIONAL MEDICINE today. Paracelsus and the so-called Galenic physicians took up the opposite position, recommending the use of natural remedies and herbal preparations.

SPAGYRIC THERAPY 'Spagyric' is an archaic word, probably invented by Paracelsus, meaning 'alchemy' and 'alchemical'. The term 'spagyric therapy' has been used as an alternative for SIGNAL-YSIS therapy.

SPINAL LESION Andrew Taylor Still, the founder of osteopathy, believed that all diseases were caused by strains, misalignments or dislocations in the spine, otherwise known as 'spinal lesion': adjusting the spine and restoring normal skeletal movement would effect a cure. He even advocated manipulation of the lower spine as a treatment for malaria and dysentery.

SPLIT-BRAIN HYPOTHESIS See BICAMERAL NATURE OF THE BRAIN.

SPLITTING Painful experiences can result in physical reactions characteristic of the FIGHT-OR-FLIGHT RESPONSE. When these become too life-threatening the experience may be forgotten – split off from consciousness – and there may also be an accompanying physical effect such as ARMOURING, when layers of muscle are held in constant tension. The forgotten feelings are then converted into physical conditions (e.g. being tight-lipped, thick-set, overweight, barrel-chested, etc.) which predispose the individual towards PSYCHOSOMATIC illness.

SPONTANEOUS REMISSION When a disease seems to be stopped in its tracks, or its progress is reversed, and this cannot be attributed to medical treatment it is 'explained' as a case of spontaneous remission. But this is no explanation at all. As Carl and Stephanie Simonton write, 'When a disease does not proceed in ways that can be explained by physical intervention, the result is called "spontaneous". The word covers today's ignorance in much the same way as the term "spontaneous generation" covered medical ignorance during the late Middle Ages.'[159] Although there cannot be adequate proof of spontaneous remission, it is often used as an explanation by mainstream medicine when no 'scientific' explanation can be given for a cure that has been effected by ALTERNATIVE THERAPIES. There is often inconsistency here: science does not understand the mechanism behind either alternative therapies or spontaneous remission, yet spontaneous remission gets the medical establishment's vote every time. The Simontons express the belief that, like spontaneous generation, spontaneous remission 'results from processes or mechanisms that are not yet understood'. Given their experience of VISUALIZATION, the Simontons would certainly expect mental factors to be involved in these processes.

STAPLEPUNCTURE Staplepuncture is an adaptation of ACUPUNCTURE. Instead of pricking the body momentarily ('tonification') or leaving the needles in the body for ten minutes or so, the acupuncturist secures a 'staple' to the body at the appropriate point (often in the ear – AURICULOTHERAPY) and the patient massages it periodically throughout the day. In recent years this has been used as an aid to giving up alcohol or smoking.

STARTLE RESPONSE In BIOENERGETICS the startle response is a form of body ARMOURING in which muscles habitually hold themselves in an inhibiting position of stress. The response is often accompanied by inhibited breathing patterns and deformed posture. A state of anxiety becomes associated with the muscular pattern and both can be eliminated by bodywork techniques.

In the ALEXANDER TECHNIQUE the term has a more restricted use, referring to the body's response when one is startled by a sudden noise or event. The shoulders and arms become distorted, the legs more tense and the torso shortened. If such a response becomes frequent or habitual it results in postural imbalance.

STATES OF CONSCIOUSNESS Reference to 'states' of consciousness can be an obstacle to gaining a fuller understanding of the range of modes of consciousness available to us. How many such 'states' are there? Waking, sleeping and trance, say some. Others would add dreaming and coma. And what about day-dreaming? And don't we sometimes feel only half-awake, whilst on some occasions we feel more awake than usual? Dr Stanley Krippner, psychologist at New York's Maimonides Hospital, has produced an even longer list: normal waking; sleeping; dreaming during sleep; hypnagogic; hypnopompic; hyperalert; lethargic; rapture; hysteria; fragmentation; regressive; meditative; trance; reverie; daydreaming; internal scanning; stupor; coma; stored memory; expanded consciousness (including four other levels – sensory level, recollective level, symbolic level, integral level).[182]

With the discovery of BRAIN WAVES it at last became possible to measure brain activity and to some extent objectify the differences between one mode of consciousness and another. But even the description of brain wave activity in terms of alpha, theta, delta, etc. tends to conceal the fact that these refer only to bands of frequencies in which there is most activity. If these frequencies were translated into light frequencies any moment of consciousness would contain many different colours and the shades would be constantly changing. Rather than considering different states of consciousness as separate box-like categories it is perhaps more fruitful to regard them as part of a spectrum, with the proviso that even this is a simplification and to some extent a 'reification' of an abstract, dimensionless phenomenon. For example, in a meditative state an increase in relaxation does not necessarily mean a decrease in awareness. We may be relaxed and alert, or relaxed and with heightened awareness of our inner world (perhaps with imagery which may be spontaneous, self-directed or guided), or our relaxation may be such that the stillness of the mind seems to cut it off from all experience of time and change. It is very difficult to place these categories of experiencing consciousness in different types of MEDITATION along one spectrum. Arranging them on a plane or graph may be a possibility, with the two axes representing degree of relaxation and degree of awareness, but this does not account for the degree of attention. The notion of consciousness in fact includes a large number of variables.

Perhaps because we *fall* asleep and talk of *heightened* awareness, some people prefer to talk of *levels of consciousness* (Colin Wilson postulates eight levels).[183] These levels are perhaps degrees of 'awakeness'. Where dreaming is concerned Erich Fromm thinks that 'We are more awake when we are asleep than when we are not. Our dreams often testify to our creative activity, our daydreams to our mental laziness.' He also criticizes the industry that has grown up around so-called personal GROWTH for providing temporary fixes rather than permanent changes in mentality and awareness. 'Binges of widened consciousness are escapes from a narrow consciousness, and after the "trip" [the participants] are no different from what they were before and from how their fellow men have been all the time: Half-awake people.'[57]

Such references to being half-awake are characteristic of many thinkers. Most spiritual disciplines involve developing a greater awareness of what Jung calls the SELF, transcending the narrow mentality of the ego, overcoming the confines of our personal conditioning and seeing things as they really are. Whether one calls this SELF-ACTUALIZATION, SELF-REALIZATION or SELF-TRANSCENDENCE, it represents a mode of consciousness which many aim for and few attain, even fewer maintaining it for long periods. In showing the distinction between this 'awakeness' and the normal well-focused consciousness, Erich Fromm writes: 'We become alert in the way and to the degree with which a vitally necessary task . . . or a passionate goal . . . requires it. Different from this partial and, as it were, pragmatic alertness is a state of total awakeness. In this state one is not only aware of that which one needs to be aware of oneself and of the world (people and nature) around one. One sees, not opaquely but clearly, the surface together with its roots. The world becomes fully real; every detail and the details in their configuration and structure become a meaningful unit. It feels as if a veil that had been in front of our eyes permanently – without our recognizing it was there – had suddenly dropped away.'[57]

STEAM, STEAM BATHS See HYDROTHERAPY.

STIGMATA Stigmata are wounds or bleeding sores which appear particularly on the hands and sometimes on the feet, side or brow, in apparent imitation of the wounds of Christ. Probably the most famous case of stigmata is that of St Francis; a more recent example is Padre Pio, an Italian Capuchin monk who died in 1968. The phenomenon usually occurs when the subject is in a state of ecstasy or trance, which may suggest that SELF-HYPNOSIS is involved. It is well known for hypnotized subjects to suffer burns on the flesh when the hypnotist suggests that they are being touched with a piece of red-hot metal, even if they are actually being touched with a feather. The phenomenon may also be related to mental imagery and VISUALIZATION. Assuming that these links are correct, it appears that the mind is not only instrumental in self-healing but also capable of harming the body. (The word 'stigmata' is also sometimes used by the medical profession to refer to marks or scars on the skin that are symptomatic of a particular disease.)

STREAMING In REICHIAN THERAPY streaming refers to the experience of energy flowing through the body, accompanied by shaking, tingling, hot flushes and even odours, which may occur with the cathartic release of pent-up emotion (ABREACTION). Similar experiences in YOGA are referred to as *kriyas*. Streaming sensations are experienced when people are in a highly charged emotional state and bodily tensions are finally relaxed. It was Reich's discovery of streamings that led him to develop VEGETOTHERAPY. He developed the notion of ARMOURING to describe the avoidance of full contact with streamings and blocking oneself off from one's emotional centre. In neo-Reichian therapies such as BIOSYNTHESIS it is considered natural to maintain awareness of these sensations. 'Those who are used to taking note of their own bodily sensations will certainly be able to sense the streamings which go through the whole body with a full and deep breathing. These wave-like movements give a feeling of being alive through and through. Those who have relaxed bodies and unclouded minds have these sensations as the regular and permanent background to all that they experience, and it is this which gives colour, taste and freshness to their whole life.'[146]

STRESS In recent decades stress has increasingly been seen as a crucial factor in the incidence of physical disease, almost to the extent that it is regarded by some as a disease itself – the plague of western civilization in the twentieth century. Most people know from personal experience that when they feel unduly stressed over a period of time, their resistance to infection is lowered and they are more likely to catch cold. West Point cadets were screened periodically and it was found that high expectation (those with 'overachiever' fathers) and poor performance – a particularly stressful psychological combination – increased their susceptibility to infectious disease. And in experiments with rats inescapable stress reduces their ability to reject tumours. The lie-detector works on the principle that most people find telling lies stressful and their mental state is betrayed by physiological responses monitored by the electronic device.

Hans Selye, the Canadian pioneer of stress research, has defined stress as 'the rate of wear and tear within the body', but this physical wear and tear is the result of essentially psychological and social factors. Major social changes such as economic instability or a recession cause psychological stress to individuals. In the *Wall Street Journal* of August 25 1980, it was claimed that with only a 1 per cent rise in unemployment 'the incidence of virtually all major diseases and all major causes of death is increased, including infant mortality, suicide, heart disorders, stroke, liver conditions, and road accidents.'[116] Many have suggested that spiritual factors (or rather their neglect) may also play a part in creating stress. 'A strong belief system can ease the fear of death and lend a sense of direction to our passage through life. Concerns such as philosophy and religion may not appear to be as stressful as trouble at the office or a difficult marriage, but the devaluation of these concerns appears to have created a malaise which is distinctly stress-inducing.'[139]

Stress is a condition in which psyche and soma, mind and body, are intimately linked. How can this psychological condition, perceived in the mind, have a damaging effect on the body? The mechanism responsible is the FIGHT-OR-FLIGHT RESPONSE. In emergencies and states of tension the fight-or-flight response activates the sympathetic nervous system so that the body is better prepared to take appropriate action. However, in modern society the panic reactions of overt aggression or hasty retreat are usually deemed inappropriate, and the body, restrained by the conscious mind, is not allowed to carry out either of the actions for which it is physiologically prepared. It is this that causes physical damage. The effects include high blood pressure, which causes strain on the heart; the reduction of the body's immune response owing to excess cortisone; a partially closed down digestive system leading to ulcers; and continuously tensed surface muscles resulting in fibrositis. Endorphins are released in the fight-or-flight response, but chronic relentless stress can deplete the level of endorphins available when they are really needed, aggravating migraines, backache and even the pains of arthritis.

Heart disease is probably the condition which researchers have linked most consistently with stress. Diet has also been regarded as an important factor in heart disease, the crucial element being cholesterol. But when Irishmen in Boston and in Ireland were compared it was found that although Boston diets were low in cholesterol, whilst those in Ireland were high, the men in Boston had a higher rate of heart attacks. Similarly there is a high cholesterol level in Navaho Indians and Masai, but little heart disease. Americans now have five times the rate of heart disease that they did in 1910, but the amount of cholesterol in their diet is roughly the same. Other factors must therefore be involved, such as dietary fibre, exercise and above all stress. For example, over three-quarters of autopsied American soldiers killed in Korea showed the first symptoms of coronary heart disease, resulting from the stress of battle. (The theory of ADAPTATION ENERGY, which is gradually used up in the general ADAPTATION RESPONSE to stress, was prompted by studies of the effects of battle and shell-shock on soldiers.)

Pioneers in this area of research were the cardiologists Friedman and Rosenman, who first noticed that the chairs in their waiting room were worn only at the front edge: their patients were literally as well as figuratively 'on edge', their physical posture reflecting their inner state. In investigating the effect of emotional stress on a patient's susceptibility to heart disease, Friedman identified what he called TYPE A BEHAVIOUR. Type A personalities tend to treat too many everyday events as emergencies, reacting inappropriately with the fight-or-flight response, thus increasing the amount of hydrocortisone secreted in the blood by forty times, pumping three times the normal amount of blood to muscles, and generating four times as much adrenalin. Friedman suggested that half the male workforce of the USA exhibited Type A behaviour.

The ways in which we can counter the physiological effects of stress include BIOFEEDBACK, MEDITATION and various RELAXATION techniques. Even relaxation in the traditional form of a holiday is beneficial. It is common knowledge that an apparently infertile couple can often benefit from a cruise or trip abroad: the absence of stress causes a resurgence in testosterone and progesterone and consequently sperm count and ovulation rates benefit. Even the relaxing effect of stroking a pet has been shown to have a therapeutic effect: in most people nervousness when reading aloud to an audience results in higher than normal pulse rate and blood pressure, but stroking a pet reduces both back to normal.

Perhaps surprisingly, switching from one stressful activity to another can also be beneficial: redirecting one's attention to something else that requires full concentration can help one to unwind and release the tension caused by the prior situation. The 'work hard, play hard' attitude is in part a reflection of this, although the same philosophy is often voiced and practised to their detriment by Type A personalities.

Experiments have demonstrated that events which most people consider positive or pleasurable can be as stress-inducing as those that are considered negative. The SOCIAL READJUSTMENT RATING SCALE is an attempt to assess the relative stress levels induced by both negative and positive events in life and work as a predictor of susceptibility to illness.

With all the emphasis nowadays on the need to reduce stress, it is easy to overlook the fact that stress is an essential part of life. 'Stress is an integral element in the biological scheme of any living organism . . . Two of the most basic characteristics of life, self-preservation and procreation, could not be realized without the innate stress mechanisms of all living organisms. Life without the challenges which induce stress would not be life at all.'[139] Furthermore, the sudden absence of stressful activity can be just as deleterious as stress itself, as can too little stress. As Dr Peter Hanson has pointed out, 'The sudden silence gained by retiring from a demanding job into a life of idleness usually causes death or senility within two years, unless new stresses and interests can be found.'[76]

This sudden absence of a necessary degree of stress may explain the unexpected results of research carried out by Rose and Marmot,[195] who analysed the cause of death among retired civil servants of different grades. One might expect people at the top to suffer from more stress, but the results showed that for every one civil servant in the highest grade who died from a heart attack, in the lowest grade four died. Making allowances for other factors such as smoking and diet, the researchers found that three out of five heart attacks were still 'unexplained', although there are several possible explanations. Those people in higher grades may have had more outside interests which they were able to continue to pursue after retirement – interests which they had perhaps taken up initially as a relief from the stress of work (an alternative stressful activity). Alternatively the crucial factor may be the individual's powers of self-expression when under stress – the ability to express negative emotions (rather than repress them resentfully) has proved to be the key factor for self-preservation among those orginally labelled TYPE A PERSONALITIES, and one would expect people in higher grades to have acquired a greater aptitude for self-expression.

It makes no sense to avoid all situations or actions which may lead to stress. People need change and challenge in their lives. We should be considering not why people break down under stress but what enables them to maintain good health when under stress. To this end, executives who exhibited a high degree of stress tolerance – so-called high stress/low illness executives – were studied to ascertain what characteristics they had in common, and comparisons were drawn with their high stress/high illness counterparts. The investigators concluded that 'the psychological hardiness of the high stress/low illness executives was characterized by a strong commitment to self, work, family and other important values, a sense of control over one's life and the ability to see change in one's life as a challenge rather than a threat. These hardy people accepted that change, rather than stability, was the norm in life and tended to welcome it as an opportunity for growth.'[195]

The high stress/high illness executives, on the other hand, were low in 'hardiness' and had a strong sense of alienation and powerlessness. They seemed threatened by change and unable to face uncertainty. Such people feel that their resources are inadequate to deal with the environmental demands. Whilst 'hardy people' transform problems into opportunities, thereby avoiding the stress response altogether, 'unhardies' react with a SYNTOXIC response, distracting themselves with drugs, television or social interaction. Such 'avoidance coping' may be useful when the problem is insoluble (as when a problem becomes simply a fact of life), but when remedial action is possible but not taken, the source of stress remains and is more likely to lead to a chronic stress reaction resulting in serious illness. Such people can benefit from so-called HARDINESS INDUCTION COURSES.

There is some evidence that stress is also experienced by an unborn child, as for example when a baby dies shortly after being born and is found to have peptic ulcers, which it is generally acknowledged are usually stress-related. It is further suggested that the mother's mental state affects the physical condition of the embryo, and the METAMORPHIC TECHNIQUE is based on this very notion. The stress of birth itself is also locked into our physical and psychological being according to the principles of PRIMAL THERAPY and REBIRTHING.

STRESS PROFILE A stress profile is a description of a person's neurophysiological responses to various degrees of stress. In a one-hour diagnosis session the subject engages in a range of normal, stressful and relaxing activities, during which various measurements are recorded. These consist of the respiration rate and pattern, the peripheral temperature of hands and feet, blood pressure; heart rate and regularity of the heart-beat are measured with an electrocardiogram (ECG), brain-wave activity is measured with an electroencephalograph (EEG), muscle activity with an electromyograph (EMG), and the galvanic skin response (GSR) is used as an indication of emotional lability.

STRESSOR A stressor is a change in our internal or external world, to which our reaction, or 'stress response', results in a state of imbalance. The word was coined by Hans Selye, the pioneer of research into STRESS.

STROKING In TRANSACTIONAL ANALYSIS 'stroking' is used colloquially 'to denote any act implying recognition of another's presence. Hence a *stroke* may be used as the fundamental unit of social action. An exchange of strokes constitutes a *transaction*, which is the unit of social intercourse.'[12]

STRUCTURAL ANALYSIS Structural analysis is the theory of psychology which underlies TRANSACTIONAL ANALYSIS. Eric Berne maintains that 'the application of structural and transactional analysis requires an esoteric vocabulary of only six words. *Exteropsyche*, *neopsyche* and *archaeopsyche* are regarded as psychic *organs*, which manifest themselves phenomenologically as exteropsychic (e.g. identificatory), neopsychic (e.g. data-processing), and archaeopsychic (e.g. regressive) *ego states*. Colloquially, these types of ego states are referred to as *Parent*, *Adult*, and *Child*, respectively. These three substantives form the terminology of structural analysis.'[13] The remaining three terms considered indispensable for transactional analysis are *pastime*, *game* and *script*.

STRUCTURAL DYNAMICS/STRUCTURAL PROCESSING/ STRUCTURAL INTEGRATION These are all alternative terms for ROLFING, or for the actual release of tension and the accompanying insight which rolfing achieves. Dr Rolf herself called her system Structural Integration. The principal aim in rolfing is also sometimes referred to as structural reintegration: the restoration in the body of normal balanced vertical alignment through deep massage and manipulation. Many of the same terms have been adopted by other bodywork therapists, for whom the reintegration is often primarily psycho-emotional rather than physical although it is achieved during the process of physical restructuring.

SUBLUXATION In CHIROPRACTIC a slight shift in the position of one vertebra in relation to the next is referred to as subluxation. It is not a complete dislocation, which may be one reason many conventional doctors do not recognize the condition at all.

SUB-PERSONALITIES See PSYCHOSYNTHESIS.

SUBHUMANISM 'Subhumanism' is Viktor Frankl's description of REDUCTIONISM: 'It is the lack of discrimination between causes and conditions that allows reductionism to deduce a human phenomenon from, and reduce it to, a subhuman phenomenon.' He also refers to it as 'the nihilism of today': 'The nihilism of yesterday taught nothingness. Reductionism now is preaching nothing-but-ness. Man is said to be nothing but a computer or a "naked ape".'[46]

SUBLIMATION In Freudian psychology the personality is ruled by drives from the id which are essentially sexual (although the LIBIDO is supposedly counterbalanced by the antithetical death instinct). The theory states that as a child grows up it passes through the oral, anal and phallic stages before reaching the mature genital stage, but an individual may become 'fixated' at the oral or anal stage, deriving satisfaction from activities that are linked with those periods. The conflicts which such fixations can provoke often lead to sublimation, the channelling of the sexual energy into some other activity, an often cited example being the preoccupation with handling money shown by someone who is fixated at the anal stage. The whole concept of sublimation seems superfluous if one subscribes to HUMANISTIC PSYCHOLOGY, which is more concerned with personal GROWTH.

SUBTLE ENERGIES See LIFE-FORCE, CHAKRAS and VIBRATIONAL HEALING.

SUCCUSSION In HOMOEOPATHY the preparation of remedies involves a particular form of shaking known as succusion. The base of the bottle or phial containing the newly diluted mixture is struck repeatedly against a hard surface. This is believed to enable the 'SUBTLE ENERGIES' of the active ingredient to spread to the whole liquid according to the process known as POTENTIZATION, even though there may be no actual molecules of that original substance left in the extremely dilute, potentized remedy.

SUGGESTION Suggestion is not the same as HYPNOSIS, although the way the mind affects the body as a consequence may well be the same. Doctors have reduced the side effects of chemotherapy in cancer treatment (hair loss, nausea, vomiting) simply by avoiding phrases such as 'toxic drugs' and 'you will lose some hair' and referring instead to 'powerful medication' and saying 'you may lose some hair temporarily'. For doctors' words to have such an effect their patients must place great trust in what they say, and the individual's belief undoubtedly plays an important part in the effectiveness of suggestion. Warts can be wished away, i.e. cured by suggestion, so long as the patient believes that the treatment will work. Warts are caused by a very common virus and the fact that we do not constantly suffer from them is a result of our immune defence system, so mental wart cures must work by activating the immune system or reducing the blood flow to the growths or both.

Suggestion can have positive or negative effects. For example, the effectiveness of relaxation training to lower blood pressure (with BIOFEEDBACK) can be affected by suggestion. If patients are told that their blood pressure will decline from some time after the third session their response will be delayed as compared with others who are told that a decline in blood pressure will be immediate. The possible negative effects of suggestion can be very serious. What are we to think when someone who constantly complains 'You make me sick to the stomach' develops stomach cancer?

Suggestion has been combined most effectively with VISUALIZATION. In one study women succeeded in enlarging their breasts by suggestion: relaxation and visualization while listening to tape recordings over a period of twelve weeks resulted in 46 per cent of the women requiring a larger bra size and 86 per cent showing measurable breast enlargement.[188] Suggestion also plays an important part in SELF-HEALING.

SUN The sun (as HELIOTHERAPY) is an essential part of many types of NATURE CURE (see also LIGHT THERAPY), but it also forms a crucial part of the preparation of certain remedies. In AYURVEDIC MEDICINE exposure to sunlight changes the effect of a remedy, and solar influence on the POTENTIZATION of ANTHROPOSOPHICAL remedies means that SUCCUSSIONS are not carried out during the two hours following noon. In many traditional systems of belief the sun and the heart are regarded as analogous; in anthroposophical medicine the heart is to the body as the sun is to the solar system, the source of warmth and light and the giver of equilibrium to the system.

SUNNING Dr William Bates, author of the BATES METHOD of eyesight training, believed that the full spectrum of natural daylight is always beneficial for the eyes. One of the recommended practices in his method of treatment is to close the eyes and let the sun shine on the closed eyelids, moving the head from side to side so that no single part of the eye gets the full force of the sun for too long. This 'sunning' should be continued for no more than two or three minutes and should be followed by PALMING.

SUPERCONSCIOUS In PSYCHOSYNTHESIS, the superconscious is not a higher state of awareness (which might be called 'superconsciousness') but a higher aspect of the unconscious. In the words of Roberto Assagioli, it represents a 'vast realm of our inner being which has been for the most part neglected by the science of psychology, although its nature and its human value are of a superior quality.'[4] It is in the superconscious that we catch glimpses of the SELF and it has much in common with Jung's notion of the TRANSCENDENT FUNCTION. 'It is both the drama and glory of man that this higher level, most often latent, sooner or later demands satisfaction; it demands to be taken into account and lived.'[5] As well as being that part of our psyche which inspires us to SELF-REALIZATION, the superconscious is the seat of intuition and creativity. Great artists and geniuses are clearly in closer touch with their superconscious than the average person; the great saints lived most of their lives at that level.

SUPEREGO According to Freudian psychology our behaviour is influenced by what we have internalized of the authoritarian attitudes of our parents and the strictures of society. This internal monitor is the superego, whose role it is to suppress the 'unacceptable' urges and desires of the ID and make sure the EGO behaves in an acceptable way, the reward being approval by society. If the superego is too strong the result can be an extremely upright and moral citizen, entrenched in beliefs and values laid down by others. Someone whose id is too strong will be extremely impulsive and relatively amoral. Freud's view of the superego and id as being in constant conflict may be a reflection of his view of the conflict between society and the individual. This contrasts with Maslow's notion of a SYNERGISTIC society in which the needs of the individual are wholly compatible with the needs of society. There is also a sharp contrast between the superego and Jung's notion of the SELF, which represents a guiding ideal to be worked towards rather than an agent of repression.

SUPRADIAN RHYTHMS Circadian rhythms affect the body in synchronization with the rotation of the earth; they are the daily cycles such as change in body temperature, change in metabolic rate, waking and sleeping, etc. Supradian cycles (for example BIO-RHYTHMS) operate on timescales greater than a day.

SURVEILLANCE THEORY A great deal of attention has been paid in recent times to carcinogenic factors in our food and in the environment, and more recently to the possibility of a cancer-prone gene, but this is not the whole story regarding the possible causes of cancer. According to the surveillance theory, everyone sometimes produces abnormal cells, whether because of external factors or because of inaccurate cell reproduction. Normally the immune system watches out for such cells (hence 'surveillance') and destroys them. Cancer may therefore be a consequence of a depressed immune system. Many alternative therapists work to improve the immune system and point out that conventional cancer treatment with radiation and chemotherapy actually has the reverse effect.

SUSHUMNA The central nervous column along which the main CHAKRAS lie is known as *sushumna*.

SWEDISH MASSAGE Peter Ling (1776–1839) was a Swedish pioneer of massage techniques and our use of the term 'Swedish massage' probably derives from the tradition which he established. Swedish massage is a particularly vigorous form of massage, involving stroking (EFFLEURAGE), friction and rubbing, kneading and squeezing (PETRISSAGE), slapping and pounding (tapotement), all of which stimulates blood circulation through the soft tissues of the body.

SWINGING In the BATES METHOD the practice of turning the head from side to side to loosen tense neck muscles is known as swinging. It is generally used in combination with PALMING.

SYMPATHETIC NERVOUS SYSTEM The sympathetic nervous system is that aspect of the autonomic nervous system which has a general excitation effect upon neural and glandular functions, acting on many areas of the body simultaneously in the FIGHT-OR-FLIGHT RESPONSE. It tenses and constricts involuntary muscles, particularly the blood vessels, activates the endocrine system, and in preparing the body for immediate action it gives rise to such sensations as 'trembling with fear', 'cold feet', 'shivers up and down the spine' and 'a racing heart'. The parasympathetic nervous system works on the same physiological structures but with the opposite effect in order to conserve energy. For example, whilst the sympathetic nervous system increases heart rate, the parasympathetic system decreases it.

SYMPTOMATIC ACUPUNCTURE/SYMPTOMATIC POINTS In acupuncture certain points are effective in treating specific symptoms. These symptomatic points are often given names according to the symptom they treat, such as the 'soothing asthma points' on the back. By learning which points can commonly be used to relieve specific conditions such as asthma attacks, migraine, earache, etc. western doctors have sometimes become proficient at symptomatic acupuncture, also called formula acupuncture, but such treatment clearly does not get to the root cause of the illness. Such methods are sometimes known as 'secondary doctor techniques'. As J. R. Worsley, the doyen of traditional acupuncture in Britain and the US, has said, 'If an adequately trained practitioner does treat on the basis of the symptom, and selects a generally applicable formula supposedly helpful for this symptom, then it is possible, even likely, that the patient's energy will become further imbalanced rather than balanced. Even if the symptom disappears, it is quite possible that in a few months' or a year's time further problems will develop that may be of an even more serious nature (owing to the worsened imbalance caused by the symptomatic acupuncture).'[186] In traditional acupuncture, such 'secondary doctor' techniques are permitted only as a temporary first aid measure.

SYNAESTHESIA Described by researchers as a 'bizarre phenomenon', synaesthesia is the rare faculty or tendency some people have to experience different senses as intimately connected. The most common form of synaesthesia is colour-hearing, which affects perhaps one in 100,000 people, more often women than men and more LEFT-HANDERS than right-handers. Such synaesthetics may see particular colours when they hear particular musical notes, or associate words, letters and numbers with particular colours. The most famous synaesthetic musician is probably the composer Alexander Scriabin, who intended to create a musical experience in which the audience would be bathed in appropriately coloured light while listening to his composition. Rimsky-Korsakov and Liszt also saw musical notes in colour.

The Oxford Companion to the Mind defines synaesthesia as 'confusion between the senses', but this sounds unduly pathological and misleadingly implies a lack of order or consistency. Most synaesthetics would not want to be without the faculty they have known all their lives. They are usually surprised when they first realize that not everyone sees what they hear in this way. It can also be a useful faculty: not only does colour-hearing help with remembering such things as telephone numbers, but synaesthetics also seem to have better than average memories and visual organization.

Elizabeth Fulford, a synaesthetic for whom words and even letters are experienced as colours, has been investigated by the Institute of Psychiatry, and because of the consistency in her responses over long periods of time researchers are convinced that her experiences are genuine. They have also identified the area of the brain where this unusual processing occurs. There is remarkable although not total consistency between different synaesthetics: all (including the novelist, Vladimir Nabokov) agree, for example, that the letter 'O', or rather the sound of it, is a rather empty shade of white. Painting under the name Elizabeth Stewart-Jones, Elizabeth Fulford has created many unique 'customized' designs using the colours conveyed by people's names.

SYNERGY Synergy is the power of working together (from Greek *syn*, 'together', and *ergon*, 'force' or 'work'), as when two systems combine to produce an effect which is greater than the mere sum of their effects when working separately. Synergy is exemplified in society when people cooperate for their mutual advantage, not necessarily because they are particularly unselfish but simply because that is the way their society works. The distinction between 'high synergy' and 'low synergy' societies was first made by the American anthropologist, Ruth Benedict (1887–1948). She decided that the basic difference between cultures she liked because they produced nice people and those she found nasty and aggressive lay not so much in their actual behaviour as in their reasons for their behaviour. In non-aggressive societies individuals act in ways that both serve themselves and benefit the group because that is the way their society is organized. As Abraham Maslow said, 'The society with high synergy is one in which virtue pays.' In societies with low social synergy, 'the advantage of one individual becomes a victory over another, and the majority who are not victorious must shift as they can.'[215] Maslow regarded American society as one of mixed synergy, generous and secure in many respects but with customs and institutions that often set people against each other. He took over Ruth Benedict's ideas and develped them, coining the name EUPSYCHIA to refer to his notion of a synergistic society. He noted that psychologically healthy people, SELF-ACTUALIZERS, are not deliberately altruistic but are selfish in a healthy way, in a way that benefits society as well as themselves.

SYNTOXIC RESPONSE There are two possible ways to respond to a stressful situation: the usual *catatoxic* response is the FIGHT-OR-FLIGHT RESPONSE; the alternative is to ignore the threat or danger – the *syntoxic* response – as, for example, when under the influence of alcohol.

T-FIELD After studying RADIONICS Edward J. Russell, an American journalist, proposed the existence of thought fields – T-fields – which are undetectable except by the human body. According to Russell's theory, the 'radiations' from T-fields, 'thought waves', are not electromagnetic and exist independently of the brain, although they may reside there, just as they may also attach themselves to other objects (as when things become so imbued with the character of their owner that psychics and sensitives can pick up information about people from their possessions). T-fields are supposedly created by our own power of thought, and telepathy is the result of T-fields linking up. Russell also suggested that radionics works because of the existence of O-FIELDS, which are natural rather than creations of the mind.

T-GROUP In the early 1940s an American psychologist, Kurt Lewin, became concerned at business people's lack of expertize in interpersonal relations. His first training group (T-group) to teach people about communication and how to deal with each other was formed in 1947. The method of instruction was experiential – i.e. learning by doing – and the participants (mainly managers and executives sent by their employers) were placed in situations in which they had to understand and relate to each other. They were encouraged to be totally honest and to be open about their feelings towards each other, so that they left the training with greater awareness of what makes people tick and with the confidence to adopt a democratic rather than authoritarian attitude to staff relations. T-groups were the forerunners of ENCOUNTER GROUPS and thus the most easily identified starting point of the whole personal GROWTH movement.

T'AI-CHI/T'AI CHI CH'UAN/TAIJI QUAN T'ai Chi Ch'uan, sometimes called Taoist or 'internal' boxing, is impossible to translate adequately: *T'ai* means 'great' or 'original'; *Chi* means 'ultimate' (not to be confused with *Ch'i* or *Qi*, which is the life-force); *Ch'uan* means 'fist' or 'boxing'. So it can be translated roughly as 'great ultimate boxing' or more loosely still as 'supreme ultimate power'. Taiji quan is the modern spelling, although it is still most commonly referred to as the abbreviated 't'ai-chi'.

T'ai-chi is an ancient Chinese system of exercise which incorporates relaxed breathing, rhythmical movement and balance. It is designed to integrate all the aspects of the person through a series of flowing movements on which the mind is completely focused. These movements, originally taken from the natural movements of animals and birds, must be like clouds – constantly changing but never appearing to change. To the casual observer they look like a dance in slow motion, an unbroken series of slowly changing postures which gradually merge into one another.

One popular version of how t'ai-chi came into being refers to a Taoist hermit who developed a series of movements to be performed after sitting for hours in meditation in order to increase his circulation and restore physical vigour without disturbing his meditative state of mind. All 108 postures of modern t'ai-chi have been developed out of those thirteen original movements. In another legend a Taoist monk,

Chang Sanfeng, invented the movements after dreaming about a snake and a bird involved in a dancelike fight: according to Taoist symbolism, the bird represents universal consciousness, the snake the regenerative powers of nature – thus the focusing of the mind on the movement of the body is a way of uniting heaven and earth.

The practice of t'ai-chi follows five principles, represented in Chinese by the words for quietly, lightly, slowly, study or practice, and perseverance. So first one becomes calm and centred ('quietly'), secondly one eliminates exertion ('lightly'), and thirdly one's pace is neither fast nor slow but consistent and without breaks. The fourth principle means that with true, attentive practice one 'studies' one's movements and is fully aware of the extent to which they match the ideal. The fifth principle, 'perseverance', refers to the commitment to practise t'ai-chi every day at the same hour and for the same amount of time.

Performing the movements of t'ai-chi leads to a sense of passive exhilaration, a calm excitement, and a sense of the unity of oneself and the universe. Practising t'ai-chi at sunrise every day, as millions do in China, enables one to experience the change in seasons day by day and a sense of the ever-changing balances of YIN and YANG in the environment. Its effectiveness in promoting health and in eliminating stress-related diseases was recognized by Chairman Mao, who was one of its strongest advocates.

Practitioners of other MARTIAL ARTS such as karate and kung fu regard themselves as in the tradition of t'ai-chi. Although t'ai-chi is usually practised alone, there is a sparring version in which one of three traditional weapons may also be used: the sword, cutlass or staff. Like all true martial arts, particularly the *nei chai* or 'inner family', t'ai-chi involves a philosophy of life. The two principles which build energy and reduce tension in the nei chai group of martial arts are known as relaxing and sinking: relaxing involves controlling muscle tension and using the minimum effort in any movement; sinking here means dropping weight through the feet, feeling and trusting the support of the ground and releasing all tension in the lower part of the body, giving the body a sense of lightness. In all this we see a fundamental concept which is foreign to most western ideas of physical exercise, that of non-exertion, non-doing, letting the body behave in a smooth natural way. Although it may take ten years to learn how to perform t'ai-chi satisfactorily, there should be no sense of striving. There are echoes of this in the ALEXANDER TECHNIQUE with its attempt to eradicate END-GAINING, as well as the total focusing of attention on the movements of the body.

TANKING The practice of tanking refers to floatation therapy, in which one floats in a SENSORY ISOLATION tank.

TELETHERAPY Teletherapy could refer to any therapy that works at a distance (RADIONICS, REIKI and other forms of spiritual healing), although it has been more specifically applied to CRYSTAL HEALING.

TEMPERAMENTS The Greek physician Galen (c.130–201) distinguished four basic temperamental human types, each associated with one of the four HUMOURS. They were the sanguine, the phlegmatic, the choleric and the melancholic. In modern times Jung developed a more sophisticated system of PSYCHOLOGICAL TYPES, categorizing people as essentially either EXTRAVERTED or INTROVERTED, with four different modes in which they orient themselves to the world, the four EGO FUNCTIONS. But some aspects of the link between basic temperament or temperamental imbalance and disease manifested in the body are now being reconsidered and redefined by researchers who link certain chronic diseases with specific PERSONALITY TYPES such as the so-called TYPE A PERSONALITY.

TENS Abbreviation for TRANSCUTANEOUS ELECTRONIC NERVE STIMU-LATION.

TERTIARY GAIN Looking after a sick member of the family can give some people a sense of being needed. This kind of psychological benefit from a patient's pain or illness is referred to as 'tertiary gain'. SECONDARY GAINS are those that accrue to the patient.

THANATOLOGY Thanatology is the psychology of DEATH and dying.

THERAPEUTIC TOUCH Therapeutic Touch (TT) is a healing technique which uses the laying on of hands to transfer human energy from the healer (who is not considered to have any special psychic gift) to the patient. It was developed by Dr Dolores Krieger, a professor of nursing at New York University, who studied the healing work of Colonel Estebany (a former Polish cavalry officer) at Montreal's McGill University. She adapted the methods of this healer and taught them in a secular form to her own nursing students. The act of healing with TT is a means of transferring

LIFE-FORCE or *prana* from the energy-body of the healthy person to the energy-body of the person whose reserves of life-force are low. Although no special expertise is required to practice TT, Krieger emphasizes that self-knowledge and correct motivation on the part of the 'healer' are essential since very close interaction is set up between the two individuals. In Krieger's terminology TT deals not with a healer and a patient but with a 'sender' and a 'receiver'. The sender, in a relaxed state, starts by sensing where there are blockages in the receiver's energy-field (by a form of hand DOWSING) and 'stroking' to 'unruffle the field', so that it can then receive an input of energy from the sender's hands. After a TT session senders shake their hands or hold them under running cold water to get rid of any lingering excess charge of energy.

THETA Theta is the eighth letter of the Greek alphabet and the initial letter in *thanatos*, Greek for 'death'. The Thetan was L. Ron Hubbard's term for the nonphysical, immortal part of the human being (see DIANETICS).

Theta was also the name given to an organization founded by Leonard Orr, an ex-consultant to EST, and dedicated to enabling people to experience REBIRTHING.

The theta BRAIN WAVE pattern, in the range of four to seven cycles per second, is characteristic of deep meditation and the state when one is drifting towards sleep in which imagery may occur.

THINKING In Jungian psychology there are four EGO FUNCTIONS, four basic faculties we can use to orient ourselves in the world, one of which we are likely to favour over the other three, thus being predominantly a particular PSYCHOLOGICAL TYPE. These four functions are thinking, feeling, intuition and sensation.

THIRD FORCE PSYCHOLOGY Abraham Maslow named his HUMANISTIC PSYCHOLOGY the 'third force', following on from the Freudian school (the 'first') and behaviourism (the 'second').

THORACIC SEGMENT In REICHIAN THERAPY the thoracic segment is one of the seven areas of the body, covering the chest and arms. (Thoracic breathing is the shallow breathing which all breathing exercises are designed to counter.)

THRUST Osteopaths often use a very short, sharp movement (also known as HVT – high velocity thrust), for example of the neck or on the lumbar spine, to mobilize joints that have stiffened. Despite the accompanying crack or pop (caused by the release of a burst of CO_2 from inside the joint) these sudden thrusts are not usually painful.

TISSUE DIALOGUE The various techniques used in OSTEOPATHY involve not only treating the affected areas of the body but also 'requesting information' from the tissues which are being manipulated. The art of osteopathy lies in being able to feel and interpret the tissues' responses to the practitioner's rhythmic, stress and thrust techniques. This so-called tissue dialogue is a particularly important aspect of most low velocity stress techniques.

TISSUE SALT THERAPY An alternative name for BIOCHEMICS.

TM The abbreviation for TRANSCENDENTAL MEDITATION.

TOBISCOPE ACUPUNCTURE points are detectable electronically because they have higher electrical conductivity (lower electrical skin resistance) than the surrounding area. The tobiscope is a Russian-designed diagnostic instrument which flashes when the sensor passes over such a point: a bright flash indicates a healthy acupuncture point; a dull flash suggests possible disease.

TONGUE DIAGNOSIS Although orthodox doctors ask patients to show them their tongue, they make much less use of tongue diagnosis than practitioners of BIOCHEMICS, who recognize a deficiency in a specific tissue salt by the exact colour of the tongue or the degree of furring. Deficiency in the various B vitamins is also diagnosable by the appearance of the tongue.

TONIFICATION In ACUPUNCTURE the therapist sometimes jabs the needles briefly into the body rather than leaving them stuck in. This is referred to as tonification.

TONING See CHANTING and MUSIC THERAPY.

TONOSCOPE A tonoscope is an instrument which converts sounds into three-dimensional images. For example, the sound of the letter 'O' pronounced by the human voice produces a sphere. The instrument was invented by Dr Hans Jenny. (See CYMATICS.)

TOUCH FOR HEALTH (not to be confused with THERAPEUTIC TOUCH) Touch for Health is the name of the British and American organizations which teach the principles of APPLIED KINESIOLOGY.

TRADITIONAL MEDICINE As a term, 'traditional medicine' is ambiguous. Many Americans use it to mean CONVENTIONAL MEDICINE, but a booklet put out by the WHO in Geneva, entitled *Potential and Development of Traditional Medicine*, uses 'traditional medicine' to mean the medical practices of non-western societies. This reflects the more common usage outside America and is akin to what is generally understood by the expression FOLK MEDICINE, which may include elements of SHAMANISM, depending on the local culture.

TRAGER WORK/TRAGERING The Trager Approach is a method of psychophysical integration similar in purpose to other body-work (or body-mind) therapies such as the ROSEN METHOD or the FELDENKRAIS METHOD. Milton Trager started a career in the 1920s as a professional boxer but his intuitive gift for massage was noticed and he gave up boxing to preserve his hands, working instead as an acrobat and dancer. He became increasingly interested in physical health, following his desire to perform difficult actions more effortlessly, for example to jump 'softer' rather than higher. After qualifying as a doctor of physical health, he treated people with neuromuscular disorders and specialized in the rehabilitation of polio patients. He left the USA to train as a medical doctor and in the 1950s set up a private medical practice in Hawaii, where he worked in relative obscurity until he demonstrated his method as ESALEN in 1975. His *Trager Mentastics: Movement as a Way to Agelessness* was published in 1987.

Like other bodywork therapies, Tragerwork aims to break down the neuromuscular holding patterns – stiffness, tension, bad posture and inefficient movement – that have their origin in unconscious mental processes. Like Alexander, Trager believes that we expend too much energy unnecessarily on simple movements. The mind has to let go so that the body behaves more naturally, and in Tragerwork the individual abandons unconscious muscular control by adopting a state of deep relaxation. The Trager practitioner also falls into a relaxed state of active meditation when working with a client. In this alert and sensitive meditative state, referred to as *hook-up*, the therapist connects with the client at a deep level, working intuitively and enabling the client to get in touch with natural movements of the body. In a comfortable and playful atmosphere the therapist uses gentle, light, steady movements, manipulating without pressure and sometimes rocking the client. After a Trager session the therapist gives the client a programme of *mentastics* ('mental gymnastics') as homework, an active, self-guided version of Tragerwork which helps to recreate and maintain the healthy, positive feeling experienced during the session.

TRANSACTIONAL ANALYSIS Transactional analysis (TA) was developed in the late 1950s by a Freudian-trained analyst, Eric Berne (1910–1970), following his rejection for membership by the San Francisco Psychoanalytic Institute. It is deterministic, in the Freudian tradition: psychological destiny is determined in the first six years of life, and people spend their entire lives following a life script composed of transactions, procedures, rituals and repetitive sets of social manoeuvres called PASTIMES, which are a result of social programming, and GAMES, which are based on early interaction within the family.

Central to TA are the three types of inner personality or ego states experienced and used by most people when relating to each other: the Parent (*exteropsychic* ego state), the Adult (*neopsychic* ego state), and the Child (*archaeopsychic* ego state). The Parent is the critical, judgmental part of ourselves, which may also be nurturing and protective; whether the inner parent is predominantly critical and blaming or supportive and encouraging depends to a certain extent on the parenting one experienced as a child. There are also two aspects to the inner Child: on the one hand it can be the demanding, frustrated part of ourselves, acting impulsively when crossed, and on the other it can be the fun-loving, playful, curious and inventive part, getting satisfaction out of exploring, taking risks and being creative. The Adult part of the personality is calm, rational and capable; it solves problems by rational analysis or 'data processing' and makes decisions.

In his debunking book, *Psychobabble*, Rosen writes of transactional analysis, 'There is nothing in it that one can't find in Freud, Adler, Sullivan, drama therapy and a few others.'[151] It is true that the three roles may be seen as a reincarnation of Freud's super-ego, ego and id, but Berne's innovation is to see them as roles – behaviour patterns that can be switched on and off at will, rather than elements that constantly struggle for supremacy. The point of TA, which is a form of group therapy, is to recognize when we switch into a particular behaviour pattern which may not be appropriate.

TRANSCENDENT FUNCTION The transcendent function of the psyche, according to Jung, is what drives us towards INDIVIDU-ATION. An important part of individuation is the transcending of the insoluble problems of life. Jung wrote that 'the greatest and most important problems of life are all fundamentally insoluble. They must be so, because they express the necessary polarity inherent in every self-regulatory system. They can never be solved, but only outgrown . . . Everyone must possess that higher level, at least in embryonic form.'[106]

TRANSCENDENTAL MEDITATION Transcendental meditation (TM) was introduced to the West in the 1960s by the Maharishi Mahesh Yogi in his book *The Science of Being and Art of Loving.* It is a form of mantra meditation, but as taught by the Maharishi it requires no adherence to any particular lifestyle or to the YOGA it is derived from and no special discipline other than fifteen minutes of meditation twice a day. The TM instructor gives the meditator a mantra, a special word known only to them, which has no meaning but a pleasing sound. During meditation the meditator thinks of this word in a relaxed, effortless way, allowing perceptions of the external world to fade away so that the focus of attention turns inward, but maintaining an alert, relaxed awareness. Research shows that during TM alpha BRAIN WAVES typical of relaxation increase, and heart rate, respiration and oxygen consumption are reduced. This led the Harvard University cardiologist Professor Herbert Benson to recommend TM or similar relaxation techniques as an antidote to stress and stress-related disease.[11]

TM has been successfully marketed, acquiring both a large following and a number of critics, among them Erich Fromm. He writes of the followers of TM, 'What is so puzzling is that they are not repelled by the unclear language, the crude P.R. spirit, the exaggerated promises, the commercialization of the salvation business – and why they retain their connection with T.M.' He maintains that in becoming one of the TM following, 'One supports an idolatrous cult and thus decreases one's independence, one supports the dehumanizing feature of our culture – the commercialization of all values – as well as the spirit of P.R. falsehoods, the no-effort doctrine, and the perversion of traditional values such as self-knowledge, joy, well-being – by clever packaging.'[57] But more than a hundred Japanese companies provide TM for their managers and executives with a consequent reduction in the number of working days lost through illness. Its positive effect on general health has also been recognized in the Netherlands, where a life insurance company (Sterpolis) has cut its premiums to TM meditators by 40 per cent.

TRANSCUTANEOUS ELECTRICAL NERVE STIMULATOR/ TRANSCUTANEOUS ELECTRONIC NERVE STIMULA- TION (often abbreviated to TENS) a transcutaneous electrical nerve stimulator is a small device used in ELECTROTHERAPY (see FARADISM) to relieve aches and pains. It has been shown that electronic nerve stimulation of ACUPUNCTURE points increases ENDORPHIN levels, and TENS has been used with acupuncture to reduce chronic and acute pain conditions and as a substitute or supplement for analgesic drugs after surgery.

TRANSFERENCE When people are in PSYCHOANALYSIS they often carry over the feelings, impressions and expectations they had with regard to someone in their past (often a parent) into the way they feel about and behave towards the analyst. This unconscious process was discovered and named by Freud as transference, the most common example being what he described as the patient's 'menacing illusion' of falling in love with the analyst. When they first met, Freud asked Jung, 'And what do you think of transference?' Jung answered that he believed it to be 'the alpha and omega of the analytical method', to which Freud responded, 'Then you have grasped the main thing.'[98]

Many aspects of the psychoanalytic procedure seem to invite transference: the anonymity of the analyst, for example, and most notably the classical situation of the patient lying on a couch with the analyst out of sight and therefore more susceptible to projections from the patient. When transference occurs during analysis or therapy the therapist may point it out to the patient, saying, for example, 'You think I am going to abandon you because that is what your father did.' The problem with such statements is that they are all too easily made and often seem predictable, whilst having little effect on the patient beyond one of irritation. They may even benefit the therapist more than the patient, since they demonstrate the therapist's superiority, reduce the therapist's anxiety rather than the patient's, and represent a means of disclaiming responsibility for any accusation made by the patient. For such reasons, some analysts have adopted a more INTERPERSONAL approach, which concedes the possibility that to some degree the patient really is reacting to the therapist.

TRANSFORMATION Many of the so-called 'growth' psychologies, and indeed much of depth psychology and psychotherapy, aim at some kind of transformation within the individual. In this sense transformation implies working on oneself and making changes in behaviour, attitude and beliefs. People who have reached this stage in their psychological development have usually realized that their behaviour is shaped by their history and wish to overcome such unconscious motivation. They have internalized conflicts that are not really their own, for example acting out the conflicts of parents. They also reproduce past conflicts: conflicts from their own past are re-enacted and they choose situations in which such conflicts are more likely to recur. Transformation involves bringing all such hidden conflicts to the surface and resolving them.

TRANSPERSONAL PSYCHOLOGY Because of its chronological position after Freud and behaviourism, Maslow referred to HUMANISTIC PSYCHOLOGY as the Third Psychology, or the Third Force. He regarded it as 'a preparation for a still "higher" Fourth Psychology, transpersonal, transhuman, centred in the cosmos rather than in human needs and interest, going beyond humanness, identity, SELF-ACTUALIZATION and the like.'[125]

In transpersonal psychology a crisis which may lead to what other therapies regard as a breakdown is seen as an opportunity for a *breakthrough*, the chance for growth on many levels including the spiritual. Within each individual it is understood that there is a spiritual essence or SELF, and the life of the personality, the everyday EGO, is a journey to find the Self. This journey of discovery is depicted in many myths and fairy tales. An integral part of transpersonal psychology is the notion that life has a purpose, that we are here to learn lessons, use our talents, develop our potential and contribute to planetary evolution, for we are all part of the whole.

Therapy in the transpersonal sense means discovering and developing the WILL, which is beyond the senses, the emotions and thinking. We learn to recognize who we really are and what we are here for, and to overcome the barriers we may have built up against the fulfilment of our potential. A variety of techniques may be used, including DREAMWORK, VISUALIZATION, GESTALT THERAPY and the techniques of PSYCHOSYNTHESIS. In some respects the aim of transpersonal psychology is closely related to Jung's concepts of INDIVIDUATION and the TRANSCENDENT FUNCTION.

385

TRANSTHERAPEUTIC ANALYSIS Erich Fromm remained convinced of the value of PSYCHOANALYSIS and saw it not just as therapy for neuroses. Because analysis could 'go beyond restoring the patient to "normalcy" ' he called it *transtherapeutic analysis*. 'The transtherapeutic goal is that of man's self-liberation by optimal self-awareness; of the attaining of well-being, independence; of the capacity to love; and of critical, dis-illusioned thinking, of being rather than having.' To some extent this sounds rather like the achievement of full humanness that is the goal of HUMANISTIC PSYCHOLOGY, and Fromm originally used the term 'humanistic psychoanalysis' for this new self-liberating function of analysis; but he dropped it, as he says, 'partly because it was taken over by a group of psychologists whose views I did not share.' There is a strong echo of Buddhist ideas in Fromm's notion of self-liberation through self-awareness; at the same time he does not dismiss Freud's theories and methods to the extent that humanistic psychologists do. Of Freud he writes, 'His great ambition did not lie in the field of therapy but in the creation of an enlightened movement, based on the last step enlightenment could make: the awareness and control of irrational passions . . . The basic aim [of transtherapeutic analysis] is that of classic psychoanalysis: the uncovering of unconscious strivings, the recognition of resistance, transference, rationalization, and the interpretation of dreams as the "royal road" to the understanding of the unconscious.' But with the additional aim of self-liberation Fromm sees transtherapeutic analysis as 'more active, direct and challenging' than classical psychoanalysis.[57]

TREPANNING Trepanning, or 'trephining', was an example of PSYCHOSURGERY practised in ancient and medieval times to treat psychiatric illnesses. Without any form of modern anaesthetic a hole was drilled in the patient's skull to release the supposed accumulation of noxious vapours.

TRIALS/CLINICAL TRIALS In the eighteenth century clinical trials were called 'medical arithmetic'. William Black (1749–1829), speaking to the Medical Society of London in 1788, said, 'The system of medical arithmetic, although it may not show the best mode of cure that may hereafter be invented, it will, however, by comparison, determine the best that has yet been discovered, or is in use.'[177] One of the earliest examples of a clinical trial was conducted by James Lind (1716–94) in 1747 on board ship: it was for the treatment of scurvy. Lind understood the possibility of the

PLACEBO EFFECT and presented his results statistically. The missing elements of randomization and double (or triple) blind came much later.

The first trial with randomization was performed in Britain in 1923 in agriculture, and the DOUBLE-BLIND technique was first used in the British Medical Research Council's streptomycin trial in 1947. It was only in the late 1960s and early 1970s that the randomized controlled trial became standard practice. Randomization means that the patients taking part in the trial are allocated at random to the treatment group or the control group. There must be a control group which receives no treatment, or a placebo. Patients are not told which group they are assigned to (single blind) and ideally the doctors administering treatment should not know who is in which group (double blind).

Whilst standard clinical trials may be suitable for assessing the value of certain ALLOPATHIC drugs, the classical scientific method is less appropriate for the study of ALTERNATIVE MEDICINE. Randomization presupposes that all subjects with a particular condition are essentially the same. This is no problem for conventional medicine: each patient is treated as an example of a particular condition and variables are either reduced to a minimum or ignored. In alternative medicine there are often too many unquantifiable variables, for each patient is regarded as a unique individual with a unique array of symptoms and underlying causes. When drawing conclusions from trials the investigators should also surely take into account patient/therapist interaction, and the variation among individual patient responses. There should also be a follow-up period to evaluate long-term results and possible side effects. Much of this is lacking in standard clinical trials.

Even if a group of patients can be found with a condition which can be regarded as common to all, without too many individual variables, there is still something of a question mark around the ethics of randomized trials: is it right that some patients should be given *no treatment at all*, as required by the scientific method? In addition, some trials may satisfy the randomization condition but not the double-blind criterion. For example, in an investigation which compared chiropractic with conventional hospital out-patient treatment for cases of lower back pain, 741 patients were allocated randomly to one form of treatment or the other, but inevitably everyone knew which type of treatment they were receiving.

In the British Medical Association report on alternative therapies the main criticism was that they were unscientific in their evaluation methods. The report defines the scientific approach of validation as including the 'normally approved method of the clinical trial', ignoring the obvious impossibility of this in many cases (not to mention the doubtful ethics). Fortunately some in the medical establishment are beginning to realize that this so-called scientific method is often inappropriate. 'The time is now overdue for researchers to question the validity of regarding patients as rigidly standardizable objects when attempting to evaluate any activity involving their person. A participatory relationship between patient and therapist is an indispensable ingredient in any treatment situation, and when research fails to follow suit it ceases to deal with reality and not infrequently runs the risk of being frankly unethical.'230

In 1983 the Research Council for Complementary Medicine was set up in Britain to provide research funding, advice (on how to set up a clinical trial, for example), and general support for researchers in alternative therapies. There are now signs of greater willingness on the part of therapists to submit to the trialling process, and the medical establishment is also more willing to concede that some of the treatments practised in orthodox medicine are administered despite not being understood. (Researchers have noted, for example, that 'The mode of action of penicillinamine in rheumatoid arthritis is unknown but it is a valuable treatment.'200)

TRIGGER POINTS Trigger points are areas of the body which become unusually tender or sensitive at the onset of a particular disease. They can be regarded as a western equivalent of ALARM POINTS in acupuncture. They are treated in Bonnie Prudden's form of MYOTHERAPY.

TRIPLE BLIND In a DOUBLE-BLIND trial both the patients and the doctors administering the drugs are unaware which patients are receiving a placebo. In a triple blind the evaluators are also ignorant of this, to ensure the objectivity of the results.

TRITURATION Trituration is a controlled grinding and mixing process by which substances are added to a base. It is used in the preparation of HOMOEOPATHIC remedies.

TRUE SELF According to the psychiatrist R. D. Laing (associated with the ANTIPSYCHIATRY movement), people who are insecure may split themselves into two systems: the FALSE SELF, a mask presented to the world, deals with the demands of a hostile environment, whilst the true self, that part of our being which has authentic experience, lies hidden. As the false self is responsible for dealings with others, the individual is seen by them as that false self, so the true self feels increasingly cut off, isolated, disembodied and unreal. The true self dreams of freedom, perhaps of revenge, but is increasingly subject to fantasy, even though it is the source of true, subjective feeling. (Laing's concept of the true self is his version of Sartre's 'imaginary self', the false self being Sartre's 'real self'.) It is not superior, but it is authentic and needs to be recognized as such. 'Patients can be helped back to fusion of their subjective experiences with the social realities seen by others, only if these true selves are first accepted as legitimate bases to build upon.'[74]

TSUBO Japanese term for an ACUPOINT.

TUI NA Tui Na is a Chinese massage technique which uses a variety of hand movements along MERIDIANS and on ACUPOINTS to stimulate and balance the flow of energy (CH'I) around the body.

TUMO In Tibetan YOGA tumo is the discipline by which yogis endure extremes of cold while naked or dressed in thin cotton. The technique involves VISUALIZATION and CHANTING. Maintaining body heat is one of the functions of the autonomic nervous system, which it was thought could not be brought under voluntary control until the research into BIOFEEDBACK in the 1960s proved otherwise.

TYPE A/TYPE B PERSONALITIES, TYPE A/TYPE B BEHAVIOUR In recent years there has been considerable interest in investigating the relationship between certain chronic health conditions and specific PERSONALITY TYPES. The result is sometimes strangely reminiscent of Galen's classical theory of TEMPERAMENTS and HUMOURS.

The Type A/Type B categorization of personalities was an attempt in the late 1960s to identify the significant character or behaviour traits in patients with heart disease, Type A being the people with heart problems and Type B the rest of the population. The initial characterization described Type A people as time-urgent (suffering from 'hurry-sickness'), polyphasic (doing several things at once), impatient and competitive. Type B people are more placid, speak more slowly, and do not try to do more than one thing at a time. The contrast between Type A and Type B is reflected in the characters of the White Rabbit and the Dormouse in *Alice in Wonderland*, or in the Hare and the Tortoise in the fable. Type A people treat too many everyday events as emergencies, damaging the body by too frequently inviting the FIGHT-OR-FLIGHT RESPONSE. Type As react to STRESS by smoking more, Type Bs by drinking alcohol.

Type A behaviour got its name because when Meyer Friedman applied for grants to investigate 'emotional stress', his applications were always rejected: the psychiatrists who considered the applications doubted whether a cardiologist was qualified to carry out such research. Calling the phenomenon 'Type A behaviour pattern' avoided the reference to psychological states and Friedman subsequently received the funding he needed.[53]

Having defined Type A, Friedman and his colleague R. H. Rosenman successfully tested their hypothesis in laboratory experiments. For example, checking the heart-rate and blood pressure of students before examinations, they found correlations with Types A and B as their theory predicted. They observed: 'The same blood abnormalities that so many of our colleagues believe precede and possibly bring on coronary heart disease were already present in our Type A subjects.' And they concluded: 'To us the logic is irresistible: the behaviour pattern itself gives rise to the abnormalities.'[52]

Subsequent research has not supported Rosenman and Friedman in the early formulation of their theory that there is a connection between Type A behaviour and the artery disease which so often precedes heart attacks. They had discovered only part of the story. In their initial analysis Type As were described as responding to challenge with hostility. 'Hostility is currently the most popular candidate in the search for the destructive Type A component; it has been linked with blood pressure reactivity, severity of coronary artery disease, and death from all causes including coronary heart disease . . . If a person is very self-involved and thinks of himself or herself as better than others in many ways, this person is vulnerable to anyone who confronts such claims or who looks better than he. Hostility may be a strategy for coping with such challenges.'[135]

It is not so much the hostility itself which is damaging, but how the individual deals with it. In further investigations potential for hostility and irritability has been found to be one of the best predictors of heart disease. But the 'level of hostility was unrelated to coronary heart disease in those patients who disclosed a willingness to express anger or hostility openly against the source of frustration.'[17] Later research concluded that it is the person who sets himself apart from the social framework, an island unto himself, and acts in a hostile way to others who is at risk from heart disease, not necessarily the extremely busy person.

So we have new conclusions on the Type A theory. 'Ambition, competitiveness or anxiety about time may not in themselves be so dangerous to the heart, unless accompanied by anger, distrust and resentment . . . As far as heart attack risk is concerned, Type A people are now being subdivided into those who express themselves well, and who are said to be less at risk, and those who fail to express themselves and so attract more risk.'[17] In view of the importance of self-expression, especially in the context of relationships with other people, it would seem that many psychological therapies, from T-GROUP to ASSERTIVENESS TRAINING, could also be valuable in protecting people from potential heart disease. This comes as no surprise to those involved in cancer research and treatment, who have also noticed the importance of certain negative EMOTIONS in their investigations into the so-called CANCER PERSONALITY.

TYPE THEORY See PSYCHOLOGICAL TYPES and PERSONALITY TYPES.

UNDIFFERENTIATED ILLNESS Also known as FUNCTIONAL ILLNESS.

ULTRASONICS Treating the body with sound waves of very high frequency, beyond the range of human hearing, is known as ultrasonics. The frequencies are so high that they cannot be produced mechanically and are generated by surrounding a quartz crystal with an electric field. The rapid expansion and contraction of the crystal produces the sound waves, the frequency of the vibrations depending on the frequency of the electric field. (Because of this use of an electric field ultrasonics is sometimes regarded as a type of ELECTROTHERAPY.) The part of the body being treated ultrasonically is either immersed in water or covered with a gel to facilitate transmission of the high-frequency sound waves, which are reflected by air. They have a warming and slightly massaging effect on body tissue and an analgesic effect on nerves, making ultrasonics a useful treatment for sports injuries, sprains and strains.

UNANI-TIBBI Unani-tibbi is a mixture of AYURVEDA and the traditional medicine of Persia and Arabia. It is practised in north west India and Pakistan.

UNCONSCIOUS Josef Breuer, an older colleague of Freud's whom Freud at one time even referred to as 'the father of psychoanalysis', discovered that the root causes of certain hysterical symptoms in his patients were painful memories and suppressed emotions, buried below consciousness. He also found that if patients verbalized these memories and emotions while under HYPNOSIS, the resulting CATHARSIS effectively cured them of their symptoms. Visiting Auguste Liébeault, who also used hypnosis in his clinic, Freud noticed that patients could not recall the suggestions given to them during hypnosis even though they could be relied on to act on those suggestions post-hypnotically. Moreover they would somehow rationalize reasons for their actions. This led Freud to the idea that much of human behaviour could be the result of unconscious motivation, with rationalization as one of the common DEFENCE MECHANISMS.

In PSYCHOSYNTHESIS the personal unconscious consists of the lower unconscious, the middle unconscious, and the SUPERCONSCIOUS. As in Jungian psychology, psychosynthesis also includes the notion of a collective unconscious, 'the precondition of each individual psyche, just as the sea is the carrier of the individual wave'.[102] Jung believed that 'the unconscious mind is capable at times of assuming an intelligence and purposiveness which are superior to actual conscious insight',[104] and that this wisdom (as well as the 'hidden motives' focused on by Freud) can be accessed in DREAMS.

URINE THERAPY/AUTO URINE THERAPY Drinking one's own urine, a practice known as *shiuambu* or *amarol*, probably first came to public attention in the West when it was revealed that President Shastri of India started each day in this way. The practice is advocated in YOGA, and, in keeping with other aspects of yoga, it is regarded as essential that the urine drinker is already vegetarian, teetotal and a non-smoker, since many drugs and toxins are expelled from the body in the urine and obviously should not be recycled. Among the ingredients of urine are urokinase, which is a preventive against unwanted blood clots, heart attacks, angina, thrombophlebitis and pulmonary embolism; prostaglandins, a group of unsaturated fatty acids which lower blood pressure, reduce hypertension and prevent ulcers; vitamin D, which also regulates blood pressure; and directin, which arrests cancer growth. The recommended morning glass of urine is said to banish constipation, and gargling with urine is a cure for sore throats. The application of fresh urine relieves mosquito bites; kept for four days it can be used in massage. Keeping urine for longer periods produces an excellent fertilizer for plants and vegetables, and many gardeners add it to their compost.

VALUES Values form an important part of HUMANISTIC PSYCHOLOGY. Abraham Maslow wrote, 'The state of being without a system of values is psychopathogenic. Human beings need a philosophy of life, a religion, or a value system, just as they need sunlight, calcium, and love.'[125] It was Maslow's belief that valuelessness was the 'ultimate disease of our times'. He originated the concept of 'Being-values', usually abbreviated to 'B-values', the motivating force in people no longer driven by deficiency NEEDS (D-needs).

VATA One of the three humours (*doshas*) in AYURVEDIC MEDICINE, translated as air, wind or movement.

VEGETOTHERAPY REICHIAN THERAPY was initially called 'vegetotherapy' because it worked directly and indirectly on muscle tensions and breathing patterns to restore the harmonious functioning of the body's so-called vegetative energies. It is the vegetative nervous system that regulates the involuntary processes in the body, such as heart beat, muscle tone, digestion and intestinal peristalsis, although some use the term 'vegetative system' in this context to refer to the whole body-mind unity. Vegetotherapy makes use of a form of deep, almost violent massage to break down muscular ARMOURING, and is also used by some practitioners of ANTHROPOSOPHICAL MEDICINE.

VIBRATIONAL HEALING/VIBRATIONAL THERAPIES

Vibrational therapies are those based on the assumption that there is a subtle energy or LIFE-FORCE underlying all living organisms. Such therapies aim to bring this energy back up to full strength or into balance by working directly on the etheric body rather than on the physical body. This may be achieved in a variety of ways ranging from the relatively tangible methods of ACUPUNCTURE and ACUPRESSURE, in which the actual flow of such energy is influenced directly by the practitioner, to the treatment from a distance that is claimed to be possible in RADIONICS and REIKI, and the use of COLOUR, CRYSTALS and AROMATIC OILS to balance the vibrations. The theory of resonance holds that when surrounded by vibrations of a particular frequency the body's vibrations fall into step. These therapies all work externally on the organism, but the same basic philosophy underlies HOMOEOPATHY, ANTHROPOSOPHICAL MEDICINE and the BACH FLOWER REMEDIES, in which remedies are introduced into the body in a more conventional way. Other ways to influence the subtle vibrations are by the actual vibrations of the physical body in CHANTING, MUSIC THERAPY and SOUND THERAPY (see also CYMATICS.) A patient's vibrations can be used diagnostically, when the AURA is felt by the sensitive hands of a HEALER, or when conditions (and treatment) are diagnosed with a pendulum.

VIPASSANA In Theravadin Buddhism, Vipassana is a form of MEDITATION intended to bring clarity and insight into reality.

VISUALIZATION Visualization is a form of mental imagery, either self-directed or guided by a therapist. In recent years it has been used increasingly as a means of SELF-HEALING, sometimes in conjunction with HYPNOSIS and always with relaxation exercises. In one experiment people were told under hypnosis to visualize their white blood cells as sharks attacking weak confused germs in the bloodstream. They were told that these sharklike cells would continue to protect them from germs even when they were not thinking about them. The same shark story was used in SELF-HYPNOSIS sessions twice a week. Blood tests were taken before hypnosis, one hour after and one week later to measure the lymphocytes present. Many people, particularly the younger subjects and those who were most easily hypnotized, showed increased responsiveness in their immune system and even increased numbers of lymphocytes.[189] The greater success of this experiment among children may have less to do with their supposed impressionability than with the suitability of the shark story for their age-group. A visualization in more scientific terms – imagining the lymphocytes more as they actually are, for example – might have been more appropriate for the adults in the group. 'The therapist must of course be creative. The same visualization exercise is not right for every patient and it is up to the therapist to find which imagery will help the patient.'[157]

The pioneers of visualization in the treatment of cancer were Carl Simonton and Stephanie Matthews, who brought this therapy to the attention of the general public in their book *Getting Well Again*.[159] Their first patient to use visualization techniques was a 61-year-old man with throat cancer. He was undergoing radiation therapy, and his visualization consisted of imagining millions of tiny bullets of energy hitting all the cells in their path: the normal cells would withstand the onslaught, but the cancerous cells, being weaker and more confused, would be damaged beyond repair. Further, he visualized his white blood cells swarming round the damaged cancer cells and carting them off to be flushed out of the body through the liver and kidneys. The radiation therapy was successful for this particular patient and he suffered virtually no negative side effects.

The Simontons have always recommended visualization as a support for conventional medical treatment and never a substitute, although centres such as the Bristol Cancer Help Centre may use it with other alternative therapies. The Simontons also stress the importance of the symbols used in the imagery. Some symbols are too negative for the visualization to be effective – imagining cancer cells as ants, for example. 'Have you ever been able to get rid of ants at a picnic?' they ask. Similarly counter-productive is visualizing cancer cells as crabs, the traditional symbol for cancer: not only are they tenacious, hanging on grimly, but with their hard shells they are relatively impregnable.

An extension of visualization techniques, known as *creative visualization*, is the process of using visual imagery not only as a form of self-hypnosis to change one's own mental attitude but also to effect changes in one's environment, achieving one's desires and projecting one's own reality. One may use AFFIRMATIONS in ways reminiscent of POSITIVE THINKING and AUTOSUGGESTION. Whether or not reality is affected by such methods, one's perception of reality may certainly be enhanced by a positive attitude. The Simontons also use a version of creative visualization – visualizing a goal as already achieved – and refer to this as 'strengthening patients' beliefs that they can meet their goals'.

VITAL ENERGY/VITAL FORCE See LIFE-FORCE.

WATER BIRTH See NATURAL BIRTH TECHNIQUES.

WATER THERAPY See HYDROTHERAPY.

WELLNESS/WELLNESS CLINIC 'Wellness' is a term often used in
holistic approaches to PREVENTIVE MEDICINE. It has been defined
by Lawrence LeShan as 'a positive movement toward greater
health, not just a curing of disease'.[116] Medical Centres in the
USA sometimes have a Wellness Clinic, which people attend not
when they are sick but as a matter of routine to maintain health
and prevent illness. Programmes at a wellness clinic may include
NUTRITION, MEDITATION, PSYCHOTHERAPY, exercise and creativity
workshops.

WILL Roberto Assagioli, founder of PSYCHOSYNTHESIS, describes
the will as 'the Cinderella of modern psychology, relegated to
the kitchen'. Freud's focus on the UNCONSCIOUS as the origin of all
psychological drives and motivation led to a determinism as strong
as any medieval belief in predestination. Assagioli reaffirmed the
freedom of the individual in the form of the conscious will. This
is not the same as will-power – a force that might be exercised
while one is still locked in unconscious patterns without having
established one's freedom as a fully self-conscious individual (hence
the use of the term 'conscious will'). It is also, and must be, a
very active force, as the WILL TO RECOVER demonstrates. Erich
Fromm distinguishes will from whim in this respect: 'Following a
whim is the result of deep inner passivity blended with a wish to
avoid boredom. Will is based on activity, whim on passivity.'[57] It
is also in a sense single-minded, for Fromm's concept of 'the art of
living' includes the condition that one must will one thing. 'To will
one thing presupposes having made a decision, having committed
oneself to one goal. It means that the whole person is geared and
devoted to the one thing he has decided on, that all his energies flow

in the direction of this chosen goal.' Rollo May makes a similar point when distinguishing between will and wish: 'Will is the capacity to organize one's self so that movement in a certain direction or toward a certain goal may take place. Wish is the imaginative playing with the possibility of some act or state occurring.'[129] (May also contends that illness can result from an inability to wish.) He describes protest as 'half-developed will'. In *Love and Will*, May sees it as our task in life 'to unite love and will'. These he describes as 'interpersonal experiences', 'ways of moulding, forming, relating to the world and trying to elicit a response from it through the persons whose interest or love we covet.' PSYCHOANALYSIS does not concern itself with this area, although Fromm's TRANSTHERAPEUTIC ANALYSIS, Frankl's LOGOTHERAPY and various forms of TRANSPERSONAL PSYCHOLOGY certainly do. (See also AUTO-SUGGESTION.)

WILL THERAPY Otto Rank was one of the first Freudians in the 1920s to reject the deterministic orthodoxy of classical PSYCHO-ANALYSIS. He maintained that no one could be restored to psychological health unless their 'will to health' were revived. Neurosis was a sign that this will had become deflated and passive. Will therapy is an approach to standard psychoanalysis which diminishes the authoritarian role of the analyst and encourages the individual's sense of independence.

WILL TO LIVE/WILL TO RECOVER 'The will to live is not a theoretical abstraction, but a physiologic reality with therapeutic characteristics.' So wrote Norman Cousins in *Anatomy of an Illness*.[29] (See LAUGHTER.) The will-to-live is obviously crucial in SELF-HEALING. When considering ALTERNATIVE MEDICINE the will-to-live could well play a more significant part in successful treatments than it does in conventional medicine: cancer patients who turn to alternative medicine are more likely to do so out of a determination to get well, a refusal to acquiesce when confronted with a pessimistic prognosis by their doctors. Dr Bernard Siegel, a professor of surgery at Yale University Medical School who has adopted the VISUALIZATION techniques of Carl Simonton, has found that about half the cancer patients he sees think in negative terms of expecting someone else to cure them, rather than asking what they should do for themselves. The will to recover is a very active force, clearly not present in passive PATIENTS. The HEALER Matthew Manning remarks that his methods may give only temporary relief unless the patient is prepared to explore self-help as a sign that they really do want to recover.

There is strong statistical evidence for the effect of the will to live among those who are actually dying: the incidence of DEATH among practising Jews falls prior to significant dates in the Jewish calendar such as Yom Kippur, and many people have seen relatives 'hang on' just long enough to celebrate some particular family event.[108] Similarly there are people who have clearly 'lost the will to live' or 'given up hope' and simply waste away. This appears to be an area unduly neglected by medical research.

WILL TO MEANING The will to meaning is the primary human motivation, according to Viktor Frankl, founder of LOGOTHERAPY. He first coined the term in 1949, partly as a result of his search for an answer to questions relating to the survival of people in concentration camps. (He had spent three years in Auschwitz and Dachau.) Why did some manage to survive against all odds? Why did some who had appeared strong suddenly give up the struggle? 'Those most apt to survive the camps were those oriented toward the future, toward a meaning to be fulfilled by them in the future.'[46] Frankl sees Maslow's hierarchy of higher and lower NEEDS as inadequate, because it was precisely when the lower needs were *not* met that the will to meaning assumed overriding importance. He contrasts the will to meaning with the pursuit of happiness: 'It is the very "pursuit of happiness" that obviates happiness. The more we make it a target, the more widely we miss.' Such a pursuit, however apparently successful to the outside observer, cannot guarantee against 'noögenic neurosis', neurosis caused by a sense of meaninglessness.

WITNESS See DIAGNOSTIC WITNESS.

WOUNDED HEALER In GREEK MYTHOLOGY Asclepius was regarded as the father of medicine. He was brought up by the centaur, Chiron, from whom he learned all his medical skills. Chiron had an incurable wound, a characteristic which in some way was seen as the source of his healing power and wisdom, and he has remained the archetypal symbol of the wounded healer.

Patrick Pietroni, a general practitioner in London who has made more effort than most to adopt HOLISTIC practices, has considered the importance of this ARCHETYPE. He notes that doctors and students often feel that their understanding and skills are enhanced by personal experience of an illness. 'In the course of their studies, medical students often "develop" the illness they are currently studying. They develop the symptoms of multiple sclerosis when first meeting a patient with this complaint . . . These internal experiences of "illnesses" are a very necessary process of experiencing "wounds" without actually being wounded. It allows the medical student to go through the modern equivalent of a shamanistic training where he acknowledges his potential for being a patient as well as a doctor. It is unfortunate that for the majority, these experiences are regarded as being "neurotic" and the student is encouraged to dismiss them as signs of weakness, so that as he matures he adopts the mantle of only one half of the archetype: that of the healer/doctor with little or no perception of the opposite pole. This opposite pole is then projected onto the patient so that feelings of weakness, dependency and helplessness are avoided by the doctor . . . It is this splitting of the archetype, or inborn potential, of the "wounded healer" that helps to produce the one-sided power relationships between doctors and patients.'[143]

A consequence of this one-sided power relationship is, as Ivan Illich has pointed out, the tendency on the part of the modern medical establishment to deprive patients of their individual illnesses and suffering by treating just the DISEASE.

WU SHU Chinese for MARTIAL ARTS, wu shu generally refers to a non-combative system of movements and exercises that includes leaps, lunges, kicks, slaps and turns. It is a popular sport in modern China. In Taiwan the term is *guo shu*, 'national' art.

XI CLEFT POINT In ACUPUNCTURE each MERIDIAN has one xi cleft point which can be used most effectively in acute conditions. For example, in cases of asthma the xi cleft point on the lung meridian could be treated. Xi cleft points are a particular group of SYMPTOMATIC POINTS.

YIN/YANG Yin and yang are the two balancing forces in the universe according to traditional Chinese teaching. They permeate the whole cosmos, and there is no separation of the individual from the environment, or of mind and body. Yin and yang are often translated as feminine and masculine respectively, but western concepts of male and female are not really helpful in understanding the full range of their complementary qualities. For example, yin may be regarded as passive, receptive, soft, wet, cold, dark, whilst yang is active, creative, hard, dry, bright. So the times of day change gradually from being all yang at noon to being all yin at midnight, and the same change occurs seasonally between midsummer and midwinter, but any particular time of the day or year is more likely to be a mixture of the two. Foods too are a mixture of yin and yang, the proportions depending on qualities such as how close they grow to the earth (which is yin) as well as their wetness and season of fruiting. This aspect of food is fundamental in planning a MACROBIOTIC diet. In ACUPUNCTURE one may describe the PULSES and the flow of CH'I as too yin or yang, the purpose of acupuncture treatment being to bring the two forces into balance. This principle is likewise followed in ACUPRESSURE and SHIATSU and has also been adopted in POLARITY THERAPY.

YOGA Yoga is essentially a spiritual discipline, a way of life through which one seeks integration or union with the universal spirit. (The Sanskrit root *yuj* means 'to bind, join or yoke'; our word 'religion' comes from a similar Latin root.) In the West, however, many people have adopted specific parts of the yoga tradition – principally breathing, posture and meditation – as a means of achieving and maintaining mental and physical well-being, without necessarily subscribing whole-heartedly to the spiritual side of the teachings.

As Patanjali said, 'Yoga is controlling the waves of the mind.' One of the first and most basic techniques employed to achieve this is the control of breathing, an essential part of MEDITATION. From the outset mind and body are inextricably linked. Perhaps this is most clearly seen in the relationship between breathing and tension: when we are emotionally tense there is a certain rigidity in the abdominal area and our breathing becomes shallower and more irregular; but if we consciously regulate and deepen our breathing pattern we also reduce the mental tension. In HATHA YOGA the breathing exercises of PRANAYAMA are combined with ASANAS (postures), sometimes using movements similar to those of T'AI CHI CH'UAN.

The psychological effects of controlled breathing and meditation lead to a yoga practitioner acquiring a certain amount of control over some functions of the AUTONOMIC NERVOUS SYSTEM. This ability, formerly associated only with yogis, was rediscovered with BIOFEEDBACK. The element of mental control in yoga has influenced or been incorporated into a variety of therapies such as COUÉISM and AUTOGENIC TRAINING. Measurement of BRAIN WAVE frequencies has shown that brain activity changes during different types of meditation, so the production of chemicals in the brain could also be affected, enhancing the body's natural immune response. Yoga is recommended as much for its preventive as its curative value.

ZAZEN Zazen is a form of seated meditation, in which the meditator uses a chair rather than sitting cross-legged or in the lotus position. The eyes are kept partially open and staring, since Zen Buddhists believe that closed eyes encourage withdrawal from life and drowsiness. The zazen meditator must not breathe too deeply, since hyperventilation causes lightheadedness and artificially induces sensations.

ZEN See MEDITATION, ZAZEN and VIPASSANA.

ZENDO A meditation hall where zen is practised.

ZONE THERAPY Like ACUPRESSURE and SHIATSU, zone therapy is based on the principle that a LIFE-FORCE flows around the body along pathways known as MERIDIANS. In the words of Joseph Corvo, 'The electromagnetic forces which animate your body run through it in ten major zones, feeding and regenerating all

401

the glands and organs in those zones. Illness, ageing and pain occur when toxins accumulate at the nerve endings so that the flow of the electromagnetic forces becomes locked, thereby causing glands and organs to malfunction and wither. Zone therapy is a unique system of pressure point massage which disperses these toxins so that the body's own animating and healing powers can course through the body at full force again.'[28] There is no direct manipulation of the back, which Corvo says can be dangerous. The massage on a succession of points is a simple circular movement with the finger or thumb, or with a rounded, blunt instrument such as the end of a pencil. One advantage of zone therapy is that it can be practised on oneself.

Bibliography

1. Ader, Robert (ed.): *Psychoneuroimmunology*, New York, 1981.
2. Alexander, F. M. *The Use of the Self*, London, Methuen, 1932; Gollancz, 1985.
3. Allport: *Becoming*, Yale University Press, 1955.
4. Assagioli, Roberto: *Psychosynthesis*, Wellingborough, Turnstone, 1965.
5. Assagioli, Roberto: *The Act of Will*, London, Wildwood House, 1974.
6. Bach, Edward: *Ye Suffer from Yourselves*, address given in 1931. (For other writings by Edward Bach, see Judy Howard and John Ramsell.)
7. Bagnall, Oscar: *The Origin and Properties of the Human Aura*, London, 1937; revised edition, New York, University Books, 1970.
8. Barlow, Wilfred: *The Alexander Principle*, London, Gollancz, 1973.
9. Bates, W. H.: *Perfect Eyesight Without Glasses*, Central Fixation Publications, 1919.
10. Bateson, Gregory: *Steps to an Ecology of the Mind*, Chandler Publishing, 1972.
11. Benson, Herbert: *The Relaxation Response*, Fount, 1975.
12. Berne, Eric: *Games People Play*, London, André Deutsch, 1966.
13. Berne, Eric: *Transactional Analysis in Psychotherapy*, New York, Grove Press, 1961.
14. Bettelheim, Bruno: *The Informed Heart*, Harmondsworth, Penguin, 1960.
15. Birdwhistell, Ray: *An Introduction to Kinesics*, University of Louisville Press, 1952.
16. Bishop, Beata: *A Time to Heal*, London, Severn House, 1985.
17. Blake, Robin: *Mind Over Medicine: Can the mind kill or cure?* London, Aurum Press, 1987.
18. Blakemore, Colin: *Mechanics of the Mind*, Cambridge University Press, 1977.
19. Blakeslee, Thomas R.: *The Right Brain*, London, Macmillan, 1980.
20. Boadella, David: *Lifestreams – An Introduction to Biosynthesis*, London, Routledge & Kegan Paul, 1987.
21. Brandt, Johanna: *The Grape Cure*, Johannesburg, Technical Press, 1929.
22. Brenner, Charles, reported in Malcolm, Janet: *Psychoanalysis: the impossible profession*, London, Pan, 1982.
23. Brohn, Penny: *The Bristol Programme*, London, Hutchinson, 1987.
24. Cannon, Walter: *The Wisdom of the Body*, New York, 1914.
25. Clark, Linda and Martine, Yvonne: *Health, Youth and Beauty Through*

Colour Breathing, US, Celestial Arts, 1976.

26. Cooper, Cary L. (ed.): *Psychological Stress and Cancer*, London, 1984.

27. Corsini, R. J. (ed.): *Handbook of Innovative Psychotherapies*, New York, John Wiley & Sons, 1981.

28. Corvo, Joseph: *Backache Cure*, London, Ebury Press, 1992.

29. Cousins, Norman: *Anatomy of an Illness*, New York, 1979.

30. Darwin, Charles: *The Expression of the Emotions in Man and Animals* (1872), Chicago University Press, 1965.

31. de Bono, Edward: *The Use of Lateral Thinking*, London, Jonathan Cape, 1967.

32. Donaldson, Margaret: *Human Minds and Exploration*, London, Penguin, 1992.

33. Donne, John: *Devotions Upon Emergent Situations*, 1623.

34. Dunbar, Flanders: *Mind and Body, Psychosomatic Medicine*, New York, 1947 and 1955.

35. Edinger, Edward F.: *Ego and Archetype*, New York, Putnam's Sons, 1972.

36. Edwards, Betty: *Drawing on the Right Side of the Brain*, USA, Tarcher, 1979; London, Souvenir Press, 1981.

37. Eisenberg, David and Wright, Thomas Lee: *Encounters with Qi – Exploring Chinese Medicine*, London, Jonathan Cape, 1986.

38. Eliade, Mircea: *Patanjali and Yoga*.

39. Eysenck, H. J.: *The Effects of Psychotherapy*, New York, International Science Press, 1960.

40. Fagan, J. and Shepherd, I. L. (eds.): *Gestalt Therapy Now*, New York, 1970.

41. Feldenkrais, Moshe: *Awareness Through Movement*, New York, Harper & Row, 1972.

42. Ferrucci, Piero: *What We May Be*, Wellingborough, Turnstone Press, 1982.

43. Ferrucci, Piero: *Inevitable Grace*, Los Angeles, Tarcher, 1990; Wellingborough, Thorsons, 1990.

44. Fosdick, Harry Emerson: *On Being a Real Person*, 1943.

45. Frankl, Viktor E.: *The Unconscious God*, New York, Simon & Schuster, 1975; London, Hodder & Stoughton, 1975.

46. Frankl, Viktor E.: *The Unheard Cry for Meaning – Psychotherapy and Humanism*, New York, Simon & Schuster, 1978; London, Hodder & Stoughton, 1979.

47. French, Neil: *Successful Hypnotherapy: An Investigation of Mankind Under the Microscope of Hypnosis*, Wellingborough, Thorsons, 1984.

48. Freud, Sigmund: *Civilization and its Discontents*, London, Hogarth, 1961.

49. Freud, Sigmund: *The Future of an Illusion*, translated by James Strachey, New York, W. W. Norton, 1961.

50. Freud, Sigmund: *Studies on Hysteria*, 1895.

51. Freud, Sigmund: *Recommendations to Physicians Practising Psychoanalysis*, 1912.

52. Friedman, M. and Rosenman, R. H.: *Type A Behavior and Your Heart*, New York, Alfred A. Knopf, 1974.
53. Friedman, M. and Ulmer, D. *Treating Type A Behavior and Your Heart*, New York, Alfred A. Knopf, 1984.
54. Fromm, Erich: *To Have or to Be?* London, Jonathan Cape, 1978.
55. Fromm, Erich: *The Forgotten Language*, New York, Rhinehart, 1951.
56. Fromm, Erich: *The Anatomy of Human Destructiveness*, London, Jonathan Cape, 1974.
57. Fromm, Erich: *The Art of Being*, London, Constable, 1993.
58. Fromm, E. and Shor, R. E. (eds): *Hypnosis: Research developments and perspectives*, Chicago, Aldine-Atherton, 1972.
59. Fulder, Stephen: *The Handbook of Complementary Medicine*, 2nd edition, Oxford University Press, 1988.
60. Garfield S. L. and Bergin, A. E. (eds.): *Handbook of Psychotherapy and Behavior Change*, 2nd edition, New York, John Wiley, 1978.
61. Gerson, Max: *A Cancer Therapy – Results of 50 Cases*, California, Totality Books, 1975.
62. Gimbel, Theo: *Healing Through Colour*, Saffron Walden, C. W. Daniel, 1980.
63. Gittelson, Bernard: *Biorhythm: A Personal Science*, Arco Publishing, 1975; 6th edition, London, Macdonald, 1990.
64. Glasser, William: *Reality Therapy*, New York, Harper & Row, 1965.
65. Goffman, Erving: *Asylums*, Harmondsworth, Penguin, 1961.
66. Gooch, Stan: *The Double Helix of the Mind*, London, Wildwood House, 1980.
67. Groddeck, Georg: *The Book of the It*, (originally *Das Buch vom Es*, 1923), London, Vision Press, 1949; New York, Funk & Wagnalls, 1950.
68. Hahnemann, Samuel: *Organon of the Rational Art of Healing*, 1810, trans. J. Kunzli *et al.*, London, Gollancz, 1983.
69. Haley, Jay: *Uncommon Therapy: The Psychiatric Techniques of Milton H. Erickson*, New York, Norton & Co., 1973.
70. Haley, Jay: *Changing Individuals: Conversations with Milton H. Erickson M.D.*, New York, Triangle Press, 1985.
71. Hall, Edward T.: *The Silent Language*, New York, Doubleday, 1959.
72. Hall, Edward T.: *Proxemics: a study of Man's spatial relationship*, International Universities Press, 1963.
73. Halliday, J. L.: *Psychosocial Medicine*, New York, 1948.
74. Hampden-Turner, Charles: *Maps of the Mind*, London, Mitchell Beazley, 1981.
75. Hanna, Thomas: *The Body of Life*, New York, Holt, Rinehart & Winston.
76. Hanson, Peter: *The Joy of Stress*, London, Pan, 1987.
77. Hardy, Jean: *A Psychology with a Soul*, London, Routledge & Kegan Paul, 1987.
78. Harold, Edmund: *Crystal Healing*, Wellingborough, Thorsons, 1987.
79. Harper, Robert A.: *Psychoanalysis and psychotherapy: Thirty-Six Systems*, Englewood Cliffs, NJ, Prentice-Hall, 1959.

80. Harris, Thomas: *I'm OK – You're OK*, London, Jonathan Cape, 1970.
81. Harrison, John: *Love Your Disease*, London, Angus & Robertson, 1984.
82. Henrik, R. (ed.): *The Psychotherapy Handbook*, New York, Meridian Books, 1980.
83. Hilgar, E. R.: *Divided Consciousness: Multiple Controls in Human Thought and Action*, New York, Wiley-Interscience, 1977.
84. Hillman, J. and Ventural, M.: *We've Had a Hundred years of Psychotherapy – And the World's Getting Worse*, New York, HarperCollins, 1992.
85. Holmes, Oliver Wendell: *Medical Essays*, Boston, 1883.
86. Howard, Judy and Ramsell, John: *The Original Writings of Edward Bach*, Saffron Walden, C. W. Daniel, 1990.
87. Hubbard, L. Ron: *Dianetics*, 1950.
88. Hulke, Malcolm (ed.): *The Encyclopedia of Alternative Medicine and Self-Help*, London, Rider, 1978.
89. Huxley, Aldous: *Ends and Means*, London, 1937.
90. Huxley, Aldous: *The Art of Seeing*, London, Chatto, 1943.
91. Illich, Ivan: *Limits to Medicine – Medical Nemesis: The Expropriation of Health*, London, Marion Boyars, 1976; Viking Penguin, 1977.
92. Inglis, Brian: *Fringe Medicine*, London, Faber & Faber, 1965.
93. Inglis, Brian: *The Book of the Back*, London, Ebury Press, 1978.
94. Jarvis, D. C.: *Folk Medicine*, London, Pan, 1961.
95. Jaynes, Julian: *The Origin of Consciousness in the Breakdown of the Bicameral Mind*, New York, Houghton Mifflin, 1976; London, Allen Lane, 1979.
96. Jensen, Bernard: *The Science and Practice of Iridology*, California, 1952.
97. Jung, C. G.: *Collected Works*, vol. 9, London, Routledge & Kegan Paul, 1959.
98. Jung, C. G.: *Collected Works*, vol. 16, London, Routledge & Kegan Paul, 1954.
99. Jung, C. G.: *Man and His Symbols*, London, Aldus Books, 1964.
100. Jung, C. G.: *Psychological Reflections*, Princeton, 1970.
101. Jung, C. G.: *Modern Man in Search of a Soul*, New York, Harcourt Brace Jovanovich, 1933.
102. Jung, C. G.: *The Practice of Psychotherapy*, London, Routledge & Kegan Paul, 1966.
103. Jung, C. G.: *Psychology and Alchemy*, Zurich, 1944; expanded in *Collected Works* vol. 12, London, Routledge & Kegan Paul, 1968.
104. Jung, C. G.: *Psychology and Religion*, New Haven, Yale University Press, 1938.
105. Jung, C. G.: *The Undiscovered Self*, London, Routledge & Kegan Paul, 1974.
106. Jung, C. G.: *Commentary on the Secret of the Golden Flower*, London, Routledge & Kegan Paul, 1962.
107. Jung, Emma: *Animus and Anima*, New York, Spring Publications, 1957.
108. Karlins, Marvin and Andrews, Lewis M.: *Biofeedback*, London, Abacus, 1975.
109. Keleman, Stanley: *Somatic Reality*, Berkeley, Center Press, 1979.

110. Kenyon, J.: *Modern Techniques of Acupuncture* vol. 2, Wellingborough, Thorsons, 1983.
111. King, Francis X.: *Rudolf Steiner and Holistic Medicine*, London, Century Hutchinson, 1986.
112. Kloss, Jethro: *Back to Eden*, California, Lifeline Books, 1973.
113. Laing, R. D.: *The Divided Self*, Harmondsworth, Penguin, 1965.
114. Laing, R. D.: *The Politics of Being Human*, Harmondsworth, Penguin, 1967.
115. Leboyer, Frederick: *Birth Without Violence*, London, Fontana, 1975.
116. LeShan Lawrence: *Holistic Health: How to Understand and Use the Revolution in Medicine*, Wellingborough, Turnstone Press, 1984. (First published as *The Mechanic and the Gardener*, New York, Holt, Rinehart & Winston, 1982.)
117. LeShan, Lawrence: *You Can Fight for Your Life*, London, Thorsons, 1984.
118. Locke, S. and Colligan, D.: *The Healer Within*, New York, E. P. Dutton, 1986.
119. Lowen, Alexander: *Bioenergetics*, Coward, McCann & Geoghegan, 1975; Harmondsworth, Penguin, 1976.
120. Luthe, W. and Schultz, J. W.: *Autogenic Training and Therapy*, New York, Grune & Stratton, 1969.
121. Malcolm, Janet: *Psychoanalysis: the impossible profession*, London, Pan, 1982.
122. Mansfield, Peter: *The Bates Method*, London, Optima, 1992.
123. Maslow, Abraham H.: *Religions, Values, and Peak-Experiences*, Ohio State University Press, 1964.
124. Maslow, Abraham H.: *The Farther Reaches of Human Nature*, New York, Viking, 1971.
125. Maslow, Abraham H.: *Toward a Psychology of Being*, New York, Van Nostrand, 1962.
126. Maslow, Abraham H.: *Motivation and Personality*, New York, Harper & Row, 1954.
127. Maslow, Abraham H.: *Eupsychian Management*, Illinois, Irwin-Dorsey, 1965.
128. Masson, Jeffrey: *Against Therapy*, New York, Atheneum, 1988; London, Collins, 1989.
129. May, Rollo: *Love and Will*, New York, Dell, 1969.
130. Meyer, Donald: *The Positive Thinkers: A Study of the American Quest for Health, Wealth and Personal Power from Mary Baker Eddy to Norman Vincent Peale*, New York, Doubleday, 1965.
131. Mole, Peter: *Acupuncture*, Shaftesbury, Dorset, Element, 1992.
132. Moss, G. E.: *Illness, Immunity, and Social Interaction: The Dynamics of Bisocial Resonation*, New York, John Wiley & Sons, 1973.
133. Moyers, Bill: *Healing and the Mind*, New York, Doubleday; London, HarperCollins, 1993.
134. Nyanaponika Mahathera: *The Heart of Buddhist Meditation*, London, Rider, 1962.

135. Ornstein, Robert and Sobel, David: *The Healing Brain*, New York, Simon & Schuster; London, Macmillan, 1988.
136. Park, James: *Shrinks*, London, Bloomsbury, 1992.
137. Parkes, C.: *Bereavement: Studies of Grief in Adult Life*, London, Tavistock, 1972.
138. Paul, Diane: *Living Left-handed*, London, Bloomsbury, 1990.
139. Pelletier, Kenneth R.: *Mind as Healer, Mind as Slayer: A holistic approach to preventing stress disorders*, New York, Delacorte Press, 1977; London, Allen & Unwin, 1978.
140. Perls, Frederick S., Hefferline, Ralph F. and Goodman, Paul: *Gestalt Therapy*, Delta Books, Julian Press, 1951.
141. Pierrakos, John: *Core Energetics: Developing the Capacity to Love and Heal*, Mendocine, California, Life Rhythms Publications, 1987.
142. Pietroni, Patrick: *Holistic Living*, London, Dent, 1986.
143. Pietroni, Patrick: *The Greening of Medicine*, London, Gollancz, 1990.
144. Playfair, G. L. and Hill, S.: *The Cycles of Heaven*, New York, St Martin's Press, 1978.
145. Polyani, M.: *Personal Knowledge*, London, Routledge & Kegan Paul, 1973.
146. Raknes, Ola, in David Boadella (ed.): *Shaking the Foundations*, Harmondsworth, Penguin, 1962.
147. Raknes, Ola, in David Boadella (ed.): *In the Wake of Reich*, Coventure, 1970.
148. Rank, Otto: *The Trauma of Birth*.
149. Rogers, Carl R. and Steven, Barry: *Person to Person: The Problem of Being Human*, USA, Real People Press, 1967; London, Souvenir Press, 1973.
150. Rosen, J. N.: *Direct Analysis: Selected Papers*, New York, Grune & Stratton, 1953.
151. Rosen, R. D.: *Psychobabble: Fast Talk and Quick Cure in the Era of Feeling*, New York, Atheneum, 1977; London, Wildwood House, 1978.
152. Rosenthal, Norman: *Winter Blues*, New York, Bantam Doubleday Dell, 1989.
153. Sacks, Oliver: *Migraine*, London, Faber & Faber, 1970.
154. Sacks, Oliver: *Awakenings*, London, Pan, 1981.
155. Scherer, K. and Ekman, P. (eds.): *Approaches to Emotion*, Hillsdale, New Jersey, Lawrence Erlbaum, 1984.
156. Schiff, Jacqui: *All My Children*, New York, Harper & Row.
157. Schneider, Meir: *Self-Healing: My Life and Vision*, New York, Methuen; London, Routledge & Kegan Paul, 1987.
158. Selye, Hans: *The Stress of Life*, New York, McGraw Hill, 1956.
159. Simonton, O. Carl, Matthews-Simonton, Stephanie, and Creighton, James L.: *Getting Well Again*, Los Angeles, J. P. Tarcher, 1978.
160. Smail, David: *Taking Care: An Alternative to Therapy*, London, Dent, 1987.
161. Smith, Manuel J.: *When I Say No, I Feel Guilty*, New York, Bantam, 1976.
162. Smuts, Jan: *Holism and Evolution*, London, Macmillan, 1926.
163. Stevens, Anthony: *On Jung*, London, Routledge, 1990.

164. Stoddard, Alan: *Manual of Osteopathic Practice*, London, 1969.
165. Stone, R.: *Health Building*, Orange County, California, Parameter Press, 1978.
166. Storr, Anthony: *Solitude*, London, HarperCollins, 1994.
167. Storr, Anthony: *Music and the Mind*, London, HarperCollins, 1992.
168. Szasz, Thomas: *The Myth of Mental Illness*, London, Paladin, 1991.
169. Thomas, Lewis: *The Lives of a Cell*, New York, Viking, 1974.
170. Tromp, S. W.: *Medical Biometeorology*, Amsterdam, Elsevier, 1963.
171. Trager, Milton: *Trager Mentastics: Movement as a Way to Agelessness*, 1987.
172. Ullman, Montague and Limmer, Claire (eds.): *The Variety of Dream Experience*, New York, Continuum, 1987.
173. Ullman, M. and Zimmerman, N.: *Working with Dreams*, Los Angeles, J. P. Tarcher, 1979.
174. Waelder, Robert: *Basic Theory of Psychoanalysis*, New York, International Universities Press, 1960.
175. Wall, Vicky: *The Miracle of Colour Healing: Aura-Soma Therapy as the Mirror of the Soul*, Wellingborough, Thorsons, 1990.
176. Watson, John: *Behaviourism*, New York, W. W. Norton, 1924.
177. Watt, Sir James (ed.): *Talking Health: Conventional and Complementary Approaches*, London, The Royal Society of Medicine, 1988.
178. Waxman, David: *Hypnosis: A Guide for Patients and Practitioners*, London, Allen & Unwin, 1981.
179. Weinberg, George: *The Heart of Psychotherapy*, New York, St Martin's Press.
180. Weiss, E. and English, O. S.: *Psychosomatic Medicine*, Philadelphia, W. B. Saunders, 1957.
181. West, M. A. (ed.): *The Psychology of Meditation*, Oxford, Clarendon, 1987.
182. White, John (ed.): *The Highest State of Consciousness*, New York, Harper & Row, 1972.
183. Wilson, Colin: *Beyond the Occult*, London, Bantam, 1988.
184. Wilson, Colin: *Access to Inner Worlds*, London, Rider, 1983.
185. Woolger, Roger: *Other Lives, Other Selves*, New York, Dolphin/Doubleday, 1987.
186. Worsley, J. R.: *Is Acupuncture for You?*, USA, 1975; Shaftesbury, Dorset, Element, 1983.

Journals

187. Andrade, Hernani: 'Psi matter' in *Energy and Character*, 12, 3, 1981; 13, 1, 1982.
188. *American Journal of Clinical Hypnosis*, 19, 1977.
189. *American Journal of Clinical Hypnosis*, 25, 1983.
190. *American Journal of Epidemiology*, 102 (1975); 104 (1976).
191. *American Journal of Ophthalmology*, 92:4, 1981.
192. *American Journal of Public Health*, 72, 1982.

193. Beecher, Henry K. in *Journal of the American Medical Association*, 176, 1961.
194. *British Heart Journal*, 1973, 35.
195. *British Heart Journal*, 1981, 45.
196. *British Journal of Dermatology*, 1977, 97; 1978, 98.
197. *British Medical Journal*, 282, 1981.
198. Engel, George: 'The Need for a New Medical Model: A challenge for Biomedicine', *Science*, 196, 1977.
199. Eysenck, H. J.: 'The effects of psychotherapy: an evaluation', in *Journal of Consulting Psychology*, 16, 1952.
200. Fisher, P. *et al.* in *Complementary Medicine*, 299, 1989.
201. Goldfarb, Driesen and Cole in *American Journal of Psychiatry*, 123, 1967.
202. Halliday, J. L.: 'Psychological factors in rheumatism', *British Medical Journal*, January 1937.
203. Holmes, T. H. and Rahe R. H. in *Journal of Psychosomatic Response*, 11, 1967.
204. *Journal of the American Medical Association*, 159, 1955.
205. *Journal of Chronic Disease*, 31, 1978.
206. *Journal of Medical Ethics*, June 1992.
207. *Journal of Neurophysiology*, 38, 1975.
208. *Journal of Optometric Visual Development*, 13 (1), 1982.
209. *Journal of the Royal College of General Practitioners*, August 1985.
210. *Journal of Transpersonal Psychology*, 7, 1975.
211. Klein, K. E. and Wegmann, H. M.: *Significance of Circadian Rhythms in Aerospace Operations*, AGARDograph no. 247, 1980.
212. *Lancet*, 1974, 1.
213. *Lancet*, 1977, 1.
214. Langer, E. J. and Rodin, J. in *Journal of Personality and Social Psychology*, 34 (1976) and 35 (1977).
215. Maslow, Abraham H.: 'Synergy in the Society and in the Individual', in *Journal of Individual Psychology*, 20, 1964.
216. Melzack, Ronald and Wall, Patrick, 'Pain Mechanisms: a new theory', *Science*, 19 November 1965.
217. Moss and Wei in *American Journal of Acupuncture*, 3, 1975.
218. *Nature*, 312, 1984.
219. *New England Journal of Medicine*, 276, 1967.
220. *New England Journal of Medicine*, 304, 1981.
221. *New Scientist*, 14 May 1981.
222. *Psychological Reports*, 49, 1981.
223. *Psychosomatic Medicine*, 2, 1965.
224. Rosenblatt, S. in *American Journal of Acupuncture*, 10, 1980.
225. Seville, R. H. in *British Journal of Dermatology*, 1977, 97; 1978, 98.
226. Simon, C. W. and Emmons, W. H. in *Science*, 124, 1956.
227. Stern, Brown, Ulett and Stetten, in *Annals of the New York Academy of Sciences*, 296, 1977.
228. *The Times*, 26 September 1991.
229. *Times Educational Supplement*, 3 July 1992.

230. Tonkin, Richard D. in *Journal of the Royal Society of Medicine*, 80, 1987.
231. Wallace, B., Garrett, J. B. and Anstadt, S. P. in *American Journal of Psychology*, 87, 1974.
232. Whatmore and Kohli in *Behavioral Science*, 13, 1968.
233. *Work in America: Report of a Special Task Force to the Secretary of Health, Education and Welfare*, Cambridge, MA, MIT Press, 1973.

Bibliographic addenda

234. Jung, C. G.: *Collected Works*, vol. 6, London, Routledge & Kegan Paul, 1961.
235. Thommen, George S.: *Is This Your Day?*, New York, Crown, 1973.

Index

In cases where the indexed item is also a headword in the Dictionary, the reference is given in italics.